WE ARE YOUR SOLDIERS

ALSO BY ALEX ROWELL

Vintage Humour:
The Islamic Wine Poetry of Abu Nuwas

WE ARE YOUR SOLDIERS

* * *

*How Gamal Abdel Nasser
Remade the Arab World*

ALEX ROWELL

W. W. NORTON & COMPANY
Celebrating a Century of Independent Publishing

For information about permission to reproduce selections from this book,
write to Permissions, W. W. Norton & Company, Inc., 500 Fifth Avenue,
New York, NY 10110

For information about special discounts for bulk purchases, please contact
W. W. Norton Special Sales at specialsales@wwnorton.com or 800-233-4830

Manufacturing by Lake Book Manufacturing
Book design by Lovedog Studio
Production manager: Anna Oler

ISBN 978-1-324-02166-7

W. W. Norton & Company, Inc., 500 Fifth Avenue, New York, N.Y. 10110
www.wwnorton.com

W. W. Norton & Company Ltd., 15 Carlisle Street, London W1D 3BS

1 2 3 4 5 6 7 8 9 0

For Youmna and Paul
In the hope that more cheerful stories are being told
by the time you read this.

Nasser is not a person. He is a unique historical phenomenon. It is impossible to consider any Arab issue without also considering this phenomenon and its impact upon it. His presence imposes itself on every problem, event, party, movement, government, and battle in the Arab world. It is a giant, oppressive presence, which has inserted itself, both negatively and positively, on modern Arab history, affecting its course profoundly, sending forth currents that have shaken the foundations of all that preceded it.

—Munif al-Razzaz,
al-Tajriba al-Murra (The bitter experience)

★

I heard Dad
Say to Mom,
"It's all thanks to Father Gamal"

—Song taught to Egyptian schoolchildren
in the 1960s

CONTENTS

WE ARE YOUR SOLDIERS

PROLOGUE

L ATE ON THE COLD NIGHT OF WEDNESDAY, FEBRUARY 3, 2021, the Lebanese public intellectual Lokman Slim was shot six times in the head and back. The fifty-eight-year-old had been visiting a friend in the remote village of Niha, deep in the sleepy green hillside of south Lebanon, before setting off alone around 8 p.m. for the ninety-minute drive in the dark up the Mediterranean coastline to the capital, Beirut. His bullet-riddled body was found at daybreak, slumped over the passenger seat of his car, near the small town of Addousieh, almost forty kilometers north of Niha.

Like many journalists in Lebanon, I had known Lokman, having met and interviewed him several times. He hailed from the Shia Muslim community, and lived in the very heart of Shia Beirut, in the urban sprawl along the city's southern fringe near the airport, known as "the Suburb" (al-Dahiyeh). Despite this choice of residence, he was among Lebanon's foremost critics of the self-styled "Party of God," Hizbullah—the Shia militia and political organization designated a terrorist entity by the UK and US governments, blamed for a laundry list of deadly attacks stretching back to the early 1980s.

Hizbullah maintains its headquarters in the Suburb, where it operates a parallel quasi-state, complete with its own armed security forces; telecommunications and intelligence networks; vehicle checkpoints; and even schools, banks, and hospitals. From the tiny sanctuary of his family villa right in the center of this quarter, Lokman voiced bold condemnations of the Party of God's conduct in

Lebanon, as well as its numerous wars abroad in Syria, Iraq, and beyond. Never mincing words, he spoke to both Western reporters such as myself, and—more dangerously—to mass-audience Arabic-language television networks broadcasting across the entire Middle East. For journalists and viewers alike, to watch and listen to Lokman was to behold the rare spectacle of Hizbullah being denounced by a member of "its own" community, speaking its vernacular, living in its very midst.

Lokman was also much more than a mere polemicist or talking head, however. A civil-society man at heart, he founded an array of cultural initiatives and NGOs, the best-known of which is devoted to the memory of Lebanon's fifteen-year civil war, for which no official museum or memorial exists. Another taught English to women in marginalized rural communities. With his German wife, Monika Borgmann, he made award-winning films about torture in Syrian prisons and killings of Palestinian refugees in Beirut. With his sister, the novelist Rasha al-Ameer, he founded a publishing house, Dar al Jadeed, which has put out original works by some of the Arab world's leading authors. He had something of the air of the Renaissance man: steeped in classical poetry; fluent in four languages; his company was humorous and ironic, a broad beam always ready to break over his ruddy face. Tobacco and drink were his redeeming vices: one friend mourned him to the author as a "hugely decent man, with whom I will miss drinking enormous amounts of whisky (over lunch)." Entire bottles of Scotch could be dispatched tête-à-tête of an afternoon. "It was like a constant test of mettle. He was a tough bugger."

He would have to be, after all, to lead the life he did. If it weren't enough to have grown up amid a gruesome civil war, multiple Israeli invasions, and decades of Syrian military occupation, Lokman then chose obstinately to remain in his great-grandfather's home even as the streets all around him filled up with his most hostile and deadly antagonists. Not long before his assassination, a mob gathered outside his house at night, shouting insults and branding him a "traitor." Two days later he woke to find his walls smothered in posters bearing explicit death threats, and declaring "Hizbullah is the honor of the nation." He responded with a written statement holding Hizbullah's leader personally responsible for any harm that should come his way.

★

ON THE ONE HAND, Lokman's murder was of a piece with a string of assassinations of leading critics of Hizbullah and its backers in Tehran and Damascus, more than a dozen of whom have been systematically picked off or maimed across Lebanon throughout the twenty-first century. At the same time, his killing also had peculiar echoes of an earlier era of violence predating the Party of God, Iran's Islamic Republic, and Syria's Assad regime, rooted in the rather different politics of the 1950s and '60s.

Lokman's own mother, Selma, was the first to note the parallels with the 1966 assassination of the Lebanese journalist Kamel Mrowa. Like Lokman, Mrowa was a prominent critic of the regimes he thought inimical to Arab life and liberty in his day. Both faced malicious smear campaigns in the gutter press, which attacked them as "traitors" and "agents" of Israel and the West. Both, incidentally, were of Shia background, albeit wholly secular in temperament. And both were killed by gunshots fired at close range, in what bore all the hallmarks of state-sponsored operations. By eerie coincidence, Lokman's late father, Mohsen—a lawyer and one-time member of parliament—had represented Mrowa's family in the trial of the four men accused of killing him. It was a perilous undertaking in its own right, bringing death threats against Mohsen himself. Decades before his son Lokman was targeted at the family home, a bomb intended for Mohsen detonated at the entrance to the same house.

On the first-floor balcony of this white villa, Mohsen's widow, Selma—Lokman's mother—points down over the courtyard to the front gates, showing me where the blast went off more than fifty years earlier. Sitting with us is her daughter Rasha, Lokman's sister, who cools us on this unseasonably hot October afternoon with glasses of chilled wine.

The gates were still wooden at the time of the explosion, Selma adds; only afterward did her husband replace them with the metal ones that stand today. "He received a lot of threats," she sighs.

No less than her late husband and son, Selma is accustomed to living dangerously. She is, indeed, a remarkable woman in all kinds of ways. Ninety years young at the time of our meeting, her memory extends as far back as her childhood in Egypt in the 1930s and '40s, when the country was still a British-occupied monarchy. After attending Cairo's American College for Girls (now named Ramses College), she studied journalism and literature at the prestigious American University in Cairo, where her teachers included Wilton Wynn, a "towering figure of American journalism in the 20th century," in the words of his Reuters obituary. Another teacher was Samir Souki, then *Newsweek* magazine's Cairo correspondent. It was through Souki that Selma landed a job at *Newsweek* herself while still in her final year of studies, joining the staff full-time upon graduation in 1956. After the Suez War of that same year, Cairo's foreign press came under mounting harassment from Egypt's new "revolutionary" rulers. By 1957, the situation was untenable. *Newsweek* closed its Cairo office, and Selma followed Souki and the rest of her colleagues to their new base in Beirut—the liberal and glamorous "Paris of the East," according to popular cliché.

No sooner had they arrived in their supposed refuge, however, than Lebanon's first civil war broke out in 1958, killing hundreds over the course of several months. In the relative stability that followed, Selma began a master's at the American University of Beirut, studying under such luminaries as professor Malcolm Kerr (who would himself be assassinated on campus in 1984). Newly married to the successful lawyer Mohsen, who was elected to Lebanon's parliament in 1960, Selma became an established figure in Lebanese society, counting the likes of Kamel Mrowa among her cohorts.

"He was very friendly," she recalls of Mrowa, still speaking the distinctive Cairene dialect of Arabic more than sixty years after leaving the city. "Warm-hearted, and always happy to talk and discuss things."

That her husband would soon face Mrowa's murderers in court may seem a morbid enough twist to the story. Yet there is a further grim irony, for the very regime that fueled Lebanon's civil war of 1958, and stood behind the shooting of Mrowa in his Beirut office, as well as the bombing of Slim's residence, was the same one Selma had thought she was escaping when she left Cairo: the military dictatorship of Gamal Abdel Nasser.

★

SIXTEEN MONTHS BEFORE LOKMAN'S assassination, Lebanon was an altogether happier and more hopeful place. On the morning of Sunday, October 20, 2019, my wife and I set off from our apartment on Beirut's eastern fringe to join the hundreds, then thousands, then tens of thousands spontaneously leaving their homes to march on the city center. Long before we arrived, it was clear we would get nowhere near the epicenter. As the pastel blue domes and sandstone minarets of the Muhammad al-Amin Mosque came into view at the end of rue Gouraud, drowning in an endless ocean of white, red, and green Lebanese flags, there were simply far too many people occupying every inch of the available space: filling not only the streets and pavements but the balconies and rooftops; standing on parked cars; scaling the billboards and lampposts.

From the very start, in our neighborhood of Mar Mikhael, the air had already been electric with improvised chants, national anthems, and unprintable obscenities yelled at the country's politicians. Yet nothing could have prepared us for the scenes downtown. Never before in Lebanese history had so vast a crowd encompassed so broad a spectrum of society. Silver-haired grandmothers; newborns slung across parents' chests; bony adolescents in Guy Fawkes masks on scooters; women in the distinctive black chadors worn by Shia; Druze men in traditional white skullcaps; wizened nuns in serge habits; bearded Marxist radicals in Che Guevara T-shirts and *kufiyas*; students switching between Arabic and American-English; bronzed white-collar professionals chattering in French—all vibrating to the bangs of drums and braving the prospect of violence to protest the corruption, incompetence, and sheer criminality of a despised political establishment that had insulted them one too many times. The colossal turnout looked well into the hundreds of thousands. And Beirut was only half the story: the same was happening that day across the length and breadth of the country, from Tripoli and Akkar in the north to Tyre and Nabatieh in the south, to Baalbek in the eastern Bekaa Valley. They called it the *thawra*: the revolt, or revolution.

Nine years on, the Arab Spring was alive and well.

To be sure, Lebanon had its own unique dynamics and dimensions, as each country does. To view every protest in the Middle East through a one-size-fits-all "Arab Spring" lens would obscure more than it clarified. In this case, however, the connection with the historic uprisings of 2010 and 2011 was asserted explicitly by Lebanon's demonstrators themselves, in the language with which they filled the streets and squares. Borrowing verbatim from the Tunisians who lit the first spark in December 2010, their megaphones and loudspeakers repeated the famous refrain that, more than any other, came to define the Arab Spring: "The people want to topple the regime!" From neighboring Syria, they borrowed the catchy jingle, "Come on, leave, Bashar [al-Assad]," replacing the Syrian president's name with those of Lebanese politicians. A third chant paid homage to Egypt, in a pun on Cairo's "Down, down with military rule," which in Beirut became "Down, down with thug rule" (they sound similar in Arabic). Punctuating these slogans every few minutes, wherever one went, came the same roar: *Thaw-ra! Thaw-ra! Thaw-ra!*

★

WE ALL KNOW THE STORY of the Arab Spring—or think we do. The Tunisian and Egyptian masses arose in late 2010 and early 2011,

peacefully toppling the autocrats under whose boots they had suffo-
cated for decades. Millions in Yemen, Bahrain, Libya, and Syria then
attempted to do the same, with varying degrees of success. Years
later, Algeria and Sudan would follow suit, overthrowing their own
ossified despots, while sustained mass protest movements would also
be seen in Iraq and Lebanon.

Each country, needless to say, had its own particular local demands
and circumstances, but as a whole the protests took aim at a common regional order: a shared curse of political repression mixed with
economic misery. Too often overlooked is the remarkable extent to
which this order was brought into being by the career of one man.
From the moment the Arab Spring began, this man—or his ghost—
cast a long, heavy shadow over events regionwide. If his presence
was not always palpable or visible, it had a tendency every so often
to come to the fore in revealing ways. At the heart of Egypt's revolution, in Cairo's Tahrir Square, protesters spoke of their parents
demonstrating against this man's regime in the 1960s. "Today, we
finished the job for them," said one with tears in his eyes on the
night President Hosni Mubarak stepped down in February 2011.
In Syria, opponents of the Assad regime disowned the national red,
white, and black tricolor flag, which was a relic of the time when,
by a quirk of history, the same man had been Syria's president as
well as Egypt's. In Libya, a large statue of him was torn down in
2012 before a cheering crowd, and the adjacent street named after
him renamed "Independence Street." Beirut is too much a city of
contradictions for that kind of clarity; its own sculpture of him still
stands today in a square bearing his name on the seafront corniche,
wedged between an Ottoman-era mosque and a McDonald's. Two
blocks away lies the giant carcass of the iconic Holiday Inn hotel,
battered to a pockmarked husk by the artillery of the same man's
followers in 1976.

He is, once again, Gamal Abdel Nasser.

INTRODUCTION

G AMAL ABDEL NASSER MAY HAVE BEEN THE MOST popular Arab leader in modern history, but he was never a stranger to criticism. Winston Churchill called him a "malicious swine." Prime ministers Anthony Eden and Harold Macmillan compared him to both Hitler and Mussolini, a habit shared by their French counterpart, Guy Mollet. "Hitler on the Nile" became the London *Daily Mail*'s taunt of choice in the 1950s.

Closer to home, Arab nationalist hard-liners suspected Nasser was secretly a Western agent. Islamists decried his rule as godless. Socialists dismissed him as a bourgeois capitalist. Capitalists denounced him as an incorrigible communist. Communists branded him a fascist.

Suffice it to say that the man divided opinion, and very much still does. "You meet people and discuss Nasser, and he's God to them," said Jordan's former interior minister to this author. "You meet others, and he's an evil man. I have not yet found a middle ground."

Indeed, for all that Nasser remains a powerful presence in the minds of millions more than fifty years after his demise, it is curious how rarely one comes across serious, rigorous, dispassionate examination of his eighteen-year reign, and the profound legacy it left, as these pertain to the Arab world of today. Certainly, we have a number of biographies and histories, almost all heavily dated now, having been written decades ago in a previous century. Such new information and scholarship as have since emerged exist mostly in scattered isolation, yet to be synthesized and incorporated into the wider conversation about Nasser.

More to the point, we have failed to update the way we think about Nasser, to bring our perception of him into the post–Arab Spring era. Twentieth-century habits of thought die hard. Thus, Nasser remains (to admirers) the plucky national liberator who slew the dragon of Western Empire, or (to detractors) the Soviet stooge who handed Moscow the keys to the Middle East. Invisible in both cases are the people over whom Nasser actually ruled, a people who did not submit tamely to his authoritarianism, who had indeed already risen up against the order he created multiple times before the spectacular eruption of 2011. The Nasser who methodically destroyed the institutions of parliamentary democracy, banned all political parties, muzzled the press, gutted the judiciary, strangled civil liberties, and jailed or outright killed his opponents, and who did all this not just at home but abroad—this is not the Nasser who tends to come to mind when most of us hear his name.

The situation is scarcely better, if at all, within the Arabic-speaking realm, where periodic debates over Nasser's legacy have taken place ever since his death in 1970. The advent of the internet naturally invigorated this process, freeing up access to information and providing new space for discussion uninhibited by the traditional constraints. The Arab Spring, likewise, fostered an iconoclastic spirit among many, not least the young, emboldening them to question the record even of this most hallowed of heroes. More recently, the social media age has even seen Nasser become a figure of ridicule in certain online circles, with comic images mocking him as a paragon of failure and calamity. "Thank God for the age of Facebook, 'trends,' and 'memes,' in which the legend of the man has worn thin and he has become a laughingstock for the new generations," wrote the young Egyptian novelist Ahmed Naji in 2020.

And yet—with honorable exceptions, such as the important books of Helwan University's professor Sherif Younis—this new zeitgeist has not generally translated into works of extended study and analysis. "I do not know of a single critical biography of Nasser published in Arabic," lamented the Egyptian journalist Khaled Mansour in 2020, adding that he found his compatriots still overwhelmingly polarized between the same old camps of fanatical supporters versus mortal foes.

If the need for a revised and expanded history of Nasser's reign was pressing before the Arab Spring, it is all the more urgent in the wake of that seismic revolt, which sought to overthrow precisely the structures produced by the Nasser era. The most cursory glance at the histories of such regimes as Mubarak's Egypt, Gaddafi's Libya, Assad's Syria, and Saleh's Yemen makes plain that the Nasser years marked the crucial stage in each one's formation. (The same can be said of Saddam Hussein's Iraq.) Yet one searches in vain for a clear and detailed account of how exactly this process unfolded in each case, systematically mapping out the specific paths that led from Nasser to the rogues' gallery of despots who went on to bring such agony upon their societies.

That is the aim to which this humble volume aspires. Focusing on seven countries in particular—Egypt, Iraq, Syria, Lebanon, Jordan, Yemen, and Libya—the book weaves the epic tale of Nasser's dramatic encounters with each, encounters more often than not drenched in blood and destruction, leaving deep scars that endure to the present day. Wherever possible, I have sought to move beyond familiar ground to tread the darker avenues—the bombings, torture camps, coup attempts, assassinations, military invasions, and chemical warfare—that are so often absent in the telling of Nasser's story, not least in the Anglosphere. I have likewise chosen to dwell only as briefly as necessary on Nasser's well-known collisions with the West and Israel, and his moves in the grand geopolitical chess matches of the Cold War, preferring to train the lens instead on his impact within the Arab domain.

In so doing, I have drawn on a combination of historical sources and my own journalistic inquiries around the region, which have taken me from Amman to Alexandria, Beirut to Beit Mirri, and Cairo to Karak. In the first instance, I have relied on Nasser's own words, whether from his writings, his interviews, or his public

speeches, more than 1,300 of which have been painstakingly transcribed verbatim and made freely accessible by the Bibliotheca
Alexandrina—an invaluable archive unavailable to researchers
before its completion in 2008. Further sources include the many
memoirs written by Nasser's colleagues, relatives, and other con-
temporaries, including sundry officials and persons of interest across
the Arab world. Press reports, biographies, court documents, novels,
films, television, and the academic literature have furnished much of
the additional input. In terms of my own reporting, it has focused
on profiling specific individual victims of Nasser's regime, several
of whose relatives were kind enough to supply me with a wealth of
privately collected information and documentation. If this book has
succeeded in adding anything of significance to the historical record,
it has only been by virtue of these remarkable individuals' courage
and generosity.

At the risk of stating the obvious, it should be stressed that a book
restricted in scope to seven countries cannot offer a comprehensive
portrait of Nasser's career. Some may well wonder why Algeria has
been left out of the picture, or Sudan, or Tunisia, or any number of
other possible arenas. So widespread were Nasser's foreign entangle-
ments that a truly exhaustive treatment would have to cover theaters
as far-flung as Congo, where he sent arms and troops in the 1960s.
To readers disappointed at finding no mention in these pages of the
Popular Front for the Liberation of the Occupied Arabian Gulf, or
Cairo Radio's Swahili propaganda in East Africa, I can plead only
that the countries were chosen as a representative sample of Nasser's
Arab dominion, and that if the point has not been made with seven
examples, the fault lies not in the quantity.

Without further ado, then, let our story begin, on the eve of Nasser's leap onto the stage of history, in the anarchic final days of the
doomed Kingdom of Egypt.

EGYPT I

THE IMMENSE
SECRET

NOT EVERY HEAD OF STATE ADMITS TO PERSONALLY taking part in an assassination attempt, then writes about it in detail in a book published under his own name. Not every head of state is Gamal Abdel Nasser.

In his 1954 manifesto-cum-memoir, *The Philosophy of the Revolution*, Nasser devoted several pages to the question of political assassination, freely confessing that in the run-up to his 1952 coup he planned many a hit on Egypt's King Farouk, his courtiers, and other "obstacles standing between our homeland and its future." In wistful tones, he recounted how he and his companions whiled away long, exciting hours finalizing the preparations to kill their enemies:

> *How many plans I sketched in those days; how many nights I stayed up late, preparing. . . . Our lives at that time were like a thrilling detective story. We had immense secrets, we had symbols, we hid in the dark. We would line up pistols side by side with grenades. The bullets were the aspirations of our dreams!*

One particular "obstacle" Nasser decided to remove was his superior within the armed forces, Maj. Gen. Husayn Sirri Amer, the attempt on whose life he wrote about at some length. A palace loyalist, Amer was accused—wrongly, as it turned out—of having caused Egypt's defeat in Palestine in 1948 by selling defective arms to the military for personal profit. Together with a few comrades, Nasser studied Amer's routine, and drew up a plot to shoot him while he was returning home at night.

The plan was straightforward: an "attack team" would open fire; a "guard team" would protect the attack team; and a third team, including Nasser, would handle the getaway.

When the chosen night—Tuesday, January 8, 1952—came around, all appeared to go as planned. The teams lay in wait undetected behind the hedges surrounding the general's villa, and opened fire on him when he arrived. As Nasser drove away, however, he heard "shrieks and laments; a woman wailing; the terror of a child; then a frantic, continuous cry for help." The dreadful sounds kept ringing in his ears, even long after he'd reached home. When he read in the next morning's paper that Amer had survived, he said it came as a relief, for he had spent the night chain-smoking, sleepless with remorse.

The official Nasserist line has always been that he renounced assassination as a modus operandi from that day on. The evidence presented in this book suggests a rather different reality. Either way, the anecdote makes plain that a readiness to use lethal violence for political ends was latent within the man and his movement from the start. The first people to experience this violence were the Egyptians.

★

BY THE STANDARDS OF the copycat coups it would later inspire across the Arab world, the Egyptian putsch of Wednesday, July 23, 1952, was a casual affair. At eleven o'clock on the night of the twenty-second, motorized infantry columns set off for the army's general headquarters in Cairo, where the chief of staff was meeting with the top brass. The building was taken with negligible resistance. Meanwhile, fellow rebel units elsewhere in the capital seized the artillery and armored headquarters, and secured the city center, taking especial care to fortify the roads in from Suez, lest British forces in the Canal Zone attempt an intervention. (They did not.)

Various police and other official facilities were likewise occupied, including the all-important radio station.

It had gone remarkably smoothly. Few shots were fired, and no lives lost. There had even been the odd moment of comedy: Nasser, the coup leader and mastermind, was mistakenly detained for a period by fellow mutineers, while Anwar Sadat—who would succeed Nasser as Egypt's president from 1970 until his assassination in 1981—missed the start of the operation altogether, being at the cinema at the time. Sadat did manage to get himself to the radio station by 7 a.m., where he read out the first broadcast delivered to the nation by its new military rulers.

This brief 181-word statement, made in the name of the new commander in chief, Maj. Gen. Muhammad Naguib, declared that the army had "undertaken to purify ourselves" of the corruption and treachery that had so sullied it in recent years, assuring Egyptians their military was now in the hands of capable and trustworthy patriots working for their interests.

No mention was made of the king or government; indeed, there was no intimation that a full-blown coup d'état was underway, much less a "revolution" (as the officers later termed it). Most onlookers, including the king himself, interpreted the event as an internal army affair with no wider ramifications for the political system as a whole. The distinguished playwright and novelist Tawfiq al-Hakim, who has been called "the creator of the modern Egyptian theatre," recalled that he was pleased to hear the broadcast over the radio that morning, but otherwise paid it little heed. He got dressed as normal and headed to downtown Cairo's Sulayman Pasha Square (now known as Talaat Harb Square) for his "usual breakfast" at the famous Groppi café. Only when he reached the square, and saw the highly unusual sight of two Egyptian army tanks parked therein, did it occur to him "the matter may be bigger than I expected." Inside Groppi, he found the patrician clientele arguing about the news in raised voices, and had the ominous sense that "events of grave importance were coming our way."

It would take two more days for the nature of those events to become clearer. On Friday, July 25, the new military junta ordered the king's entourage to vacate the seafront Ras al-Tin Palace in Alexandria, where the monarch was holed up, trying to negotiate what suddenly looked a most uncertain future. Al-Hakim, who was also in Alexandria by then, watched a giant convoy of army vehicles fill the length of the coastal corniche, to the enthusiastic applause of bystanders. He too became swept up in the passions of the moment, for "there was no one in Egypt who wasn't thrilled for this army, which had managed by itself to stand up to that king; that person loathed by all for his repugnant morals and bloated, porcine physique."

The next day, the monarch formally abdicated the throne, on the junta's orders. He was luckier than he realized to escape with his life. Several officers within the junta had pushed for his execution, but Nasser had countered that execution would require a trial, consuming valuable time and distracting them from more urgent priorities. "Let us spare Farouk and send him into exile," Nasser told his colleagues. "History will sentence him to death."

Physically unharmed, Farouk was even granted a twenty-one-gun salute, and permission to use the royal yacht when he set sail that evening for Naples. A dynasty tracing its origins to the illustrious Ottoman conqueror Muhammad Ali Pasha was finished, and a profoundly new Middle East was born.

But who was its master?

★

GAMAL ABDEL NASSER WAS born on January 15, 1918, in the Bakos neighborhood of Alexandria, a short stroll from the brilliant turquoise water of the sea and its fresh, cooling breeze. His father, Abdel Nasser Husayn, who hailed from the village of Bani Murr in Upper Egypt, worked for the postal service. His mother, Fahima Hammad, also of Upper Egyptian roots, was the daughter of a coal merchant. This placed the family within Egypt's middle class, if toward the lower end in terms of income and social status. The family home, at 18 Qanawati Street, was a single-story villa with wooden shutters over the windows in the Mediterranean style.

Gamal's childhood could not be described as stable. At age three, the family relocated to Asyut, 550 kilometers south of Alexandria. It was the first of no fewer than eight moves, which saw him shunted between sundry relatives, attending schools everywhere from Khatatba in the Nile Delta to Helwan south of the capital to Alexandria (twice) to the historic Nahhasin School in the heart of Cairo's medieval quarter, a stone's throw from the world-famous al-Azhar Mosque. A tragic further disruption came with the death of his beloved mother when he was eight, which he described as "a cruel blow that was imprinted indelibly on my mind."

As a student, he was not without intellectual promise, showing an especial interest in history and literature, and reading widely. From the Western canon, he took on Dickens, Voltaire, Hugo, Rousseau, and the lives of Napoleon, Alexander, Lawrence, Bismarck, and Clausewitz. Biographers have understandably been tempted to see significance in the fact that he played Julius Caesar in Shakespeare's eponymous tragedy for a school production in 1935. In Arabic, favorite authors included the pioneering Egyptian nationalist Mustafa Kamil, the nineteenth-century reformist Abd al-Rahman al-Kawakibi, the "prince of poets" Ahmad Shawqi, and above all Tawfiq al-Hakim, whose 1933 novel *The Return of the Soul* was perhaps Nasser's most cherished book of all.

If his academic performance fell short of his potential, this was in large part because his teen years saw him slide increasingly into the turbulent street politics of the period. He was coming of age just as the revolutionary dreams of Egypt's previous generation were fading into frustration and humiliation. Full independence from the British yoke, demanded by the leaders of Egypt's 1919 revolt in the wake of World War I, had failed to materialize. The political class in whom the nation had vested its hopes for liberation had disappointed. It fell to the youth to revive and reinvigorate the struggle.

Nasser joined his first protest in 1933, while still in his early teens in Alexandria, studying at the Ras al-Tin school in the shadows of the very palace from which he would banish the king to exile nineteen years later. Walking through the waterfront Manshiya Square in the heart of the city, he happened upon a student demonstration and immediately joined in, "without," he later said, "having the slightest idea as to what they were demonstrating for." As the police put down the protest, a truncheon struck him on the head, leaving him bloodied. He spent the night in jail.

A more dangerous encounter came two years later in 1935, when he was the seventeen-year-old leader of the student movement at Cairo's al-Nahda secondary school. At a demonstration against the suspension of Egypt's constitution, British troops shot and killed a university student. Nasser quickly organized a protest outside the British army barracks at Ismailia Square (now Tahrir Square), which met again with police batons. The following day, at a larger protest, police opened fire on a bridge off Cairo's Rawda Island, their bullets grazing Nasser on the forehead and killing two of his friends.

It was shortly after this that Nasser made his first foray into party politics. Since 1919, the main party representing Egypt's national aspirations was known as the Wafd, meaning "the Delegation," named for the group of Egyptian leaders who had sought British permission to attend the Paris Peace Conference to press for independence following the First World War. Britain's refusal to grant this permission, and its arrest and deportation to Malta of those who requested it, led to a nationwide uprising and, ultimately, the establishment in 1922 of the quasi-independent—but still British-occupied—Kingdom of Egypt.

If the Wafd had been the heroes of Nasser's parents' generation, by the 1930s they looked less impressive to younger Egyptians yearning for full independence and a more muscular confrontation with the British. The Wafd began to lose hearts and minds to newer, more militant movements.

One of these was the Muslim Brotherhood, founded in 1928,

which called for a wholesale reorganization of state and society in line with its founder's conservative interpretation of Islamic laws and values. Secretive and violent, responsible for a number of assassinations and indiscriminate bombings of civilian targets, with time it grew into the largest opposition force in Egypt, boasting hundreds of thousands of active members across the country by 1949.

Another newcomer was Young Egypt, founded in 1933 by a lawyer named Ahmad Husayn, who drew inspiration from the fascist parties then flourishing across Europe. With its "God, Fatherland, and King" motto, and green-shirted paramilitaries modeled on Mussolini's Blackshirts, Young Egypt would even forge links with Nazi Germany. It was this party that the eighteen-year-old Nasser opted to join in 1936, the same year its leader attended the Nuremberg Rally in person. Nasser remained a member until 1938, when he left because, in his words, they had "achieved nothing substantial." (Despite this, the party's cofounder Fathi Radwan—who sported a Hitler moustache—was given a prominent cabinet seat after the 1952 coup, and became a leading propagandist for Nasser's junta and against democracy throughout the 1950s.)

A third force on the rise in the 1930s was communism, which gained ground among certain intellectuals repelled by the same European fascism that inspired Young Egypt. While communists succeeded from around 1936 onward in gradually rebuilding their movement, which the authorities had forcibly dismantled a decade earlier, they and the left as a whole would remain essentially marginal to Egyptian politics for the rest of the 1930s.

It was also in 1936 that Nasser first attempted to join the army. The Anglo-Egyptian Treaty negotiated by the Wafd government that year was criticized for granting Britain the right to retain troops in the Suez Canal Zone, and to avail itself of Egyptian ports, roads, and airports—essentially to reoccupy the country—in the event of war (as indeed it did three years later). The treaty also, however, enabled Egyptians of the middle class to join the Military Academy for the first time. Nasser quickly applied, but was rejected, seemingly on account of his politics, as well as his lack of well-placed connections. Disappointed, he enrolled without enthusiasm at Cairo University's law school instead, where he lasted just six months.

In early 1937, he learned of another intake of military cadets, and applied again, this time making sure to secure a contact first. He paid a visit to the war ministry's undersecretary, Gen. Ibrahim Khayri Pasha, who agreed to help, apparently impressed by the strapping young lad and sincerely wishing to improve the officer corps. This time, Nasser's application was accepted.

Entering the academy in March 1937, Nasser gave it his all, and rose quickly through the ranks. In 1938, he was charged with mentoring a new recruit, Abd al-Hakim Amer, who became his best friend. Passing his final exams in July of that year, he was posted as a second lieutenant to Manqabad in Upper Egypt, only a few kilometers from his father's hometown. It was here that he and Amer made the acquaintance of Anwar Sadat and Zakaria Muhieddin. The nucleus of Egypt's future military junta was already taking shape: all four would go on to be key participants in the 1952 coup, and pillars of the regime it produced.

The outbreak of World War II in 1939 brought Egypt military and economic injury combined with political insult. Invoking its treaty rights, Britain quickly returned to Cairo in full martial force. Though initially spared the fighting, Egypt would become a battlefield of the highest importance in 1942, when the Nazi field marshal Erwin "the Desert Fox" Rommel charged across North Africa, driving the Allies eastward out of Libya into northwest Egypt, threatening an advance on the Nile Delta and, ultimately, the grand strategic prize of the Suez Canal. Were Rommel to succeed, the British Empire would be sawed in half. Not for nothing did Churchill vow, "We are determined to fight for Egypt and the Nile Valley as if it were the soil of England itself." To his mind, nothing less than the fate of the free world hung in the balance.

Not everyone in Egypt agreed. A sizable segment of public opinion was either indifferent to what it viewed as a turf war between one European hegemon and another, or else positively supported the Axis, seeing in it the hope of deliverance from British dominion. When in early 1942 it appeared King Farouk might appoint Axis sympathizers to his next government—amid chants of Rommel's name in Cairo's streets—Britain dispensed with the niceties of the Anglo-Egyptian Treaty and behaved like the colonial master it was no longer supposed to be. On the evening of February 4, British tanks rolled up to the gates of Farouk's Abdeen Palace in the heart of the capital. Britain's ambassador, Miles Lampson, barged his way through the doors and into the king's private quarters to inform him he would appoint the government of Britain's choosing or else lose his throne then and there. Farouk opted for the former.

Rommel's advance continued regardless for another five months, until it was stalled at El Alamein in July, then rolled back across Libya into Tunisia, where the last Axis foothold in North Africa fell in May 1943. Whether or not Lampson's performance at Abdeen Palace made any material difference to the course of the war, in its brazen disregard for Egypt's sovereignty and disrespect for the very person of its head of state, it unquestionably succeeded in outraging nationalist opinion. Nasser, who was serving in Sudan at the time, was incensed, though also pleasantly surprised at the reaction of the officers around him. "When your letter first arrived I almost exploded with rage," he wrote to the friend who had broken the news to him. But "the army . . . has been thoroughly shaken. Until now the officers only talked of how to enjoy themselves; now they are speaking of sacrificing their lives for their honour. . . . This event—this blow—has put life into some. It has taught them there is something called dignity which has to be defended."

With Egypt no longer an active war zone after El Alamein, Nasser found time to focus on private affairs upon his return to Cairo in late 1942. For years, he had known of a girl, Tahia Kazem, whose mother was old friends with his aunt, and whose brother was an acquaintance. Her father was a successful merchant of Iranian origin. Nasser went about his mission in traditional fashion, sending

his uncle and aunt to the Kazem home to make the necessary inquiries. There were some initial obstacles—it was thought improper for
Tahia to wed before her elder sister had done so—but once these
were resolved, the couple were able to marry on June 29, 1944. Their
wedding photo shows a slim, dapper Nasser in dinner jacket with
winged collars and black bow tie, a restrained smile just discernible,
his right arm around the back of his bride in white dress, her expression decorously staid. A daughter, Hoda, was born two years later, to
be followed by her sister Mona (who went on to marry the famous
spy Ashraf Marwan) and brothers Khaled, Abd al-Hamid, and Abd
al-Hakim. Nasser was by all accounts an unimpeachably faithful
husband and loving father throughout his life, enjoying films, pho-
tography, and games of chess with the family when he was able to
spend time with them.

Happiness at home was paired with progress on the professional
and political fronts. In February 1943, the newly promoted Captain
Nasser became an instructor at Egypt's Military Academy. Impress-
ing recruits and peers alike with his knowledgeable conversation
and fervent nationalist convictions, he built up a growing coterie of
friends and admirers—one could almost say disciples. However, he
had still not yet formally created the organization that was by then
less than a decade from seizing power. Instead, he and his closest
associates were drawn to what had become the most powerful and
militant opposition force in the country.

The nature and extent of Nasser's involvement with the Muslim
Brotherhood in the 1940s and early '50s has been the subject of considerable debate, confusion, distortion, and mythmaking on all sides.
The facts as best as they can be ascertained are as follows. In 1943
or early 1944, Nasser, Amer, and several other future junta members allowed themselves to be recruited into a particular unit of the
Brotherhood created specifically for infiltration of the military and
police, known as the Special Organization (al-Tanthim al-Khass).
An important feature of this unit and the cells it spawned was that
recruits were not required to become full, card-carrying members of

the Brotherhood. This was how Nasser was later able to deny having ever joined the Brotherhood, a claim both true and disingenuous.

Initially, Nasser's activities within these Brotherhood cells were largely limited to weekly discussions in private homes and the distribution of pamphlets. With time, they are said to have extended to military training for guerrillas attacking British forces in the Suez Canal Zone. Particularly illuminating in this regard is the testimony of the Free Officer Khaled Muhieddin, a fellow soldier within Nasser's entourage at the time who later played a prominent part in the coup and junta. According to Muhieddin, in 1947 he and Nasser met the Brotherhood's founder and leader, Hassan al-Banna, in person at the latter's home, where they swore allegiance to him, placing one hand on a Qur'an and the other on a pistol. It was, he says, a matter of practical rather than ideological considerations: "We joined the [Brotherhood] underground because it was the only potential paramilitary network that could carry out effective attacks against the British." Senior Brotherhood officials from the time, such as Farid Abd al-Khaleq, have corroborated the substance of Muhieddin's claims.

Revelations of this kind may seem scandalous to those accustomed to thinking of Nasser as the arch-secular scourge and nemesis of political Islam par excellence, but they should not be so surprising. At the time, there was not nearly so rigid a delineation between the "secular" and "Islamist" categories as prevails today. Nasser's own stance was far more protean and mercurial than the one-dimensional "secular" label permits. To all appearances a believing Muslim who prayed regularly and made the pilgrimage to Mecca, he wrote in *The Philosophy of the Revolution* of the importance of Islam to his political thinking and to Egypt as a whole. As we shall see, Brotherhood members were granted seats in Egypt's first post-coup cabinet, and the Brotherhood was the only party not to be banned within the first two years of the military regime. It's true that this would change by the mid-1950s, when Nasser suddenly jailed thousands of Brothers and ridiculed their leader in public speeches. But even then, he was not above donning religious garb himself when it suited him. At the height of the Suez War, on November 2, 1956, Nasser stood at the pulpit of the thousand-year-old al-Azhar Mosque after Friday prayers to tell the nation: "Our slogan shall always be, 'God is Greatest.' May God strengthen us. May God grant us victory. We depend upon God and upon ourselves. We shall wage jihad, struggle, and fight. We shall be victorious, with God's permission. God is greatest, God is greatest."

In any event, Nasser's stint in the Brotherhood's cells came to an end in the late 1940s, when a new development of seismic importance took center stage.

In September 1947, Britain announced its intention to withdraw from Palestine, which it had occupied and administered since the First World War. On May 14, 1948—one day before British rule was due to expire—Israeli statehood was proclaimed in Tel Aviv, to widespread condemnation throughout the Arab world. The following day, military forces from Egypt, Jordan, Syria, Iraq, and Lebanon commenced hostilities against the nascent Israeli statelet.

The Arab armies could scarcely have been less prepared for war. Egypt's prime minister had no enthusiasm for the fight, arguing in cabinet meetings that Cairo's energies were better spent getting the British out of Suez than battling a third party outside Egypt's borders. The other Arab states each had misgivings of their own. When the Arab League did finally decide on joint military action, mere days before the war began, it was on account of its members' mutual dislike and distrust more than any warm feelings of pan-Arab fraternity. Taking victory as a given, they were already looking ahead to the post-war power squabbles. Some aimed to block Jordan's King Abdallah I from annexing Palestine and/or Syria to his kingdom, while others sought to ensure that King Farouk, or indeed Palestine's own Mufti al-Hajj Amin al-Husayni, would not gain at their expense. As one historian put it, "the Arabs entered Palestine more at war with each other than with the Jewish state."

The Egyptian war plan was to head northeast from the Sinai

Peninsula through Gaza and the Negev desert to link up with Jordanian forces on the West Bank. The Israelis stalled their advance in less than a month. Soon, more than four thousand Egyptians were encircled by the village of Faluja, northeast of Gaza, where they would remain for the rest of the war until the Egyptian-Israeli armistice of February 1949.

Among these Egyptians was Maj. Gamal Abdel Nasser of the Sixth Brigade. The impact of the war on his life trajectory should neither be dismissed nor overstated. He makes a point of stressing in *The Philosophy of the Revolution* that the Palestine defeat was *not* the root cause of the 1952 coup, which he insists would have happened regardless. At the same time, the experience was bound to leave a lasting imprint. Like most of his peers, Nasser had seen no real action in World War II; Palestine was the first war he and his generation of Egyptian soldiers had ever fought. To have spent the time holed up for months under Israeli siege, attacked at will by artillery and air strikes, could not have failed to leave a bitter taste. What is interesting is that the bitterness was directed principally inward, at Cairo. The chief political consequence of the war for Nasser and his fellow officers was a hardening of their resolve to challenge the status quo back home, if and when they made it out alive.

"We were fighting in Palestine, but our dreams were all in Egypt," wrote Nasser, recalling how he would sit around under fire in the Faluja trenches discussing Egyptian politics with the likes of Zakaria Muhieddin, Salah Salem, and Kamal al-Din Husayn—all future junta members. A stab-in-the-back narrative proliferated, blaming the king, government, and military high command for sending the nation's finest to battle with inadequate planning, arms, ammunition, and supplies of all kinds. The words attributed to a fallen comrade, Ahmad Abd al-Aziz, as he lay dying became something of a mantra and mission statement: "The larger jihad is in Egypt."

For the Israelis themselves, meanwhile, Nasser seemed to harbor a grudging respect, bordering on admiration. He freely admits in his book to meeting with an Israeli officer, Yeruham Cohen, when a

small Israeli delegation appeared in Faluja in the autumn of 1948 to
negotiate a truce with the besieged Egyptians. Per his own account,
Nasser quizzed Cohen with interest about Israel's "struggle against
the British," how they had organized their "secret resistance movement" in Palestine, and how they succeeded in gaining global sym-
pathy for their cause. Other, more detailed accounts of the meeting
describe future Israeli prime minister Yitzhak Rabin also being in
attendance, along with future acting prime minister Yigal Allon.
The three Israelis are said to have met with Nasser and his superior, al-Sayyid Taha, at the nearby Kibbutz Gat, where they shared
a meal and essentially all agreed Egypt would have been better off
staying out of the war and focusing on its confrontation with Britain
at home. According to Rabin, Nasser told him they were fighting
"the wrong war against the wrong enemy at the wrong time." One
sees here, perhaps, the early roots of the more conciliatory attitude
Nasser was to take toward Israel in the final years of his life.

★

THE CAIRO TO WHICH Nasser returned from Palestine in early
1949 was a city in turmoil. While he had been away, a series of
deadly blasts had shaken the capital, including one in the historic
Jewish quarter in September 1948 that killed twenty. There had been
two attempts on the life of the Wafd's leader, Mustafa Nahhas. On
December 4, 1948, Cairo's police chief Gen. Selim Zaki was killed.
Blaming the Muslim Brotherhood for this and much of the other
bloodshed besides, Prime Minister Mahmoud al-Nuqrashi banned
the movement four days later. Nuqrashi was himself then assassinated by a Brotherhood member, Abd al-Magid Ahmad Hassan, on
December 28. In reprisal, the Brotherhood's founder and "Supreme
Guide," Hassan al-Banna, was gunned down in the street in February 1949—the month Nasser returned from Faluja—by assailants
working for the authorities.

With the Brotherhood so squarely in the crosshairs, it was only
prudent for the returning officers to keep their distance. The moment

had come at last for them to create their own independent organization, which they did in the second half of 1949. They called
themselves the "Free Officers," adopting the moniker already used in
some of the earlier pamphlets distributed by the Brotherhood's army
cells. By October 1949, they had formed an executive committee of
eight members (later expanded to ten), of which Nasser was elected
president. These were the men who would carry out the 1952 coup,
form the junta that ruled in its wake, and change the course of Arab
history. Not one was older than thirty-five.

They were an ideologically diverse bunch, spanning the full
spectrum of Egyptian opposition politics. Some, such as Khaled
Muhieddin, leaned toward the socialist left, while others such as
Abd al-Munim Abd al-Rauf were of Muslim Brotherhood persuasion. The majority, however—including Nasser—had little ideological zeal of any kind, aside from general hostility to British dominion
and an abiding sense of injured national pride.

Nor did they hold uniform or clearly articulated objectives. They
agreed Britain had to leave Egypt. Beyond that, the three military
coups that took place in rapid succession in Syria in 1949 opened
their eyes to the possibilities available to them. But the pamphlets
they began distributing in November of that year said nothing
about repeating the Syrian experience in Egypt. Instead, they kept
to vague slogans about combating imperialism, reforming parliament, and building up a strong army serving the national interest. At
times, they even lauded certain government policies. The question
is begged: Were these determined conspirators hell-bent on toppling the king and seizing power for themselves, or simply a pressure
group hoping to reform the army from within, and foster a more
wholesome, patriotic esprit de corps? If the executive committee
themselves agreed on the answer, they kept it from the rank-and-
file members, who numbered around three hundred at their peak,
and knew nothing of the coup plans until the final hours. For his
part, Nasser later said a coup was always the ultimate goal, though
at first he hadn't envisioned it taking place until about 1955. The

vertiginous tailspin into which Egypt plunged in the early 1950s compelled him to move much sooner than anticipated.

In October 1951, the Wafdist prime minister Mustafa Nahhas unilaterally abrogated the Anglo-Egyptian Treaty, removing the legal basis for the continued presence of British troops on Egyptian soil. The Suez Canal Zone transformed into a battlefield as militants launched guerrilla attacks on Britain's forty-thousand-strong force. On January 25, 1952, British Centurion tanks surrounded an auxiliary police compound in the city of Ismailia on the banks of the canal. When the police refused British orders to surrender, they met with a punishing assault that killed at least forty-four of their men.

The following day, as news of the slaughter spread, downtown Cairo went up—literally—in flames. Known ever after as Black Saturday, it was "a vision of horror unforgettable to all who lived" it, in the words of the author Anouar Abdel-Malek, who did. In the heart of Cairo's most glamorous and cosmopolitan district, scores of cinemas, restaurants, cafés, clubs, theaters, offices, banks, casinos, and hotels were put to the torch by arsonists following earlier, nonviolent protests against the Ismailia attack. At Groppi café, where Tawfiq al-Hakim liked to breakfast, "rioters toss[ed] cakes and chocolates into the street and then set fire to the place." At the world-renowned Shepheard's Hotel, where royals, celebrities, and spies mingled at cocktail hour on the terrace, the mob burst into the lobby and set the lavish carpets and furniture ablaze, sending guests—including an opera singer, the Egyptian film star May Medwar, and the *New York Times* correspondent A. C. Sedgwick—running for their lives. The ugliest scene was at the Turf Club, a members-only British establishment founded in the nineteenth century after the manner of a Victorian London gentlemen's club. As the mob rammed through the locked doors and set the club alight, members scrambled to shelter on higher floors. Some managed to jump to safety, albeit with burns and broken bones. Others were seized upon landing in the street and beaten and stabbed to death. The rest were killed inside by the smoke and flames. In all, nine Britons and one Canadian lost their lives at the club, including an eighty-four-year-old economist, James Craig, and a woman, Margaret Crawford, found under a table on the fourth floor, so charred she could be identified only by clothing and jewelry. Elsewhere across the city, several Greeks and at least sixty Egyptians were also killed in the mayhem.

Though it would not have been at all apparent at the time, the most consequential event to take place in Egypt that month had actually happened three weeks earlier, when the Free Officers swept to victory in the elections for the Officers Club board, defeating the candidates backed by the palace. It was this seemingly marginal development, soon overshadowed by Ismailia and Black Saturday, that triggered the sequence of moves that led directly to the coup six months later.

The king had not been amused to see his influence challenged in the open, and within the military, of all institutions. In the immediate aftermath of Black Saturday, however, he had what he thought were more pressing matters to deal with, such as the increasingly elusive task of finding a prime minister to run a government. By the summer, he was turning his attention once more to the army issue. On July 16—one week before the coup—he ordered the elected Officers Club board dissolved, and appointed palace loyalists to replace it.

The Free Officers' executive committee met as quickly as they could to decide their response. Even at this late hour, they were unsure how to proceed. They contemplated (not for the first time) a spree of assassinations of senior officers. In the end, they decided on a coup in early August, based on contingency plans they had tentatively begun drawing up a few months prior.

That time frame had to be hastily revised when word arrived on July 20 that the king planned to appoint as war minister none other than Husayn Sirri Amer—the man Nasser had failed to assassinate in January—with a specific mandate to hunt down the rebels within the officer corps. Learning also that the high command possessed a list of their names, they understood that it had become a now-or-never situation. The coup was brought forward to the soon-est possible date, the night of July 22.

Underprepared, unsure of success, and acting as much out of self-preservation as anything else, the young Free Officers nonetheless pulled off their coup with stunning ease. In retrospect, it is clear that power had already long slipped loose of the king's grasp, and was floating amorphously in the ether, waiting for somebody else to find it and pick it up. Having taken it firmly in hand, the officers never let it go.

◆ 2 ◆

THE TRANSITION
PERIOD

T HE FOURTEEN-MAN JUNTA THAT RULED EGYPT AFTER
July 23, 1952, lost little time eliminating all conceivable
sources of opposition. In the process, they steamrolled the old order
in its entirety, dispensing alike with its colonial and monarchical
aspects as well as its liberal cosmopolitanism, and all "the democratic freedoms so laboriously evolved by the Wafd" in the three
decades since the 1919 revolt. The end result was a profoundly
repressive dictatorship, which by late 1954 had come to be embod-
ied in the sole person of Nasser, around whom a cult of worship
was systematically constructed.

The junta's first casualty, as we have seen, was the king himself,
shipped off to exile in Italy three days after the coup. Two months
later, the officers began their frontal assault on the political class.
Their principal target was the liberal Wafd, which, for all its faults
and failings, remained the most popular party in the country, and
thus the greatest potential threat. On September 5, the junta ordered
the arrest of sixty-four leading politicians—"a virtual 'who's who'
of the old regime"—including the Wafd party secretary, Fuad Sirag
al-Din. The next day, they dismissed the token civilian they had
installed as prime minister, replacing him with their preferred frontman, the popular, middle-aged Major General Naguib. Three days
later, a new "Party Reorganization Law" dissolved all parties and
obliged them to reapply for certification.

When Egyptian law required the release of the arrested politicians in early December—since no formal charges had been brought against them—the junta's solution was to annul the constitution, removing all further legal obstacles to their ambitions. A brand-new "Treason Court" was then created on December 22, ostensibly to prosecute crimes of corruption. Indictments were issued to Sirag al-Din and twelve other Wafdists on January 1, 1953.

January was, indeed, a busy month. On the sixteenth, the junta banned all political parties and declared a three-year "transition period" of military rule. The parties were denounced as a "grave danger" to the country, conspiring with foreign powers to engineer the return of their "corrupt" rule. The once-mighty Wafd saw its funds confiscated, its headquarters closed, and its media outlets muzzled. Over two hundred arrests were made in the following days in connection with this alleged plot, encompassing Wafdists, communists, and eighty-seven university students.

At the same time, the junta announced the creation of a so-called Liberation Rally, a state-sanctioned political movement designed to supplant the parties of old. In practice, the Rally became little more than an organized pro-regime mob, used to "deploy thugs from among its ranks to either stage street demonstrations supporting the Officers or face-off against Wafdists, leftists, or Muslim Brothers when necessary."

Still in January, with an irony lost on none, the junta arrested thirty-five army officers for supporting an opposition candidate in the annual Officers Club elections—one year since the Free Officers had done the very same against Farouk's people. On January 18, as the Marxist left incurred the junta's mounting displeasure, a military decree forbade the publication of all communist media.

It was in January, too, that the junta began referring for the first time to their coup as a "revolution." Until then, they had dubbed it the "blessed movement," or simply the "army movement." Now, suddenly, they were "revolutionaries," Naguib was the "Commander of the Revolution," and the junta became the "Revolutionary Command Council."

This was more than a matter of branding or nomenclature; its implications were far-reaching. Its purpose was to resolve the twin problems of legitimacy and accountability. In its initial weeks and months, the junta had gone to some trouble to appear to be acting within the bounds of Egypt's preexisting constitutional system, adhering to the law of the land. Farouk's abdication, for instance, was—in constitutional terms—undertaken by royal decree signed by the sovereign himself, rather than any peremptory order from the military, which would have had no legal basis under the system as it then existed. Only when this charade of "constitutionality" could no longer be sustained did the junta dispense with the constitution and rule by fiat. The declaration of "revolution" was their attempt to legitimize this brazen move—for "revolutionaries," by definition, are not bound by the rules of the systems they overthrow, nor accountable to any of their institutions. What the officers were really announcing was that they were no longer subject to any authority higher than their own—for there no longer existed any such authority. Never mind that it was proclaimed only retroactively, after the fact: "revolution" licensed them to rule with absolute, unchecked authority thereafter. (This was a lesson not lost on the military men who soon seized power in other Arab countries, who made sure to style their coups as "revolutions" from the start.)

If the junta represented the "revolution," it followed that its opponents were "counterrevolutionaries" or even "enemies of the revolution," with all the concomitant tightening of the screws of repression that implied. Vowing to "strike with all ferocity the hand of any who stand in the way of our aims," the officers now expanded their political targets and pursued them with redoubled zeal. March and April 1953 saw increasing arrests of communists, who had taken to denouncing the junta in typically colorful terms as a reactionary, fascistic, and imperialist military dictatorship. Specific bones of contention included the officers' refusal to prosecute Farouk; their failure to officially abolish the institution of the monarchy (Farouk had abdicated to his infant son, Fuad II, who was thus still king at the time); their conspicuously cordial relationship with the US embassy; their banning of political parties; and their hanging of two textile workers on charges of inciting riots in the Delta town of Kafr al-Dawwar the previous year. The communist detainees were tried in closed military court sessions, some ending up in prison camps. It was the first of multiple rounds in a long duel between the regime and the left that would culminate in gruesome bloodshed at the end of the 1950s.

As though sensitive to the left's critique, in June 1953 the officers did abolish the monarchy, declaring Egypt a republic, with Naguib its first president (as well as prime minister). Nasser, who still preferred to shun the limelight at this point, became deputy prime minister and interior minister. The levers of internal security were now directly in the junta's hands, all the more so after the interior ministry merged the military and civilian intelligence services together under its unified command.

The media, already accustomed to threats and intimidation from the junta, began now to see its landscape change irreparably. Purges were conducted of the communications ministry and national broadcasting administration. By the end of the year, two venerable newspapers, *Al-Zaman* and *Al-Balagh*, closed down; more would follow. In their place arrived the junta's official daily, *Al-Gumhuriya* (The republic).

September 1953 witnessed the creation of yet another new court, the Revolutionary Tribunal, which, unlike the Treason Court, had the power to inflict capital punishment. That its three judges were all junta members with no legal qualifications—Anwar Sadat, Abd al-Latif al-Baghdadi, and Hasan Ibrahim—perhaps says all that need be said about its independence and impartiality. Its first show trial was of the former prime minister Ibrahim Abd al-Hadi, who did indeed receive a death sentence, later commuted to life imprisonment. Various Wafdists and palace cronies followed him into the dock, usually receiving fifteen-year sentences. Notable exceptions were the thirteen citizens accused of collaborating with Britain, four of whom were hanged.

After several false starts, the dramatic trial of the Wafd strongman Sirag al-Din finally began in December. The farcical proceedings "admitted any sort of damning testimony," whether or not it was of relevance to the corruption charges against him. Ultimately, he too was sentenced to fifteen years' imprisonment.

In spite of all that had happened, at the end of 1953 Nasser managed to say with a straight face to an audience in Alexandria, "The first objective of this revolution is liberation and democracy . . . we have not thought for a moment of dictatorship, for we do not believe in it. . . . We did not undertake this revolution, which calls for freedom and democracy, in order to rule over you." Risible as the claim was, it was true that the repression—though considerable—had still not quite reached the point of no return. Nor had power yet been wholly concentrated in the sole person of Nasser, who indeed remained mostly unknown to the public. Both of these would change during the watershed year of 1954.

The year began with the junta abruptly turning on the Muslim Brotherhood, to whom it had been only friendly until that point. It is no small irony, in light of Nasser's reputation for secularism today, that he in fact struck both the liberal Wafd and the godless communists long before laying a finger on the Islamists. Two Brothers had been given seats in the first Naguib cabinet of September 1952. When all other parties were banned in January 1953, the Brotherhood was the only group exempted, on the questionable grounds that it was a mere "religious association" with no political character. The junta pardoned the Brother who had assassinated Prime Minister Nuqrashi in 1948. It also threw its weight behind the Brotherhood's candidates in the Cairo University student elections of November 1952, arresting their Wafdist and communist opponents when they emerged victorious. In return, the Brotherhood gave the junta its warm endorsement, naturally applauding the assault on the Wafd, and issuing statements of support at critical moments, such as the annulment of the constitution and the Kafr al-Dawwar affair.

And yet, in mid-January 1954, the junta banned the Brotherhood and arrested over four hundred of its leaders and members. Tensions had brewed behind the scenes for some time. The creation of the Liberation Rally had irked the Brothers, not least when it was suggested they might dissolve their movement and join the Rally instead. A personality clash between Nasser and the Brotherhood's new leader, Hassan al-Hudhaybi, was aggravated further by Nasser's efforts to undermine the latter from within his own ranks. At the heart of the matter was a simple power struggle. The Brothers thought themselves rightful inheritors to a significant stake in the new regime, and sought to influence policy on something like equal terms with the officers. Nasser had no intention of allowing anything of the sort.

With the Brotherhood repressed, by February 1954 the officers had managed to make enemies of every one of Egypt's key political forces. The stage was set for a momentous confrontation. For the first (and last) time, the entire political class united with civil society in a grand collective effort to rescue the traditions and institutions of parliamentary democracy from the jaws of military dictatorship.

At the center of the action was Muhammad Naguib, Egypt's president and prime minister. Conscious of their youth and total lack of public profile, the Free Officers had decided months before the coup that it would be prudent to have an elder figure of reputable standing as their public face. A grinning, pipe-smoking war hero in his early fifties, wounded three times in Palestine, Major General Naguib fit the bill. The success at the Officers Club elections of January 1952, when Naguib led the Free Officers' list to victory, showed the partnership was a winning one. Though he had no part in planning the coup, Naguib was brought in as the figurehead as soon as it happened. The junta's first broadcast was delivered in his name; it was he who ceremoniously saw Farouk off at the port on July 26; and he became the first president of the Egyptian republic. He knew perfectly well it was a theater performance, but, as far as the public was concerned, Naguib was the man in charge, the "Commander of the Revolution."

The arrangement suited Nasser fine—until it didn't. By late 1953, Naguib appeared to be enjoying the act a little too much. The face was growing to fit the mask. Worse, the people seemed genuinely to like him, or at least to prefer him to the humorless younger officers they occasionally saw scowling by his side. When he began not only to delude himself that he possessed real power after all, but to try to wield this power against the junta, he brought about his own downfall.

The rupture came on the heels of the Brotherhood ban in January 1954, which Naguib had opposed (as he had also opposed the creation of the Revolutionary Tribunal and the prosecution of Sirag al-Din). By this point, Nasser was losing patience with him. When Naguib learned the next month that Nasser had been convening junta meetings without him, he tendered his resignation. The officers accepted, and denounced him as a megalomaniac when breaking the news to the public on February 25.

To the junta's surprise, demonstrations then erupted in the street in support of Naguib, as political forces from across the spectrum— Wafdists, leftists, Muslim Brothers, feminists, workers, intellectuals, and even a segment of the army—saw the opportunity to mount a joint stand against the cabal that was tyrannizing them. It didn't matter that Naguib had been a participant in that tyranny at every step; he was simply the cannonball with which the opposition sought to sink the officers' ship.

The vehemence of the protests stunned the officers, who had not understood the depth and breadth of ill will their brief rule had engendered. Outside Farouk's old Abdeen Palace, which had become the seat of the presidency, demonstrators called for the fall of the junta and the jailing of Nasser specifically. When word spread that Naguib was to be reinstated, victory for the opposition appeared within reach.

Catching their breath, the officers bought time by announcing several apparently major concessions on March 5. Parliamentary elections would be held, after a constituent assembly had finalized a new constitution. Martial law would end, as would the censorship of the press. Hundreds of political prisoners (mostly Muslim Brothers) were freed.

What followed has been described as a "renaissance of open political discourse." The now-unbanned parties sprang immediately back to life, and set about organizing for the coming elections and issuing statements of their positions and proposals. Prominent intellectuals, such as the journalist and novelist Ihsan Abd al-Quddus, took to the pages of leading newspapers to write openly against the junta, demand the officers return to their barracks, and debate the ins and outs of the future constitution and parliamentary system. Professional syndicates spoke out; the bar association issued a memorable statement decrying martial law as "an assault on human dignity and civil rights," insisting on a full return to civilian rule. Feminists, led by the famous Dorya Shafik, went on an eight-day hunger strike to protest the exclusion of women from the constituent assembly. Various trade unions stood with the opposition, especially the communist-led ones in Alexandria and the Delta. Workers demonstrated in the industrial towns of Helwan and Shubra al-Khayma.

On campus, teachers and students alike threw themselves into the movement. The Alexandria University faculty set the tone with a bold statement demanding an end to martial law and the dissolution of the junta. Their colleagues at Cairo and Ain Shams Universities soon followed suit. Students, meanwhile, were a crucial force on the ground from the very start, having braved police gunfire on Cairo's Qasr al-Nil Bridge to lead the march on Abdeen Palace in late February. On March 15, over one hundred women students rallied outside the same palace in solidarity with the hunger strikers.

The junta looked, for a moment, to be on the ropes. By March 25, however, it had readied its decisive counterattack. In a duplicitous feint, the officers gave the appearance of conceding total defeat, then worked immediately and ruthlessly to engineer the exact opposite. The junta would permanently dissolve itself by late July, they announced to a shocked nation. Free and fair elections would take place, with all parties welcome to participate. Those convicted by the Treason Court and Revolutionary Tribunal would see their political rights restored.

Needless to say, none of this came to pass. The officers' true plans were already in motion before the announcement was made. Five days earlier, they had set off as many as six bombs around Cairo to sow chaos and scare the crowds off the streets. One went off at Groppi café. Another detonated on Cairo University campus while hundreds of students were demonstrating, chanting, "Down with fascism" and "Down with the one-ruler regime."

When the bombings failed to clear the streets, the junta unleashed its Liberation Rally goons upon protesters. Chanting, "Down with freedom" and "No political parties and no democracy," Rally members assaulted demonstrators, attacked newspaper offices, and almost killed the country's top jurist, the State Council president Abd al-Razzaq al-Sanhuri, who has been described as "one of the most influential legal figures of Arab history." So badly was the latter beaten he required hospitalization; had the junta's Salah Salem not intervened just in time, he may have lost his life. The shocking incident became "etched in public memory as marking a rupture with the old institutions and ways of doing things."

Meanwhile, away from the streets, Nasser worked deftly to neutralize the Muslim Brotherhood, thereby knocking much of the wind out of the opposition's sails. He released over two hundred jailed members of the movement, including the Supreme Guide, with whom he then had dinner. When he gave him a personal promise to re-legalize the Brotherhood, he received the leader's assurance they would pose no further trouble to the junta.

A final coup de grâce was the regime's weaponization of trade unions. Some of these, as mentioned, had already come out against the officers, but others were more amenable to inducements, not least of the pecuniary variety. The heads of the oil, tobacco, and transit work-ers' unions were paid to put on a strike with the stated demands that political parties be banned once again and the junta rescind its decision to dissolve itself. Nasser "later boasted that he bought the working class for £E 4,000" (worth then around $11,500, or $125,000 today).

This combination of bribery, backroom dealing, and brute vio-lence soon achieved the desired result. By the end of the month, there was no one left on the streets but the students, who kept their protests going until police forced them off campus in early April, by which time the game was already up. On March 29, the offi-cers announced that military rule would continue after all until the end of the three-year "transition period"; that is, until January 1956. Egypt's short-lived "renaissance" was quashed, and with it perhaps the last chance to save the country's democracy.

It had been a near thing, at least for a few days. The most danger-ous moment for the regime had actually been at the very start, in late February, when around two hundred officers from the armored corps held a protest at their barracks against Naguib's resignation, demand-ing he be reinstated and parliamentary elections held. This was par-ticularly worrisome as the armored corps was among the most crucial and influential pillars of the armed forces. A pro-Naguib coup was not beyond the realm of possibility. It took two days of Nasser's direct intervention—he went in person to the barracks—to get a handle on the situation and ultimately arrest the insubordinate officers.

With the army secured, the truly existential threat to the junta had passed. The civilian protests that followed, while certainly inconve-nient, proved easy enough to disperse with a classic pairing of stick with carrot—or what Nasser described to a US State Department official as teaching the country a lesson.

The defeat of the March uprising brought about profoundly far-reaching changes for Egypt, and by extension the Arab world. It triggered the transformation of what had been a military autoc-racy run by a council of officers into the personal dictatorship of an all-powerful Nasser. The process involved not only an intense tightening of repression at all levels but also a fundamental restructuring of Egypt's state and society.

First came changes at the top of the power pyramid. In mid-April, Nasser became prime minister, displacing Naguib, who had collapsed of exhaustion in late March, requiring several weeks in the hospital to recover. The ailing general was permitted to remain president in name until November, when Nasser assumed that position too.

As prime minister, Nasser arrogated the powers of the junta to himself, though the Revolutionary Command Council continued to exist on paper for another two years. By appointing its members as ministers in his cabinet, Nasser formalized their subordination to him, and his seniority over them. Where once they had all theoretically been equals, making decisions by consensus, he began treating them as mere advisers, whose counsel may be appreciated but was in no sense binding. For good measure, he added "military governor-general" to his titles.

A purge of the army soon followed, after the discovery in late April of continued dissent within the armored corps. Sixteen officers were arrested and court-martialed on charges of plotting a coup; nine were jailed for up to fifteen years. So extensive were the subsequent removals of personnel that British intelligence assessed that the military capabilities of the corps had been significantly degraded.

The purges then extended far and wide in every direction, as the junta—or, rather, Nasser—moved to drain the public sphere of all conceivable sources of dissent. The March revolt had shown him the habits and instincts of democracy were embedded much deeper in the Egyptian soil than he had realized. Plainly, it would not suffice to just annul the constitution and jail a few party bosses, for, as the Egyptian historian Sherif Younis writes, "behind the parties and constitution were traditions of political participation that sprang from many different institutions." To be sure, plenty more Wafdists and other politicians would be persecuted in response to the March events. But the crackdown had to go much further. The only way for Nasser's "revolution" to succeed was to "tear democracy out from its roots."

Thus the judiciary, for one, had to be "purified," in the official terminology. The country's top jurist, Sanhuri—who had been beaten to within an inch of his life by the Liberation Rally—was removed from his post as head of the State Council (akin to Egypt's supreme court), to be replaced by a pliant functionary.

The press saw the last remnants of its freedom snatched away. *Al-Misri*, the country's largest daily, which had been "the spokesman for the whole of democratic sentiment" during the March revolt, was shut down. The prominent journalist Ihsan Abd al-Quddus, who had penned a stinging denunciation of the junta at the height of the uprising, was imprisoned, as were others including *Al-Misri*'s managing editor Mahmud Abd al-Munim Murad and Abu al-Khayr Naguib, owner of the *Al-Gumhur al-Misri* publication, which was also closed. The press syndicate was thoroughly purged, and junta member Salah Salem made its head, in what Younis calls an act of "total contempt for the profession." A new law forbidding the practice of journalism by anyone not a member of the syndicate completed the stranglehold. The once-vibrant and free-spirited Egyptian press was reduced to just three official or semi-official papers, not one critical of the regime.

Another focal point of "purification" was the universities, which had long boasted a proud tradition of political activism. It was from Cairo University's law school that the 1919 revolt against the British had erupted. As we have seen, it was on campus that the struggle in the spring of 1954 endured longest. A measure of Nasser's personal displeasure at this was his remarking "several times" to the British diplomat Anthony Nutting in later years that he "had never forgotten" how Cairo University stood against him in that critical hour.

The retribution was firm. Students were arrested, and scores of professors were fired across Cairo, Alexandria, and Ain Shams Universities, in a flagrant and frontal assault on the fundamentals of academic freedom. As with the press syndicate, the regime seized direct control of university administrations via the education ministry, granting itself the power to appoint or dismiss deans and other senior faculty members hitherto chosen by the universities alone. The education ministry also appointed officials to sit on the universities' councils. Beyond simply dissuading dissent or oppositional activism, the regime sought to depoliticize university life altogether, encouraging students to channel their extracurricular hours into sports and other unthreatening pursuits. Sure enough, Nasser succeeded in extinguishing student activism for over a decade, from 1954 until a subsequent uprising in 1968.

While this was all still going on, a dramatic event on October 26, 1954, thrust it into overdrive. Nasser was giving a speech at downtown Alexandria's seafront Manshiya Square to celebrate the signing one week earlier of a new Anglo-Egyptian Agreement. Though this agreement obliged Britain to withdraw all its forces from Egypt within twenty months, it inflamed public opinion by granting the British the right to return in the event that Turkey or an Arab League state were attacked. "From university professors to porters, from students to Nubian doormen," critics of all political stripes decried the agreement as little different from the despised 1936 treaty abrogated by the Wafd in 1951. Ending the truce it had reached with the regime during the March revolt, the Muslim Brotherhood added its loud voice to the condemnations. Tensions spiked sharply; the regime raided several Brotherhood mosques, and the group's Supreme Guide went into hiding.

As Nasser spoke on the podium in Alexandria, reminiscing to the crowd about his first protest in the same square back in the 1930s, a Brotherhood member named Mahmud Abd al-Latif approached him and fired eight shots from a pistol in his direction. None hit its target. So Hollywoodesque were the next moments that conspiracists have ever since maintained the whole scene must have been staged.

Unscathed, and still standing in place, Nasser tried to calm the panicked crowd, though the high pitch of his own voice betrayed the adrenaline charging through his veins. Telling everyone to stay where they were, he then extemporized the following:

> My blood is a sacrifice to you. . . . My life is a sacrifice to you. . . . Let them kill me, let them kill me. . . . I would die right now with peace of mind, for all of you are Gamal Abdel Nasser. . . . If Gamal Abdel Nasser dies, or Gamal Abdel Nasser is killed, then go forth with God's blessing towards glory, towards might, towards dignity. . . . Let the traitors and deceivers know that Gamal Abdel Nasser is not alone in this nation, for each one of you is Gamal Abdel Nasser, after you felt glory, and after you felt freedom, and after you felt dignity. . . . I was one of you, and I still am; I used to protest with you in this square; and I speak to you today as your leader; but, my brothers, my blood is of your blood, my soul is of your soul, my heart is of your heart, and my feelings are of your feelings. . . . If they manage to kill Gamal Abdel Nasser . . . they will not manage to kill your souls, nor your hearts, nor your proud spirits, nor your pure blood, you free people.

It was his first notable public oration. Until then, his speeches had been forgettable affairs, a far cry from the spellbinding performances of later renown. He had already begun building up his personality cult in the few months before the attack, ordering that his photos replace Naguib's in the papers, and publishing *The Philosophy of the Revolution* in September. But the results had been modest. He "confessed" to Anthony Nutting that "he had not as yet established any great popular following," and "his position therefore depended almost entirely upon the army's support." It was the high drama at Manshiya that struck a real chord with the public for the first time. The propaganda harvest extended beyond the usual outlets into popular culture, as the diva Umm Kulthum—famed and adored across the Arab world—was prevailed upon to mark the occasion with a song titled "Gamal, You Epitome of Patriotism":

*Gamal, you epitome of patriotism . . . with your survival
at Manshiya . . . we delight, and those who betrayed you
despair. . . . A perfidious traitor sought to strike, and fire upon
a beloved chest, at a heart filled with patriotism. . . . You faced
the fire with faith and stood firm. . . . The stance of the brave
moves not for cowards.*

As shall be seen, the song became an instrument of torture in
Nasser's prison camps, where inmates were forced to sing it on pain
of physical punishment.

Politically, the Manshiya attack sparked Nasser's final, decisive
break with his former friends in the Muslim Brotherhood. Now,
there would be no more dealmaking or ambiguity: the movement
had to be obliterated. The Liberation Rally torched the Brotherhood's Cairo headquarters the very next day. The Supreme Guide,
Hassan al-Hudhaybi, was arrested. Yet another new court, this time
called the People's Tribunal, was set up to try the assailant along with
Hudhaybi and other key Brotherhood figures.

This court surpassed even the Revolutionary Tribunal in brazen
disregard for elementary judicial standards. Defendants routinely
bore clear marks of physical torture, and the head "judge"—junta
member Gamal Salem—"assumed the role of inquisitor, harassing
and threatening defendants and witnesses" alike. Despite this, the
shooter's testimony, in which he described being tasked with the
mission by a militant arm of the Brotherhood known as the Special Apparatus (al-Nitham al-Khass), is generally taken to be truthful, and has been corroborated by Brotherhood sources outside the
courtroom. More controversial were the court's efforts to implicate
Hudhaybi and the political leadership directly in the plot, when in
fact they may not have known or approved of the operation.

The court sentenced the assailant, Hudhaybi, and five others to
death in December. Hudhaybi's sentence was commuted to life
imprisonment, but the other six were hanged within the week.
Meanwhile, the regime swept across the country, arresting over a

thousand Brothers, going for the first time beyond the major cities into the remoter provinces. If they didn't quite succeed in extirpating the movement entirely, they nonetheless dealt it a "staggering blow."

While they were at it, they extended their crackdown to other targets. It was now that Naguib was finally removed from the presidency and placed under house arrest, ostensibly for Brotherhood ties. Even leftist journalists and intellectuals were jailed for good measure. Indeed, "in the months after their suppression of the Muslim Brotherhood the officers arrested nearly every major opponent" of the regime, and "cleared the path for long-term dictatorial rule."

As 1954 rolled into 1955, Nasser's takeover of Egypt was complete. It had been a busy two and a half years since the coup. Fourteen people had been executed, and a conservative estimate put the number of political prisoners at three thousand. Parliament was gone; the judiciary decapitated. The country that just months earlier bore witness to a democratic "renaissance" was now a political wasteland: no parties, no protests, no press, no civil society, not even any campus activism. Egypt's long political winter had set in.

★

WITH THE DOMESTIC FRONT sewed up, Nasser began in 1955 to turn his attention to foreign affairs, which would consume much of his energies for the rest of his life. Insofar as these concerned the Arab world—where Nasser now sought to export his "revolution" abroad and work actively to undermine, and even overthrow, regional rivals—they will be treated in later chapters. For the moment, only those international engagements that also held domestic significance need be considered.

In April 1955, a first-of-its-kind gathering of leaders of newly independent states from Asia and Africa was held over the course of a week in the Indonesian city of Bandung. Largely the brainchild of India's prime minister, Jawaharlal Nehru, it brought together the heads of twenty-nine states collectively representing over half the world's population, in what was billed as an effort to forge a new power bloc independent of both the West and the Soviet Union in the context of the global Cold War. It marked an important milestone in the developing notions of decolonization and "Third-Worldism," and was a precursor of the Non-Aligned Movement later associated with the likes of Tito, Fidel Castro, and Nelson Mandela.

Nasser, who had already hosted Nehru in Cairo, was invited to head Egypt's delegation to the conference, and leapt at the opportunity of a first performance on the international stage. Wearing full military uniform (he had not yet switched to the suit, tie, and pocket square that later became his trademark), the thirty-seven-year-old charmed the statesmen and crowds alike, becoming one of the stars of the show alongside Nehru, the Chinese premier Zhou Enlai, and Indonesia's president Sukarno. "His body is so virile, his hand is so strong that it can destroy steel," remarked one excited onlooker. Despite his youth, he was made chair of the committee that decided the conference's final communiqué.

More important than the official outcome for Nasser were the conversations he was able to hold in private. Invited by Zhou Enlai to sit at his table at one of the functions thrown by Sukarno, Nasser inquired about the prospect of China selling Egypt arms. Zhou advised him to take the matter up with the Russians, and offered to pass the request on personally. Sure enough, upon Nasser's return to Cairo, the Soviet ambassador reached out to say Moscow would be only too happy to provide whatever aid Egypt might require. From this fortuitous encounter Nasser was able to eventually secure not just Soviet arms but financing for major infrastructure projects and, ultimately, a tight-knit strategic partnership with Moscow lasting for the rest of his life.

At home, great hay was made of the Bandung trip's success. Arriving at the Cairo airport, Nasser was greeted by crowds of "workers" bused in by the Liberation Rally, then driven in an open-top car for sixteen kilometers through "triumphal arches" and banners proclaiming, "Welcome, hero of Bandung, champion of peace and liberty! Welcome champion of Africa and Asia!"

Gratuitous bombast it may have been, but it reflected a real change in Nasser's self-perception and amour propre. Junta members attest he came back from Bandung a different man. No longer could they address their old friend as "Gamal"; it was now "Boss" or "Mr. President." Where once they thought nothing of staying seated when he entered the room, they were now obliged to stand.

At the same time, the conference inaugurated what has been dubbed Nasser's "Bandung period," during which he eased some of the pressure off the domestic left, and took tentative steps toward an apparent liberalization of Egypt's political climate. In part this was a matter of courting the new Soviet benefactors—the fortunes of Egypt's Marxists had a tendency to fluctuate with the vicissitudes of Cairo-Moscow relations. It was also a result of Nasser feeling more secure in his position, and realizing his new celebrity as a Third World icon might enable him to make friends out of erstwhile foes.

The process gathered pace in the landmark year of 1956. In January, a draft new constitution was published that appeared to promise a measure of democratization. It referred to Egypt as a "democratic republic"; pledged to guarantee the freedoms of opinion, assembly, and the press "within the limits of the law"; and provided for a parliament of sorts, albeit one the president had the power to dissolve. The president was also given the sole authority to appoint and dismiss cabinet ministers. This constitution was approved in June in a pantomime referendum that also saw Nasser "voted" in as president, "the first of his famous 99.9 percent victories." The junta, which now held neither de jure nor de facto authority, was formally abolished.

One month later, Nasser gave the speech that secured his place in history. On July 26—the fourth anniversary of King Farouk's abdication—Nasser returned to Alexandria's Manshiya Square, site of the 1954 assassination attempt, to announce the nationalization of the Suez Canal Company, the foreign-owned enterprise that had controlled shipping in the strategic waterway ever since it was constructed in the nineteenth century.

His primary motive, as he made plain in the speech, was financial.

He had set his mind on a grandiose infrastructure project: a giant dam on the Nile near the city of Aswan, which would significantly expand Egypt's arable land while also generating hydroelectricity, enabling his ambition to industrialize the economy. The project was technically sound but, with an estimated cost of $1 billion, more expensive than Egypt could afford.

As such, Nasser had entered into talks with the World Bank, ending in an offer for external financing. The Bank would provide a loan of $200 million for the project, on condition that the US and Britain collectively do the same, starting with $70 million for the first phase of construction. The remaining $600 million would be paid by Egypt.

The plan initially appealed to London and Washington, who thought it a way to one-up the Soviets and pull Nasser away from the Bandung club into the Western "sphere of influence." No sooner had Nasser agreed to the offer in February 1956, however, than the US and UK began to get cold feet. The dismissal of the British general John Glubb from Jordan in March alarmed the prime minister, Anthony Eden, who mistakenly believed it to be Nasser's doing. Two months later, Cairo's recognition of the communist People's Republic of China spooked Washington, already fearful that Nasser was "going Red." When the US formally dropped its offer to finance the dam on July 19, the deal collapsed, since the World Bank loan had been contingent on Washington's participation.

Nasser was out of options. The Soviets were not prepared at the time to plug the $400 million gap in the project's financing. There was only one play left, it seemed to Nasser: to nationalize the Suez Canal Company and use its considerable income to fund the dam. The company earned $100 million in revenue every year, he said in the speech at Manshiya, of which Egypt received just $3 million. Were it to be nationalized, the company would provide Egypt $500 million over five years, dwarfing the $70 million offered by the US and UK, he told the crowd with a chuckle.

This was, of course, populism, not accounting. For one, it ignored the much larger sum of $200 million that had been, but was no longer, due from the World Bank. For another, it overlooked all the Suez Canal Company's expenses—the operating and maintenance costs, wages, insurance, allocations for expansions and improvements, depreciation, and so on—which left net proceeds very much lower than the gross revenue figure: somewhere in the region of $30 million per annum. For a third, it neglected the compensation Nasser pledged to pay the company's shareholders for their nationalized holdings, which ended up totaling $65 million. Taking that payment into account, the actual sum available to spend on the dam over the following five years would amount not to the $500 million boasted by Nasser but to something closer to just $85 million—less than 10 percent of the project's cost. In the end, the dam was built only with substantial Soviet aid.

Then again, such bean-counting and nitpicking were beside the point, for there were powerful nationalist passions involved too. The canal was an Egyptian waterway, situated in sovereign Egyptian territory, as even Britain had affirmed in the 1954 Anglo-Egyptian Agreement. One hundred twenty thousand Egyptians had died building it, Nasser claimed. The Suez Canal Company, moreover, was legally an Egyptian joint-stock enterprise. For a hundred years, he thundered, Egyptians had been denied the rich fruits of their own garden by the Dickensian robber barons of European colonialism.

No longer, said Nasser, as he announced the nationalization to the roaring crowd. "The money is ours. . . . We'll build the High Dam! We'll regain our usurped rights!" And if the Americans didn't like it, they could go and "die of rage."

As it turned out, it was not the Americans he had to worry about. That the nationalization would infuriate Britain he knew well enough. What he failed to sufficiently foresee was how much it would also anger France, the largest shareholder in the company, whose prime minister Guy Mollet already loathed Nasser for his support of the Algerian independence movement. It was at Mollet's initiative that the infamous plan was laid for a three-way French,

British, and Israeli invasion of Egypt to topple Nasser's throne and forcibly restore international control of the canal.

The attack commenced on October 29, 1956, when 398 Israeli paratroopers were air-dropped onto the Mitla Pass in Egypt's Sinai Peninsula, sixty kilometers east of the Suez Canal. At the same time, Israel began a ground invasion of the Sinai, sweeping southwest from Eilat toward Sharm al-Sheikh; west from the Negev toward Suez; and northwest for the Mediterranean coast.

Eight days later, Israel held the Sinai in its entirety, as well as the Gaza Strip. The Egyptian city of Port Said at the northern entrance to the canal had been conquered by British and French forces arriving by sea from Malta. British Canberra warplanes had decimated the Egyptian air force, and struck targets in Cairo itself. Perhaps as many as three thousand Egyptians had been killed, and Nasser's worst nightmare—a British reoccupation of Egypt on his watch—had become reality.

And yet, the very next day, the invaders were compelled to declare a cease-fire and bring their advance down the canal to a halt. A deus ex machina had arrived in the form of US president Dwight Eisenhower. Whatever his own reservations about Nasser, Eisenhower was incensed that a military operation of this magnitude had been undertaken by his closest allies without his knowledge—not least after he had expressly warned Eden from the start against so much as "contemplating" the use of force. It appeared the Europeans had still not grasped the geopolitical fact that the sun had finally set on their former empires, and the great powers in the Middle East were no longer London and Paris but Washington and Moscow. Eisenhower therefore took the opportunity to impress this upon Eden, first by securing a UN General Assembly vote for a cease-fire by an overwhelming majority, then by checkmating him economically: refusing to sell Britain desperately needed oil in exchange for sterling unless and until the attack was called off. The cease-fire came on November 7, and the British and French were gone before the year was out.

It would be difficult to overstate the seismic effect the Suez War had on Nasser's celebrity, not just at home in Egypt but across the Arab world and beyond. More than any other single episode, it established his legend in the popular imagination, bestowing upon him the numinous aura of the superhuman. It mattered not at all that his army had been demolished in a week, that he owed his survival to Uncle Sam, or that Israel had succeeded in ending Egypt's blockade of the port of Eilat. It sufficed that Nasser had fought Europe's two mightiest colonial powers simultaneously, plus Israel to boot, and come out of it alive. It helped, too, that he had displayed physical courage throughout the war, appearing in person at al-Azhar Mosque two Fridays in a row to rally the nation's spirits in their darkest hour. Reminding them of his experience under siege in Palestine, he assured them, "I'm here with you in Cairo. . . . I'm not leaving," vowing in Churchillian tones to "never surrender" but instead fight the enemy "everywhere, from house to house, village to village . . . to the last drop of blood."

Suddenly, the man protesters had wanted locked up two years earlier was now feted as the new Saladin, vanquisher of the Crusaders and liberator of Jerusalem. His "photograph was to be found in souks, cafés, taxis and shops from the Atlantic to the Indian Ocean." So fervent was the admiration he inspired that people in other Arab countries began talking of merging their own states with Egypt under his leadership.

Domestically, apart from securing Nasser's grip on power as never before, the Suez War changed the nature of the country in other ways. For generations, Cairo and Alexandria had been thoroughly cosmopolitan cities, bustling with large Greek, Italian, Armenian, Syrian, and other communities, as well as sizable indigenous Christian and Jewish populations. The Egyptian scholar Louis Awad—a Coptic Christian himself—recalled the Alexandria of the 1930s and '40s as having still "had something of Lawrence Durrell's *Alexandria Quartet*," while it was "not much of an exaggeration" to liken downtown Cairo to "the Baghdad of al-Mutanabbi, where you heard every language spoken except Arabic."

After Suez, however, these "foreigners"—most of them born and bred in Egypt—fell prey to a vengeful xenophobia, formalized in official legislation expropriating their financial assets and stripping their citizenship. Around 1,000 Egyptian Jews were arrested, and some 500 Jewish families then expelled from the country. Some 2,700 British and French citizens paid for their governments' actions by being deported. An exodus of tens of thousands of other international residents began, as those who weren't removed by force read the winds and made their own way to the exit. The Greek community, which had numbered 140,000 in the early 1950s, fell to 30,000 by the late 1960s. Of the 80,000 Jews who had once lived in Egypt, only 2,500 remained by 1967. Even fellow Arabs were affected. The family of the famous Palestinian American intellectual Edward Said was one of many that relocated to Beirut, which then began to supplant Cairo as the capital of Arab letters and culture. As we have seen, Lokman Slim's mother, Selma, made the same journey at the same time. The resulting brain drain cost Egypt "both invaluable economic and technical know-how and some of the most liberal and intelligent members of her society."

Nor did the "Bandung period" deliver on its ostensible promise of democratization. It is true that a very narrow, strictly limited political space of a kind opened up temporarily between 1956 and 1958. Various "Communists, progressives and leftist liberals" were released from prison. A newspaper, *Al-Messa* (The evening), was created as a regime-sanctioned platform for the loyalist left, under the editorship of Nasser's old friend and former junta colleague Khaled Muhieddin. A number of new publishing houses were also established. Through these new avenues, as well as in magazines, plays, and radio broadcasts, the Marxist intellectuals suppressed and jailed after March 1954 were permitted to speak again for the first time. The left-wing author Anouar Abdel-Malek, who lived in Egypt at the time, argues it was a missed opportunity for Nasser to build a more dynamic and successful regime. After Suez, he "enjoyed an overwhelming popularity. . . . No one challenged his power." Had he wished to do so, he could have channeled the energies of these professors, novelists, journalists, and philosophers to his advantage.

But it was not to be. As the intelligentsia cogitated on democracy, Nasser proceeded as normal to fortify his authoritarian castle. His appointment in 1957 of a new intelligence chief, Salah Nasr, saw an apparatus intended to protect the nation from external threats turn instead into a tool of internal repression. The "parliament" created by the 1956 constitution, which lasted from its first session in July 1957 until its dissolution the following year, witnessed not a single piece of legislation come into force.

The short-lived experiment in rapprochement with the left came to an end over the course of 1958. This was the *annus mirabilis* of Nasser's pan-Arab glory; the year the colossal wave unleashed by Suez reached its high-water mark. In February, Egypt formally merged with Syria into a "United Arab Republic" under Nasser's presidency. Five months later, a coup in Iraq carried out by self-styled "Free Officers" toppled that country's monarchy and established a republican dictatorship similar in many respects to the Egyptian junta's. For reasons explored in coming chapters, the combination of these two events led to a violent rift between Nasser and communists across the Arab world, not least within Egypt itself. The Bandung period "vanished in terrorism" as the regime ended the decade with one of the most macabre chapters in its history. It is a story rarely told in the detail it merits.

3

THE GRAVEYARD OF
THE LIVING

O N THE SIXTH FLOOR OF AN OTHERWISE UNREMARK-
able building in Cairo's Heliopolis district resides the man
many would call Egypt's greatest living novelist. Now in his mid-
eighties, Sonallah Ibrahim remains little known to Anglophone
readers, though critics have sung his praises in high places. The *London Review of Books* has called him "a major voice of Arab modern-
ism," while *The New Yorker* has hailed his "superbly austere style."
(He has acknowledged a debt to Hemingway.) If the late Nobel lau-
reate Naguib Mahfouz is the Egyptian novelist everyone has heard
of, Ibrahim is the more off-piste connoisseur's choice. Experimen-
tal in form, gritty and existentialist in theme, his unflattering and
sexually forthright depictions of modern society have been getting
banned, unbanned, and rebanned ever since he began writing them
in the 1960s.

Adding to his countercultural credentials is his lifelong political
activism. An inveterate Marxist, he has been agitating against capi-
talism and Western imperialism since the early 1950s. His involvement with the communist Democratic Movement for National
Liberation (DMNL) landed him in far deeper trouble with Nasser's
regime than his fiction did. The first of several brief imprisonments
came during the March 1954 revolt, while he was a law student at
Cairo University, for co-organizing debates on democracy and economics in which opinions at variance with the junta's policies were
expressed. Further arrests followed in 1956, including one—oddly

enough—for distributing leaflets in *support* of the regime during the Suez War. There was some violence; he once had his head beaten and his glasses smashed by a security official who ended up at a senior position in the state-run Socialist Union. Yet the comprehensive crackdown inaugurated in 1959 was of an incomparably darker, bloodier, and deadlier nature. In its determination to stamp out the challenge from the left once and for all, the regime went to the extent of interning Ibrahim, along with hundreds of his comrades, in what have been fairly described as concentration camps.

Concentration camps? In Nasser's Egypt? One may be excused for wondering if the term is not sensationalist. After all, few people even inside Egypt at the time were aware of what was happening within the black box of the prison system. As another novelist, Waguih Ghali, had the protagonist of his 1964 classic *Beer in the Snooker Club* say to a fellow Egyptian: "Do you know the number of young men, doctors, engineers, lawyers in concentration camps? Or don't you know that we have concentration camps?"

The *Oxford English Dictionary* defines a concentration camp as one "in which large numbers of people, esp. political prisoners or members of persecuted minorities, are deliberately imprisoned in a relatively small area with inadequate facilities, sometimes to provide forced labour or to await mass execution." The Abu Zaabal camp— dubbed the "Graveyard of the Living"—to which Ibrahim and his fellow socialists were sent more than meets this definition.

★

THE DECISIVE ATTACK ON Egypt's left began at dawn on January 1, 1959. In a coordinated series of simultaneous raids across the country, from the major cities to the small towns of the Nile Delta and Upper Egypt, some 280 suspected communists were seized and hauled off to detention. In the days that followed, their number grew to over 1,000. Sonallah Ibrahim was taken first to the famous Citadel, an eight-hundred-year-old fortress overlooking Cairo built by Salah al-Din al-Ayyubi (aka Saladin), later used for centuries as a prison by Egypt's various Mamluk, Ottoman, British, and finally Egyptian rulers, until President Hosni Mubarak turned it into a museum in 1984.

After three months in this surreal space—part of which looked out directly onto the site of a historic massacre of Mamluk leaders in 1811—Ibrahim and his cellmates were relocated. He spent the next year shuffling among numerous facilities: Egypt Prison in Cairo; al-Qanatir al-Khayriyya Prison in the Nile Delta; and the Oases Prison deep in the southwestern desert. In February 1960, he found himself before a military court in Alexandria, facing trial on charges of conspiring to overthrow the regime. The trial ended on June 14, 1960, with no judgment or sentence delivered. That same night, he was taken to Abu Zaabal, where the event he would later describe as the "ugliest" in Nasser's entire reign took place the following day.

★

IT WAS PAST MIDNIGHT when the prisoners set off from Alexandria, chained together like chattel in large vehicles. Not until 5:30 a.m. did they reach the camp, more than two hundred kilometers away, on the northeastern outskirts of Cairo.

Stepping out of the vehicle, Ibrahim found himself in an outdoor yard walled with piles of putrid rubbish. Before him were soldiers armed with machine guns, as well as officers on horseback wielding whips, sporting distinctive moustaches twirled upward. Rudely, he was ordered—amid a stream of insults—to squat down on his heels and bow his head. He could hear the thumps of sticks colliding with human flesh and bone around him. Sneaking a glance, he spied a friend being whipped and called a "son of a bitch." For an hour and a half, Ibrahim stayed in this position, till he could no longer feel his legs. But this was only the beginning.

Suddenly, he heard his name called out, and was ordered to stand up. Casting his eyes around, he caught sight of men sprinting while being chased by the mysterious horsemen.

"Run, you son of a dog!" yelled a voice at him.

Following the lead of three others whose names had also been called out, he began running between two long parallel lines of soldiers attacking him with clubs, bats, and cudgels of all different sizes. "I can still recall the face of one young man," he writes in his memoir of the experience, "totally expressionless as he pummeled my body with a stick as thick as a tree trunk." Reaching the end of the lines, he found himself before a large table at which several men sat wearing dark sunglasses, some in military uniform, others in civilian attire.

One asked Ibrahim his name. Before he had a chance to reply, an officer yelled, "Your name, you son of a bitch!" When he did respond, the officer barked, "Louder! Say *efendim* ['my master']!"

"Take him away," muttered the man at the table.

Within seconds, Ibrahim was stripped naked, insulted, and beaten with more sticks. A man came and shaved his head and pubic hair, all while the flogging continued.

"Lie down on your back," ordered a voice. "Say, 'I'm a woman.'"

More beatings followed. Eventually, a voice said, "Enough," and Ibrahim was dragged along the ground, then ordered to run to a large hangar with an open door. Inside, he found his fellow inmates, dazed and bloodied, wincing and groaning, some leaning against the walls, others slumped on the bare ground. The ordeal was over at last: they had survived what Abu Zaabal's wardens found it amusing to call the *tashrifa*, or "welcoming ceremony."

The most prominent member of their group, however, was missing.

SHUHDI ATTIAH AL-SHAFII WAS a giant of the Egyptian left in all senses of the word. An Oxbridge-educated intellectual in his late forties, he was a decorated veteran of the struggle against the ancien régime, having been arrested in 1947 and sentenced to years of hard labor for his communist activism. Editor in chief of *Al-Gamahir* (The masses) magazine and founder of a publishing house, he had authored a number of books, most notably *The Development of the*

Egyptian National Movement, 1882–1956, published in 1957. He was tall and broad shouldered, a magnetic figure to whom others instinctively turned for leadership. Ibrahim writes frankly of looking up to him like a father or elder brother.

At the military court in Alexandria, Shuhdi took it upon himself to mount a spirited defense of his fellow accused. The gist of it was that the partisans of the DMNL—which he had cofounded—were stalwart patriots who supported Nasser's regime, and deemed themselves allies thereof, even if they also had reservations about certain less-than-fully-democratic practices. More to the point, for the regime and the communists to break ranks would be in the interests of none but their common enemies: the reactionaries and imperialists. In summation, he asked the judges to set the defendants free, that they may dutifully assist "our national government and our president Gamal Abdel Nasser" in building the progressive Egypt of tomorrow that all agreed they sought.

It was worth a try, one might say. But if Shuhdi truly believed his romantic appeal to revolutionary solidarity would carry weight with the unsmiling men of the military, he was fatally mistaken. Indeed, it appears in retrospect that his court performance contributed directly to the fate that befell him at Abu Zaabal the very next day.

★

BY CHANCE, IT HAPPENED that Ibrahim sat next to Shuhdi on the night drive from Alexandria to the camp, their hands shackled together at the wrists. He recalls they spent the journey discussing Hemingway. When they arrived, and the *tashrifa* began, they were initially near each other. Due to his height, Shuhdi's head stuck out above the others while they squatted on their heels, and Ibrahim saw an officer club Shuhdi on the neck, telling him, "Lower your head, boy."

Soon after, Ibrahim heard someone ask which one of them was Shuhdi. Without hesitation, Shuhdi replied, "Me." It was the last time Ibrahim heard his voice. As they were separated moments later,

Ibrahim was not a direct eyewitness to what happened to Shuhdi next. Another inmate, however, saw everything.

From the start of the *tashrifa*, it was clear Shuhdi had been singled out for especially cruel treatment. His beatings were longer and harsher; the verbal abuse more vituperative. When he reached the table of men in dark glasses, where the other detainees were sent off to the hangars, he was taken instead to a separate area by a warden named Abd al-Latif Rushdi. The latter was infamous in the camp for having clubbed an inmate's head open on the day that came to be known as Bloody Wednesday. That the men in glasses chose Rushdi to take care of Shuhdi was ample indication of their intentions.

"Say, 'I'm a woman'!" Rushdi yelled while bludgeoning Shuhdi's back, sides, and head with his stick.

"Say, 'I'm a woman'!"

But Shuhdi would not say he was a woman. He "took the beatings in silence, never opening his mouth in a single cry of pain."

"Say, 'I'm a woman'!"

Shuhdi fell to his knees. The beatings continued.

"Say, 'I'm a woman'!"

He fell flat on the ground. Still, the beatings rained down on his naked, motionless body.

"Say, 'I'm a woman'!"

Finally, Rushdi stopped, and summoned the camp doctor to check the body. The atmosphere in the camp changed palpably in an instant. The men in dark glasses hurried off and sped away in cars. Those still undergoing the *tashrifa* were given a few hasty last whacks and then swept into the hangars, where the word was already spreading:

Shuhdi was dead.

★

SHUHDI WAS NOT THE FIRST to be killed at Abu Zaabal. Indeed, he and Ibrahim had arrived at what turned out to be the tail end of the bloodbath. Ten days later, Ibrahim was moved to another prison, and the camp was soon closed.

For the less fortunate, who had by then spent many months in the camp, the *tashrifa* had merely been the start of the ride, and by no means the worst of it. A fuller picture of the camp experience is provided by the author Ilham Sayf al-Nasr, who arrived seven months prior to Ibrahim, in his memoir, *Fi Mu'taqal Abu Za'bal* (In Abu Zaabal Camp).

Ilham had spent most of 1959 much as Ibrahim had. Arrested on January 1, he passed through the Citadel and Oases prisons before winding up at the same military court in Alexandria. Upon arrival at Abu Zaabal on November 8, his *tashrifa* was the same in its essentials: whippings by the men on horseback; running through the parallel rows of officers swinging truncheons; the beatings, slappings, and floggings while naked and shorn in front of the men in dark glasses.

Unlike Ibrahim, however, Ilham was destined to spend seven more months at the camp, undergoing days much worse than his *tashrifa*. His memoir provides a trove of information about all conceivable aspects of the camp, from the physical layout to the food to the individual wardens' names and backgrounds to the wide variety of torture and forced labor practiced, including in-depth accounts of especially unpleasant episodes, like Bloody Wednesday.

The camp comprised a large square containing six elongated hangars. Around the perimeter stood high yellow walls, with armed guards on wooden platforms in each of the four corners, watching and listening round the clock. There was only one way in or out, through a heavily guarded ironclad gate on the eastern wall.

Each hangar had a lockable door at one end, and a toilet at the other. Between the two was nothing but bare ground, flanked by two parallel strips of asphalt upon which as many as one hundred prisoners slept without mattresses. Air was provided by several iron-barred openings in the walls, far above head height, which also enabled the guards to listen in at all times.

Torture occurred daily. The bare minimum one could expect,

at the best of times, was to be lined up against the wall upon waking in the morning and clubbed on the back, a daily routine repeated in the evening before the hangar was locked for the night. No visits were permitted; no books, pens, or paper; no radios; and no shoes. The food was abominable: a handful of beans caked in muck and crawling with flies and worms was often an entire day's nourishment. There was no medical care, and—since there were also no showers—diseases such as eczema, scabies, and anemia soon grew rife. One inmate, Rushdi Khalil, perished from typhoid, having been "simply left to die with no treatment." These were the conditions in which Nasser saw fit to intern university professors, mathematicians, lawyers, engineers, doctors, teachers, and poets.

It only got worse as time went on, and new innovations in the torture were gradually introduced. Instead of simply facing the walls for their morning beating, the inmates might one day be made to lie down on the ground in a line and be bludgeoned one by one. That was called "the piano." Next, they might be told to do push-ups while the guards ran over their backs, drubbing anyone who collapsed for "failing to follow orders."

Then there was the night an officer burst into the hangar at 2 a.m. and started clubbing them all senseless while laughing hysterically, apparently high on drugs. Another time, the same officer had taken a keen interest in one inmate, Saad Zahran, who had a wooden foot; the officer made a point of incapacitating his one good leg by kicking it repeatedly and walloping the sole of its foot. It was this same officer, again, who in late November 1959 put a rod to the skull of Dr. Farid Haddad—a childhood friend of Edward Said—during his *tashrifa*, splitting the bone apart. Ilham watched Haddad die in front of him, "on the ground, naked; his head smashed; his brain fluids soaking the sand."

Worse even than the beatings, however—for those who survived them—was the forced labor, according to Ilham. Half an hour's march north of the camp was a large basalt rock quarry known to inmates as "the mountain," though it was actually beneath ground, not above it. Several meters deep, and over a kilometer in diameter, its giant cavities are still visible today with satellite imagery.

It was here that common criminals—murderers, thieves, drug dealers—who had been formally sentenced to hard labor would come to carry out their duties. After the inner walls of the quarry were blasted with dynamite, the prisoners would break the large basalt blocks into smaller pieces using hammers and other hand tools, then carry the fragments in leather pouches to a machine that pulverized them. The end product would ultimately be used to pave Egypt's roads and streets.

Ilham and the other communists, however, were not common criminals, nor had they received sentences of any kind. Kept apart at all times from the other prisoners, they were brought to the quarry not to work, but simply to be abused—in other words, to be tortured.

It began a few weeks after their arrival at the camp. One morning, following the ritual beating, they were surprised to be ordered out of their hangars into the main courtyard, where they found all the camp's other inmates lined up in three rows. Joining them, they were escorted en masse by guards armed with automatic rifles, and officers on horseback, through the camp's exit to the outside world. Forced to march—barefoot—for half an hour, they finally arrived at the quarry, and were led down into its depths.

A tense silence was broken by a loud whistle from a guard, at which dozens of his colleagues descended upon the prisoners with clubs and cudgels, dishing out vicious beatings. When this stopped, they were made to congregate at one end of the quarry, fill up leather pouches with rocks, and then run with them to the other end through two parallel rows of guards battering them with sticks the entire way. Anyone who paused to catch his breath, or who tripped and fell down, was walloped all the harder until he was running once again.

This went on for an hour, until another whistle brought matters to an end, and they were led back to the camp. But that was merely the "rehearsal," to quote Ilham. The next day, the procedure was repeated from morning till sundown. The same happened the following day, and the days after. With time, they came to realize they had collectively shifted several tons of rock and earth from one end of the quarry to the other, only to then carry it all back to where they'd started. It was an exercise in utter futility: the sole purpose was to break them, physically and mentally.

It was "the greatest torture" of all, writes Ilham: "days that wouldn't end," as "ribs were shattered" and "bodies were turned into blue bruises, suppurating wounds, and swellings."

On Wednesday, February 17, 1960, the pain reached its pinnacle.

The day known to the annals of Abu Zaabal history as Bloody Wednesday began with an act of rebellion. The inmates of Hangar No. 1—who included Ilham—had been forced to line up standing in three rows of twenty, one row behind the other, in imitation of a choir. Sitting before them were all the other inmates of the camp, numbering several hundred in total. The selection of Hangar No. 1 was no accident, for it contained the leaders and foremost personalities of the communist movement nationwide. Clearly, an example was to be made of them in front of their juniors, *pour encourager les autres* and to crush the morale and cohesion of the group as a whole.

Conducting the show was the camp's senior warden, Hasan Munir, flanked as usual by officers and soldiers bearing rifles and heavy truncheons.

"I am pleased with you, children," said Munir, addressing the choir. "As such, I've decided to teach you how to sing. Do you know the song, 'Gamal, You Epitome of Patriotism'? Go on, children, sing!"

No sound came forth.

"Sing, children, or I shall be upset with you!"

Silence. The tension was mounting fast. Soldiers squared up to the inmates, brandishing their weapons. Munir gestured to a man standing in the front row, who happened to be Dr. Ismail Sabri Abdallah, a trilingual professor of economics at Alexandria University, who had earned his doctorate from the University of Paris and would go on to become a cabinet minister under President Anwar Sadat.

"Sing, child!" spat Munir.

But, instead, Abdallah launched into an impromptu speech. This camp, he said, was no place for patriotic songs. Their place was outside its walls, in the air of freedom. As proud Egyptian patriots, he and his comrades would be honored to sing for their nation, but not under duress. "We refuse to sing before rifles and truncheons. We refuse to sing on command."

That he could not have failed to anticipate exactly what would happen next only made Abdallah's words that much more astounding. As Munir erupted in apoplectic obscenities, the bats and cudgels rained in torrents upon the professor, who fell to the floor, still and silent, blood pouring from his head.

The flailing truncheons then turned on the rest of Hangar No. 1. Bloody Wednesday had begun.

After that initial beating, the men were marched off to the quarry, well aware that a vengeful retribution was in store. As they neared the craters, they saw long rows of guards wielding sticks already waiting for them at the bottom. The routine was as normal—sprint from one end to the other carrying rocks while being battered the entire time—but the intensity was like never before. Thirty men fainted; it's a wonder none was killed. When the sun finally set, half the inmates had to be carried back on the shoulders of their fellows. Upon arrival at the camp, yet another beating was administered.

For all its agony and terror, Ilham recalls Bloody Wednesday as the left's finest hour in Abu Zaabal; the day they were subjected to their most grueling test, and came out with honor fully intact, and iron mettle displayed. No one, after all, had sung the song. They had dared to defy the camp's tyranny, and taken everything it could throw at them, and survived. For that reason, spirits were paradoxically high in the hangars once night fell, and the doors closed, and the tales of heroism circulated. The stoic courage of the aforementioned literature scholar and public intellectual, Dr. Louis Awad, went on to become the stuff of legend. A forty-four-year-old graduate of Cambridge and Princeton, Awad was no communist at all, but had been jailed all the same for being vaguely leftish and insubordinate. Upon arrival at the hangar that night, bloodied and breathless, his thick spectacles shattered, this prolific author and translator of Joyce and Aeschylus dryly remarked, "Today I discovered Egypt does not respect habeas corpus."

★

THE BRUTALITY AT ABU ZAABAL continued unabated until the killing of Shuhdi Attiah, which, given his prominent profile, could not easily be ignored by the regime, at least at first. Nasser happened to be in Yugoslavia as Tito's guest at the time, and was embarrassed to have to answer questions from his hosts about the death of a distinguished socialist and patriot in his custody. He made a point of ordering an official inquiry into the matter. It was a charade, quickly buried, but the torture did in fact stop at Abu Zaabal thereafter, and the inmates were permitted family visits and medical care for the first time. Within weeks, the camp was closed.

Only after he had already left Abu Zaabal was Sonallah Ibrahim finally sentenced to seven years of hard labor, and taken back to the Oases Prison in the desert. This was certainly no picnic in itself—in 1963, one of its inmates, Louis Ishaq, was shot dead by a guard. Yet it was not on the level of Abu Zaabal. Books, newspapers, magazines, and writing implements could be smuggled in from outside, or improvised on-site. Lectures, plays, live music, poetry nights, and even soccer matches were organized by the inmates. For Ibrahim, who wrote several short stories between its walls, it was a formative experience of the highest order: the place where "I decided to become a writer."

In 1964, Nasser drew closer than ever before to the USSR. Khrushchev paid a high-profile sixteen-day visit to Egypt in May of that year, participating in a grand ceremony at Nasser's flagship infrastructure project, the Aswan High Dam, built largely with Soviet aid. As a goodwill gesture—or possibly at Khrushchev's insistence—Nasser at last released the communists from jail. Ibrahim was freed on May 10, one day after Khrushchev arrived, and went off to write his semi-autobiographical debut novella, *Tilk al-Ra'iha* (That smell), about a young man struggling to adjust to newfound freedom in Nasser's Cairo after years in prison.

But the Egypt of the 1960s shall be left for a later chapter. To grasp how and why it differed so markedly from the 1950s—and why the horrors at Abu Zaabal happened in the first place—we must first explore what Nasser had been getting up to elsewhere in the Arab world.

IRAQ

4

THE BANNER OF
FREEDOM

BY SEVEN O'CLOCK ON THE MORNING OF MONDAY,
July 14, 1958, the Iraqi royal palace was in flames.

Half an hour earlier, the young King Faysal II had listened to
Baghdad Radio—now renamed Free Iraq Radio—as a military
officer declared the country "liberated" from "the corrupt clique
installed by imperialism" and "the tyrannical class that scorned the
rights of the people." The reference was to Faysal's own royal house
and its political entourage, in whose place a "people's republic"
would now be established: "the Republic of Iraq."

The shelling of the palace began shortly afterward. Their guards
having surrendered, the fleeing royal family made it as far as the palace courtyard before an insurgent soldier mowed them down from
behind, killing the twenty-three-year-old sovereign along with
Crown Prince Abd al-Ilah, Queen Nafisa, Princess Abadiya, and
their accompanying staff. In the orgy of violence that lasted the full
day and well into the night, the crown prince's body came in for special treatment: "hands and feet hacked off, mutilated, dragged naked
through the streets, hung up as a spectacle, driven over repeatedly
by cars, until nothing was left but a piece of spine and flesh." It took
one more day to track down Prime Minister Nuri al-Said, who had
slipped across the Tigris on hearing the gunfire. Spotted in the street
disguised as a woman, he was shot dead, before his corpse too was
dragged along the roads, strung up, dismembered, and set on fire.

Unsavory as the spectacle looked to many, one notable observer expressed satisfaction with the result. "The banner of freedom is raised today in Baghdad," declared Gamal Abdel Nasser to a crowd in Damascus four days later. This banner of freedom (a phrase used eleven times in the speech), which already flew high over Cairo, would soon—Nasser vowed—be hoisted up also in Amman, in Beirut, and indeed "all over the Arab world."

★

HAVING CONSOLIDATED HIS RULE by late 1954, it would have been perfectly possible, in theory, for Nasser to content himself with Egyptian affairs, leaving other Arab countries to govern themselves as they pleased. Historically, Egyptian nationalism had been exactly that: Egyptian, attending to the particular interests of the people of the Nile Valley, with little or no special consideration given to the disparate concerns of other peoples elsewhere. Conscious of their unique Pharaonic heritage, on the one hand, and the indigenous identity and language of Egypt's Coptic Christians on the other, the intelligentsia were undecided as to whether Egyptians were Arabs at all. Influential nationalists such as Ahmad Lutfi al-Sayyid saw the Egyptian nation as a distinct entity, while Taha Husayn went so far as to assert that Egyptians were actually Europeans.

At all events, radical pan-Arabism of the kind that resonated in places like Syria made very little headway in Egypt in the first half of the twentieth century. The Free Officers themselves were "Egypt Firsters" almost to a man, and their original six-point program was wholly domestic in scope. Even Nasser was never rigorously ideological in his Arab nationalism. His intellectual formation owed far more to Egyptian nationalists such as Mustafa Kamil and Lutfi al-Sayyid (to whom the junta twice offered the presidency) than to such pan-Arab zealots as Sati al-Husri or Michel Aflaq.

It was for reasons fully known only to himself, then, that Nasser chose in late 1954 to barge his way so aggressively into Arab affairs, against the natural inclinations of his compatriots and closest colleagues alike. Scarcely had he bundled President Naguib off to house arrest than Egypt's new "Commander of the Revolution" put the Arab world's statesmen on notice that he expected them to follow his lead and dance to his tune—or else. The first of the many clashes to which this attitude inevitably gave rise took place in Iraq.

★

THE INITIAL TRIGGER OF the great Arab showdown of 1955 seems so innocuous in retrospect that it's difficult to believe it could have generated as much rancor as it did. In February of that year, Iraq and its neighbor Turkey signed a "pact of mutual cooperation," which came to be known as the Baghdad Pact. Its stated terms were as dry and unremarkable as the name suggested: the two states would cooperate in matters of security and defense; they would not inter-fere in each other's internal affairs; they would settle any disputes between themselves in a peaceful manner. And that was about it. Left to their own devices, few people anywhere would have found much cause to be exercised about the news. Inside Iraq itself, opposi-tion to the pact was "remarkably feeble." There was, after all, a clear strategic rationale from the Iraqi perspective for friendly ties with the northern neighbor, not least given lingering fears of Turkish designs on Mosul, and the perennial potential for Ankara to destabilize Iraq's restive Kurdish region. To many minds, it was only natural that two states sharing a border, along with centuries of historical, cultural, and religious bonds, should seek improved bilateral relations.

And yet, from 1,300 kilometers beyond the horizon in Cairo, a howling thunderstorm of apoplectic vituperation rose forth, washing over all corners of the Arab world, propelled by Egypt's popular new "Voice of the Arabs" radio broadcasts, which hit the airwaves just as transistor radio sets had become readily available and affordable on a mass scale.

The Iraqi–Turkish Pact, proclaimed Cairo Radio, spelled the end of Palestine. It meant the end of Arab unity. Its architect, the Iraqi prime minister Nuri al-Said, was committing an act of "bare-faced treason . . . an act of treachery against Arabism far more damaging . . . than anything done by Israel or Zionism." The Iraqi people would defy him and "destroy this filthy piece of paper."

The level of vitriol was truly unprecedented in the Arab politics of the time, which generally set great store by rhetorical courtesy and decorum. The coarse, abusive new tone from Cairo, more redolent of Leninist fanaticism than the genial etiquette of the court and *majlis*, took everyone by surprise. What was going on?

It was true that the Baghdad Pact was rather more than an exclusively Iraqi-Turkish affair. Two months later, Britain added itself to the pact, under the articles of a new "special agreement" signed with the Iraqi government on April 4, 1955. This was a more substantial document, granting Britain the right to maintain military personnel and aircraft in Iraq ("at the request of the Government of Iraq") for as long as both states remained parties to the pact. By the end of the year, Iran and Pakistan had also joined the pact, meaning its members formed an unbroken chain extending from the edge of Europe to the borders of India and China. To all outward appearances, a solid wall of British allies now linked NATO (via Turkey) to its Asian counterpart, SEATO (via Pakistan), blocking Soviet expansion from the north and cementing Britain's primacy in the Middle East.

Nasser had known something of this kind was afoot in advance of the Iraqi-Turkish Pact, since Iraq's prime minister, Nuri, had told him as much in his own home in Cairo in September 1954. According to the Free Officer and junta member Salah Salem, who was present, Nasser told Nuri he was "free to do whatever you wish," but Egypt would chart a separate course. In reality, Nasser had no intention at all of leaving Nuri a free hand. This was a crucial point of principle, lying at the heart of so many of Nasser's dustups in the years to come. For Nasser, it was never enough to agree to disagree, for him to head one way and other Arab states another: everyone had to fall in line behind Cairo. The "revolution" had to be exported beyond Egypt's borders—by direct intervention and, if necessary, by force.

Thus, no sooner had Nasser bid Nuri farewell than the Voice of the Arabs called on Iraqis to "raise your heads from the imperialists' boots." In January 1955, Nasser upped the ante, summoning all Arab League heads of state to Cairo for a summit aimed at nipping the Baghdad Pact in the bud. This was the first active bid for Arab leadership by the thirty-seven-year-old premier, who was still largely an unknown entity outside Egypt. (He had not yet made his great splash at Bandung.)

The results were mixed. While no state other than Iraq was prepared to say it would join the pact, most were equally reluctant to condemn Iraq for doing so, taking the conventional diplomatic view that, as a sovereign state, Iraq was entitled to determine its own foreign policy. Naturally, the meeting failed to prevent the pact going ahead: Iraq signed it the following month. Still, the summit had lasting significance in one respect: it drew up the battle lines that would divide the Arab world for years thereafter into a "revolutionary" camp, led by Nasser, and a "reactionary" one headed by Iraq's Nuri. (That the "revolutionary" camp included at that point the ultraconservative Kingdom of Saudi Arabia was not the kind of detail the Voice of the Arabs chose to emphasize.) Though the members of each clique varied over time, the basic framework remained until the end of Nasser's life—and indeed lingered on after his death, as new contenders vied for his mantle and bludgeoned their own foes with his same rhetorical flourishes.

It remains to be explained why Nasser's antipathy for the pact was quite so vigorous. Certainly, a self-styled "revolutionary" and "anti-imperial" regime such as his own, which claimed the expulsion of Western armies from Arab soil as a raison d'être, could hardly applaud an agreement extending Britain's presence in Iraq indefinitely. Even in Farouk's day, the Wafd had opposed participation in Western military alliances as a point of principle. It's also true that Nasser was at this time much swayed by India's Nehru, who had his own parochial reasons for opposing the pact, in light of Pakistan's membership. But none of these suffices to fully account for the sheer toxicity of the venom emanating from Cairo. Two further factors merit a mention.

The first concerns Nasser's position at home in Egypt, which he evidently thought still precarious. It will be recalled that, just three months before the January 1955 summit, Nasser had met with stinging denunciations from all quarters for the agreement he himself had signed with Britain in October 1954. He had, indeed, quite literally come under fire for it, nearly paying with his life in Alexandria.

Significantly, the terms of Nasser's Anglo-Egyptian Agreement had one conspicuous point in common with the Baghdad Pact: both granted Britain the right to reoccupy local military facilities in the event of an attack on Turkey. To the extent that the Baghdad Pact linked Iraq with NATO, the Anglo-Egyptian Agreement could be said to do the very same with Egypt. Indeed, the domestic attacks on Nasser in the autumn of 1954 found uncanny echoes in Cairo's onslaught against the Baghdad Pact only weeks later. The charge by the Brotherhood's Supreme Guide Hassan al-Hudhaybi that Nasser had, in effect, extended Britain's presence in Egypt by five years, since the original 1936 treaty was due to expire anyway in 1956, mirrored the observation that the 1930 Anglo-Iraqi Treaty would have terminated in 1957, had the Baghdad Pact not replaced it. When Egypt's communist DMNL decried Nasser's new Anglo-Egyptian Agreement as a "treaty of ignominy and shame, of treachery, imperialism, and war," it might have been quoting a Voice of the Arabs broadside against Nuri al-Said.

Suffice it to say that the subject of pacts with Britain was a sore and sensitive one for Nasser, and so, when the Baghdad Pact materialized, he felt he could ill afford a stance of anything less than maximum enmity. He all but admitted as much in private to Anthony Nutting, the British diplomat who signed the 1954 agreement on London's behalf, to whom he confessed that a defense arrangement with Britain would indeed be in Egypt's interests, but he lacked the domestic support needed to make it happen.

The second, and not unrelated, factor was Nasser's fear the Baghdad Pact would render Iraq preeminent on the Arab stage, especially if it were accompanied by the provision of the kind of modern

Western weaponry Nasser had been notably incapable of procuring himself. The January 1955 summit had exposed the limits of his own regional clout, raising prickly questions of "prestige," not least as it had taken place on his home turf. Having personalized the dispute by going after Nuri by name on the airwaves, Nasser transformed the issue into a duel between himself and the Iraqi premier, only one of whom could prevail. When Nuri insouciantly ignored all of Cairo's protests and signed the pact as planned in February, Nasser set his mind to bringing him down.

This would have seemed a considerable task at the time, for Nuri was a towering figure—perhaps *the* towering figure—of early twentieth-century Arab politics. Born in 1888 in Baghdad to a minor local official in the administration of the Ottoman Empire that then ruled Iraq along with much of the Arab world, he rose from unexceptional beginnings to become prime minister of his country no fewer than fourteen times. Along the way, friends and foes alike acknowledged his boundless drive and energy, and his extraordinary ability to know everyone and be everywhere at exactly the right time—until, of course, the fateful day in 1958 when his luck ran out.

As a young soldier in the Ottoman army in 1910, he had befriended Atatürk—the future founder and first president of the Turkish Republic—who was then his senior captain. In the town of Babaeski, by the Bulgarian border, the two spent one particularly memorable evening of merriment, ending with Nuri bandaging the great man's head and helping him to bed after a bottle of *raki* brandy had been smashed over his skull. (Aside from his native Arabic, Nuri spoke fluent Turkish, solid French, and passable English.)

By the time the First World War broke out four years later, Nuri had imbibed the Arab nationalism then thick in the air, and joined the historic Arab Revolt against the Ottomans when it kicked off in 1916. Proving his mettle by helping to drive the Turks out of the Hejaz, he soon found himself fighting shoulder to shoulder with the famous T. E. Lawrence ("of Arabia"), who wrote glowingly of Nuri's "courage, authority, and coolness" on the battlefield in his celebrated account of the revolt, *Seven Pillars of Wisdom*. The two made quite a pair: storming Turkish positions in the heights over the Dead Sea; sheltering from bombers under rocks in the Hawran; Nuri giving Lawrence the signal to blow up a bridge outside Daraa. When he wasn't charging the enemy, Nuri spent his evenings with the band of Iraqis and other Arabs under his command, swigging Scotch and playing poker for gold coins. After their triumphant arrival in Damascus in October 1918, when Lawrence made Nuri overall commandant of the troops, he pressed the advance farther north through Homs and Hama, finally chasing his old friend Atatürk out of Aleppo just days before the armistice.

For Nuri, the war transitioned seamlessly into a political career. It had put him on intimate terms with the two forces destined to reign supreme in Iraq for the next four decades: the British; and the Hashemite dynasty, guardians of Islam's holy city of Mecca, who had formally led the revolt. In the post-war settlement, the Hashemite princes Faysal and Abdallah became kings of Iraq and Jordan, respectively. As chance would have it, Nuri had enjoyed a warm friendship with Faysal since they first met in the Hejaz in 1916. From the moment the fighting stopped, he remained by Faysal's side, accompanying him on trips to London, Italy, and Egypt. Once established on the Iraqi throne, Faysal made Nuri his chief of staff, then deputy commander in chief of the armed forces (Faysal was ceremonially commander), as well as defense minister, in which capacities Nuri oversaw the creation and expansion of Iraq's national army. But loftier stations beckoned. In 1930, he became prime minister for the first of fourteen times, bringing Iraq into the League of Nations and signing a new Anglo-Iraqi Treaty. Though his fortunes waned following Faysal's death in 1933, the Second World War brought him to the fore once again, and from the end of the war until his own death in 1958 he was the unsurpassed dynamo and strongman of Iraqi politics—ruling, it should be said, with a pronounced authoritarian streak.

Given the life he had led, it is perhaps small wonder Nuri felt little inclination to submit meekly to Nasser's dictates. It wasn't only a matter of believing he needed few lectures on Arab nationalism from a man thirty years his junior—younger than his own son—with no military accomplishments to his name, who was not even alive at the time Nuri was leading troops into battle to liberate occupied Arab land. ("I am not a soldier in 'Abd al-Nasir's army," he had politely but firmly told the junta's Salah Salem in early 1955. "Please tell him that I will never obey his orders.") It was also the generational and circumstantial gulf that separated the two men's perspectives. For if Nasser, coming of age in the Egypt of the Lampson Affair and Ismailia massacre, had known the British only as imperious occupiers who gunned down students at protests, Nuri saw Britain as something else entirely: an indispensable ally of the Arabs against the Ottoman despots (and, in later years, the twin menace of Nazism and communism).

Yet if Nuri vowed never to serve as a soldier in Nasser's army, there were others in Iraq who felt differently. His controversial Anglophilia, combined with his iron-fist methods, plus the unpopular alliance with large landowners and tribal elders on which his narrow power base rested, had earned Nuri no shortage of domestic opponents by the 1950s. At the civilian level, these ranged from communists to Arab nationalists to liberal constitutionalists to Kurdish parties. However, just as it had been junior army officers who brought down Farouk in Egypt, so in Iraq it was in the ranks of the very military Nuri had helped build up that his most dangerous foes emerged, and resolved to emulate their Egyptian counterparts.

It took just two months for Egypt's coup to inspire an Iraqi franchise of the "Free Officers." The first secret cell was founded in September 1952 by Maj. Rifaat al-Hajj Sirri and his close friend, Maj. Rajab Abd al-Majid, at the engineering barracks at al-Rashid Camp in southeast Baghdad. Like Nasser himself, both officers were in their early to mid-thirties, and hailed from modest backgrounds. That the Egyptian putsch was their model and inspiration was stated explicitly by Abd al-Majid in his memoirs. They sought, in short, to topple the Iraqi monarchy by means of a military coup, and install in its place an Arab nationalist republic in the Nasserist mold.

At first, progress was slow. Abd al-Majid was transferred to England, and, though Sirri secured some high-profile recruits, he was also compromised by leaks. Soon enough, however, other cells began spawning in the barracks spontaneously and independently of one another. The most important of these coalesced around Brig. Abd al-Karim Qasim and the brothers Col. Abd al-Salam Aref and Col. Abd al-Rahman Aref. This group would eventually merge with the Sirri–Abd al-Majid conglomerate and go on to play the decisive role on the day of the coup. All three men—Qasim and both of the Aref brothers—were destined to become leaders of the Iraqi republic in due course.

The Baghdad Pact drama, with its attendant incitement by Cairo against Nuri, breathed new life into the Iraqi Free Officers just as their movement had begun to flag. But it was the Suez nationalization and subsequent war in 1956 that fired up the officer corps as never before. For if it had still been possible in 1955 to argue Britain was a friend of the Arabs, how could this conceivably be maintained after it had invaded, bombed, and reoccupied Egypt by force, killing thousands in a matter of days, in open partnership with the Israeli archenemy? Overnight, Iraq's official association with Britain turned from a source of controversy into a mortal danger to Nuri and the entire monarchical system. It was a mark of how much the aging Nuri's political instincts were deserting him that he failed utterly to see this coming. With characteristic timing, he was at Downing Street dining with Prime Minister Eden when word of the canal's nationalization arrived. His advice was to "hit [Nasser] hard and hit him now."

In the wake of Eden hitting Nasser, membership of the Iraqi Free Officers swelled so rapidly it was found necessary to formalize the organizational structure. A ten-man Supreme Committee was created at the end of 1956, and a body of rules put in place. A few months later, in May 1957, Brigadier Qasim merged his group with the main movement, and became chairman of its Supreme Committee by virtue of his military rank. The key protagonists of the coup were now all united under one umbrella. All that remained was to finalize arrangements for the big day.

It was in early 1958 that contact was first made between Nasser and the Iraqi conspirators. The latter were in the habit of using the Sorbonne-educated lawyer Siddiq Shanshal as their liaison with Iraq's civilian opposition, of which he was himself a prominent member. At the officers' prompting, Shanshal flew to Cairo in February and met with Nasser, who gave him "definite assurances" he "would back the revolution without reserve." Nasser also raised the matter with the Soviet ambassador to Cairo, who expressed his own approval. Naturally, both these developments gave the officers great encouragement.

At around the same time, Qasim is said to have written to Nasser apprising him of the officers' intentions and requesting guidance and, if possible, material support. In response, Nasser is reported to have said he would supply them with whatever they needed, but only after they had successfully established their new regime. To an extent, this is indeed what transpired shortly after the coup.

The year 1958 was Nasser's *annus mirabilis*: a dizzying time of seismic, historic, rapidly moving events across the Arab world, all of them to his apparent advantage. February saw Egypt's merger with Syria into a "United Arab Republic" (UAR), with Nasser as its president. The move was billed as a first step in the eventual unification of all Arab states, the hallowed dream of every true-believing Arab nationalist. In Iraq, it stoked further fire in the bellies of the Free Officers, many of whom yearned to see their own country join in.

Their chance would arrive at last on the night of July 13, when at nine o'clock the army's Twentieth Brigade departed its base at Jalawla by the Iranian border, 140 kilometers northeast of Baghdad. Its orders were to pass through the capital and head for Jordan. The commander of its Third Battalion—the ardent Nasserist and Free Officer Abd al-Salam Aref—had other ideas.

Seizing control of the brigade with the help of its First Battalion commander, a fellow Free Officer, Aref charged on to Baghdad. Reaching its outskirts at dawn's first light on the fourteenth, he paused to address his troops and explain what was about to happen. "Those who wish to join us in this patriotic honor may do so; those who don't should leave now," he told them. ("Not one soldier left us," he wrote in his memoir.)

Sending the First Battalion to secure the ministry of defense, Aref led his own Third Battalion to take the radio station, where he personally read out the famous "Proclamation No. 1" at 6:30 a.m. It was also Aref's men who seized the royal palace, where the massacre occurred, as well as the home of Nuri al-Said (who, it will be recalled, managed to escape across the Tigris). Elsewhere, other Free Officers took possession of key military sites such as al-Rashid Camp and the Habbaniya air base west of the capital, detaining senior personnel, including the chief of staff. Qasim, who had waited out the initial hours at al-Mansur Camp ninety-five kilometers away, rolled into Baghdad at noon and ensconced himself in the defense ministry. The coup was complete. After forty years, it had taken no more than a handful of young officers and an hour of shelling for Britain's strongest ally in the Arab world to crumble to dust.

The day was far from over, however. From the moment of Aref's first broadcast, in which he urged the public to "support" the army "in the wrath that it is pouring" on the royal palace and Nuri's residence, a huge crowd estimated at no smaller than one hundred thousand had flooded the streets of Baghdad, ranging from organized communist and Arab nationalist partisans to the penniless inhabitants of the slums on the eastern fringe of the capital. A scene reminiscent of Cairo's Black Saturday in January 1952 proceeded to unfold. The British embassy was attacked and torched, its comptroller killed and its building heavily damaged, until the army itself felt compelled to chase the mob away. At the prestigious New Baghdad Hotel, foreign guests, including the Jordanian deputy prime minister Ibrahim Hashem and defense minister Sulayman Tuqan, as well as three Americans, were beaten to death. A German was battered with iron rods and then beheaded. Royal palaces were looted, and a Turkish war cemetery desecrated. Chants were heard against Jews and Christians. In the words of one eyewitness, the city was "ablaze in fires and drenched in blood, the corpses of the victims scattered in the streets." Only the enforcement by the new military rulers first of a curfew, then of martial law, managed finally to restore a semblance of order by 9 p.m.

Born in blood, the Iraqi "revolution" was a profoundly transformative moment in the country's modern history. Much like Syria before it, having now joined the military coup club, Iraq was destined to tumble down the treacherous path of further coups, countercoups, assassinations, and all-out warfare, ending inexorably in absolute dictatorship of the darkest kind—in Iraq's case, the genocidal regime of Saddam Hussein. It is of no small significance that Saddam's relative and chief political patron, Brig. Ahmad Hasan al-Bakr, who went on to become president of the republic from 1968 to 1979, was a Free Officer and participant in the 1958 coup.

5

A PROGRESSIVE
PEOPLE'S REVOLUTION

AT FIRST, NASSER COULD BE EXCUSED FOR BELIEVING all was going his way in Iraq. His nemesis Nuri was dead, and the Baghdad Pact consigned to the dustbin. In the streets, the thronging masses on July 14 had chanted, "We are your soldiers, Gamal Abdel Nasser"—a neat inversion of Nuri's words to Salah Salem three years earlier. Demonstrations clamoring for union with the United Arab Republic and raising giant portraits of Nasser became a daily fixture; the *New York Times* published a photo of an Iraqi tank bearing Nasser's face. King Faysal Street, a major Baghdad thoroughfare, was renamed Gamal Abdel Nasser Street, in a gesture of self-evident symbolism.

Nasser also had powerful supporters at the top of the new regime, most particularly the hero of the coup, Col. Abd al-Salam Aref, who now occupied the posts of deputy prime minister, deputy commander in chief, and interior minister. Less than a week after the coup, Aref was embracing Nasser in Damascus, making ebullient public statements about Arab unity, and signing a mutual-aid agreement between Iraq and the UAR. "I felt we had known each other a long time," recalled Aref fondly of this emotional first encounter with his idol. In subsequent appearances at demonstrations across Iraq, Aref made a habit of referring to Nasser as "our elder brother." Aref himself was hailed as the "Nasser of Iraq" by a crowd in Basra.

The initial actions taken by the new regime gave every indication the country was following the Egyptian playbook. The monarchy and parliament were abolished, and figures associated with them arrested. The army appointed a cabinet led by Free Officers, placed military men in charge of key civilian institutions, and re-declared martial law for good measure. The armed forces, police, judiciary, and civil service were purged, and a "People's Tribunal" instated to conduct show trials of ancien régime luminaries, some of whom were executed. Diplomatic relations were swiftly established with the Soviet Union and China. Land-reform legislation was passed to expropriate large agrarian holdings. A foreign policy of strict non-alignment was professed; the junta even vowed to uphold the "resolutions of the Bandung Conference" in its first proclamation on the morning of the coup.

For his part, Nasser made good on his pledge to support the "revolution" from day one. He not only extended the new regime immediate recognition but stated he would regard any attack on it as an attack on Cairo itself. Within days, military aid in the form of small arms and artillery was dispatched to Iraq through the neighboring Syrian "province" of the UAR. The Habbaniya base then received a UAR air force detachment comprising two squadrons of Soviet-made MiG-17 fighter jets; Ilyushin transport planes; anti-aircraft guns; radar equipment; and some two hundred personnel. Beyond the military sphere, economic and other ministerial delegations were soon seen in Cairo, where they met Nasser and discussed plans to develop Iraq along Egyptian lines. An agreement was reached to coordinate the two countries' education systems and school curricula.

That Iraq was on course to join the UAR, or at the very least become its firmest of allies, seemed a foregone conclusion. There was only one snag: the man at the very top in Baghdad, the eccentric and mysterious Brig. Abd al-Karim Qasim.

As prime minister, commander in chief of the armed forces, chairman of the Free Officers' Supreme Committee, and minister of defense to boot, Qasim outranked his right-hand man, Aref, even if only slightly, and even if Aref himself didn't always appear to acknowledge the fact. Though fully on board for a "revolution-ary" regime sharing much in common with Nasser's, Qasim had never envisaged going the full distance of actually joining the UAR, with the surrender of national sovereignty this would entail. Having clasped the reins of Iraq in his fingers, Qasim discovered he had no intention of handing them to Nasser. This placed him at irrecon-cilable odds with his deputy, whose growing swagger and evident fondness for the limelight were beginning to unnerve Qasim. When rumor swirled in the Arab and international media that Aref—"the Nasser of Iraq"—would soon oust Qasim, just as Nasser had Naguib, Qasim took preemptive action and brought about the reverse instead.

The fall from grace was swift and dramatic. In September and October 1958, Aref was relieved of his duties as deputy commander in chief, stripped of all political roles, and appointed ambassador to Bonn. Returning defiantly to Baghdad in November, he was arrested, tried at the People's Tribunal, and sentenced to death. Nor was he alone: Qasim moved at the same time against other leading Arab nationalists and advocates of UAR membership, including the head of the Iraqi Baath Party, Fuad al-Rikabi, and Ahmad Hasan al-Bakr, the influential Baathist Free Officer and relative of Saddam Hussein. As well as being a deep blow to the pan-Arab camp, the purge consolidated power in the single person of Qasim, who from October onward was styled the "Sole Leader" (al-Za'im al-Awhad).

Needless to say, Nasser followed these developments with great consternation. He had made no small investment of his own prestige in the Iraqi "revolution," which rendered the defeat of his partisans a personal humiliation before the eyes of the Arab world. Worse, the very integrity and legitimacy of the entire UAR project were now open to question. If the heroes who toppled Nuri al-Said wanted no part of Nasser's venture, there was clearly trouble in paradise. Nasser was not yet ready to denounce Qasim in public and go on the open attack—though that day would come soon enough. Before it did, he embarked on the first of what ended up being multiple experiments in covert action against the Sole Leader.

The first plot was hatched in November 1958, meaning it took just four months for Nasser to go from championing the new regime to working for its downfall. At the center of the conspiracy was the venerable figure of Rashid Ali al-Gaylani, a sixty-six-year-old former Iraqi prime minister lionized in the annals of Arab nationalism for his role in a short-lived coup in 1941—backed by Nazi Germany and Fascist Italy—that had sent Nuri and the regent Abd al-Ilah into exile, and took Britain a month of military action to undo.

Gaylani was living in the UAR at the time of the July 14 coup, and was a vocal advocate of Iraq joining the union thereafter. On September 1, he left his adopted home to return to Baghdad for the first time in seventeen years. Before doing so, he met Nasser in person to say farewell, and to discuss various details of Iraq's envisaged membership of the UAR.

Arriving in Baghdad just in time to witness the fall of Aref, Gaylani was aghast at the turn of events. His home soon became a hub of informal political gatherings, where Arab nationalists explored ways to reverse their dwindling fortunes. By November, Gaylani had formed a concrete plan of action, using contacts cultivated within tribal circles, the officer corps, and the UAR embassy.

It went as follows: On December 9, tribal insurgents would create unrest in the Euphrates Valley, blocking roads, derailing trains, cutting telephone lines, and fomenting general disorder. In return for their services, they would be paid from the UAR coffers. Ten thousand Iraqi dinars (equivalent to $28,000 at the time, or almost $290,000 today) were indeed deposited into a Baghdad bank account, 4,500 of which made their way into the hands of one Abd al-Rida Sikkar, a member of the al-Fatla tribe from the town of al-Mishkhab, near Najaf, in southern Iraq. Arms, too, would be supplied by the UAR from depots in the Syrian village of al-Susa by the Iraqi border, with transport planes ready to air-drop further supplies if and when needed. As the provinces fell into chaos, anti-regime demonstrations would be organized in Baghdad.

At this point, a group of officers would approach Qasim in person to demand his resignation, on the grounds that there was no other way to restore order. (They would include the original founders of the Free Officers, Sirri and Abd al-Majid.) If Qasim refused, he was to be killed. Once he was gone one way or the other, the radio would announce the creation of an Egyptian-style "Revolutionary Council," and the formation of a cabinet headed by Gaylani, who would become president, prime minister, and foreign minister. The new government would proceed to join the UAR.

It was a shoddy venture both in conception and execution. The notion that a provincial tribal uprising far removed from the capital would force Qasim to his knees was frivolous. At any rate, the plan never got off the ground. So poor was the conspirators' discipline that Qasim's intelligence agents caught wind of it a mile off, and managed to infiltrate the group posing as volunteers. So persuasive was their performance they were even given 2,500 dinars of the UAR's money by the plot's masterminds. Arrests were finally made on December 7. Gaylani was tried at the People's Tribunal and sentenced to death ten days later.

Far from deterring Nasser and his Iraqi acolytes, the plot's bungling only redoubled their drive to scheme against Qasim, who in turn was further steeled in his resolve to eradicate the Nasserist threat decisively. In this quest he found a natural ally in the faction that had long been Iraq's strongest and most effective organized political force: the communists.

The Iraqi communists' view of Nasser had chiefly been determined by the experience of their comrades in neighboring Syria, who felt—not without reason—that they had gotten a raw deal out of union with Egypt. Since all political parties had been banned in Egypt since 1953, Nasser insisted as a prerequisite for union that the same apply in the Syrian "province" of the new state. The head of Syria's Communist Party opposed this, and was exiled to Eastern Europe for his troubles. Leaderless and endangered, the party was forced underground, its members eventually subjected to mass arrests, torture, and killings.

In consequence, from the moment the first calls for Iraq to join the UAR were made on the morning of the July 14 coup, Iraq's communists were already set against the idea, knowing full well it would mean the end of their party. They had not endured decades of imprisonment and executions under the ancien régime to now go gently into Nasser's good night. Their difficulty lay in preventing union at all costs while at the same time flaunting their "revolutionary" credentials and winning the hearts and minds of Nasser's many fans on the street. To do this, they hit on the formula of a "federal union" with the UAR, whereby Iraq would maintain its independence, as opposed to full unification. The distinction was a subtle one, especially when expressed in Arabic, where the two terms shared a grammatical root and were virtually identical at the etymological level (*al-ittihad* versus *al-wahda*).

Though no communist himself, Qasim quickly saw the logic of a marriage of convenience with the party, and the decisive muscle it could bring to bear against their shared Nasserist rival. Over the course of the next year, he gave the party almost unlimited rein to take the fight to the Arab nationalists, and their power swelled to levels never before enjoyed by communists in an Arab country. Their political prisoners were released, and exiled members allowed to return. Mass rallies drawing crowds in the hundreds of thousands were staged, calling for federal union and other communist demands. Baghdad Radio came under their sway, as did several leading newspapers, trade unions, professional associations, and student groups.

Most ominously, the communists took over the "Popular Resistance" militia created by Qasim in August 1958 to "stand by the army in the defense of the homeland." Thousands of communists were given weapons and military training, and empowered by the state to set up checkpoints, raid homes, and detain ordinary citizens in makeshift prisons. The climate of fear this engendered was of course anathema to the Nasserists, who bore its brunt. Vigilante revenge attacks on communists by Arab nationalists became a feature of life—one communist member of the militia, Aziz Swadi, was stabbed to death in December 1958, while many more were wounded in similar street assaults. The young Saddam Hussein himself is thought to have murdered his very first victim two months earlier: a provincial communist party official named Saadun al-Tikriti. In these developments lay portents of ugly days ahead.

As Iraq's communists grew in strength and confidence, it wasn't long before they were emboldened to oppose the UAR more vocally. In a statement in September 1958, they enumerated the "negative results" of the union between Egypt and Syria, highlighting in particular "the want of freedom of opinion and of party and social organisation," concluding that "a merger would have an unfavourable effect on Iraq." Soon afterward, Syria's Communist Party called for free parliamentary elections in both Egypt and Syria, and the provision of "democratic liberties: freedom of the press, assembly, demonstration and the right to strike, freedom of trade unions and the right of all the people and patriotic forces to free political association."

These were fighting words. To call for elections in Egypt itself was to go well beyond critiquing the union; it was to attack the very foundations and legitimacy of Nasser's rule at home in Cairo. Nasser interpreted these developments not as isolated initiatives by the Syrian and Iraqi communist parties acting alone, but as a concerted and coordinated campaign by Arab communism as a whole. He came out swinging in a landmark speech in late December 1958, accusing the communists by name of joining forces with "Zionism" and "reaction" against Arab unity. "For the sake of Arab unity and Arab nationalism," he vowed to "wage war against all who raise the banners of secession and partition."

Syria's communists were arrested by the hundreds, and their newspapers closed, while Damascus Radio assailed them as "foreign agents and traitors." Days later, on January 1, 1959, the crackdown was extended to Egypt's communists, leading to the torture of Sonallah Ibrahim and Louis Awad at Abu Zaabal, and the killing of Shuhdi Attiah and others.

It remained for Nasser to settle his score with Iraq's communists, who, with Qasim's backing, grew only more dominant in the first months of 1959. For Iraq's Arab nationalists, who of course shared Nasser's disgust with Qasim and the communists, the death sentence handed to Aref by Qasim's kangaroo court in February 1959 was the final straw. A mass resignation of Arab nationalist cabinet ministers, including Fuad al-Rikabi of the Baath Party and Siddiq Shanshal—the lawyer who had met Nasser on the Free Officers' behalf before the coup—came two days later. In close coordination with their UAR contacts, the officers accelerated plans for a sequel to the Gaylani plot.

The new conspiracy was, in essence, the same as the old one, but on steroids. Once again it involved a three-way collaboration among the UAR, the Iraqi officer corps, and prominent tribes. The officers were in many cases the same people. The tribes, this time, were in the northwest; chief among them was the Shammar confederation, whose members and influence extended from in and around Iraq's Mosul across the border into eastern Syria. On the UAR side, the key figure was the notorious Syrian security and intelligence czar, Abd al-Hamid al-Sarraj, a ruthless pioneer of clandestine operations who had had notable success running guns to pro-Nasser rebels in Lebanon the previous year. Assisting Sarraj on this occasion were Muhammad Kabbul of the UAR embassy in Baghdad, who had played a significant role in the Gaylani plot; Col. Abd al-Majid Farid, the UAR's military attaché in Baghdad; and Lt. Col. Burhan Adham, a senior military intelligence officer under Sarraj in Damascus.

As before, the basic idea was for the tribes to stage an armed uprising, providing the pretext for intervention by the officers. Arms had been flowing across the Syrian border into the tribes' hands since as early as January 1959. By the first week of March, their transfer had "assumed the regularity of an organised shuttle service."

Among the Iraqi officers, the central figure would prove to be Col. Abd al-Wahhab al-Shawwaf, commander of the Fifth Brigade based near the city of Mosul. An early Free Officer who had also been involved in the Gaylani plot, Shawwaf epitomized the class of Arab nationalist officers who felt personally sidelined and disregarded by Qasim following the July 14 coup of which, in their view, they had been the original architects.

Rather than meekly call on Qasim to resign once the tribes were up in arms, this time the officers planned to send their units into the streets, taking Mosul by force before broadcasting word of their "revolution" to the nation. At that point, Colonel Sirri—the Free Officers' cofounder—would take the defense ministry in Baghdad, kill or exile Qasim, and seize the reins of power.

As well as the weapons, the UAR would supply the radio equipment for the broadcast, along with a "battalion of commandos" and a squadron of MiG fighter jets, should the need for them arise.

★

CATCHING WIND THAT SOMETHING was afoot in Mosul, the communists decided to put on a mass rally in the city on March 6, as a show of force. That this was done with Qasim's blessing is clear from the special rail discounts offered to participants coming from out of town, and the prominent coverage given to the event on state television and radio. In all, some 250,000 communists and fellow travelers descended on Mosul, comfortably outnumbering the city's entire population of 180,000.

If their presence was intended as a warning, it served instead as a provocation. Marching through conservative, pro–Nasser, and pro–Aref neighborhoods, the demonstrators bellowed their signature rhyming chant: "*Maku za'im illa Karim*" (There is no leader except [Abd al-]Karim [Qasim]). The livid officers contained themselves for one day, until the rally was over and the crowds began to depart. On the night of March 7, Shawwaf set the wheels in motion.

By dawn on the eighth, the insurrection was underway. Armed Arab nationalists and Shammar tribesmen took to the streets and began abducting communists, some of whom were summarily executed. Shawwaf's Fifth Brigade rolled into town. The good news was proclaimed over Mosul, Cairo, and Damascus Radios: Shaw-waf was named "Leader of the Revolution," and Qasim decried as a "mad tyrant" who had betrayed the glorious values of July 14. UAR flags were raised around the city.

From the very beginning, however, things went wrong. The reb-els couldn't get the radio working properly; many more Egyptians and Syrians learned of the "revolution" than did Iraqis. Shawwaf coordinated poorly with Sirri in Baghdad, who in the end made no move. In Mosul itself, some soldiers refused orders and chanted Qasim's name in the streets. The UAR's promised commandos and MiGs were nowhere to be seen.

By the next morning, it was clear the revolt was doomed. Shaw-waf himself at that point was "completely dejected, and only eager to achieve an honourable death," according to an officer who was with him. In despair, he ordered two Fury aircraft to take off and try to bomb Baghdad Radio outside the capital. Qasim, meanwhile, sent four Venom fighters to strike the Fifth Brigade headquarters, wounding Shawwaf, who was on his way to the hospital when he was intercepted and killed. The rebellion fizzled out just as suddenly as it had begun, the Shammar vanishing like ghosts over the hori-zon. Of the two pilots sent by Shawwaf to bomb Baghdad, one was arrested upon landing back at the base, while the other tried to fly to Syria, crashed, and shot himself.

Shawwaf's "revolution" was over, but the violence in Mosul was only beginning. There followed three dark days of diabolical blood-letting, as communist militiamen went house to house, butchering residents on the mere suspicion of supporting the revolt, stringing their bodies up on lampposts and dragging them through the streets. Officers attempting to flee to Syria were cut down; they included Capt. Abd al-Jawad Hamid, famous for capturing the royal palace in Baghdad on July 14. The Arab nationalists, for their part, slaugh-tered communist captives, including the well-known lawyer and poet Kamil Qazanchi. All the while, local police stood idle.

In the delirium of the bloodbath, long-bottled ethnic, sectarian,

and class passions were uncorked, overlapping with local and personal feuds, spreading the fever of murderous hatred far beyond
Mosul throughout the surrounding province. Armed Kurdish and
Yazidi tribesmen from the countryside, joined by Aramean peasants, descended on the city intent on killing Arabs. Rival Arab
tribes set upon one another, and also on Kurds. Christians versus Muslims; peasants versus landlords; soldiers versus officers; rich
versus poor; families versus rival families: a chaotic and utterly lawless free-for-all ensued, fueled by every conceivable motive and
grievance. Killings took place as far away as Duhok and Tal Afar,
more than seventy kilometers from Mosul. Not until March 12,
when battalions of the First Brigade arrived, was the madness gradually brought to an end. No fewer than two hundred lives had
been taken.

★

THE FAILURE OF THE Shawwaf revolt was the greatest humiliation yet faced by Nasser on the Arab stage. A rebellion behind which
the Voice of the Arabs had very publicly thrown its full weight had
been put down in a day. Qasim was showing the Arab world it was
possible to lead a successful "revolutionary" regime without joining
the UAR or bending the knee to Nasser. Indeed, Mosul is often
regarded as a turning point in Arab nationalist history: the moment
Nasser's star first began its slow but irreversible decline.

There is no doubt he was rattled. Two days after Shawwaf's death,
on March 11, Nasser went after Qasim by name for the first time in
a series of ill-tempered speeches from Damascus. No term of abuse
in the Nasserist lexicon was spared. Qasim, the "divider" of Iraq—a
pun on the literal meaning of the word qasim—was an enemy of
Arabism; a collaborator with foreigners, terrorists, and imperialists. He was another Nuri al-Said: after all, Iraq was still officially a
Baghdad Pact member state. In a revealing indication of what was
worrying him, Nasser insisted the "divider" would never succeed
in dividing the UAR. That Nasser combined all this with a furious

attack on communists as "foreign agents" and "terrorists" further explains the grisly events that were about to unfold at Egypt's Abu Zaabal, as well as in Syria, over the following months.

As for Iraq's Arab nationalists, they were in utter despondence. From the moment it became clear on the morning of March 9 that all was lost, "everyone" felt "the bloody tragedy had struck them to their depths," wrote the Baath Party's secretary-general Fuad al-Rikabi. They were scarcely able to move: "Our steps felt so heavy it seemed our feet were stuck to the floor."

Forced into hiding, the Baath's leaders were nonetheless able to meet days later to discuss what could be done. They were unanimously agreed: the only option was to assassinate Qasim.

★

SHORTLY AFTER 6:30 P.M. on October 7, 1959, Qasim was being chauffeured along Baghdad's al-Rashid Street from his office at the ministry of defense to a function marking East Germany's Republic Day.

Standing on the same street were six young men pretending to examine shop windows, concealing the submachine guns and hand grenades they carried under their clothes. As the prime minister's Chevrolet approached, they opened fire, killing the driver and wounding both Qasim and his aide-de-camp, who lost consciousness.

Things then went awry. A grenade hurled at the vehicle missed its target and exploded in the open street. As the car veered to a halt and the gunmen moved unthinkingly in different directions, three were struck by friendly fire, one fatally so. Panicking, they retreated from the scene, leaving Qasim bloodied but alive inside the car. (He went on to make a full recovery.) Of the two wounded militants, one was a twenty-two-year-old from a village near Tikrit, on the Tigris between Baghdad and Mosul. Despite his age, he had already earned renown in Baathist circles for his willingness to commit murder in the cause of Arab nationalism. His name was Saddam Hussein.

★

THE EXTENT OF UAR involvement in the Baath's attempt on Qasim's life that day is unclear. At the "People's Court" in Baghdad, where seventy-eight people were tried in connection with the attack between December 1959 and February 1960, the state prosecutor alleged a dramatic conspiracy going all the way to the top in Cairo.

Nasser had personally approved a request from the Baath for assistance in the operation sent through his Syrian henchman Sarraj, the prosecutor said. Four thousand Iraqi dinars were sent to the conspirators via Tawfiq Sulayman Abaza, second secretary at the UAR embassy in Baghdad, who was their key point of contact. (Abaza was declared persona non grata and expelled from Iraq one month after the attack for "endangering the safety of the state.") The name of another embassy official, Muhammad Kabbul—previously implicated in both the Gaylani and Shawwaf plots—also came up. The money was said to have been used by the Baath to buy arms, ammunition, and a car, and to rent an apartment near the site selected for the attack. In presenting his case, the prosecutor drew on an impressive roster of witnesses, including several of the six gunmen themselves.

A somewhat different version of events was later provided by the then head of the Iraqi Baath, Fuad al-Rikabi, in a book he wrote about the operation published in 1963. Here, the Baath are presented as acting alone, with no mention of money from the UAR, nor indeed of any direct UAR role at all. Rikabi does say the hit squad tried at first to source weapons from the "Syrian province" of the UAR, but it was felt that since the guns they sought were of a type used only by the armed forces, "their use could lead to complications if the operation were to fail." In the end, Rikabi writes, the weapons were acquired through smugglers and unspecified "Arab nationalist and allied groups and friends."

Where exactly the truth lies between these two accounts is uncertain. In a rare interview in 2002, the aforementioned Sarraj— Nasser's right-hand man in Syria—said he had "naturally" been "in

the picture" with regard to the operation. Though he did not elaborate further, the statement may be taken as an admission that the
UAR had—at the very least—foreknowledge of the plans.

Beyond that, one may only speculate. There are excellent reasons, in principle, to treat the claims of the Baghdad People's Tribunal with profound skepticism. A notorious circus of the crudest and
most vitriolic propaganda, the court's own officials abused Nasser
during the trial as, variously, a "dog," a "pharaoh," a "Hitler," and a
"Freemason, Zionist, imperialist dictator." Despite this, the essence
of the prosecution's case need not be thought implausible—provided
one discards its more lurid aspects, such as the claim the gunmen
planned to send Qasim's severed head to Nasser as a souvenir.

The UAR had, after all, already sponsored two other armed conspiracies against Qasim just months previously, since which time
Nasser's quarrel with the man had only intensified. More to the
point, the court's narrative actually tallied with Rikabi's in many
of the smallest and most particular details. It was true, as the prosecution and various witnesses said, that the gunmen included Samir
al-Najm, Abd al-Wahhab al-Ghurayri, Ahmad Taha al-Azooz,
Abd al-Karim al-Shaykhli, and, of course, Saddam Hussein. It was
also true that the hit squad had bought a car and rented an apartment near Baghdad's al-Rashid Street; that preparations had begun
immediately after the Shawwaf fiasco; that the gunmen had been
trained in the desert outside of al-Haswa, south of Baghdad; that the
code word to signal to the team that Qasim was on the move was
"Mahmud"; and that the Baath had contacted Iraqi Free Officers to
sound them out on the plan and propose the latter seize power once
Qasim was gone, to install an Egypt-style junta that would bring
Iraq into the UAR. There can be no doubt at all, in other words,
that the court's case rested at least in part on truthful witness testimony. There is also reason to believe Qasim's intelligence agencies
had some prior knowledge of the plot, just as they had in the Gaylani
and Shawwaf cases.

What, then, should one ultimately conclude about the UAR's role in the operation? We have it on Sarraj's authority that they knew something about it, at minimum. Splitting the difference between the court and Rikabi down the middle, one might surmise Cairo sent funds, too, while the bulk of the conception, planning, and execution was undertaken by the Iraqi Baath. Of course, this is at best no more than an educated guess. Given the clear limitations and partisanship of all accounts in question, and in the absence of facts emanating from independent and disinterested sources, the full truth remains unknown.

What is certain, on the other hand, is the UAR did provide money and asylum to those conspirators who managed to make it across the border into its territory, including Rikabi and the young Saddam Hussein. Rikabi fled through Iraq's western desert, driving off-road from Fallujah to the crossing at Husayba, helped by a Bedouin guide who navigated at night by the stars and moonlight shining on the sand. From Syria's Deir al-Zor he continued on to Aleppo, then Damascus, before finally ending up in Cairo.

Saddam also wound his way to Cairo, taking a different route north up the Tigris to his hometown of al-Awja by Tikrit before proceeding to Syria. In the Egyptian capital, he lived as a privileged guest of Nasser's regime, paid an allowance by the intelligence services and protected whenever his violent behavior landed him in trouble, as it often did. Having no qualifications, he attended the Qasr al-Nil secondary school for a year before enrolling at Cairo University's law college in 1961—the very college Nasser himself had briefly attended twenty-five years earlier.

Saddam's spare time was spent mostly with fellow Iraqi Baathists in his favorite café, Indiana, a modest establishment that still exists on the bustling Doqqi Street north of the university. Its owner later recalled him as "an undesirable person . . . a bully, always picking fights with my customers." But there was nothing he could do. After an incident in which Saddam pulled a knife on someone, he was briefly detained by police, only to be released after word came down from above that he was "under Nasser's protection."

In all, Saddam would spend more than three years in Cairo, returning to Iraq only after his comrades back home had finally succeeded where Gaylani, Shawwaf, and Saddam himself had failed before them.

★

Just after eight o'clock on the morning of February 8, 1963, the Nasserist hero of the 1958 coup, Col. Abd al-Salam Aref—back from the dead after a pardon by Qasim two years earlier—arrived at the Fourth Tank Regiment headquarters in Abu Ghrayb, and climbed into a tank. Next to him was Ahmad Hasan al-Bakr, the veteran Free Officer and relative of Saddam Hussein. Together, they set off to carry out their second coup d'état in less than five years.

This time, the plan had been laid patiently and properly, over the course of ten months. There was to be no more messing around with rural tribes or amateur assassins: now, the officers themselves would take the lead, and strike with overwhelming military firepower at the beating heart of Qasim's regime in central Baghdad.

The prime mover of the coup was the Baath Party, reconstituted in Rikabi's absence under the leadership of one of his protégés, the young and energetic Ali Saleh al-Saadi. In collaboration with sympathetic Free Officers, including Aref and Tahir Yahya—a veteran of both the Gaylani and Shawwaf plots—the Baath developed a comprehensive plan of action, encompassing not just the military specifics of the D-day itself, but also the details of the junta and cabinet that would rule the country thereafter.

The morning of February 8 got off to a successful start. While Aref and Bakr were seizing the radio transmitter, Hawker Hunter fighter jets from the Habbaniya base were bombing Qasim's heavily fortified headquarters at the defense ministry in Baghdad. Planes also struck the al-Rashid airfield, grounding the MiG fighters that might otherwise have come to Qasim's aid. The customary "Proclamation No. 1" was broadcast at 9:40 a.m., declaring the end of "the regime of the enemy of the people Abd al-Karim Qasim," and pledging to "continue the triumphant march of the glorious July Fourteenth Revolution" and bring about "national unity," "public freedoms," and "rule of law."

Qasim was still alive, however. At 10:30 a.m., he entered the defense ministry, determined to fight it out. Sensing the mortal danger that awaited them in the event of Qasim's fall, the communists rapidly organized demonstrations in support of the "Sole Leader" outside the ministry, demanding weapons to "crush the reactionary imperialist conspiracy." A grim scene unfolded when army tanks and Baathist paramilitaries appeared an hour later and proceeded to disperse the crowds with pitiless lethal force. The death toll from this alone ran into the hundreds.

The final battle for the defense ministry began at 3 p.m. Against the rebels' tanks and planes stood Qasim and approximately one thousand loyalists. The latter put up stiff resistance, even shooting down a plane with an antiaircraft gun. But with the complex surrounded, and Qasim's radio and phone communications bombed out, it was only a matter of time. Even so, it took till noon the following day for the fighting to end. Qasim was apprehended at half past noon and executed by firing squad one hour later.

Despite Qasim's death, communists kept their resistance going for several more days in isolated areas: Baghdad's al-Kathimiya, Aqd al-Akrad, and the port of Basra. They fought "as only men could fight who knew that no mercy was to be looked for in defeat." Sure enough, the new junta's Proclamation No. 13, issued on the evening of February 8, had authorized the army, police, and Baathist death squads to "exterminate" communists. By the time the guns at last fell silent, the total body count since the start of the coup was well over a thousand.

★

THE NEW IRAQI REGIME was run by a junta styling itself the National Revolutionary Command Council, self-evidently modeled on Egypt's Revolutionary Command Council. Aref became president of the republic. Real power, however, lay for the moment with the Baath, who occupied most other key positions. Bakr was prime minister, Saadi his deputy, while the minister of defense was Saleh Mahdi Ammash—a Baathist Free Officer who had played a role in the attempt on Qasim's life in October 1959. Besides the junta, there was also a cabinet, again heavily Baathist, but with three of the twenty-one seats going to the unaffiliated Free Officers Naji Taleb, Fuad Aref, and Mahmud Khattab.

A third instrument of power was the "National Guard" militia developed under Saadi in the run-up to the coup, which had assisted the army on the ground when D-day came. This was the Baath's riposte to the communists' "Popular Resistance" militia, and its members lost no time exacting payment in kind for the blood spilled in Mosul in 1959. Now it was the Baath's turn to go door to door, shooting suspected opponents on sight, or else dragging them off to be tortured with the special sadism for which the Baath would ever after be renowned. Their most infamous detention center was the palace where the royal family had been massacred in 1958, now aptly renamed the "Palace of the End." Here were later "found all sorts of loathsome instruments of torture, including electric wires with pincers, pointed iron stakes on which prisoners were made to sit, and a machine which still bore traces of chopped-off fingers."

★

THE NEW COUP WAS hailed by Nasser as a "courageous revolution," a "progressive people's revolution," and a "great victory for the Arab struggle." Speaking in Cairo alongside "the brother" Saadi—that is, Iraq's new deputy prime minister, secretary of the Iraqi Baath Party, and head of the National Guard death squad—Nasser gushed how, on the day of the coup, "every member of this nation was with you in the battle. . . . We all praised God that your revolution was victorious in Iraq, or rather that *our* revolution was victorious in Iraq, because it was the revolution of the entire Arab nation and of free people everywhere." Going further, he dropped strong hints that Egypt might now unite with Iraq as it had with Syria, "abolishing the artificial borders" to become "one Arab nation" at last.

Indeed, apparently concrete steps were soon taken in this direction. Syria had seceded from its union with Egypt in 1961, effectively bringing an end to the UAR (though Nasser insisted on retaining the name in Egypt). However, one month after the Iraqi Baath seized power in February 1963, its Syrian counterpart did the same in Damascus. Suddenly, the prospect of reviving the UAR, this time with Iraq as a third member, was up for discussion.

No fewer than thirteen trilateral meetings were held in Cairo to explore this possibility in March and April 1963. Nasser personally represented the Egyptian side, while the Iraqi delegation comprised Saadi and foreign minister Talib Shabib. The end result was a joint declaration on April 17 of the three countries' intentions to form a federal union, to be known as the UAR, with Cairo as its capital. Signed by Nasser, Iraq's prime minister Bakr, and Syria's president Luay al-Atasi, the thirty-page agreement envisaged full unification of the countries' armed forces and foreign policies, though each of the three "provinces" would elect a form of local parliament.

No sooner had the agreement been signed than it was buried in the rubble of a violent breakdown in Nasser's relations with the Syrian Baath, a feud from which Iraq's Baath largely steered clear. Meanwhile, back in Baghdad, the situation was unstable, and would remain so for the next five years, as the internal conflicts and contradictions of the motley crew who had taken power rose to the surface. The extreme brutality and thuggery of the National Guard so tarnished the Baath's name that Prime Minister Bakr took to using quiet backstreets to avoid members of the public and "their looks of hate." The party's own founder and chief ideologue, Michel Aflaq, deplored the "great harm" done by all the "bloodshed and torture," saying "our differences with the communists cannot possibly justify such means" as had been used.

The Baath's larger problem, however, lay in the Iraqi military, where its support base had always been slender, and was thinning by the day. Already disgruntled at the rapid rise of a parallel army—the National Guard—answering not to the generals but to a political party, officers of all persuasions were incensed by the treatment they suffered at the hands of the Guard's goons, who made sport of stopping, searching, and even abusing them in the streets. The Baath itself grew polarized internally between a younger camp of Saadi loyalists supportive of the Guard, suddenly professing to be "Marxists," on the one hand, and a more conservative opposing camp of old-guard officers such as Bakr, Ammash, and Yahya, on the other.

The inevitable rupture came on November 11, 1963. At a party meeting, armed officers burst in and abducted Saadi, bundled him into a car at gunpoint, and threw him on a military plane to exile in Madrid. A week of borderline civil war followed, in which the National Guard raged in the streets, and Saadi loyalists managed to seize planes and launch airstrikes on al-Rashid Camp and the presidential palace. Eventually, army units commanded by President Aref—who naturally sided with his fellow officers—moved in on November 18 and crushed the Guard for good. Having served as a merely ceremonial president until that point, Aref now came into his stride, and finally assumed the leadership role he had felt was his due since 1958.

At last, Iraq's Nasserists were to have their day in the sun, unencumbered by Qasim, the communists, or even the Baathists, whom Aref had little difficulty sidelining over the following weeks. Under his regime, for the better part of two years, Iraq all but became a de facto province of the UAR. In May 1964, a "Joint Presidential Council" was created, aimed at closer coordination between Baghdad and Cairo on a wide range of issues, as well as preparing the ground for an eventual constitutional union. Two months later came a raft of decrees applying in Iraq several major economic and political measures recently introduced in Egypt. On July 14, at the stroke of a pen, dozens of Iraqi banks, insurance companies, and large industrial and commercial enterprises were nationalized, just as their Egyptian counterparts had been. The same day, an Iraqi version of Nasser's "Arab Socialist Union" movement—the successor to the old Liberation Rally—was established, becoming the sole legal political organization. In September, following a Baathist coup attempt, Nasser dispatched a force of six thousand men to Iraq to bolster Aref's position. October 1964 brought another unity agreement, the "Iraq-UAR Unified Political Command," which envisaged full union within a period of no more than two years. Finally, in November, a cabinet reshuffle saw a doubling of seats for Iraq's Nasserists, who acquired key ministries, including the interior, justice, economics, and industry portfolios.

To ask why, at this stage, the two countries did not go all the way and officially unite would be to misunderstand what each really wanted out of the relationship. As far as Nasser was concerned, he now had everything he needed from Iraq: a staunch friend and ally who could be relied on to support the Cairo line at all times in Arab and international affairs. Responsibility for the day-to-day governance of other peoples' *domestic* concerns was a burden he had learned from the Syrian experience to avoid at all costs. As for Aref, he was perfectly content to enjoy the prestige and legitimacy conferred by association with the masses' hero without, at the same time, having to relinquish his throne at home.

Such "moderation" on Aref's part, however, won him enemies among die-hard advocates of full and immediate union. One of these was Brig. Aref Abd al-Razzaq, commander of the air force, whose "revolutionary" credentials included taking over the strategic Habbaniya air base on the morning of the 1958 coup, and enabling its transfer into rebel hands during the 1963 coup. A zealous Nasserist and "unionist" who had sided with Aref in the standoff against the Baath, he was appointed prime minister, as well as defense minister, in another cabinet shake-up on September 5, 1965. When Aref traveled to Morocco the following week, Abd al-Razzaq made an attempt to seize power himself, on the grounds that the president had strayed from the unionist path. It was an abject failure: one of his men betrayed him after the order to move was issued; President Aref's loyalists were alerted; and the operation was nipped in the bud. Abd al-Razzaq fled with over a dozen co-conspirators to Cairo, where he was given asylum and a stipend of two hundred Egyptian pounds.

Abd al-Razzaq would later say the Egyptian authorities had had no role in this first attempt to topple Aref. His second coup attempt, however, the following year, was a joint venture with Cairo from start to finish, in his telling. Aref had died in a helicopter crash in April 1966, and his successor—his brother, Maj. Gen. Abd al-Rahman Aref—was felt not to be steering the ship to Cairo's satisfaction. Not the least of the problems was the new prime minister, the civilian Dr. Abd al-Rahman al-Bazzaz, who incurred Nasser's displeasure by his talk of liberalizing the country politically and economically, permitting free expression, ending political imprisonment, and preparing the ground for eventual free parliamentary elections. The impression that Bazzaz was also "tilting" away from Egypt in the direction of Saudi Arabia proved too much to tolerate, and plans were set in motion for a correction of course.

The plot began with a personal visit to Abd al-Razzaq in Cairo by Egypt's powerful military official, Shams Badran, who proposed that Abd al-Razzaq make haste back to Iraq to lead a coup in collaboration with other Nasserist officers already in touch with Cairo. This was followed by a visit from Nasser's senior aide Sami Sharaf—a man so close to Nasser the latter had him on speed dial on the phone in his home office. Sharaf discussed the plans further and handed Abd al-Razzaq three hundred British pounds (equivalent to five thousand today). Fake Egyptian passports were also provided for him and his entourage, as was transportation from the Egyptian embassy in Kuwait into Iraq using Egyptian diplomatic cars. Abd al-Razzaq entered Iraq on June 4, 1966, and made his move on the last day of the month. It was every bit as feckless as his first attempt, and this time he wound up in prison. His exit from the Iraqi stage marked the end of Nasser's direct influence over the country.

★

THE FEEBLE AND MORIBUND regime of Abd al-Rahman Aref was put out of its misery in a 1968 coup by the Baath, who had spent the last five years systematically plotting their comeback. The coup—which was really two coups, one on July 17 and another thirteen days later—was an uncharacteristically bloodless affair.

It began with a palace putsch arranged by three pillars of Aref's regime: military intelligence director Col. Abd al-Razzaq al-Nayef, Republican Guard commander Col. Ibrahim al-Dawud, and Tenth Armoured Brigade commander Col. Saadun Ghaydan. The men were not Baathists themselves (though Ghaydan had "briefly flirted" with the party in 1963); instead, it was largely fear of the Nasserists that prompted them to depose their boss. Both Nayef and Dawud had played roles in foiling Aref Abd al-Razzaq's June 1966 coup attempt, and were convinced, as Dawud put it, that sooner or later the Nasserists would succeed in seizing power and "send us to the gallows." (The implied faith in Baathist benevolence was poorly placed: Nayef was later assassinated in London by Saddam Hussein's military intelligence branch.)

On the morning of July 17, 1968, the Baath's Ahmad Hasan al-Bakr, Saleh Mahdi Ammash, and others simply drove into the Tenth Armored Brigade headquarters at Ghaydan's invitation and assumed control. Dawud, meanwhile, took the radio station, while Nayef occupied the defense ministry. No resistance whatsoever was mounted. President Aref conceded defeat with sportsmanlike good grace, reportedly wishing his friends every success before boarding a plane to exile in England. Bakr was proclaimed president of the republic, while—for the time being—Nayef and Dawud became prime minister and defense minister, respectively.

That was round one. Spectacularly misapprehending the nature of the people with whom they were doing business, Nayef and Dawud failed completely to grasp that the Baath were only waiting for the first opportunity to do away with them. That moment came when

Dawud traveled to Jordan at the end of the month. After a lunch at the presidential palace with Bakr, Nayef was arrested at gunpoint by Saddam Hussein himself—emerging even then as the real strongman and driving force of the regime. (According to his official hagiographers, Saddam told the whimpering Nayef, "Nothing will happen to your children if you behave sensibly.") Both Nayef and Dawud were banished to exile. Ghaydan, who had read the winds more capably, had an overnight conversion to Baathism, and was permitted to stick around. It mattered nothing: the Baath were now sole masters of Iraq, and the road was cleared for the unstoppable rise of Saddam.

The new rulers' relations with Nasser were marked by studied ambiguity. It will be recalled that it was none other than now-president Bakr who, five years earlier, had signed the agreement with Nasser and Syria's President Atasi on a three-way Egyptian-Syrian-Iraqi union. In theory, the Baath were supposed to yield to none in their unswerving pursuit of total Arab unity within a single state extending from the Atlantic to the Arabian Gulf. In practice, they had no more intention of sharing power with Cairo than had Qasim in 1958.

They therefore played the now-familiar game of mouthing the correct niceties about Nasser and Arab unity in public, while quietly going about a very different agenda in private. Bakr described the new coup as a "profound reassertion of the *unionist* progressive leanings for which the 8 February 1963 revolution was carried out" (emphasis added), while at the same time closing down the committee tasked with bringing union about. A "firm commitment" to upholding the "joint Iraqi-Egyptian political line" came two weeks before Iraq's branch of the Arab Socialist Union was closed. "Fulsome congratulations" were sent to Nasser on the anniversary of Egypt's July 23 coup, shortly before Nasserists were rounded up in the Baath's all-encompassing campaign of terror against every conceivable opponent or competitor. Still, in one mark of the enduring influence of Nasserism in form if not necessarily in content, the Baath's junta named itself the "Revolutionary Command Council"—the exact

wording used by Egypt's Free Officers. The RCC would remain
Iraq's supreme executive and legislative body all the way until 2003,
when it was dissolved by the Coalition Provisional Authority's Paul
Bremer on May 23.

The forest, however, ought not to be missed for the trees. By
1968—sixteen years into Nasser's reign—the damage from Cairo
had already been done some time ago. In the historical course of
events that took Iraq from Nuri al-Said to Saddam Hussein in just
over a decade, Nasser's decisive part had by then already been played.
From the last days of the monarchy until the Baath deposed Aref in
1968, Iraq witnessed three successful coups d'état, at least five failed
coup plots, and at least one attempt to assassinate its head of state.
Of these nine events, it can definitively be said that Nasser's regime
provided moral and/or material assistance in at least four, while an
Iraqi court accused it of involvement in a fifth. If Nasser did not literally install Saddam on the throne, he nonetheless did a great deal to
create the conditions that enabled him to get there—not least during
the three years he hosted, paid, and protected him as his guest in
Cairo. Along the way, Nasser facilitated the spilling of rivers of Iraqi
blood, empowered many of the country's most violent and authoritarian actors, and made a pivotal contribution to the long-term devastation of its society and politics.

Iraq was by no means the only country of which this could be said.

SYRIA

• 6 •

THE DAWN OF
ARAB LIBERATION

O N THURSDAY, JUNE 25, 1959, THE VETERAN LEBA-
nese communist leader Farajallah al-Helu made a fateful decision to travel to Damascus.

He knew the risk was severe. The war being waged on communism by Nasser's UAR had reached its lethal apex, following the
bloodbath in Iraq's Mosul three months earlier. It was at this very
time that, in Egypt, communists were being rounded up and herded
into Abu Zaabal Camp, while in Syria they disappeared into the
notorious dungeons of the military intelligence bureau. Already, in
February, a Syrian comrade, Saeed al-Droubi, had been tortured to
death in the latter's custody.

Yet the fifty-two-year-old Helu had been tasked by the unified
Lebanese-Syrian Communist Party with running its underground
cells inside Syria, and he was not a man to shirk his party duties.
He had, in fact, already made the perilous journey from Lebanon to
Syria and back again several times in the preceding months, under
a false identity. As he packed his bags for another trip, his wife Vir-
ginie begged him not to go. He told her it would be the last time.
He wasn't wrong.

On the southern outskirts of Damascus, by an intersection leading
to the Kafr Susa suburb, stood the residence Helu had used several
times before as a safe house. Arriving around 7 p.m., he rapped on
the window, as agreed with the trusted party colleague who lived
in the property. When the door opened and Helu stepped inside,

however, he was greeted not by communists but by Syrian intelligence officers. Unbeknownst to him, they had recruited two of his Lebanese comrades, who had given him up in exchange for avoiding prison and torture. The godfather of Syrian intelligence at the time, Abd al-Hamid al-Sarraj, would later boast Helu had been followed at every moment of his journey, "from the doorstep of his home" in Lebanon.

Bundled into a car, Helu was taken to an intelligence branch in Damascus's Salihiya district, near the Italian Hospital, where his interrogation commenced immediately. Of especial interest to his captors was a set of keys they found on him, which they surmised were for other safe houses they had not yet uncovered. Helu, however, was made of sterner stuff than the other Lebanese communists they had arrested, and refused to give away any information. According to one eyewitness, Helu told the head of the Political Division of Syrian General Intelligence, Capt. Abd al-Wahhab al-Khatib, that he had "seen plenty like you before" in his decades of communist activism, and never once had he betrayed his comrades.

This defiance earned Helu a strong dose of the sadism for which Sarraj's men had a well-founded reputation. He was punched in the face, kicked, and caned until he snapped the rod. Stripped to his underwear, he was lashed with whips on his bare torso, back, and limbs. Tied by the ankles to a pole known as a *falaqa*, he was beaten and whipped on the soles of his feet. When this failed to loosen his lips, his toes were electrocuted with a cable plugged into the wall socket. A pump was inserted into his anus and inflated, while a boot pressed down on his stomach.

For twelve straight hours this went on, interrupted only whenever Helu lost consciousness. By the early morning, he was lying in a pool of his own blood. Witnesses described his body as having turned blue, his face and eyes swollen grotesquely, the skin on his back flayed and shredded by the whippings. His breathing was slow and labored. Shortly before dawn, he asked for a sip of water, which he had been denied throughout the ordeal. These would be his last words: moments later, he passed away.

This was not a turn of events the UAR authorities were prepared to make known to the world. The killing of so prominent a man as Farajallah al-Helu—a public figure in Lebanon, who had led the Lebanese Communist Party in the 1940s, and played a role in winning the country's independence from France in 1943—was not an incident that could escape notice or rebuke. Cairo's relations with Moscow were strained enough as it was, already jeopardizing negotiations for Soviet funding of Egypt's all-important Aswan High Dam project. The disclosure of Helu's death was a scandal Nasser could not afford.

The body, therefore, had to disappear. At first, this was accomplished by burying it in a shallow grave in the village of Dayr Salman, twenty kilometers east of Damascus, by a patch of farmland belonging to the head of the intelligence branch in which Helu was killed, 1st Lt. Sami Jumaa.

This was soon deemed an insufficiently permanent solution, however, and so it fell to one of Jumaa's underlings, Wajih Antakli, to carry out the task that, perhaps more than any other, etched Sarraj's name in Syrian minds as a byword for horror. Thanks to an official investigation into Helu's killing led by a Syrian judge in 1961–62, we have Antakli's own account of the macabre deed he was ordered to undertake.

It began in mid-July 1959, some twenty days after Helu's burial, when Antakli returned late at night to the grave in Dayr Salman accompanied by four colleagues. After stuffing wads of cotton in their noses and mouths to block the smell, they dug up and exhumed Helu's decomposing corpse. Reaching for the saw he had brought along for the purpose, Antakli then proceeded to cut off the body's legs and arms, then the head, before splitting the torso in four. Placing the pieces in a large bag, he hauled it into the trunk of his car, and dropped his colleagues back in Damascus.

That was the first half of Antakli's task. He then drove to his house in the countryside southwest of the capital, on the road to Daraya, where the gruesome final act would take place. From the souks of Old Damascus, he had recently purchased a white bathtub, the plughole of which he sealed with cement. From the same souks, he also bought a large glass vessel of acid, which came enclosed in a metal cage stuffed with straw. Pouring the acid into the bath, he added the severed pieces of Helu's remains, covered the tub with an old wooden door, and waited.

After "three or four" days, he decided to inspect the results. Pulling back the wooden cover, he found an oily, black, frothy substance in the tub, giving off a diabolical stench. Stirring it, he was surprised to see even the bones had dissolved entirely. He alerted his superior, Capt. Naasan Zakkar, director of the intelligence services' Seventh Branch, who drove to the house with Jumaa to see for himself. Pronouncing himself satisfied, Zakkar told Antakli to dispose of the liquid right away. Scooping it up with a jug, he poured some of it into a small hole he dug next to the house, and the rest into a nearby river.

With Helu now well and truly gone without a trace, the lying began in earnest. Many years later, Sarraj told an interviewer he phoned Nasser after the disposal of the corpse, and they agreed to deny everything: not just that they had killed Helu, but that Helu had ever entered UAR territory to begin with. They held firm to the lie even as the case garnered global attention. The Soviet leader Nikita Khrushchev, India's Prime Minister Nehru, and Cuba's Fidel Castro were among those who pressed Nasser personally for information on Helu's fate. An international committee comprising French, Italian, Indian, Swedish, and Arab luminaries campaigned into the 1960s for his release from prison—not knowing he was already long dead.

Eventually, decades later, Sarraj admitted the truth—or part of it—as did Jumaa, who wrote a colorful memoir of his years as Sarraj's sidekick.

Nasser maintained the lie to the day he died.

★

SYRIA HOLDS THE DISTINCTION of being the only country other than Egypt to have been ruled by Nasser directly. It was not a happy experience by anyone's reckoning. A marriage that began in 1958 in a drunken ecstasy—watched by the rapt eyes of the Arab world—collapsed three years later in the bitterest acrimony. The very public divorce was a blow from which neither partner fully recovered.

Four years prior to this ill-fated union, Syria looked to be on an altogether happier and healthier trajectory. In February 1954, army officers overthrew the repressive dictatorship of Col. Adib al-Shishakli, who had ruled in despotic fashion since seizing power in a military coup in 1949. By 1953, Shishakli had managed to unite a broad coalition of opponents against him, ranging from the urban elites who had won Syria's independence in 1946 to Arab nationalists, communists, and rural Druze chieftains. The final weeks of his reign witnessed something of a national uprising, as students demonstrated in the four largest cities of Damascus, Aleppo, Homs, and Hama, clashing with police, while lawyers, other professionals, and small business owners went on strike. A state of emergency was declared, and the former president Hashim al-Atasi was placed under house arrest. When the army finally moved to depose Shishakli on February 25, it could claim with a degree of sincerity to be responding to the popular will.

Most Syrians were certainly not sorry to see the back of Shishakli. Having endured no fewer than three military dictators since 1949, they had had more than their fill. They sought now to turn the page and write a new chapter in their national story, reviving the civilian-led parliamentary democracy of which they had been robbed five years earlier.

For a brief moment, it appeared they would get their wish. The parliamentary elections held in the wake of Shishakli's fall, in September 1954, were billed "the first free elections in the Arab world." Undoubtedly they were freer than any seen in Syria before or since.

The open and orderly manner in which they were conducted, and the unprecedented breadth of political persuasions they brought into the new parliament, showed Syria to enjoy a "constellation of parties and . . . richness of political life" unsurpassed by any other Arab state.

The election results revealed a marked decline in support for the traditional parties of the post–World War I era, in favor of newer and more radical upstarts. Whereas candidates loyal to the old National and People's Parties had held two-thirds of the seats in the 1949 parliament, their share now fell by half, to just one-third. Into the vacant seats came the Arab nationalists of the Baath—who alone now commanded 15 percent of the total—as well as various social-ist, Syrian nationalist, and nonideological figures. The election of an openly communist member of parliament, Khalid Bakdash, marked a notable first for the Arab world. Still, the radical new-comers remained a numerical minority overall. With the presidency and premiership in the familiar hands of Hashim al-Atasi and Faris al-Khuri, respectively, Syrians could be forgiven for believing they were entering a bright new era, combining stable civilian rule and constitutional order with the healthy pluralism and diversity of a free liberal democracy.

Two powerful forces blocked the path to this future. The first was the military, which, despite appearances, never truly returned to its barracks after toppling Shishakli, and continued to act as a higher authority or "deep state" pulling levers behind the scenes, unanswerable to civilian politicians and institutions. The second was Gamal Abdel Nasser, whose presence on the Arab stage began to make itself inescapable only weeks after Syrians went to the polls. It was the fusion of these two powers—Nasser and Syria's officers—that would deal the death blow to Syrian democracy four years later.

★

AS WITH IRAQ AND other Arab countries, Syria's first significant encounter with Nasser came during the Baghdad Pact saga of 1955.

It will be recalled that Nasser sought to prevent the pact's creation by rallying his fellow Arab leaders against its key champion, the Iraqi premier Nuri al-Said.

Given its strategic position at the heart of the Arab world—between Cairo to the west and neighboring Baghdad to the east; bordering also Israel, Jordan, Lebanon, and the NATO member Turkey; connecting the desert to the Mediterranean—it was felt by all concerned that a great deal was riding on whether or not Syria would join the pact. "Syria enjoyed what amounted to a casting vote on the Pact's future: had she applied for membership, other Arab states would have followed." As the battle lines were drawn up in January 1955, when Nasser summoned the Arab heads of state to Cairo to debate the pact, the Syrian delegation came under especial scrutiny.

Syria's venerable prime minister at the time, the seventy-seven-year-old Faris al-Khuri, was unmistakably a man of the Nuri al-Said generation. A founding father of the independent Syrian republic, he had distinguished himself in the battles against first the Ottoman, then the French occupations, being imprisoned for his part in a 1925 revolt against the French. A polyglot and polymath, trained as both a lawyer and a mathematician, he had previously served as speaker of Syria's parliament, founded the Damascus University law faculty, and led the Syrian delegation to the inaugural United Nations Conference in San Francisco in 1945. To this day, he remains the only Christian to have held the post of Syrian prime minister.

Few were in any doubt that Khuri privately sympathized with Nuri's position vis-à-vis the Baghdad Pact. Yet, in recognition of the dissenting view taken by the likes of the Baath—Syria's new rising stars, who had performed so well in the recent elections—he declared his government would remain neutral in the affair, neither joining the pact nor condemning Nuri for doing so. To Cairo and its supporters in Syria, this was not good enough. When, in an unguarded moment in early February 1955, Khuri remarked that Nuri would have no need for the pact if the Arab armies were capable of defending Iraq, the Egyptian press hounded him. Sensing their opportunity, the Baath and other Syrian factions raised a noisy fuss at home. When cabinet ministers started resigning, the aging Khuri tendered his own resignation, to cheers from Cairo Radio.

It was a watershed moment, prompting Syria's decisive entrance into the Nasserist camp, where it would faithfully remain for the next six years. Moreover, the episode marked the birth of Nasser's special relationship with the Baath in particular, a relationship of paramount importance in determining the course of subsequent events.

With Khuri gone, what might be termed the "Nasserization" of Syrian officialdom occurred at a swift pace. In March 1955, Syria's new prime minister, Sabri al-Asali, signed an agreement on a military alliance with Egypt, providing for the integration of the two countries' armed forces. Finalized seven months later, the alliance placed the militaries of Egypt, Syria, and Saudi Arabia under the joint command of the Egyptian Free Officer Abd al-Hakim Amer. While its significance was more symbolic and diplomatic than military per se, the agreement did see Syrian troops undergo training in Egypt. Among them was a young air force pilot named Hafez al-Assad, the future long-standing dictator who would eventually bequeath power to his son Bashar, Syria's current ruler.

Around the same time, Egypt's ambassador to Damascus, Brig. Mahmud Riyadh, began to wield extraordinary influence in Syria, earning him comparisons to the Ottoman governors and colonial French High Commissioners of bygone days. His office overlooking the Tora River in Damascus's prestigious Abu Rummaneh district became the indispensable address for all Syrians seeking to win Cairo's affections, turning the ambassador into the "beating heart of Syrian political life." On intimate terms with presidents, prime ministers, and military men alike, he did his utmost to promote Nasser's allies—the Baath above all—and undermine his foes. Allegations abounded of him bribing the Syrian press with monthly stipends, while tasking spies and undercover agents with all manner of skulduggery.

Most important of all the developments at this time were those taking place within Syria's military, of which the alliance with Egypt was just one aspect. The emergence of Nasser during the Baghdad Pact saga, and the attending defeat of the Khuri government and all it represented, put a spring in the step of not a few Syrian officers. In Egypt's military dictator they perceived a kindred spirit, who had no more time than they did for the irksome constraints of parliament and democratic accountability. Nasser's rise emboldened them to intervene more assertively in Syrian politics. Indeed, it had been the officers themselves—specifically, the chief of staff Shawkat Shuqayr and his deputy Adnan al-Malki—who had engineered the military alliance with Egypt in March 1955.

The shocking assassination in April 1955 of the latter officer, Malki, at the hands of a Syrian nationalist extremist sent this process into overdrive. The gloves came off, and the army made no bones about cracking down with violence, not just on the Syrian nationalist movement, but on all quarters deemed hostile to the new era represented by Cairo, the Baath, and (to a lesser extent) the communists.

Leading the charge was the head of military intelligence, Col. Abd al-Hamid al-Sarraj, whose campaign of terror in the wake of the Malki assassination earned him a name for brutality still spoken of with dread by Syrians of a certain age to this day. Over the following three years, Sarraj methodically extended his personal grip over the security and intelligence apparatuses, until he was widely regarded as the single most powerful and fearsome man in the country. This was the person in whose hands Nasser opted to place Syria once the union occurred, granting him full and free rein to take his talents to entirely new depths of depravity, going beyond Syria's borders to sow death and destruction across Lebanon, Jordan, and Iraq.

★

ABD AL-HAMID AL-SARRAJ WAS born in 1925 in a low-income neighborhood of Hama, Syria's fourth city, slightly nearer to Aleppo than to Damascus. His father owned a small corner shop. According to his brother-in-law, who wrote a biography of him, Sarraj's childhood was an unhappy one, seething with resentment of the local aristocracy, whose children enjoyed a way of life very different from his own. Even at the height of his power decades later, he would still recall with bitterness how he was forbidden as a child to swim in the Orontes River alongside the sons of the wealthy families, who would pelt him with stones if he approached them.

Sarraj began his career in the days of the French occupation as a humble gendarme guarding the entrance to the historic souk of Aleppo, near the medieval citadel. After asking to see shoppers' IDs, he would pat them down for drugs or weapons before sending them on their way. Among the few stories of interest from this time is one that may be apocryphal just as easily as it may be completely true. It holds that Sarraj grew attached to a prostitute from the red-light district near his guard post. So fond did he become of the woman that he kept on seeing her for years after leaving Aleppo, moving her to an apartment in Damascus to continue their trysts even after marrying another woman and rising to become Syria's interior minister. The arrangement endured until the day came in 1959 that he decided she was an inconvenient burden, and had her killed and dumped on the banks of the Barada.

In 1947, one year after the French departure, Sarraj enrolled at the Syrian military college. While some accounts state he fought in Palestine the following year, his brother-in-law quotes him as saying his request to fight was actually turned down, on grounds of insufficient experience. At any rate, he was in Syria by 1949, when he found work as a bodyguard for the country's first military dictator, Husni al-Zaim. He remained a member of the presidential security detail under Syria's third dictator, Shishakli, who took a strong liking to him, eventually appointing him head of the so-called Premier Bureau, in charge of personnel. When Shishakli was overthrown in 1954, the army's chief of staff, General Shuqayr, placed Sarraj in charge of military intelligence, officially known as the Deuxième Bureau.

It was in this role that Sarraj first developed his reputation for tyranny, and established what went on to become the "norm"—so to speak—of extreme cruelty practiced by the Syrian state against political dissidents.

Sarraj had been in the job for only one month when Malki, the deputy chief of staff, was assassinated. Malki was an Arab nationalist close to the Baath, while his killer was a proponent of "Greater Syria" nationalism. This peculiar ideology asserts that all the land between Egypt's Sinai Peninsula and what are now southern Turkey and western Iran—including the island of Cyprus—belongs to the ancient "Syrian nation," who are a people wholly distinct from the Arab nation. Together, these two opposing nationalisms—Arab and Greater Syrian—were the strongest ideological currents within the Syrian officer corps at the time of Malki's killing.

Accordingly, the assassination was seized on by Sarraj and his fellow Arab nationalists as a pretext to expunge the Syrian nationalists from the military, and indeed from public life altogether. The leading Syrian nationalist officer, Maj. Ghassan Jadid, was driven into exile in Lebanon, where he was later assassinated himself. More than one hundred other party members, including all the civilian leadership, were formally indicted for murder and other grave crimes. The party was banned, its members purged from the public sector, its printing press burned down by a mob. The witch hunt extended to people with only the loosest connection to the movement, who plainly posed no security threat, such as the poets Adonis and Muhammad al-Maghut, two major figures of modern Arabic literature who were both imprisoned at the time. Adonis later described the experience as "a year of torture, a true hell," while Maghut spoke often of the lifelong fear it instilled in him:

> In prison, all beautiful things collapsed in front of me, leaving nothing but panic and terror. Instead of seeing the sky, I saw a boot; the boot of Abd al-Hamid al-Sarraj, which left its imprint on me for the rest of my life.

Military checkpoints sprang up on roads all over the country, stopping and searching passing vehicles. Homes were raided by the infamous "dawn visitors" of Sarraj's Deuxième Bureau. As we have already seen with Farajallah al-Helu, those unlucky enough to be pulled away to detention entered a sealed-off world where the quaint notions of human rights and legal protections did not exist. Methods of torture included beatings, whippings, electrocution, being dipped naked into barrels of ice or diesel, and the removal of fingernails with blades. Sarraj is credited—if that's the word—with introducing two practices that became especially notorious. The first, known as the "tire" (*dulab*), involved forcing detainees inside a car tire, painfully contorting the body and rendering them helpless to defend against further violence. The second, dubbed the "ghost" (*shabah*), would see them tied by their wrists to the ceiling and left in place without food or drink for hours or even days, causing excruciating swelling and discomfort, interspersed with regular beatings. In recent years, rights groups such as Human Rights Watch and Amnesty International have documented that many of these methods, including the ghost and the tire, continue to be practiced extensively against Syrian detainees to this day.

As the lurid tales of Sarraj's torture dungeons spread from house to house, a general atmosphere of fear and anxiety crept in. Social life in Damascus retreated, as people went out less and came home earlier. The optimism of just a few months prior was already beginning to dissipate, as it grew clearer by the day that Syria had once again turned down a dark path, and was heading for worse still. Even foreign visitors could sense it: passing through in May 1956, the American journalist Joseph Alsop left predicting Sarraj would be Syria's next dictator.

★

JULY 1956 BROUGHT NASSER'S nationalization of the Suez Canal Company. War came three months later. For Syria, already by then Nasser's closest Arab ally, the experience was transformational.

As soon as the company was nationalized, Damascus declared its "strong and absolute support" for Nasser's decision. When the war began, Syria severed diplomatic relations with Britain and France in a gesture of solidarity. It even offered to send troops of its own to fight alongside the Egyptians, an offer Nasser graciously declined. Instead, in early November, Syrian officers blew up three crucial pumping stations on the Iraq Petroleum Company's pipeline from Kirkuk to Tripoli, significantly disrupting Europe's oil supply chain.

When the war ended and Nasser was lionized across the Arab world, his supporters in Syria received the boost of a lifetime. The Baath, who had already called for union with Egypt before Suez, now set about actively making it happen.

To do so, they knew they would have to win over the real decision-makers in Damascus: the military top brass. Certain key officers, including Sarraj, were already close to the Baath, as well as to Egypt's powerful ambassador, Riyadh. Others, however, were old Shishakli cronies, and/or nonideologues driven by pure self-interest, with no particular attachment to Cairo.

Two key developments in the course of 1957 converted a critical mass of the officers to the cause of union. The first was the rising tide of communism in the country. Just as Nasser had been successfully courting Damascus since 1955, so Moscow had made inroads of its own since the election to Syria's parliament of the Arab world's first communist MP, Khalid Bakdash, in 1954. Trade agreements inked in August 1955 were followed the next month by Soviet arms sales to Syria, encompassing tanks, planes, and armored vehicles. In July 1956, Syria recognized Communist China. When the Suez War broke out three months later, Syria's president, Shukri al-Quwwatli, flew to Moscow and received assurances of Soviet support in the event of an attack on Syria.

The second development was the international response to this apparent creeping Sovietization of Syria. This was, after all, the heyday of the Cold War. The US was committed to the "containment" of Soviet influence around the world, to which end President

Eisenhower had announced his signature doctrine in early 1957, offering both economic and military assistance to any country in the Middle East requesting them in confronting communism. It was no secret that Syria was among the countries Eisenhower had uppermost in mind when formulating the policy.

Approved by Congress in March 1957, the Eisenhower Doctrine was scorned by the Syrian government, whose defense minister Khalid al-Azm signed a substantial economic and technical agreement with Moscow five months later. Within days, Syria also expelled three US diplomats accused of intriguing against the regime, and appointed as army chief of staff a Col. Afif al-Bizri, who was suspected—not very accurately, as it turned out—of communist sympathies.

This was all too much for Washington, now convinced Syria had become an all-out Soviet satellite state. In early September, plans were announced to airlift US arms to Jordan and fortify Iraq and Lebanon, on the grounds that they were threatened by Syrian communism. At the same time, Turkey began mobilizing troops on its southern border with Syria.

It was now Moscow's turn to flex its muscles. The Soviet premier, Nikolai Bulganin, warned darkly that an armed conflict in Syria would not be limited to Syria. Washington responded with statements backing Turkey's right to self-defense. When two Soviet warships then showed up at the Syrian port of Latakia, a full-blown Cold War standoff had arisen, pitting NATO (represented by Turkey) nose-to-nose with Soviet troops.

Into this combustible fray suddenly stepped Nasser, who sent a contingent of his own forces to Latakia to take up positions facing the Turks on Syria's northern frontier. The gambit paid off handsomely: the crisis came to an end, allowing Nasser to pose as the gallant Arab knight who had seen off a NATO invasion of Syria, while also stealing the initiative from both the Soviets and Saudi Arabia, whose King Saud had tried to mediate a diplomatic resolution of the dispute.

In the wake of this triumph, Syria's unionists decided the time had come to make their decisive move. The drama had led the officers as a whole to believe Syria required a guarantor against external aggression, as well as an arbiter for their own ceaseless squabbling and factional feuding. All things considered, they preferred for this role to be played by Cairo rather than Moscow. Not only was Nasser a fellow Arab and Muslim, he was a military man, a creature of their own world of coups, conspiracies, and juntas. A closer alliance with Egypt would, it seemed, offer them the best means of ensuring their own continued primacy in Syria going forward.

The officers were therefore receptive when the Baath's cofounder Salah al-Din al-Bitar suggested to Sarraj that they send a delegation to Cairo to ask Nasser in person for a union. It was still far from clear what precise form this union might take; certainly, few at this point had in mind the wholesale surrender of Syrian sovereignty that in fact came to pass.

Acting on Bitar's suggestion, with Sarraj's encouragement, fourteen officers led by Chief of Staff Bizri boarded a flight to Cairo on January 12, 1958. The Syrian cabinet had neither been consulted nor so much as informed in advance. Nor had the views of the Syrian public been sought in any way. The future of Syria was about to be decided by an entirely unelected and unaccountable cabal of soldiers, colluding with the leader of a foreign country. When he heard what the officers had done, President Quwwatli not inaccurately called it a military coup.

Receiving the delegation, Nasser heard the officers' proposal, then set out his conditions for acceptance. These amounted to the complete dismantling of Syria's democracy: parliament had to be abolished, and all political parties dissolved, so as to harmonize the Syrian political system with Egypt's own. The Syrian presidency and government as they then existed would likewise come to an end, their powers subsumed under Nasser's supreme authority. No democrats themselves, the officers raised no objections. After hammering out the details for a week, a final agreement was reached on January 20, following a four-hour meeting among Nasser, Bizri, and Bitar, who had joined the delegation midway through.

Only when Bitar and the officers returned to Damascus the next day did the magnitude of what was happening finally dawn on Syria's civilian politicians. As the Lebanese writer Hazem Saghieh has put it, Syria's parties were being asked to volunteer willingly for that which Egypt's parties had only been forced into against their will. The Baath, nonetheless, were prepared to go along with it and dissolve themselves, on the belief—sorely mistaken, as it turned out—that, as the architects of the union, they would be granted a preeminent role in the governance of the new state.

Far less sanguine about the situation were the likes of President Quwwatli, Prime Minister Asali, and the veteran statesman Khalid al-Azm, who grasped all too late in the day that not only would they personally be consigned to political oblivion, but the very entity of the independent Syria they had devoted their lives to building was to be abolished at the stroke of a pen. In a panic, they quickly hashed out a counterproposal for a looser federal union that would preserve at least a modicum of Syrian autonomy and independence. When they sent Bitar to Cairo on January 25 to put this to Nasser, however, it met with flat rejection. "It was to be total union on his terms or nothing at all."

The clock had now run out. His patience with the politicians exhausted, Colonel Bizri strong-armed them into submission, threatening any further dissenters with imprisonment at Sarraj's infamous Mezze jail. Ordering the cabinet onto a plane on January 31, Bizri set off with them for Cairo. At a joint session of the Egyptian and Syrian governments the following day, full union between Egypt and Syria was formally proclaimed to the world. The two countries— henceforth to be known as the "United Arab Republic"—would share a single capital in Cairo, as well as a single flag and army, with Nasser as the new state's sole president. It was, Nasser declared, the "dawn of Arab liberation."

Four days later, on February 5, the union was approved by both the Egyptian and Syrian parliaments, a foregone conclusion noteworthy only for the abstention of Syria's communist MP Bakdash. Pointedly remarking that no communist party had ever dissolved itself, Bakdash boycotted the session. Here was an early milepost in the rift between Nasser and Syria's communists that would—as we have seen—give rise to ferocious bloodshed in more than one country.

February 21 saw ostensible "referenda" conducted in both Egypt and Syria, purporting to grant democratic legitimacy to the union and Nasser's presidency thereof. While it is possible that a large plurality or indeed a majority in both countries truly did favor the union at first, the "referenda" can in no way be adduced as evidence for this. No less a figure than Bashir al-Azma, who served as the UAR's health minister (and later Syria's prime minister), recalled in his memoir how he "participated in the rigging of the referendum" by casting votes in multiple ballot boxes. The official results came out at 99.99 percent for union in Egypt, versus a mere 99.98 percent in Syria.

If this was an ominous start to the union, for Syria the even darker portent came on March 6, when the UAR cabinet lineups were announced. Coming in as interior minister for the Syrian "province"—a post enjoying full control over the instruments of domestic repression—was none other than the torturer-in-chief himself, Col. Abd al-Hamid al-Sarraj.

7

THE DAMASCENE
CONVERSION

THE MONTH OF THE UAR'S ESTABLISHMENT—FEBRUARY 1958—marked the absolute pinnacle of Nasser's pan-Arab power and popularity. Visiting Syria for the first time (in his life) that month, he was swarmed by giant crowds of tens if not hundreds of thousands, coming from not just all across Syria but Lebanon, Jordan, and beyond. For three days and nights, every hotel in Damascus was fully booked, causing people to sleep outdoors in the streets and gardens. So dense were the throngs when Nasser's car attempted to drive the short distance from outgoing president Quwwatli's home to al-Dhiyafa Palace that a journey that should have taken minutes lasted an hour and a half.

The spectacle would recur for months afterward. The late Lebanese American scholar Fouad Ajami, then in his early teens, was among the many in Beirut who made the trip to see the living legend in the flesh. "I braved the fury of my elders," he later wrote, "and went to Damascus, aboard a bus with my friends, to attend a rally for the Egyptian leader Gamal Abdul Nasser. We caught a glimpse of the hero-leader of Arab nationalism as he made an appearance on the balcony of a guest-palace. . . . Around the corner, it was believed, lay a great Arab project, and this leader from Egypt would bring it about."

The speed with which Nasser proceeded to squander this adulation was remarkable. By the following year, the crowds at his Damascus speeches had so dwindled that Sarraj's colleague, Sami Jumaa, recalled they had to bus in factory workers, school students, government employees, and random public-transit passengers to make up numbers. Two years later, the union collapsed altogether, felled in a bloodless coup by officers who were themselves then cheered in the streets of Damascus.

How could this happen?

At root, the fundamental problem was the mismatch between Nasser's intentions and Syrians' expectations. Imagining they were entering into a merger between equals, Syrians quickly discovered they were unmistakably the juniors in the relationship—that is, when they were taken into consideration at all. Whereas Syrians had believed they would at least continue to govern their own affairs, Nasser conceived of the union as a straightforward extension of his dominion, an addition of a new Syrian "province" to Egypt's preexisting state and system, which would essentially go on operating as before, cosmetic adjustments notwithstanding. This came as a particular shock to Syria's Baath, who had indulged the fantasy that they might govern not just Syria but Egypt, too. Yet the discontent was soon felt by all strata of Syrian society, from politicians to soldiers, leftists to conservatives, the wealthiest land barons to the humblest shopkeepers. Even Sarraj, the only Syrian to whose opinion Nasser listened, despaired of the union in the end, resigning in its final days. Brief though the experiment proved, the fallout of the damage it wrought remains with us to this day, for—as shall be seen—it was in the gloomy midst of the union's dysfunction that the nucleus of the future Assad regime first took solid form.

THE FORMAL STRUCTURE OF the new UAR regime was revealed in early March 1958, when its constitution and government system were declared. There was to be a single, unified cabinet for the entire UAR, based in Cairo, in addition to two "executive councils," one for each of the Egyptian and Syrian "provinces." Right away, it was clear where Nasser's priorities lay, for while Sarraj was given the vital interior ministry portfolio for Syria, the Baath's Bitar—arguably the foremost engineer of the whole union—received the underwhelming post of minister of state. True, the Baath's Akram al-Hawrani was also named vice president of the republic and chairman of the Syrian executive council, but the former was a purely ceremonial role, while the latter also carried less weight than it appeared to.

Meanwhile, the constitution provided for the creation of a quasi-parliament, the "National Assembly," whose six hundred members (four hundred Egyptians and two hundred Syrians) would each be appointed directly by Nasser. In lieu of political parties—already banned in Egypt, and now in Syria too—a "National Union" movement akin to Egypt's old Liberation Rally would be formed in due course. As for Syria's erstwhile president Quwwatli and premier Asali, whose offices were abolished upon the union's establishment, the latter joined Hawrani as the second of four vice presidents in Cairo, while the former retired with the honorific title of "First Arab Citizen."

If the Baath took umbrage at what they felt was their undersized representation in the new halls of power, they kept up cordial appearances for the time being. The first volleys of open dissent came instead from Syria's communists. They had not been opposed in principle to the union; their objection was to dissolving their party. Throughout 1958, they made multiple attempts to reach an understanding with Nasser, offering to lend the union their full support in exchange for the party's survival—all in vain. The mood steadily soured, not least after the July coup in Baghdad, which, as we have seen, proved highly favorable to Iraq's communists at the expense of its Nasserists. Finally, in December, the Syrian communist leader Bakdash issued his forthright call for free elections and full civil and democratic liberties across the entire UAR. This was met with Nasser's furious speech in Port Said, in which he vowed to "wage war" against the treacherous communists, singling out the Syrian party for especial abuse.

Thus began Nasser's determined quest to crush communists

wherever he could reach them: in Egypt, where hundreds were sent to Abu Zaabal; in Iraq, where guns were sent to fight them in Mosul; and in Syria, where Sarraj was given carte blanche to extirpate them by any means. According to Sarraj's colleague Sami Jumaa, Sarraj summoned the heads of Syria's security agencies to a meeting in Damascus on December 30, 1958, at which he announced the start of a campaign to utterly eliminate the communist movement in Syria. He distributed lists of party members to arrest, detailing their home addresses and places they were known to frequent. The arrests began within hours. Among the results was the torturing to death of one Saeed al-Droubi in Homs on February 15, 1959, a fate shared also by a Pierre Shadarfian in Aleppo. Riad al-Turk, the communist dissident dubbed "Syria's Mandela" on account of his lengthy prison stints under numerous Syrian regimes, was also arrested during the period. It is notable that, despite enduring eighteen years of solitary confinement under Hafez al-Assad, Turk attests that the physical torture he underwent in Sarraj's custody was the most "brutal" of all.

And then came the killing of Farajallah al-Helu in June 1959. Once again, Sami Jumaa provides illuminating details, particularly on how the Deuxième Bureau was able to snare Helu. After the first wave of arrests starting in late December 1958, the remaining communists went underground, conducting their activities in secret using people the Bureau had not yet managed to apprehend. Many were based next door in Lebanon.

Eventually, the Bureau did arrest a senior communist helping to run these clandestine cells in Damascus. His name was Rafiq Ridha, a sixty-year-old member of the party's central committee hailing from Lebanon's Tripoli, living at the time at a secret location in the Syrian capital.

Searching for a weakness to exploit while interrogating his detainee, Jumaa found it when Ridha mentioned his beloved and beautiful young wife, then pregnant with their first child, who he could not bear to imagine fending for herself while he spent years behind bars.

That did not need to happen, responded Jumaa, handing the man a packet of Gauloises. There were two options before him, Jumaa said. He could "remain a communist leader, and bear the consequences" of that decision, or else choose his new bride, and the child she would deliver in just a few months' time. The next day, Ridha gave the Bureau everything: names, addresses, safe houses, the entire secret network in Damascus. Placing himself at the Bureau's disposal thereafter, he was paid a monthly salary and granted an apartment to live in with his wife in the very same building as Jumaa's intelligence branch.

Ridha's assistance quickly proved invaluable. As the Bureau chipped away at the remnants of the communist cells, they succeeded on June 19 in arresting another Lebanese member from Tripoli, Subhi al-Habal, in a Damascus café. When they brought him in for questioning, he and Ridha immediately recognized each other, and struck up a conversation. Before long, Habal offered to divulge all his information in exchange for being spared torture. Most significantly, he told them where to find the safe house used by the senior party officials running the underground activities during their periodic visits from Beirut. The next comrade due to arrive in the coming days was "Abu Fayyadh"—the nom de guerre, explained Ridha, of the famous Farajallah al-Helu.

Jumaa promptly deployed four of his men to the location, where six days later they arrested Helu upon arrival. Within twelve hours, he was dead.

★

IF THE COMMUNIST CHALLENGE was largely quelled by the summer of 1959, Nasser soon found he had other problems on his hands in Syria.

One month after Helu's killing came the elections for the National Union, the body envisaged as the official state-sponsored political movement, taking the place of the parties of old. From the beginning, the Baath had pinned their highest hopes on this Union, which they expected to be given control over as a matter of course, in recognition of their sacrifice in agreeing to disband their party, not to mention their pivotal role in bringing the UAR into existence to begin with. "We will be officially dissolved," the Baath's leader Michel Aflaq had said, "but we will be present in the new unified party, the National Union. As the child of the union of the two countries, this movement cannot be animated by principles other than those of the Baath." In other words, the Baath saw themselves supplying the political and ideological platform of the new state, with Nasser being merely the charismatic leader and enforcer of the program.

Needless to say, Nasser had no more time for this kind of talk than he had had when Egypt's Muslim Brotherhood entertained similar delusions back in 1953. The Baath performed pitifully in the Union elections, winning less than 3 percent of the available seats. To this painful slap in the face, further humiliations came thick and fast. In September, Nasser dismissed the Baathist culture minister Riyadh al-Malki from the Syrian executive council. In October, he sent the Egyptian army commander, Field Marshal Amer, to Syria to act as his viceroy, making a mockery of the UAR constitution and doing away with even the pretense that Syrians were in charge of their own "province." Seeing they had spectacularly misjudged the nature of Nasser and his attitude to power-sharing, the Baath resigned en bloc two months later.

The departure of the Baath in December 1959 placed the union on far thinner ice than Nasser appears to have appreciated at the time. The Baath, after all, were the only organized political force in Syria that had ever been deeply enthusiastic about the union in the first place. With them gone, there was very little holding it together beyond Nasser's personality and Sarraj's repression.

Sure enough, throughout 1960, Nasser invested ever greater powers in Sarraj, who became chair of the Syrian executive council—effectively Syria's prime minister—as well as head of the National Union in Syria, and the leading Syrian in the Union's Higher

Executive Committee. More than at any time in the past, Syria became the personal fiefdom of Sarraj, who held not just the security and intelligence services but also the cabinet, the media, and various sectors of the economy in an iron grip.

No amount of coercion, however, could enamor Syrians of a union to which they were growing more opposed by the day. By 1960, the discontent had spread well beyond communist and Baathist circles, afflicting the political class as a whole. Even technocrats who had kept an open mind about the arrangement at first were now dismayed by how it had panned out. Dr. Bashir al-Azma was a politically unaffiliated physician from Damascus called on to serve as UAR health minister in a cabinet reshuffle in October 1958. His memoir provides one of the more enlightening, not to say darkly entertaining, accounts of the period.

Showing up early on his first day at the health ministry in Cairo, Azma told the guard at the entrance, "Minister of health."

"He doesn't get here before eleven o'clock," came the reply.

When Azma clarified that he was, himself, the new minister of health, the bewildered guard stared at him with deep suspicion before reluctantly letting him in. Azma was later told by his office manager that it would be preferred if he observed the ministerial custom and refrained from arriving earlier than eleven o'clock. For the commoners to see too much of His Excellency might detract from the gravitas attached to his office.

Indeed, Azma soon discovered he was not expected to perform work of any kind. With the innocence of a political novice, he had come to Cairo believing he was being tasked with leading a "health-care revolution" to raise the living standards of tens of millions of Arabs. Yet when he undertook surprise visits to local hospitals to inspect conditions—which he found "indescribably and unimaginably" appalling—his Egyptian colleagues were aghast. On the sole occasion he was able to secure a personal meeting with Nasser to discuss the healthcare situation in the UAR, the president interrupted him midway through reporting what he had seen in one hospital.

"That's not true, not possible," said Nasser. "I visited that hospital myself and found it decent." In vain did Azma try to explain that a prearranged visit by the president was a different matter from an unannounced one.

With time, Azma learned to while away his mornings reading the papers and solving the crosswords, before heading in the afternoons to the exclusive Gezira Club for tennis, squash, and bowling. This was the club memorably described by the late Waguih Ghali in his 1964 novel, *Beer in the Snooker Club*:

> There is something about that club. Just walking along the drive from the gate to the club-house, seeing the perfectly-kept lawns on either side, the specially-designed street-lamps hovering above you, the white stones lining the road, the car-park, and then the croquet lawn—croquet! a place where middle-aged people play croquet. Imagine being a member of a place where middle-aged people play croquet. This ease; this glide from one place to another; the crispy notes in crocodile wallets; the elegant women floating here and there. Mobile sculptures. And then into the club-house, through it, and out to the swimming-pool where members move as though they were a soft breeze.
>
> The strange thing about this club is that in the early days of the revolution, it was condemned as a symbol of exploitation and was taken over by a committee or something like that. Well, all the members are still members, with a few additional military members.

Should he tire of the Gezira, Azma was also welcome at the Police and Hunting Clubs. When he felt like escaping the city, his office manager arranged hunting and fishing excursions to the Red Sea and Suez Canal.

One might say there were worse ways to live. Yet the novelty soon wore off, as it dawned on Azma and his fellow Syrians that they were not really cabinet ministers at all, but mere props to be wheeled out to smile and clap at official functions. "We began whispering and complaining among ourselves, wondering: what do they want from us?" They came to feel they were being held "hostages" in a "gilded cage," and that the so-called union had amounted in reality to an annexation. Missing his life and medical practice back in Damascus, Azma resigned and left Cairo in August 1960.

★

MORE DANGEROUS FOR NASSER than the grumbling among civilians such as Azma were the similar thoughts occurring at the same time to the Syrian officer corps. Accustomed ever since their first coup in 1949 to wielding supreme authority over Syrian affairs, they, too, had cause to resent the way things had unfolded in the short life of the UAR thus far.

There was, for a start, the haughty and disdainful manner with which many Syrian officers felt they were treated by their Egyptian counterparts, each of whom—it was said—strutted about Damascus as though he were Nasser himself. Peers who only yesterday were the picture of courtesy and geniality, addressing Syrians with almost blushing deference as *efendim* ("Sir"), turned overnight into petty tyrants, barking orders in "pharaonic" fashion, according to Sami Jumaa. Syrian officers quickly acquired the impression of being occupied by a foreign power, as vital military decisions such as senior appointments and troop movements were made by the Egyptians without their consultation.

No less objectionable were Nasser's efforts in parallel to rid the Syrian officer corps of its influential figures and ideological undesirables, so as to reduce it to a pliant and docile instrument of Cairo. Scarcely had the UAR existed for a month when in late March 1958 the Syrian army commander Bizri—the man who had personally frog-marched the Syrian cabinet onto the plane to Cairo to declare the union—was dismissed and replaced by his little-known deputy, Jamal Faysal. This met with open protest from several Syrian officers, some of whom were jailed and tortured in consequence.

The incident was later cited by the Syrian colonel who brought an end to the union in 1961 as the starting point of the officer corps' disillusionment with the UAR experience. The purge soon extended well beyond the top brass to encompass even junior officers suspected of unwelcome political inclinations.

No faction felt this more keenly than the Baathists. To scatter them and forestall the possibility of their intriguing against the regime in Damascus, a variety of methods were employed. Some were made ministers, such as Mustafa Hamdun and Abd al-Ghani Qannut, both members of the historic officers' delegation that flew to Cairo on January 12, 1958. Others were given ambassadorial or other diplomatic posts abroad. The majority, however, were transferred on military pretexts to Egypt, where a closer eye could be kept on their activities.

Here, they lived well enough. Earning double pay, with a free apartment and sometimes a car, "they spent much time lounging in Groppi's and Lappas, cafés where British officers before them had once whiled away off-duty hours." The politically zealous among them, however, seethed with rage at the calamity that had befallen the Baath, blaming the civilian leadership for agreeing to dissolve the party and selling the cause down the river. By 1960, a young contingent of these officers had formed a small and highly secretive group that would go on to change the course of Syrian history.

Calling themselves the "Military Committee," they comprised five key figures above all: Lt. Col. Muhammad Umran, Majors Salah Jadid and Ahmad al-Mir, Capt. Abd al-Karim al-Jundi, and a certain Capt. Hafez al-Assad, then twenty-nine years old, whose squadron of MiG-19 fighter jets had been transferred to Cairo the previous year. As the eldest and highest ranked, Umran was the *primus inter pares*. They would meet outside the city, or at one another's homes, or in a quiet corner at Groppi—a vastly more patrician establishment than the Indiana coffeehouse on the other side of the Nile where Saddam Hussein was getting into knife fights that same year. (It's fascinating to reflect there was a time when both Assad and Saddam were on Nasser's payroll, and all three men lived in the same city.)

The initial aims of the committee, so far as they were defined with any clarity, were directed internally within the Baath. The men were not plotting Syria's secession from the UAR; instead, they hoped to reform and reconfigure the union on more favorable terms. Above all, their fixation was on the Baath's civilian leadership. Seeing the party founder Michel Aflaq and his cronies as feckless saps unfit to carry the torch any longer, they resolved to work in full secrecy and independence from them, essentially regarding themselves as the true Baath leaders thenceforth. "We felt the problem lay in the leadership," Umran later wrote, "and so there was a need to move beyond its rule from above, and to free ourselves of its personal squabbles."

Three years later, this handful of young officers would carry out the coup that brought the Baath—*their* Baath—to power in Damascus, leading ultimately to the establishment of the Assad dynasty that still rules Syria today.

For the moment, however, the UAR kept plodding forward, sleepwalking to the edge of the cliff.

★

BY EARLY 1961, NASSER himself was acknowledging the disaffection then practically ubiquitous across the Syrian "province." Rather than take the criticism on board, however, he attacked its authors as saboteurs, fifth columnists, and enemies of Arabism. In a speech in February at the Latakia Officers Club, he mocked those who said, "We want freedoms, we want democracy, we want political parties," asking rhetorically in return: "What did parties do for us in the past? Was anyone able to pass a land reform law through parliament? Were they able to pass any law for social justice through parliament?" It was a revealing moment, in which the depth of his lifelong contempt for parliamentary democracy was on plain display.

Whether in denial, or truly deluded by the yes-men with whom he surrounded himself, Nasser declared in the same speech that what he saw with his own eyes in Syria left him certain the union had never been stronger. "Every time I visit you . . . I see the Syrian people are keener than ever on the union."

Away from the Potemkin villages wheeled out for Nasser's stage-managed tours, however, the reality could not have been more different. Over and above Syrians' political grievances, a laundry list of economic complaints had also accumulated since February 1958. For all its flirtations with Moscow, Syria's economy had remained broadly liberal and laissez-faire in the years before the union. The application since then of Egyptian-style statist measures had been anathema to much of the Syrian middle class.

Increased duties on commodity imports raised the cost of living. Stringent currency-exchange controls led to a major flight of capital out of the country. Land expropriations in 1958 naturally alienated affected landowners, not least as the proportion of cultivated land seized was double in Syria what it was in Egypt. The wealthy were by no means the only ones penalized: all businesspeople down to the corner shopkeeper were saddled with onerous and unfamiliar bureaucratic red tape, forced "to follow the maddeningly complicated and interminable procedures for which the government of Egypt has long been famous." Nor was any of this alleviated by the severe drought that happened to befall Syria during the three years of union, slashing its national income by a third in 1960.

Against this backdrop, the "bombshell" announcement in July 1961 of mass nationalizations of Syrian (and Egyptian) banks, insurance companies, shipping enterprises, and other industrial firms, as well as the introduction of a progressive income tax reaching 90 percent in its highest bracket, among other measures collectively dubbed "the socialist decrees," sent tensions spiraling. That the decisions had been made without consulting Syria's economy minister was an additional sting, though by this stage not an unusual one.

Discontent in Syria now reached fever pitch. In a too-little, too-late attempt to cool the temperature, Nasser finally reined in Sarraj, transferring him to Cairo in August and awarding him the grand-sounding but largely meaningless title of vice president of the republic for internal affairs. Far from rescuing the collapsing union, this only had the effect of untying the last knot holding it together. With Sarraj gone, Nasser's Syrian flank was undefended, and though Sarraj resigned in disgust the following month and returned to Damascus, the die was already cast. Two days later, a handful of Syrian officers brought the union crashing to the ground.

★

THE COUP OF SEPTEMBER 28, 1961, was not Sarraj's doing, though it's possible he had an inkling of the plot's existence, and may have been right to claim—as he did to the British diplomat Anthony Nutting—that had he not been removed to Cairo the month before, he could have prevented it.

In point of fact, it was the brainchild of one Lt. Col. Abd al-Karim al-Nahlawi, a politically unaffiliated Damascene officer in his mid-thirties serving at the time as director of the office of Nasser's viceroy in Syria, Field Marshal Amer. In a lengthy interview with Al Jazeera aired in 2010, Nahlawi said he first conceived of the operation in mid-1961, around the time of the socialist decrees. Early co-conspirators included a Maj. Fayez Rifai and Capts. Zuhayr Hamawi, Hisham Nashawi, and Jamal Baalbaki. Their grievances were those of the Syrian officer corps in general. As Nahlawi put it to Al Jazeera, before the union, "Syrian officers felt a sense of dignity, of self-esteem," but then "the Egyptian officers came and lorded supreme over them. There was no longer any value attached to any Syrian officer, from the army commander on down."

Asked to state the specific factors that drove him to take action, Nahlawi cited the "arbitrary discharge" of Syrian officers by their Egyptian superiors, the transfer of capable Syrian officers to civilian diplomatic missions or idle posts in Egypt, allegedly wasteful expenditure by Cairo of funds from the Syrian treasury, and what he called the "looting" by the Egyptian army of Syria's arsenal. The icing on the cake was a rumor, one week before he made his move, that the Syrian central bank's gold reserves were to be relocated to Egypt. It was then that he decided on Thursday, September 28, as D-day.

In the final twenty-four hours, on September 27, Nahlawi says he approached his boss Amer—Nasser's closest friend since 1938—in a last-ditch attempt to resolve matters through official channels. The situation in Syria had become critical, he told Amer in the latter's office. Trust between Syrian officers and their Egyptian counterparts had broken down completely. Amer seemed not to believe him. Was it really that bad? he asked. It's worse, said Nahlawi. Amer suggested they speak to some Syrian officers to hear their views firsthand. No Syrian would speak freely in the presence of an Egyptian, replied Nahlawi, for fear of being discharged, if not arrested. Could it really be that bad? asked a skeptical Amer again. The conversation ended where it had started, with no decisions made. That night, at one o'clock in the morning, Nahlawi's crew went into action.

From the Qatana base southwest of the capital emerged the tanks of the Seventieth Armored Brigade, led by Capts. Nashawi and Baalbaki, as well as the Seventy-Second Infantry Brigade, commanded by Muhib Hindi and Hisham Abd Rabbuh. Ironically, the Egyptians were counting on precisely these two crucial brigades to guard against potential coup attempts, placing them on round-the-clock alert for this purpose. Elsewhere, a tank column led by one Hassan Hijazi made for the military police building, while a Zuhayr Barazanji took the radio station. Others were also in on the plot at the Mezze military airport outside Damascus, in the Mediterranean port city of Latakia, and in the eastern desert region.

By 4 a.m., Nahlawi was standing in downtown Damascus's Umayyad Square, surrounded by tanks, staring at the army command headquarters, where Amer was holed up with a number of officers. Aside from light clashes with the guards outside Amer's residence on Adnan al-Malki Street north of the square, causing one injury, it had been a smooth and bloodless affair. At 7 a.m., a fellow rebel officer,

Lt. Col. Bassam al-Asali, broadcast the inevitable "Proclamation No. 1" over the radio.

This statement had harsh words for the "corrupt" and "criminal clique" of "quasi-tyrants and imperialists" and "deviants" who had "betrayed the Arab nation," spread terror, stripped the army of its "heroes," wasted public funds, and issued "so-called revolutionary decrees of which the revolution is innocent"—a clear allusion to the July 1961 laws. Yet the statement pointedly did not declare Syria's secession from the UAR, and indeed made frequent reference to the "sacred" cause of Arab unity, pledging devotion to union "from the [Atlantic] Ocean to the [Arabian] Gulf," but only "on a solid basis of parity, equality, liberty, and fraternity."

Similarly, in his telling of his conversation with Amer inside the now-besieged army command headquarters that morning, Nahlawi says he made no mention of secession, instead affirming that he and his men continued to regard Nasser as their rightful president and Amer as their commander; they sought merely to "rectify the situation within the framework of the union." Amer was apparently receptive to this, even approving a proposed list of names for a new joint military command. To what extent this was a sincere, good-faith agreement as opposed to a tactical chess move played by one or both sides became a moot point once Nasser learned what had happened back in Cairo.

Racing to his own radio station, Nasser delivered a thunderous attack on the mutineers who had "stabbed Arab unity in the back," vowing the UAR would prevail even if blood had to be shed, and indeed claiming that army units all over Syria were descending upon Damascus at that moment to crush the insurrection.

Syrian units were doing no such thing. In the blindness of his rage, however, Nasser did dispatch Egyptian forces—2,000 airborne paratroopers, and five warships in the Mediterranean—to Latakia. Only when word came back that Latakia itself was with the rebels did he call off the operation at the last moment. The 120 troops who had already touched down on Syrian soil were ordered to give them-selves up without resistance.

Back in Damascus, meanwhile, the radio war of words had soured the mood at Umayyad Square. As turbulent anti-Nasser demonstra-tions broke out in the capital's streets, it was decided that Amer and his coterie had overstayed their welcome. A plane was arranged to fly them to Cairo, and, once Amer was in the air, the fall of the union was a fait accompli. Two days later, the independent Syrian Arab Republic was formally proclaimed, restoring the old national anthem and replacing the green-starred red, white, and black UAR flag with the red-starred green, white, and black tricolor of the democratic pre-1958 republic. (It's no accident that these are the same flags adopted today by Syria's Assad regime and its opponents, respectively.) The final pillar of the UAR regime fell on September 31, when Sarraj was arrested and tossed in Mezze Prison, the same place he had incarcerated and tortured so many of his enemies over the years.

A new era had arrived in Arab politics as a whole. For Nasser, his defeat in Syria was a monumental blow, a definitive end to the golden era symbolized by his triumphant arrival in Damascus three years earlier. He was a changed man thereafter: gloomier, angrier, colder, crueler. For his regional foes—Iraq's Qasim, Jordan's King Hussein, Saudi Arabia's King Saud—the union's breakup was nat-urally a delight. For Syria itself, it was another chance—the last chance, as it turned out—to restore the parliamentary democracy that had now been trampled twice under military boots. As events would soon show, however, Nasser's friends in the Syrian officer corps were not quite prepared to call it a day just yet.

8

NASSERISTS
AGAINST NASSER

IN THE WAKE OF NAHLAWI'S COUP, SYRIA'S POLITICAL
system briefly returned to something approximating that which
had prevailed between the overthrow of Shishakli in 1954 and the
establishment of the UAR in 1958. That is to say, the country once
again had a civilian president and prime minister, and the institu-
tional trappings of a democracy, including an elected parliament. At
the same time, supreme power—also once again—rested in practice
with a small and unelected cabal of military officers, in this case
the Nahlawi junta. The tenuous modus vivendi improvised between
these parallel civilian and military authorities held together by a
thread through seventeen tumultuous months before yet another
group of officers—Baathists in common cause with Nasserists, much
as in 1958—sprang forth to sweep both Nahlawi's men and the civilians aside, burying the corpse of Syrian democracy once and for all.

★

IT HAD GOTTEN OFF to a seemingly promising start, all things
considered. The very first day after the coup, on September 29,
1961, Nahlawi and his officers called on a civilian, Dr. Mamun al-
Kuzbari—a law professor and former parliament speaker from Aleppo—to form a temporary cabinet, the principal task of which was
to prepare for parliamentary elections as soon as possible. Vocal support for the new order flooded in from virtually all of Syria's foremost political figures, including former president Quwwatli, former

prime ministers Asali and Khuri, the Druze leader Sultan al-Atrash, Khalid al-Azm, and even the Baath's Bitar and Hawrani.

Sure enough, relatively free elections were held just over two months later, on December 1. The results brought a diverse spread of characters to the new parliament, from the Baath's Hawrani to the Muslim Brotherhood leader Issam al-Attar. As one might expect, the party that did best in 1954—the People's Party, particularly strong in Aleppo and Homs—came out on top again. Its leader, Nazim al-Qudsi, became president of the republic, while his colleague Maaruf al-Dawalibi became prime minister, forming a coalition cabinet in which the People's Party held the key ministries.

Scarcely had the members of this new cabinet and parliament buttoned up their shirts before they fell into a major crisis with the officers. The bone of contention was the controversial nationalizations decreed by the UAR authorities in the final months of the union. In February 1962, the new parliament voted to repeal these decrees altogether. Fearing dissent among the army rank and file, Nahlawi objected to this, demanding that only some nationalizations be repealed. Summoning President Qudsi on March 25, Nahlawi ordered him to dismiss Dawalibi's cabinet, dissolve parliament, and form a government himself to implement the officers' program. When Qudsi refused, on grounds of the flagrant unconstitutionality of such a move, Nahlawi took matters into his own hands.

On March 28, 1962, military police units acting on Nahlawi's orders arrested President Qudsi, Prime Minister Dawalibi, all but one of Dawalibi's cabinet ministers, Parliament Speaker Kuzbari, and at least seven MPs, among other figures. Khalid al-Azm describes the almost comical experience of being driven to Mezze Prison at half past two in the morning, to be led into a large room with thirty-five other senior statesmen, among them five former prime ministers. As they huddled together under woollen blankets drinking tea, shivering in the cold, they heard a martial broadcast over the radio to the effect that the army had taken a "patriotic" step to rescue the country from reactionary imperialism by dissolving parliament, arresting cabinet members and MPs, and "accepting the resignation" of President Qudsi.

Nahlawi had, in effect, carried out a second coup, this time against the democratic institutions he had himself put in place just six months earlier. If he imagined this would stabilize the situation, he was sorely mistaken. Many Syrians—including some in the room with Azm at Mezze—misinterpreted the broadcast as an Egyptian-backed coup against the secessionist regime as a whole, officers and civilians alike. Within the junta itself, a fierce split broke out, with the result that Nahlawi and his closest associates were exiled to Switzerland. The new junta, whose key figure was now the army commander Gen. Abd al-Karim Zahr al-Din, announced that civilian rule under President Qudsi would soon be restored.

In the midst of this chaos and confusion, a group of Nasserist and other self-declared "Free Officers" in Aleppo decided to roll the dice. On April 2, they stormed the city's historic citadel, killed the garrison commander, raised the UAR flag, and requested arms and funds from the Egyptian embassy in Beirut. Led by the prominent Nasserist Col. Jasim Alwan, they included the young Hafez al-Assad and his secretive Baathist cell formed in Cairo two years earlier. The junta responded with air strikes on Aleppo's radio station and other sites, also dispatching forces from Homs. The insurrection was quashed, at an unknown cost of lives—Damascus Radio reported two officers killed by "Nasserist agents," while rumors swirled in the regional press of as many as 150 slain by the aerial bombardment.

As matters gradually calmed over the following week, the politicians began to be released from Mezze, where they had whiled away the time reading books from the prison library and playing backgammon and chess. On April 13, Qudsi was restored as president. As prime minister, the junta called on Bashir al-Azma, the former UAR health minister.

Invited to meet Qudsi at the presidential palace on April 14, Azma was told by the nominal head of state that "the brothers" had requested he head the new cabinet. Who are the brothers? asked

Azma. "The group," replied Qudsi. "I don't understand," said Azma. An aide had to interject to clarify that the brothers were "the officers of the army command."

Two days later, Azma's cabinet was formed, comprising two ministers each from the People's Party, National Party, Baath, and Muslim Brotherhood, plus some unaffiliated technocrats. With parliament still dissolved, the cabinet assumed both executive and legislative powers, leaving it open to accusations of unconstitutionality.

The purpose of Azma's government, as he well knew, was to try to ease tensions with Cairo, not least after the events in Aleppo. It was also expected to undo the policies of its predecessor that had angered the junta in the first place. Thus the cabinet renationalized various companies, and repealed certain amendments to the land-reform laws. It also permitted Egyptian newspapers to enter Syrian territory again. Statements were even made expressing regret about the secession and pledging to work to revive the union in future.

These overtures were not reciprocated by Cairo. When Syria's foreign minister, Adnan al-Azhari, flew to Egypt to meet Nasser's minister for presidential affairs, Ali Sabri, he was told in no uncertain terms that Cairo was not interested in union talks with the present Syrian government. In a speech on July 26 marking ten years since Farouk's abdication, Nasser laid into the authorities in Syria, or "the northern province of the UAR," as he made a point of calling it. Reaching for every insult in the book, he described Syria's rulers as reactionaries, imperialists, opportunists, feudalists, and monopolists, who threw workers, lawyers, and intellectuals in prison. In fact, the Syrian people as a whole had been "placed in one large prison."

Azma's cabinet responded with a complaint to the Arab League, which then held a notoriously shambolic meeting in the Lebanese town of Shtura in August. Cairo set the tone, "in a well-calculated needling gesture," by sending among its delegates two Syrians who had defected to the UAR after the secession. Syria's own delegation also came prepared, passing around copies of a "Black Book" enumerating the crimes of the UAR, and accusing the Egyptians of collaborating with Washington to sell out Palestine. At that, the Egyptians walked out, and the circus was over. So mortifying was the spectacle that the Arab League secretary-general "broke down in tears."

Clearly, the plan of using Azma to appease Nasser had not been an unmitigated success. Partly for this reason, the junta began to look favorably on a plan B devised by the canny Damascus aristocrat and four-time former prime minister Khalid al-Azm.

The latter had spent the period of Azma's premiership hosting endless gatherings of politicians at his stately homes in Abu Rummaneh and Dummar. The purpose of these meetings was to find a way to restore the constitutional and parliamentary life suspended by Nahlawi's March 28 coup—and, in the process, usher in a new cabinet headed by Azm himself. Over dinner with President Qudsi in the scenic resort town of Zabadani, in the hills northwest of the capital, Azm and fellow diners Hawrani, ex-premier Dawalibi, the Muslim Brotherhood's Attar, and the current prime minister Bashir al-Azma succeeded in winning the president over to the idea. (The miserable Azma had been begging the president to let him resign for some time.)

Thus it was that, on September 13, 1962, all but 15 of Syria's 172 MPs convened at Azm's house and held a de facto parliament session in which they voted in favor of his heading a new cabinet. Azma resigned the same day, and, after four further days of wrangling over cabinet seats, Azm's government was officially formed on September 17.

In political terms, the new cabinet marked no drastic shift from its predecessor; indeed, Azma stayed on as deputy prime minister. While the majority of ministers were independents, there were also three from the People's Party, three from the Baath, and two from the Muslim Brotherhood. Tellingly, the army commander Zahr al-Din sat as defense minister. The two main differences were the constitutional legitimacy claimed by Azm's government, and the fact he was a political heavyweight, where Azma had been a virtual unknown.

Enunciating the outlines of his government's policy, Azm pledged to uphold the nationalizations and land-reform laws as they were; to pursue a course of "positive neutrality" in foreign affairs; and to work toward realizing eventual Arab unity. Reflecting on the moment in his memoir, he writes, "It was thought the cabinet would live a long life, and parliamentary elections would be held, and the country would enjoy calm and stability."

That was not quite how matters panned out.

★

AZM AND THE PARLIAMENTARIANS were not the only ones making plans in the latter half of 1962. Bouncing back from their defeat in Aleppo in April, Assad and his secret Military Committee quickly set about formulating a more sophisticated coup plot that stood a serious chance of success.

For want of a better alternative, they turned once again to their Nasserist counterparts within the officer corps, and managed to win two senior recruits to their conspiracy: the head of military intelligence, Col. Rashid al-Qutayni, and the commander of a key brigade in Homs, Col. Muhammad al-Sufi. To expand their clique further, they approached a prominent independent officer, Col. Ziad al-Hariri, who commanded the Israeli front, and offered to make him their leader. Their timing was fortuitous, as Prime Minister Azm was about to relieve Hariri of his command and send him to Baghdad as a military attaché.

By these means, a six-man junta-in-waiting came together in late 1962, comprising Assad, Umran, and Jadid from the Military Committee, plus Qutayni, Sufi, and Hariri. Their great spur to action arrived with the February 8, 1963, coup in Iraq, where fellow Baathist and Nasserist officers toppled the Qasim regime and established their Egyptian-inspired "National Revolutionary Command Council." The tide, it seemed, had suddenly turned back in favor of Cairo's brand of Arab nationalism, at the expense of the so-called "provincial" and "isolationist" stances of Qasim and the Qudsi-Azm government in Damascus. Exactly one month later, on March 8, Syria's own Baathists and Nasserists emulated their Iraqi comrades.

Their action plan followed what was by then an all-too-familiar playbook in Syria. The first step was to neutralize the crucial Seventieth Armored Brigade south of the capital, which had so often done the heavy lifting in past coups. As Colonel Hariri brought tanks up from the Israeli front to meet with another brigade en route from Suwayda, they trapped the Seventieth Armored in a pincer movement, prompting its surrender and takeover by the Military Committee's Umran. Rolling unopposed into Damascus, they seized the usual sites: the defense ministry, the radio station, the bureau of officers' affairs. Assad himself took the Dumayr air base northeast of the capital, home to Syria's entire air force. General Zahr al-Din and President Qudsi were arrested, while Prime Minister Azm barricaded himself in his home above the Turkish embassy, invoking the building's diplomatic immunity for his own safety. He writes in his memoir that a baying mob assembled outside on the day of the coup, pelting the house with rocks and waving thick ropes, vowing to drag him through the streets as had happened in Baghdad in 1958.

In actual fact, the coup was carried off without bloodshed. Just as their Iraqi counterparts had done the previous month, Syria's new masters promptly set up a "National Revolutionary Command Council" (NRCC), once again echoing the terminology of the Egyptian junta. Its twenty initial members comprised twelve Baathists alongside eight Nasserists and independents. As chairman, commander in chief, and president of the republic, they appointed Col. Luay al-Atasi, a veteran of the Aleppo coup attempt whom they released from prison on March 8 and promoted to lieutenant general. The following day, the NRCC tasked the Baath's cofounder Bitar with forming a new government.

So far, so smooth. Beneath the outward camaraderie, however, ticked a time bomb with a short fuse. March 8 was the third occasion on which Syria's Baathists had teamed up with Nasserists to mount a coup, and the relationship was burdened with the baggage of past experience. Neither trusted the other in the slightest. At the same time, there was nothing in particular either could pinpoint that separated them in ideological terms. Theirs was the special enmity that exists only between former best friends. At root, it boiled down to a pure power struggle. The Baath had learned the hard way that Nasser would never relinquish an iota of his authority to anyone. Indeed, at the tripartite Syrian-Egyptian-Iraqi union talks that began later that month, he insisted once again on the full dissolution of all political parties as a sine qua non—his position had not budged an inch since 1958. For all that Syria's Baathists waxed militant about their unshakable devotion to union, the hard fact was they were no more willing to hand their country to Nasser than had been Iraq's Qasim, or indeed Syria's own endlessly maligned "secessionist" government. As such, from the very beginning of the new post–March 8 era, the Baath—or more precisely the Military Committee, which in practice worked independently of the party's formal leadership—made sure to gain the upper hand on their Nasserist partners, in preparation for the inevitable showdown.

Thus, while they appeared to grant senior cabinet positions to the Nasserists Sufi and Qutayni, and the independent Hariri (defense minister, deputy chief of staff, and chief of staff, respectively), the Military Committee retained the most crucial levers of hard power for themselves. Their leader, Umran, became commander of the all-important Seventieth Armored Brigade. Jadid controlled the officers' affairs bureau, through which he was able to hire and promote friendly officers, while demoting or purging rivals. A late recruit to the Military Committee, Ahmad Suwaydani, assumed control of military intelligence. A friend of the committee since their Cairo days, Mazyad Hunaydi, was made head of military police. The important Military Academy in Homs came under the Baath's control, and quickly admitted hundreds of Baathist recruits, including Assad's brother Rifaat. Assad himself became de facto head of the air force, as commander of the Dumayr base. A strategic final touch was the appointment of the non-Baathist Col. Amin al-Hafez—another

Cairo acquaintance—as interior minister. Before long, he would replace Atasi as president and act as the Military Committee's frontman, playing a role somewhat akin to that of Egypt's Naguib between 1952 and 1954.

In a bid to win the "legitimacy" conferred by Nasser's blessing of their new regime, the Syrians entered into union talks with both Egypt and Iraq in late March. We have seen that these came to no more than a stillborn agreement on April 17 worth less than the paper on which it was written. A sign of how unseriously the Military Committee took the charade was that none of their members bothered to attend the talks at all, with the exception of Umran, who joined only at the final stage in an observer capacity.

An even stronger sign of the committee's real intentions came eleven days after the agreement, on April 28, when it began its systematic purge of Nasserist officers. More than fifty pro-Cairo officers were dismissed over the course of the next week, prompting the NRCC's two leading Nasserists, Sufi and Qutayni, to resign along with five Nasserist cabinet ministers. The showdown had arrived.

As a first response, turbulent protests against the purge broke out in Damascus and Aleppo on May 8 and 9, led by the Arab Nationalist Movement (ANM), a Nasserist organization with branches in multiple Arab countries. On the Military Committee's orders, interior minister Amin al-Hafez responded with an iron fist: fifty protesters were shot dead, and the ANM was crushed, its offices and newspaper shut down, its leaders imprisoned or exiled. From then on, "Nasser loyalists were purged from every sector of public life" in Syria, and replaced with Baathists. Likewise, the independent Hariri and his followers were easily dispatched in late June while he was traveling in Algeria.

As July rolled around, the Baathists of the Military Committee looked to be the uncontested masters of Syria. Once again emulating their Iraqi comrades, from late June they had built up their own "National Guard" militia, in the mold of the force that had struck such terror in Iraqi hearts with its finger-choppings and electrocutions in Baghdad's "Palace of the End." They would not have to wait long to see action.

For the Nasserists had one round left in them yet. Their leading officer, Col. Jasim Alwan, from the eastern town of Deir al-Zor, was a man of no small stature in the Syrian army. In the UAR days, Nasser's viceroy Amer had tapped him to succeed Jamal Faysal as the next chief commander of Syria's armed forces overall. When the union fell, he had led the ill-fated coup attempt in Aleppo in April 1962, in which Assad and the Military Committee had also participated.

A staunch Nasser devotee and advocate of restoring full union with Egypt, Alwan naturally watched the purge of his comrades in arms in the spring of 1963 with utmost revulsion. He decided something had to be done, no matter how long the odds. Using the limited time and resources available to him, he cobbled together another of his half-baked coup plans. He himself estimated its chance of success at "thirty percent in the best-case scenario."

Undeterred, he flew to Cairo to meet Nasser and discuss the proposal face-to-face. Some sources allege Nasser promised him air and radio support if and when the coup went ahead, along the lines of the Shawwaf plot in Mosul. Alwan himself was coy about the details in an interview with Al Jazeera, saying only that Nasser gave him to understand he was "still keen on restoring the union," and that "this was the thing that encouraged us to do everything we could" to bring that to fruition.

And so it came about that, at eleven o'clock on the morning of July 18, gunmen under Alwan's command opened fire in broad daylight on the Syrian army headquarters, as well as the Damascus radio station, killing and wounding some twenty pro-regime forces in the opening salvo of their coup attempt. The gunmen included ANM militants as well as Palestinian fighters reportedly dismissed from the intelligence services in the recent purge. They managed to take over and occupy at least three army brigades before interior minister Amin al-Hafez, personally wielding a submachine gun, led their bloody subjugation, using the full force of the army as well as the new

National Guard. It was a "slaughter such as Syria had not known since the struggle against the French." Hundreds were killed or wounded, including innocent bystanders. Twenty-seven Nasserist officers taken into custody were summarily executed on the spot. Alwan himself managed to hide out in the Damascus suburb of Ghouta for ten days before he was discovered, thrown in Mezze Prison, tortured, and sentenced to death. Only a deal secured by Nasser through the mediation of Algeria's president, Ahmed Ben Bella, enabled Alwan to leave in 1964 for Cairo, where he spent forty-one years in exile until being permitted to return to Syria in 2005.

Such uneasy amity as had obtained between Nasser and the new Syrian regime since March 8 was hurled to the wind after the slaughter of July 18. In a two-hour speech four days later devoted almost entirely to the subject, Nasser slammed Syria's rulers as "fascists" (a word he used seventeen times) who tyrannized every true Arab nationalist and unionist among their noble compatriots. The tripartite union agreement of April 17 was as good as scrapped. "We have decided that this agreement . . . binds us to Syria, but it does not in any way bind us to this fascist Baathist government ruling Syria today." There could be "no union with the fascist Baath Party"; indeed, to proceed with the agreement on such terms would be "treason against the cause of Arab unity."

The "special relationship" between Nasser and Syria's Baath had met a grisly end. Never again would Nasser play the central role in Syrian domestic politics that he had done, on and off, since 1955. Henceforth, Syria's power struggles would be internal affairs, following a dizzying course of fratricidal cannibalization. Interior minister Amin al-Hafez replaced Luay al-Atasi as president until 1966, when he and the erstwhile Military Committee leader Muhammad Umran were ousted in a bloody palace coup by fellow committee members Salah Jadid and Hafez al-Assad. The latter then became Syria's two most powerful men, and promptly fell into a feud of their own.

To be sure, there were moments of rapprochement with Cairo.

In late 1966, as the prospect of war with Israel loomed, Egypt and Syria exchanged ambassadors for the first time since 1961, set up a joint military command, and signed a bilateral defense pact. In 1969, then–defense minister Assad visited Nasser in Cairo, and shared a cordial conversation. Nasser asked after various Syrian Baathists he had known in the good old days, to which Assad replied they were all either killed, imprisoned, or exiled. "You Baathists," chuckled Nasser, "you're so harsh with each other!"

To the end, then, Nasser was never entirely absent from the Syrian picture, and the rulers of Damascus continued to regard him with a complex mix of envy, disdain, and respect. The late British author Patrick Seale, who interviewed Assad at length and penned what many consider his definitive biography, wrote that the future Syrian president was "undoubtedly . . . influenced by the model of Nasser . . . whose regime he had observed at first hand." Ever since their earliest days in Cairo's cafés under the UAR, the Military Committee had agreed with Nasser that civilian politicians were feckless, that parliaments and other democratic institutions were to be trounced, and that the only way was absolute military dictatorship, established by means of a coup. They were, in other words, committed Nasserists in method, or what the Baath's former secretary-general Munif al-Razzaz called "Nasserists against Nasser." Their essential guiding principle, said Razzaz, was that they could rule exactly as Nasser did, only better.

Less than two months after Nasser's death in September 1970, Assad ousted Jadid and assumed sole control of Syria, instituting a dynasty that continues to rule the country to this day.

LEBANON

9

THE SUMMER
OF BLOOD

I T WAS LATE ON THE NIGHT OF MONDAY, MAY 16, 1966, but Kamel Mrowa was still at his desk in downtown Beirut. The fifty-one-year-old editor in chief of *Al-Hayat* (Life), widely regarded at the time as the Middle East's leading paper of record, known for cutting against the grain of Arab nationalist orthodoxy, was finalizing the following day's paper before it was to be sent off for printing. It had been a relatively slow news day by Lebanese standards—the story du jour was a visit by the Senegalese president Léopold Senghor. Scarcely could Mrowa have imagined that the headline of the paper he was editing, when it came out just a few hours later, would read, "Kamel Mrowa Assassinated in His Office."

Shortly after 9 p.m., Mrowa was on a phone call with Lady Yvonne Cochrane, a Lebanese aristocrat and wife of the Irish diplomat Sir Desmond Cochrane, when Adnan Shaker Sultani walked into his office. Posing as a courier, the twenty-three-year-old handed Mrowa an envelope, then pulled out a silenced 6 mm Beretta pistol and, from a distance of one meter, fired a single round into his chest. The bullet slipped between two ribs, puncturing Mrowa's left lung, and ended up in the right ventricle of his heart.

A scuffle then ensued between the two men, overheard by the alarmed Lady Cochrane. Sultani fired two further rounds, breaking the glass of the office balcony and drawing the attention of staff throughout the building in Beirut's bustling city center. As Mrowa slumped to the floor, bleeding to death, Sultani threw down his pistol and managed to escape to the street. A chase ensued between him and the newspaper's staff, who yelled "Thief!" to attract the notice of passersby. Their efforts succeeded: when Sultani jumped in a taxi and ordered it to take him to the Egyptian embassy, he was followed in a second cab by a concerned citizen named Rafiq Elias al-Mir, who intercepted him a few blocks later and forced him into a police station. He quickly confessed to his crime.

"The mistake," as Nasser's Syrian intelligence czar Sarraj would reflect in conversation with Sultani in Cairo ten years later, "was not having a getaway car."

★

THE ASSASSINATION OF KAMEL MROWA may have been among the most shocking acts of violence linked to Nasser in Lebanon, but it certainly wasn't the first, nor would it be the last. Indeed, it was possible at all only because Nasser had by then spent over a decade muscling his way into a position of unequaled authority over Lebanon's political leadership, military and security forces, intelligence agencies, judiciary, and criminal underworld. The story of Mrowa's killing is inseparable from that of the wider suzerainty enjoyed by Nasser over Lebanon, which was in turn a fundamental chapter of his eighteen-year quest for mastery of the Arab world as a whole. Before seeing how he was able to have a media mogul gunned down in the center of the Lebanese capital, we must first understand how he acquired so much power in the country.

★

IF THERE WAS ANY Arabic-speaking head of state in the mid-1950s who irked Nasser almost as much as Iraq's prime minister Nuri al-Said, it was Lebanon's president, Camille Chamoun. A law graduate and longtime parliamentarian with a distinctive head of slicked-back silver hair, he had been among the founding fathers of the Lebanese Republic imprisoned by the French on the eve of independence in 1943. An unabashed Anglophile and laissez-faire capitalist fond of white suits and cigars, Chamoun made no secret of his disdain for revolutionary socialism and anti-Western militancy. As for Arab nationalism, like many of his fellow Maronite Catholics, he tended to view it through the prism of Lebanon's peculiar sectarian frictions, seeing it above all as an Islamic phenomenon, which threatened to sweep away the protections and privileges enjoyed by Lebanon's Christians if left unchecked.

This is not to say Chamoun commanded the unanimous support of Lebanese Christians. His presidency may have had its merits, including an economic boom, infrastructural development, and the vote granted to women. Yet it was also marred by corruption, and a certain high-handedness that alienated not just a majority of Lebanese Muslims but no small number of Christians too, the powerful head of the Maronite Church among them. Suffice it to say he was a controversial figure, though not without a significant popular base. Given all this, it was inevitable that, as Nasser's star rose in the latter half of the 1950s, he would butt heads with Chamoun at every turn. In 1958, their feud would plunge the young Lebanese republic into its first civil war.

As with Iraq, the bad blood began in 1955, during the Baghdad Pact dispute. At the Arab League conference called by Nasser in Cairo in January, Chamoun's representatives flatly declined to denounce Prime Minister Nuri. Lebanon was committed to strict neutrality in foreign affairs, they held, and so would neither join nor oppose the pact. If Iraq found it advantageous to enter into it, it was not for little Lebanon to stand in its way.

This vexing refusal to come to heel earned Chamoun a prominent spot on Nasser's blacklist. From then on, Cairo's Voice of the Arabs broadcasts grouped the Lebanese president together with Nuri in the clique of reactionaries and imperialists whom the masses were called on to overthrow.

From this inauspicious start, matters only grew worse. If Chamoun displeased Nasser over the pact, his conduct during the Suez Crisis the following year incurred the full fire of his wrath. Even as British,

French, and Israeli invaders were occupying Egypt's soil and killing its citizens by the thousands, Chamoun would give only the most perfunctory and half-hearted rhetorical support to Cairo. (This while neighboring Syria and even Jordan's King Hussein were offering to send their own troops to fight alongside the Egyptians.) When Chamoun further refused to join other Arab states in severing diplomatic relations with London and Paris, his own prime minister, Abdallah al-Yafi, resigned in protest in mid-November 1956, bringing down his cabinet.

Lebanon now stood at a critical junction. A large slice of public opinion looked favorably on Nasser's brand of Arab nationalism and was outraged by the Suez aggression. Chamoun could, conceivably, have tried to accommodate this constituency, and by doing so defuse domestic tensions and avert the coming bloodshed. Instead, he aggravated them further. Days after Yafi's resignation, he appointed a cabinet including such staunch anti-Nasser hawks as the former ambassador to Washington, Charles Malek, whose yearning for an alliance with the West made Chamoun look moderate by comparison. With Malek goading him on as foreign minister, Chamoun accepted US aid in early 1957 under the terms of the Eisenhower Doctrine, decried by Nasser as the American successor to Britain's Baghdad Pact. Having formerly pledged neutrality, Chamoun now sided openly with the West.

If that weren't enough to antagonize his opponents, Chamoun then proceeded to rig the parliamentary elections of June 1957, with reported assistance from the CIA. Votes were purchased on election day in broad daylight, with one voter cheerily telling the *Manchester Guardian*, "There's money for anyone who wants to sell his vote." The result was a brazenly fraudulent landslide that unseated all of Chamoun's most influential rivals, from former premiers Yafi and Saeb Salam to the Druze chieftain Kamal Jumblatt to the Shiite strongman Ahmad al-Asaad. This breached the gentlemen's agreement by which the elite families in charge of Lebanon's many religious communities were each supposed to receive their due slice of the political pie. Chamoun was playing with fire, and the flames of communal violence lost little time in kindling.

Already, even before the elections, an opposition protest in Beirut on May 30, 1957, had turned deadly when security forces fired on demonstrators, killing at least six and wounding dozens, including the former premier Salam. Soon afterward began a wave of bombings that would ravage the country for the better part of the next year and a half, often occurring several times per day. On July 30, 1957, for instance, four bombs went off in Beirut, targeting the offices of Voice of America and the US Information Service as well as the Jordanian embassy. In early November, the *Manchester Guardian* reported that "bomb explosions and political murders" had been ongoing in Lebanon "at the rate of one each week for the past two months," with targets including "two newspaper offices, a newspaper distributor, a Jewish school, [and] two private houses." In December, an explosion shattered the windows of the British Council's lecture hall in the capital, while the following month saw the first fatal bombing, when three were killed by a blast in a Beirut apartment.

Who was behind these attacks? The Lebanese government blamed Sarraj's Deuxième Bureau in Damascus, and we have it on the authority of none other than Sarraj's colleague, Sami Jumaa, that the Bureau was indeed supplying matériel to Chamoun's opponents from an early stage. "It was natural," wrote Jumaa in his memoir, "that Syria should assist the revolution with weapons and money." He went on to recount the colorful anecdote of a bombing in the pro-Chamoun town of Zahle in Lebanon's Bekaa Valley, undertaken on Sarraj's direct orders, using a donkey whose saddle had been stuffed with plastic explosives by the Bureau's men.

Such was the general atmosphere in Lebanon when news came in February 1958 that Syria had officially united with Egypt, rendering Nasser president of both countries—one of which shared a lengthy and porous land border with Lebanon. If the political temperature in Beirut had already been uncomfortably warm, it now came to a furious boil. To many minds, the question was no longer one of foreign policy, or whether Chamoun should stay or go, but whether Lebanon itself would continue to exist as an independent entity. Master of two historic Arab capitals, Nasser seemed to have the winds all at his back, the Arab world putty in his palms. That tiny Lebanon should be next on his trophy cabinet did not by any means look an overly fanciful prospect. Chamoun himself believed this was Nasser's intention. Not a few Lebanese dearly hoped for it. "Frequent and often violent" demonstrations broke out to demand Lebanon join the union. On one revealing occasion in March, a crowd in the southern city of Tyre trampled the Lebanese flag. At a prominent Beirut school linked to the Salam family, the portraits on classroom walls were of Nasser rather than President Chamoun.

If Chamoun understood how combustible the situation had become by the spring of 1958, with a triumphal Nasser on his doorstep vigorously fanning the flames of dissent, he gave little indication of it. Opting yet again for needless provocation, he allowed rumors to circulate that he would move to extend the term of his presidency beyond its constitutional six-year limit. At this, Nasser saw his opportunity to rid himself of the Chamoun headache once and for all. He had already developed friendly ties with the president's many domestic opponents, including the aforementioned Salam and Yafi in Beirut, Jumblatt in his mountain fiefdom southeast of the capital, and another former premier, Rashid Karami, in the northern port city of Tripoli. Now, with their full connivance, the UAR's arming and funding operations took on a new scale and intensity, as the anti-Chamoun insurgency made preparations for all-out war.

Once again, Sarraj's colleague Sami Jumaa, who was actively involved, provides rich firsthand details. The Bureau began by creating arms depots in strategic locations close to the Lebanese border. One in the Syrian town of Talkalakh, west of Homs, for instance, was used to supply Karami loyalists in the north, who controlled the rural terrain between Tripoli and the Syrian border. Others in Damascus and the border village of Serghaya fed the crucial pipeline to Jumblatt, who, given his proximity to the Syrian capital, was best placed to distribute the arms not just to his own men but to others around the country.

In the crucial theater of the capital, Sarraj's Bureau created its own militia, the story of which is illuminating. In November 1957, a Lebanese journalist named Ghandur Karam, known for his anti-Nasser stance, was shot dead in southern Beirut. The man who shot him, a Lebanese Nasserist named Rasheed Shihab al-Din, showed up not long afterward in Damascus, on the run from the Lebanese authorities. When Jumaa learned he was in town, he contacted the fugitive and made his acquaintance, even gifting him a 9 mm pistol. He then told Sarraj what had happened, to which Sarraj said the Bureau was "in need of someone like that." At Sarraj's request, Jumaa introduced Shihab al-Din to the head of the Bureau's Lebanon desk, Burhan Adham. After a series of meetings between Sarraj, Adham, and Shihab al-Din, agreement was reached on creating a so-called "popular resistance" militia in Beirut, led by Shihab al-Din, and funded and armed by the Bureau. The foot soldiers would be the young Nasserists and street toughs from the lower-income neighborhoods south of Beirut's city center who already formed the natural muscle of the opposition to Chamoun in the capital.

By the late spring of 1958, the UAR had showered Chamoun's opponents with money and weapons, turning Lebanon into a powder keg in search of a spark. It arrived on May 7, with the assassination of an opposition journalist, Nasib al-Matni. Barricades sprang up in the streets of Beirut, Tripoli, Sidon, the Shouf, the Bekaa, and beyond, as gun battles broke out between insurgents and government forces, backed in some areas by pro-Chamoun paramilitaries. Tripoli's historic Old City slipped quickly into rebel hands, and calls for Lebanon to join the UAR blared from its mosques during Friday sermons. A United Press reporter allowed into the city by Karami's fighters found that "on every corner and in most shops there were pictures of United Arab Republic President Gamal Abdul Nasser." Lebanon's "Summer of Blood," as it would be known thereafter, was underway.

For the next three months, the skies would ring daily with the crackle of bullets and booms of explosions. In military terms, the fighting was largely inconclusive, with little in the way of territorial advances or concrete gains by either side. Plenty of lives were lost nonetheless, with a daily death toll often in double figures. Perhaps more horrifying than the shooting were the bombings, which now took on an altogether deadlier nature. On May 15, three were killed and thirty-five injured by a bomb thrown from a passing car at Beirut's bustling main square during lunchtime. On July 8, at least six were killed and forty-five injured by a truck bomb outside a busy Beirut department store. Ugliest of all was the bombing of a crowded streetcar in Beirut's city center on May 26, killing at least eleven and gravely wounding fifteen others. Six more were killed on July 29 by a roadside bomb seemingly intended for Prime Minister Sami al-Solh, whose car was just meters from the blast, and who had to be treated for shock and bruises.

Throughout, the UAR kept the arms flowing in. As Sarraj himself put it in a rare interview decades later, "It was incumbent on us to remove Camille Chamoun and Charles Malek by any and all means, and that is what we did." The Bureau certainly did not lack for determination, or imagination. When the Lebanese authorities caught on to their use of fuel tankers to smuggle weapons in, they had the brainwave of strapping guns to herds of mules, which would wend their way across rocky mountain paths from the border village of Dayr al-Ashair to Jumblatt's men farther inland. These, too, were intercepted before long: a report in Lebanon's English-language *Daily Star* newspaper in late May bore the title, "Planes Hit Armed Donkey Caravan." The convoy in question was carrying arms, ammunition, and "four cases of bombs" before it was brought to a halt by the Lebanese air force.

Supplementing these efforts were those of the UAR embassy in Beirut, which "became virtually the opposition's headquarters." With flagrant contempt for all semblance of diplomatic decorum, Cairo's notorious ambassador Abd al-Hamid Ghaleb was "deplorably ham-handed in his dealings with the rebels, allowing trucks to be loaded with rifles for Salam's and Karami's guerrillas in front of the gates" of the embassy.

For sheer head-scratching absurdity, however, it was hard to top the UAR's recruitment to its cause of the Belgian consul general in Damascus, Louis de San. Described by *Time* magazine as a "millionaire eccentric," de San is said by Sarraj's colleague Jumaa (who knew him well) to have been a Buddhist convert and staunch antisemite who enjoyed yoga and meditation, and who vowed to Sarraj when they met that he would help him "against the West and the Jews."

Taking him at his word, the Bureau asked the consul general if they might possibly make use of his diplomatic-plated car to deliver an urgent consignment of matériel to the "resistance" in Beirut. To Jumaa's surprise, the Belgian was only too happy to agree. The car made multiple trips back and forth from Damascus to Shihab al-Din's fighters in Beirut, until the day came in mid-May that it was stopped and searched by the Lebanese border guard—tipped off by British intelligence—with the consul general himself at the wheel. In the trunk were thirty-three submachine guns, twenty-eight revolvers, 14,650 rounds of ammunition, and one time bomb. The Belgian was arrested and tried in a Lebanese court, sentenced to death (later commuted to twenty years), and imprisoned, until Nasser prevailed on Chamoun's successor as president to release him. De San lived the rest of his life in Syria, practicing his daily yoga, eventually dying in the village of Bmalka, near Tartus, in 1995.

In all, Jumaa estimates the Syrian province of the UAR alone spent over fifty million Syrian pounds on Lebanon's war. So liberally did the Bureau avail itself of the state's coffers that it fell prey to scam artists. Con men would show up in Damascus claiming to represent this or that "resistance" group in Beirut, only to sell the weapons they received, or gamble the money away on blackjack and baccarat at the casino resorts of Bloudan outside the Syrian capital.

★

KNOWING FULL WELL he was up against a state-sponsored insurgency, Chamoun made efforts of his own to enlist the help of outside powers. The terms of the Eisenhower Doctrine entitled him to request military intervention by the US in the event Lebanon was threatened by "overt armed aggression from any nation controlled by international communism." Applying an elastic definition of "communism," Chamoun and his foreign minister lost few opportunities throughout the Summer of Blood to make exactly this request of their interlocutors in Washington.

At first, their pleas fell on skeptical ears. The US was in no hurry to repeat the blunder Britain had committed in Suez two years earlier. The Lebanese army, it felt, was fully capable of putting down the rebellion if and when its commander chose to give the order (as he thus far had not). Even so fervent a Cold Warrior as Secretary of State John Foster Dulles worried privately that intervention risked aggravating sectarian strife, perhaps even leading to Lebanon's partition. In short, Washington did not regard Chamoun's predicament as strategically compelling enough a reason to put boots on the ground in a Middle East military adventure.

What changed their calculus entirely, in an instant, was the Iraqi Free Officers' coup of July 14, with its stunningly gory massacre and mutilation of the royal family and Prime Minister Nuri. To Washington, this seemed to confirm all the darkest warnings of Chamoun and Malek about Nasser, who suddenly appeared capable of pulling the entire Arab world into the Soviet camp. Sensing his moment had come at last, Chamoun told the US ambassador his own regime would fall within forty-eight hours if Washington didn't act immediately. The very next day, the Sixth Fleet landed the first of fifteen thousand marines on the beaches south of Beirut, whence they rolled north onto the capital.

At first glance, this would seem to have saved Chamoun's skin. Sure enough, the fighting soon stopped, and Chamoun served out the remaining two months of his presidency in full. On closer inspection, however, the much more lasting and consequential outcome of Washington's intervention was to cement and normalize Nasser's primacy in Lebanon for the rest of his life. Once the marines were ashore, Eisenhower despatched an envoy, Robert Murphy, to negotiate a resolution to the conflict, which in practice meant finding a successor to Chamoun agreeable to Nasser, Washington, and the Lebanese elites. The name of Gen. Fouad Chehab, the commander of the Lebanese army and Chamoun's defense minister, had already been floated by Nasser to the US ambassador in Cairo as early as May. Chehab had impressed Nasser, and much of the Lebanese opposition, by his studied refusal to involve the army in the street battles, as Chamoun had pressed him to. Having dismissed Nasser's proposal at the time, the Eisenhower administration suddenly discovered it could live with a President Chehab after all. With both Washington and Cairo in agreement, Chehab's path to the presidency was cleared, and Lebanon's parliament duly voted him in on July 31. As a bonus, it was decided that Rashid Karami—the Tripolitan leader of the rebellion in the north—would be Chehab's prime minister. With his mission thus accomplished, Nasser instructed Sarraj to halt the flow of guns and money, and the insurgency was wound down.

The official line in Beirut was that the Lebanese republic's first civil war had ended with "no victor and no vanquished." Cairo's Voice of the Arabs disagreed. "As Chamoun goes home, he takes imperialism with him," it declared triumphantly on the final day of his presidency. "The entire Arab world rejoices with newly-liberated people. Today Lebanon, tomorrow Jordan." Events would indeed soon confirm that the Lebanese version of events was a polite fiction.

Chamoun had been vanquished, and Nasser was victorious.

★

PRESIDENT CHEHAB WAS HARDLY a doctrinaire Nasserist—he had served in Chamoun's last cabinet, after all. Nonetheless, he calculated that for Lebanon to survive in the post-1958 Middle East required coming to working terms with the most powerful man in the region, who also happened now to be his neighbor.

To that end, one of Chehab's early moves as president was to meet Nasser face-to-face in March 1959, in a tent straddling the border between Lebanon and the UAR, the symbolism of which was lost on none. It was at this meeting that the basic equation of the Nasser-Chehab relationship was laid down. Its essence was an end to UAR meddling in Lebanese domestic and security affairs, in exchange for Beirut toeing the Cairo line as far as foreign and defense policy were concerned. Chehab agreed, in effect, to surrender a core component of Lebanon's sovereignty, acknowledging the reality of the immense power imbalance between the two men. Thereafter, Nasser would have no qualms about exploiting this imbalance to the full, even as Chehab went above and beyond in keeping up his end of the bargain.

A dramatic case in point was Chehab's role in Sarraj's escape from Mezze Prison in Damascus, where he was placed upon his arrest following Syria's secession from the UAR in September 1961. In May 1962, Nasser authorized an audacious plan to break Sarraj free and smuggle him to Cairo. The scheme was possible only due to the direct participation of Lebanese military intelligence, acting with Chehab's full knowledge and consent. Other key players in the plot, as affirmed by Sarraj himself, included the Egyptian embassy in Beirut, the Druze warlord Jumblatt, and a renegade Jordanian Nasserist "Free Officer," Nadheer Rasheed, who had taken up asylum in Syria in 1957.

It was Rasheed who managed to make the acquaintance of Sarraj's cell guard, Mansur al-Rawashida, and to bring him on board. On the night itself, the guard simply opened Sarraj's cell, gave him a military uniform to wear and the password needed to get through the various gates, and the pair of them walked unchallenged out of the prison, where Rasheed was waiting in a car to drive them to the nearest part of the Lebanese border.

The next leg of the journey has been described by Nasser's senior intelligence aide and secretary, Sami Sharaf, who was personally

in the car with Sarraj as he arrived at the Beirut airport to board
his plane to Cairo, as well as Lt. Sami al-Khatib, a senior Lebanese military intelligence officer (and later interior minister), who
drove the car.

Entering Lebanese territory in the dark of night from the Syrian
side of the rocky, mountainous border zone west of Damascus, Sarraj
and his former cell guard rode camels procured for the purpose by
Jumblatt. They reached the border village of Dayr al-Ashair, tracing the route taken by the mules who hauled guns across in 1958.
There they were met by a local Jumblatt crony, Shibli al-Aryan, who
escorted them to Jumblatt's hometown of Mukhtara in the heights of
the Shouf, where they spent the night. The next morning, they set
off for the home of an Egyptian embassy official in Beirut's seafront
Raouche district. From there, they were picked up in a Lebanese
army jeep driven by Khatib. Sharaf sat up front in the passenger seat,
while Sarraj was in the back with the cell guard and one of Sharaf's
aides. All wore official Lebanese military uniforms. ("I still have
mine in my wardrobe here in Cairo," said Sharaf in a 2007 interview.) Upon arrival at the Beirut airport, they entered through a
gap in the perimeter created by Lebanese military intelligence, and
delivered Sarraj to an Egyptian plane waiting on the tarmac.

Thus did a man responsible for the slaughter of countless Lebanese in the 1958 war—and a great deal of other bloodshed besides—
escape accountability for his actions, and manage to live the rest of
his long life a free man in Cairo. The operation was facilitated by
Lebanon's own authorities, and granted full "political and security
cover" by President Chehab himself.

★

As THE EPISODE PLAINLY ILLUSTRATES, the Chehab era saw
close cooperation and collaboration between Lebanese and Egyptian intelligence. In parallel, there was an expansion in the power of
Lebanon's intelligence apparatus in general, especially military intelligence (which, as in Syria, was known as the Deuxième Bureau).

As these phenomena intertwined, the Lebanese Bureau became in many ways tantamount to an extension of Nasser's own sprawling intelligence network. Its head, Col. Antun Saad, along with key colleagues such as Gaby Lahoud and—especially—the aforementioned Sami al-Khatib, were all on excellent terms with Cairo. In their hands, the Bureau became something of a Lebanese "deep state," interfering in everything from the press to the arms trade to workers' unions to parliamentary elections. Among its methods was the recruitment of the armed street gangsters and neighborhood toughs who had done the serious fighting against Chamoun in 1958 (and who, it will be recalled, had previously been armed and funded by Sarraj's Bureau in Damascus). These men were now turned into Lebanese Bureau agents and informants in exchange for pay and other privileges, such as arms licenses and protection from prosecution. Almost all of these quasi-militiamen now brought onto the Lebanese state payroll were Nasserists. Many would go on to form a key fighting force in Lebanon's second, and far more devastating, civil war starting in 1975. One in particular played a starring role in the Kamel Mrowa assassination.

The increasingly interwoven relationship between the Lebanese and Egyptian regimes, plus Chehab's general attitude of "maximum possible accommodation to Nasserist policy," led to a blurring of the lines in Beirut as to where Chehab's authority ended and Nasser's began. The figure of Cairo's ambassador to Lebanon, Abd al-Hamid Ghaleb—the man who had loaded guns onto trucks outside the embassy in broad daylight in 1958—served to further cement Nasser's influence at the expense of Chehab's. Acting with even more temerity than his former counterpart in Damascus, Mahmud Riyadh, Ghaleb would "summon" Lebanese cabinet ministers and MPs and "dictate to them his wishes," or at other times pay them bribes, or woo them with offers of access to Nasser. Small wonder that he, too, was compared to the French overlords of colonial times, and described by one Lebanese historian as acting "virtually as a High Commissioner, intervening even in the details of the

Lebanese political process to keep the country strictly in line with Egyptian policy."

All this, Chehab simply accepted as his lot. So much did Nasser come to value his loyalty that, when the time came for Chehab's presidential term to expire in 1964, Nasser pressed him in private to extend it, heedless of the irony that it had been precisely Chamoun's rumored desire to do the same that formed the pretext of the 1958 rebellion. Chehab, at any rate, was unprepared to take this step, and the presidency passed to his chosen successor, Charles Helou, a weak compromise candidate who assiduously maintained his predecessor's faithful deference to Cairo. Helou would, indeed, be the first Lebanese president to visit the Egyptian capital in an official capacity. Devoid of any significant popular base, and mercilessly lampooned in the press, Helou rendered Lebanon more beholden to Nasser and his men in the Deuxième Bureau than any president before or since.

Such was the official and political climate in the country at the time of Kamel Mrowa's assassination, two years into Helou's presidency. As we shall now see, the story of Mrowa's murder is a neat encapsulation of the Lebanon-Nasser relationship at its most malign, one in which several characters already encountered play decisive parts, including Ambassador Ghaleb and the Bureau's Sami al-Khatib. Before returning to the grisly tale of Mrowa's death, however, it is perhaps apt to recall something of his life.

10

A MISSION
VERY IMPORTANT
FOR NASSERISM

IN THE STUNNING GREEN HILLS OVERLOOKING BEIRUT and the glistening Mediterranean beyond is a villa quite unlike any other. The Hollywood star Robert Mitchum was photographed there with his wife, Dorothy, in 1962. The year before, sixteen Miss Europe contestants popped by for a shoot. The current king of Saudi Arabia, Salman bin Abdulaziz, recalls playing on swings there in his youth. Every Sunday was "open house," with any number of politicians, diplomats, exiles, and writers dropping in to lunch, laugh, and debate with the home's famous owner. In this fabled glamour of prewar Beirut in the Swinging Sixties—when the city was frequented by Frank Sinatra, Marlon Brando, and Brigitte Bardot—the Mrowa Villa was a magnet for Lebanon's high society and intelligentsia, and a fashionable port of call for well-connected international guests.

"The house was constantly full," recalls Mrowa's son Malek, now in his mid-sixties, sitting by a terrace near the villa's artfully asymmetric pool. In appearance, Malek is unnervingly similar to his father, his blue eyes and jet-black eyebrows crowned by a full head of gracefully silvering hair. I ask about the luminaries who passed through the premises in his father's day. Clearly reluctant to boast, he shuffles in his seat, casts his eyes toward the sea, takes a drag on a Gitanes, then says finally, "I've met three [Saudi] kings": Fahd, Abdallah, and Salman. All three, he says with a chuckle, asked him the same questions: "Do you still have the house? Is it still as beautiful? *Do you still have the swings?*"

Entering the vast grounds of the estate today, it is indeed still beautiful, and remains more or less as it was in Kamel's time, though Malek and his siblings have extended and modernized it in places. (They do still have the swings, Malek confirms.) Following the natural gradient of Mount Lebanon on the fringes of the town of Beit Mirri, the property comprises multiple distinct but interconnected levels, nestled into the fir and pine forests that blanket the surrounding mountainside. The uppermost section contains the villa itself, a futuristic structure of angled concrete beams designed in the 1950s by the renowned architect Raymond Ghosn (who, by morbid coincidence, would himself be assassinated in Beirut in 1976). Farther downhill, accessible by a separate driveway, lie the pool and an adjacent stone outhouse, surrounded by a series of large grass lawns punctuated with stone-tiled seating areas. Birds chirp as they hop from lofty palm trees to cypresses. The pièce de résistance, however, is not strictly speaking part of the house at all. It is the unobstructed view that can be enjoyed from all parts of the sea-facing estate, wherever one happens to be at any given moment. From its commanding position more than seven hundred meters above sea level, around a quarter of Lebanon's entire coastline can be seen, from Amchit in the north to well beyond Khalde to the south. Not for nothing did Israeli Merkava tanks choose to park outside the villa's entrance in 1982, from which vantage point they could shell Syrian convoys rolling along the Damascus highway down the valley to the south.

Beirut extends before the eye in an isosceles triangle spearing into the great silver mass of the Mediterranean, so huge from this angle one fancies one can almost glimpse the tip of Cyprus on the shimmering horizon. "It's just a magnificent piece of land," says Malek's brother Karim—not bragging, simply stating the obvious fact. "I don't think there's any other place that has such a spectacular view or setting."

How, then, did a boy of modest background, from an undistinguished rural village in Lebanon's impoverished deep south, end up owning some of the best real estate in the country, where he would entertain beauty queens, Hollywood icons, and royalty? It's a tale of adventure, innovation, and commercial savvy, combined with sheer drive and determination. Above all, it was one man's quest to create the Arab world's foremost news organization—a quest that would cost him his life.

★

KAMEL MROWA WAS BORN on January 19, 1915, in the small village of al-Zreriyeh, in what was then still the Ottoman Empire and is now south Lebanon. Drawing his first breath amid a World War, in a land that would soon pass into French colonial hands, the boy born into the Shia Muslim underclass might easily have gone on to lead a life of invisible penury and hardship, unnoticed by history. His father, Muhammad Jamil Mrowa, was a relatively successful trader of agricultural produce in the nearby city of Sidon, until he died at the age of just forty-two in 1925, when Kamel was ten. His untimely death was a great blow to the family, not least for his widow, Badia Muhieddin, who then had to raise the children alone. Though Kamel did well academically at school in Sidon, even winning a small scholarship to study at the prestigious American University of Beirut (AUB) in 1932, the family's financial situation prevented him from completing his studies.

Determined to stay in Beirut regardless, Kamel found a job teaching at a philanthropic association that worked to reduce illiteracy among the Shia community. It was to journalism, however, that he felt the strongest pull. After a brief first stint at *Al-Nidaa* (The call) newspaper, he moved in 1934 to a brand-new paper that would go on to become a pillar of the Lebanese media landscape: *Annahar* (The day), founded by Gebran Tueni, which remains widely read to this day.

It was a formative time for Mrowa on many fronts. At AUB, his political consciousness was awakened, and he began identifying with the pan-Arab currents then prevalent in much of the country that was, after all, not yet independent of its French occupiers. He joined a secret organization called the Arab Movement (*al-Haraka al-'Arabiyya*), affiliated with the prominent Princeton-educated Syrian intellectual Constantine Zurayk, then a professor of history at the university.

He also began to travel, and to make use of his natural talent for networking. In 1938, he suggested to the head of the charity college at which he was teaching that they go to West Africa to solicit donations from the continent's wealthy Lebanese expatriates. He agreed, and the pair set sail from the Beirut port to Alexandria, Marseilles, and then on around the Strait of Gibraltar to Senegal, Guinea, Sierra Leone, Liberia, the Ivory Coast, Ghana, and Nigeria. The funds raised enabled the college to move to a larger building in Beirut's Ras al-Nabaa neighborhood, where it remains today. Quite apart from that, the contacts Mrowa made in Africa would prove invaluable when he later decided to launch his own news venture.

First, though, came the Second World War. Lebanon was initially spared the fighting, and indeed, Mrowa—who was by then *Annahar*'s editor for Arab and international affairs—had success with a special magazine he produced to cover it, called *The New War in Pictures*. In June 1941, however, the war came to Lebanon, when the Allies launched Operation Exporter against the Vichy French authorities in Beirut and Damascus. Mrowa left for what he imagined to be the safety of neutral Istanbul, where a number of his fellow Arab nationalists had taken refuge. There he would have happily stayed for the remainder of the war, but, after seven months, he and other Arabs were abruptly thrown in prison, the Turks suspecting them of covert political activities. Released a week later, he was ordered to leave the country. He decided to try to make his way back to Senegal, where he had friends and relatives, and boarded a train to Sofia, the Bulgarian capital.

What he hadn't fully reckoned with was that Bulgaria was Axis territory, meaning he was unwittingly placing his fate at the mercy of the Third Reich. As he crossed the border by the town of Svilengrad in February 1942, he saw his first steel-helmeted Nazi soldier.

Unbeknownst to him, he would spend the next three years as, in effect, a prisoner of the Gestapo, who followed him around, controlled his movements, and forbade him from traveling without their permission. Later that month, they ordered him to travel to Vienna, without explanation. The train journey took him through war-ravaged Serbia, then a hellscape of wrecked planes and tanks dotting the countryside.

Vienna, however, was still intact. Mrowa stayed at the famous Hotel Imperial, where Hitler had worked in his youth, and to which he returned triumphantly after the 1938 *Anschluss* that annexed Austria to Germany. Mrowa was now very much in Nazi territory. Unthinkingly violating the forced blackout by opening his curtains on his first night, he was told by a policeman who burst into the room moments later that he would be executed if he did it again. In the streets, he saw elderly Jews wearing the infamous yellow stars. (Younger Jews had already been sent to the camps by that point. Later, in Berlin, he would astonish fellow passengers on a train by offering his seat to an old Jewish woman, who declined, as it was against the law for Jews to sit. Later still, in Slovakia in 1943, he would witness a train deporting Jews from Thessaloniki to Poland, a sight he described as "painful in the extreme.")

After two months in Vienna, the Gestapo ordered him to travel to Berlin to meet with a foreign ministry official, still not explaining why. He arrived at the Anhalter Bahnhof train station, walking through its famous underground tunnel that connected it to the no-less-renowned Hotel Excelsior—all now gone, having been destroyed later in the war.

The Nazi capital played host to a community of several hundred Arab nationalist exiles, many of whom hoped an Axis victory would clear the British and French empires out of the Middle East and bring independence to the Arab world. They included Iraq's former prime minister Gaylani (who, it will be recalled, later received UAR backing for an unsuccessful coup attempt in 1958). There was also the Grand Mufti of Jerusalem, al-Hajj Amin al-Husayni, a prominent figure in Palestinian and pan-Arab politics, who would disgrace himself by his public meetings with Hitler and Mussolini. While Mrowa did not share these exiles' enthusiasm for a Nazi victory, many were nonetheless old friends from Beirut, to whom he had written to see if they might intercede with officials in Berlin to help him on his way to Senegal.

At the meeting he was obliged to attend with the foreign ministry's Fritz Grobba—an Arabist and former German ambassador to Iraq and Saudi Arabia—Mrowa was told his movements had been restricted due to the authorities' discomfort at his neutral stance toward the war, and his contacts with Allied-linked persons while in Istanbul. Nonetheless, his friends in Berlin had vouched for his bona fides, and the issue was now resolved. He was free to relocate to Sofia; a prospect that pleased him, given its proximity to Turkey and the Arab world.

He left Berlin the next day, heading for Sofia via Vienna, Zagreb, and Belgrade. As he entered Croatia, he felt a deep relief, believing the "nightmare" was over. Little did he know the worst of his war experience was still ahead of him.

The Bulgarian capital became his base for the next two years, until he was finally able to leave for Istanbul and ultimately Beirut. During that time, he traveled widely around Axis Europe, visiting Budapest, Bucharest, Bratislava, and Dresden, as well as returning to Berlin and Vienna. It was in Berlin in 1943 that he experienced his first Allied air raid, catching him unawares on Kurfürstendamm Street on the evening of November 22:

> *Where were the shelters? Where was the street? The lights had gone out, and the bombs' glare was obscured by the smoke from the blasts and dust of the destruction. . . . Explosions came from all sides, and fires broke out everywhere, sparked by the hundreds of thousands of falling phosphorus munitions. I was running with all my strength, choking on the stench of arsenic, as the smoke thickened and shrapnel rained all around me. The buildings—all made of brick—wobbled like playing cards from the air pressure caused by the explosions.*

Only by taking shelter under the famous Kaiser Wilhelm Memorial Church did he miraculously escape harm.

What exactly Mrowa got up to between his return to Sofia in April 1942 and his departure for Istanbul in October 1944 is hard to pinpoint in detail, for he died without completing that section of his memoir. What is known is he spent a period roaming around with the Grand Mufti's entourage, and also worked for a time at a Nazi-sponsored Arabic media outfit, though his heart was not in either enterprise. In a letter to a friend written in early 1943, he voiced his skepticism about the Axis's promises to liberate the Arab world. "I have come to believe [their] intentions [toward us] were never once benevolent at any time."

In September 1944, the Soviet Red Army entered Bulgaria, driving out the Nazis and perpetrating widespread atrocities in the process. Mrowa fled by train to Istanbul, where he stayed around a month before boarding a train to Syria. Arrested upon crossing the border on suspicion of Axis sympathies, he was taken to Aleppo, then Beirut, where he was detained by the French for over two months before finally being freed on February 3, 1945.

The war left a lasting mark on the worldview of the young man, who had only just turned thirty. Having seen both Nazism and Stalinism up close with his own eyes, he would vigorously oppose the military dictatorships that were soon to make their first appearances in the Arab world. "I learned a lot about military regimes in Germany," as he put it dryly. By a similar token, having seen how disastrously the Mufti's bet on Hitler had played out, he would have no patience thereafter for the Arab states and parties that threw their lot in with Moscow. If the West was far from perfect, he concluded, it nonetheless represented the Middle East's best hope for a brighter future.

A new man, with a new vision, in a new world: the time had come, Mrowa also decided, for a new newspaper. Tueni, his boss at *Annahar*, generously offered him space at the office to get started. After borrowing some start-up capital and obtaining a license, he and six colleagues launched the first edition of *Al-Hayat* on January 28, 1946.

The paper quickly proved popular for a number of reasons. It came out at dawn, while most of its competitors didn't appear until noon. It specialized in region-wide Arab and international affairs, rather than the local Lebanese coverage that dominated Beirut's other papers. Its articles were succinct, with attractive charts, maps, and other visuals. Later, in 1964, it would be the first paper in the Arab world to adopt color printing.

Soon it was time for the team to move out of *Annahar's* offices into a dedicated space of their own. To this end, Mrowa returned to Senegal in late 1946 to reconnect with his well-heeled émigré contacts. Having raised a healthy sum, on his return to Beirut he purchased a property in the city center, near the Azarieh complex, close to what is now the large landmark Muhammad al-Amin Mosque. (Along with almost everything else in downtown Beirut, *Al-Hayat's* building was later destroyed in the 1975–90 civil war.) To design *Al-Hayat's* office, Mrowa commissioned Raymond Ghosn, the same architect who would later build his Beit Mirri villa. The French designer Jean Royère did the furnishing, while the Lebanese artist Saloua Raouda Choucair decorated the walls. After a trip to Europe to procure state-of-the-art printing machinery and other hardware, the team finally moved into their new premises in 1950.

From then on, Mrowa's rise was exponential. In 1952, he launched the English-language *Daily Star*, which remained Lebanon's flagship English paper until its closure in 2021. Four years later, he started the French-language *Beyrouth Matin*, which subsequently merged into what is now *L'Orient-Le Jour*, Lebanon's leading Francophone daily. His private life, too, was flourishing. Having married Salma Bisar in 1948, the couple went on to have five children: Hayat (named after the paper), Jamil, Lina, Karim, and Malek. To accommodate the family in the style he could now afford, he tasked Ghosn with creating the Beit Mirri villa, to which the Mrowas moved in 1959.

By the 1960s, *Al-Hayat* was a name as big as any other in Arab journalism. The paper "used to sell in Jeddah the second day as much as Beirut," says Malek, who has inspected its financial records from the time. "In Jordan even more. Iraq was a huge market. Morocco and Tunisia" too. The comparative freedom and quality of Lebanon's press in general made Beirut's papers the gold standard of the Arab world as a whole. "If you wanted a piece of news or an opinion to reach the widest number of Arab readers, you had to ensure it was published in a newspaper or weekly in Beirut," writes the historian Fawwaz Traboulsi. Inevitably, though, the same success that earned Mrowa friends, fame, and fortune also made him no shortage of enemies—some of them exceedingly powerful, and dangerous.

Foremost among these was none other than Nasser himself, whom *Al-Hayat* "had a special talent for annoying, to the point of causing him to lash out against [it] in his public speeches." An avid reader of the press, foreign as well as Arab, Nasser had long set especial store by the Beirut papers, "which he regarded as the surest barometer of Arab opinion." That a daily as prominent and widely read as *Al-Hayat* stood against him was a source of profound irritation. Nor was Nasser the only one displeased by Mrowa's biting editorials, and the paper's coverage more generally. Within Lebanon, *Al-Hayat* also had its run-ins with the Deuxième Bureau, whose agents would tail Mrowa's car around town, and had his managing editor, George Shami, arrested some six months before the assassination. "It was a message to *Al-Hayat*," says Mrowa's son Karim. "I'm sure my father read it for what it was: a message and a warning." Evidently, there were elements within the Bureau who shared Nasser's interest in seeing Mrowa's pen fall silent.

In the spring of 1966, a man with links to both would bring about precisely that outcome.

★

BY 1966, IBRAHIM ABD al-Qadir Qulaylat was an established strongman in his Beirut neighborhood of al-Tariq al-Jadideh, at the age of just thirty. Despite his relative youth, he could already boast nearly a decade's experience as a full-time Nasserist militant.

He had earned his stripes in the 1958 Summer of Blood, when he was among the "resistance" fighters paid and armed to wage war on the Lebanese government by Sarraj's Deuxième Bureau in Damascus. Three years later, he and Rasheed Shihab al-Din were granted the dubious honor of sheltering Capt. Abd al-Wahhab al-Khatib—the former head of Syrian General Intelligence's Political Division, who had personally tortured Farajallah al-Helu on the day of his death in 1959—while he was on the lam in Beirut before moving finally to Cairo. When the UAR fell in 1961, Qulaylat was arrested by Lebanon's own Bureau for lobbing a hand grenade at the home of a cabinet minister who had just returned from talks with the new "secessionist" leadership in Damascus.

Qulaylat's zeal for the Nasserist cause was, indeed, boundless. In the years to come, he would work his way up Beirut's violent underworld to become the preeminent Nasserist warlord in all of Lebanon, meeting with the boss himself in Cairo, and heading his own party, which he called the Independent Nasserist Movement. The armed wing of this movement, known as al-Murabitun, would play a central role in the early fighting of Lebanon's second civil war, occupying much of the western half of Beirut at the peak of its power. Especially notable was its part in the destruction of the glamorous five-star hotels that had hosted the capital's famous visitors in years past. An official party poster from the time depicts a fighter smashing his rifle butt into the Holiday Inn, with a quote from Qulaylat boasting that "on 21 March [1976], al-Murabitun demolished the symbol of fascist treason." The battered skeleton of the Holiday Inn still stands in place to this day, an unofficial monument to the stunning devastation visited on the city.

But that was all later. In the mid-1960s, Qulaylat was still clawing his way to the top—and was about to carry out his most consequential operation yet.

It was in early April 1966, at a social gathering to mark the occasion of Eid al-Adha, that Qulaylat took the twenty-three-year-old Adnan Sultani aside and told him he required his assistance with an important matter. Sultani had been a junior figure within Qulaylat's network of loyalists since 1963, after which the latter helped him get a job as a doorman at a bank. To be handpicked for a mission by "Abu Shaker," as Qulaylat was known to his followers, was no small honor; certainly, it was not to be turned down.

Sultani agreed to meet Qulaylat at the latter's home within the next few days. When he did, he was briefed on the objective of assassinating Kamel Mrowa, whom Qulaylat described to him as a "dangerous servant of imperialism, opposed to the Arab cause, and an agent of the reactionaries." His elimination was "very important for Nasserism." Sultani was invited to take some time to think it over. But there was never any question of his refusing.

"Ibrahim assured me this was an issue that concerned Nasserism," Sultani later told a judicial investigator. "So I was emboldened on that basis to carry out the crime, as I'm a Nasserist Arab nationalist."

On the afternoon of April 20, the ball was formally set in motion. Qulaylat had just returned from the second of two three-day trips to Egypt he had made since bringing Sultani into the plot earlier in the month. Now, Sultani met Qulaylat and his driver, the twenty-eight-year-old Ahmad Fuad al-Muqaddam, on Beirut's seaside corniche, near the American University, where they picked him up in a white 1962 Fiat 1500 and drove together to the hills of Beit Mirri to scope out Mrowa's home. The initial plan was for Sultani to shoot him at or near the villa, by blocking the road in front of him and pretending his car had broken down. The premises were studied closely, so much so that staff at the villa reported seeing strangers in the vicinity. Karim and Malek Mrowa themselves can still recall spotting a flashlight beam in the dark one night upon their father's return from work. In the end, however, Sultani felt uneasy about the location, being a born-and-bred Beirut townie unfamiliar with the mountain environment, which would also necessitate a lengthy getaway.

Plan B, then, was to do it at the *Al-Hayat* offices downtown. By a stroke of chance, Sultani recalled he had a friend, twenty-four-year-old Mahmud al-Arwadi, who had once worked at *Al-Hayat* in an

administrative role, and so knew the office layout. Qulaylat agreed
to bring him into the conspiracy, and, after making a few calls and
pulling some strings, Arwadi managed to get himself rehired at the
office as a telephone operator, seated just a few paces from Mrowa's
personal office.

With the plan now taking solid shape, it was time for Sultani to
learn how to commit a murder. On May 1, Qulaylat drove him
in the same Fiat to a remote, uninhabited area in the forested hills
of Aramoun, some twenty kilometers south of Beirut. Sticking a
torn-off piece of newspaper on a wild plant as a target, Qulaylat
showed him how to use the silenced 6 mm Beretta pistol that had
been brought by an unnamed Egyptian man from Cairo especially
for the mission. Sultani fired off dozens of bullets. On May 6, they
did the same again.

Meanwhile, on May 9, Qulaylat's driver Muqaddam used a fake
name to rent an apartment on Ardati Street in the Ras Beirut neighborhood, to be used by Sultani and Arwadi as a hideout after the killing, until a car could be sent from the nearby Egyptian embassy to
collect them. (If things went wrong at any point, Qulaylat told them,
they were to make their way immediately to the same embassy.)
Muqaddam gave Sultani a set of keys to the apartment and showed
him around it two days later.

By the night of May 14, the final pieces were all in place. The
four principal conspirators—Sultani, Qulaylat, Muqaddam, and
Arwadi—met at the apartment to rehearse the details. Qulaylat gave
Sultani a small indigo satchel containing the silenced 6 mm pistol,
ammunition, and an unsilenced 8 mm pistol. He also gave Arwadi a
7 mm pistol, telling him to keep it on him as a backup. Sultani acted
out exactly what he would do. They decided the big day would be
the sixteenth or the seventeenth. In either case, Qulaylat told them
he would fly to Egypt on the fifteenth to provide himself an alibi.
Sure enough, he boarded a plane the next morning.

At 8 p.m. on May 16, Sultani walked into a corner shop in the
Ain al-Mreiseh neighborhood, wearing a beige suit and spectacles,

carrying his indigo satchel. As per the plan, he told the shopkeeper he was expecting a phone call from a woman named Samira. Forty minutes later, "Samira"—who was in fact Arwadi—rang the phone. Mrowa's secretary, Yvonne, had left the office, said Arwadi, and Mrowa had finished his last meeting. No potential eyewitnesses remained except the office doorman, Jamil Khreis. As they had rehearsed, Arwadi now told Khreis there was a phone call for him. Taking the receiver, Khreis was told by Sultani, posing as a police-man, that there had been a fire at his home. Two women had been taken to the hospital and he should make his way immediately to the Nabaa police station. The alarmed Khreis took off at once.

The coast was clear. Sultani hitched a ride on his brother's motor-cycle to the *Al-Hayat* offices, arriving just before 9 p.m. Walking up to the building, he was nearly stopped at the last moment by the night watchman, Ali Rammal, who asked him where he was going. By another stroke of chance, the nearby telephone operator, Lutfi Idris, recognized Sultani from when he had accompanied Arwadi for his job interview. Replying that he was going to see Arwadi himself, he was waved through with no further fuss.

No human being now stood between Sultani and Mrowa. Arriv-ing at the first floor, he was shown into Mrowa's private office by Arwadi, who told his boss an employee from Intra Bank had come to deliver an envelope. Sultani walked in, greeted Mrowa as practiced, placed his indigo satchel on his desk, and opened it.

★

KAMEL MROWA DREW the last breath of his life just as he was entering the emergency ward at the American University of Beirut Hospital. With a punctured lung, a bullet lodged in his heart, and extensive blood loss, he never stood a chance. The very first official telegram of condolences received by his family came from Nasser himself, arriving one day after Mrowa's demise. The joke that then made the rounds in Beirut was that it was a good thing it hadn't arrived one day before it.

At around the very moment Mrowa passed away, Sultani was being hauled into police custody, thanks to the extraordinary actions of Rafiq al-Mir, the passerby who took it upon himself to follow and apprehend the man being chased by people in the street shouting "Thief!" Arwadi, on the other hand, had disappeared the moment the noisy scuffle broke out in Mrowa's office, making his way directly to the Egyptian embassy, where he was joined by Muqaddam. The pair remained in the embassy for weeks until being extracted in secret to Egypt, where—much like Sarraj—they lived the rest of their lives as guests of the authorities, and fugitives from justice.

Sultani would not be quite so fortunate. Within minutes of being apprehended, he confessed to policemen Sgt. Sulayman Mansur, Azar al-Tayyar, and Abbas Mughniyeh that it was he who had shot Mrowa. He was then taken to Beirut police headquarters to be interrogated by the chief investigator assigned to his case, Judge Amin al-Harakah. By the morning, he had given up the name of Ibrahim Qulaylat. The rest of the details came out over the following days. Sultani would even physically reenact the crime in person at the Al-Hayat office for the investigators, and show them to the site in Aramoun where Qulaylat had trained him with the pistol. Here the police managed to find twenty-five spent bullet casings that matched the weapon recovered from the scene of the murder.

Once Sultani's testimony was wrapped up, it remained for police to apprehend Qulaylat himself, who had been in Cairo since the assassination. It took six months of wrangling with the Egyptian authorities before a deal to extradite him was agreed upon, on condition that he be held on remand, rather than imprisoned.

The trial of Sultani and Qulaylat—plus Arwadi and Muqaddam in absentia—was then able to begin, on December 5, 1966. The occasion was marked by the detonation of an explosive device at the Al-Hayat offices, neither the first nor the last of its kind. Indeed, acts of violence and intimidation, including death threats sent to the judges and prosecutors, would become routine throughout the two years of the trial. (It will be recalled that a bomb also exploded at Mohsen Slim's house.)

Having confessed to shooting Mrowa to police moments after the crime, then repeating and elaborating on this confession on at least five subsequent occasions to Judge Harakah, not to mention physically reenacting the crime at the *Al-Hayat* office on May 25, 1966, Sultani later made a clumsy attempt to retract these confessions during the course of the trial. It had actually been Arwadi who killed Mrowa, he suddenly claimed; Sultani had merely been Arwadi's accomplice. As for Qulaylat, the man Sultani had described in such exhaustive and cinematic detail as the mastermind of the plot, he had had nothing at all to do with it whatsoever, he now asserted. How exactly Sultani knew Qulaylat flew out of Beirut the day before the crime—as investigators were able to independently confirm—Sultani could not say. Bereft of logic at the best of times (for who in their right mind confesses repeatedly to a murder they didn't commit?), Sultani's shaky new story sank on occasion into farce. Asked why he told the taxi driver to take him to the Egyptian embassy (as investigators also corroborated), Sultani said it was a slip of the tongue; he had meant to tell him the American embassy.

Such was the caliber of argument advanced by Sultani and his defense lawyers, who were led by the pro-Jumblatt politician MP Bahij Taqi al-Din. The plain objective was to shift blame away from Sultani and (especially) Qulaylat onto the two defendants being tried in absentia, Arwadi and Muqaddam.

Weeks before the final verdict in 1968, the unusual step was taken to replace one of the five judges adjudicating the case, Shafiq Abu Haydar, with another, Butrus Nujaym, known for his friendliness with Cairo's powerful ambassador, Ghaleb. This new judge quickly set about pouring further cold water on the evidence incriminating Qulaylat.

On March 15, 1968, the verdict was issued. Sultani was found guilty of premeditated murder, and sentenced to death (later commuted by President Helou to twenty years' imprisonment, of which he would ultimately serve just ten). His efforts to change his story and blame Arwadi failed to impress the judges, who noted—among other things—that no eyewitnesses saw Arwadi in the building after the sound of smashing glass, whereas they did see Sultani walking away from Mrowa's office. The building guard, Lutfi Idris, also testified that he saw Sultani walking in with the satchel later found on the bloodstained floor by Mrowa's desk.

Arwadi and Muqaddam were both sentenced to death in absentia, though Muqaddam's sentence was immediately commuted to fifteen years' imprisonment with hard labor.

As for Qulaylat, he got off scot-free. Having ruled, in effect, that Sultani was telling the truth in his original testimony, the judges nonetheless chose to disregard the wealth of incriminating statements he had made about Qulaylat, acquitting the latter of any involvement at all on grounds of insufficient evidence. Qulaylat did receive a one-year sentence for possession of unlicensed firearms, but since he had already served more than that period in custody, he was freed on the day of the verdict.

Unsurprisingly, many observers thought Qulaylat's acquittal smacked of a flagrant cover-up. The court's head judge himself, Justice Albert Farhat, formally dissented against his four fellow judges, saying there was plenty of evidence to convict Qulaylat. *Al-Hayat* published a full-page spread of extracts from Sultani's original confessions to Judge Harakah, in which he had mentioned Qulaylat's name more than ninety times. On its own terms, the verdict made no sense. Did it stand to reason that Qulaylat's personal driver and constant companion, Muqaddam, should have partaken in an assassination of which his boss was innocent? Was it believable that the twenty-three-year-old Sultani, earning a doorman's monthly salary of 145 Lebanese pounds (then around $47), had conceived of and executed such a sophisticated plot all on his own initiative, using his own funds, acquiring a silenced pistol with zero assistance from the warlord of whose entourage he was a confirmed member? Why did Qulaylat travel repeatedly to Egypt in the weeks leading up to the crime, including just one day before it? (And how did Sultani know about that travel, if Qulaylat didn't tell him in the apartment while finalizing the assassination plan?) Why, for that matter, did all three of the men found guilty either flee or attempt to flee to the Egyptian embassy—and why did the embassy provide them shelter? These were only the most obvious of the many questions the verdict failed to answer persuasively.

In the view of the Mrowa family—and many others besides—the most reasonable conclusion to be drawn from the available facts is that Mrowa was killed on Nasser's orders, at Sarraj's direction, with Qulaylat managing the operation on the ground, and then escaping conviction due to Nasser's far-reaching influence in Lebanon. (Sarraj, who had lived in Cairo since escaping prison in 1962, was officially an "adviser" to Nasser on Lebanese, Syrian, and Iraqi affairs at the time.)

Among those who shared this assessment was Washington's then ambassador to Lebanon, Dwight J. Porter, who cabled the following to the State Department twelve days after the verdict came out:

> *The acquittal of Koleilat [sic] is a clear travesty of justice and by all evidence was arranged, in fact fixed, by the UAR Government and UAR Ambassador Ghaleb for political reasons. There is little doubt that Mrowa was murdered by UAR or UAR-supported agents. The Embassy has received various reports that the assassination of Mrowa was orchestrated by Abdul Hamid Sarraj, the former Minister of Interior of the Syrian Region during the Egyptian-Syrian Union and at one time the most powerful man in Syria. Since 1962 he has been an advisor of President Nasser on Syrian affairs. According to these reports, Sarraj, with the full support of UAR Intelligence, planned and directed the assassination of Mrowa. The agent who actually instigated the crime in Lebanon was Ibrahim Koleilat. Adnan Sultani was merely the tool to carry out the actual murder. . . . The Embassy has also received reports*

*that three of the judges of the Judicial Council, Amin Talih,
Munir Mahmassani and Boutros Nujin [sic], were pressured
by Ambassador Ghaleb to pass the verdict of non-guilty on
behalf of Ibrahim Koleilat. There are also reports that Ghaleb
approached both outgoing Prime Minister Rashid Karame and
Prime Minister Yafi at the time of the formation of Yafi's cabinet in February 1968, to assure that the GOL [Government
of Lebanon] would use its influence to have Koleilat set free.*

Beyond the evidence presented above pointing to this general
conclusion, interviews later carried out by Mrowa's sons Karim
and Malek, and various Lebanese journalists including Najem El
Hachem, have unearthed further details. They suggest that Egypt's
General Intelligence apparatus, headed by Salah Nasr, was also
involved in the operation; that a senior Egyptian intelligence officer, Fuad Huwaydi, flew to Beirut from Cairo specifically to super-
vise the course of events from Egypt's embassy; that Lebanon's own
military intelligence played a role in the cover-up, with Lt. Sami
al-Khatib attempting to intervene in the investigation from the
very night of the crime onward (Khatib, it will be recalled, was the
Deuxième Bureau's liaison with Cairo, who had personally driven
Sarraj to the Beirut airport during his 1962 prison break); and that
Sultani was regularly visited in jail by Egyptian embassy staff, who
paid him a monthly stipend.

Of dozens of interviews carried out by El Hachem in the course
of his journalistic investigations into the Mrowa killing, perhaps the
most significant was his face-to-face encounter with Sultani himself
in Beirut's Clemenceau neighborhood in 1999. Sultani had escaped
jail in 1976, amid the chaos of Lebanon's civil war, when a militia seized control of the prison in which he was held in Roumieh,
ten kilometers east of Beirut, and simply let the inmates go rather
than assume the burden of running the facility itself. Back on his
home turf by the Beirut seafront, Sultani fought for a Nasserist
group known as the Arab Socialist Union in his neighborhood of

Ain al-Mreiseh, where a sculpture of Nasser stands to this day. By the time El Hachem met him in 1999, the war had been over for nine years, and the fifty-six-year-old Sultani passed his days working at a Libyan publishing house.

The conversation was casual and relaxed, recalls El Hachem. Sultani freely admitted it was he who killed Mrowa, and Qulaylat was the manager of the operation, as per his original confessions to the police and Judge Harakah. "He said that, at the time, when he carried out the mission, he did it with absolute conviction, and that if Abdel Nasser had asked him for his own children, he'd have given them to him," El Hachem tells me in a café outside Beirut. "He was prepared to carry out more operations than this one."

It was also at that 1999 encounter that Sultani informed El Hachem of his meeting with Sarraj during a visit to Cairo in 1976, when the latter opined that the great error had been the lack of a getaway car.

"He and Sarraj conducted a review of the operation, and agreed this was the mistake. Had there been a car waiting to take Sultani away afterward, he would never have been caught, and the perpetrators would have been recorded as unknown. . . . Neither the role of Egyptian intelligence nor that of Ibrahim Qulaylat would have been uncovered."

★

WHAT WAS THE MOTIVE for the crime? That Mrowa angered Nasser by what he published in *Al-Hayat*—causing him to "lash out" against the paper in public—we have already seen. With Mrowa gone, *Al-Hayat* would never again concern Nasser to the same extent. The assassination "had a devastating effect" on the publication, according to Mrowa's son Karim, leaving it "a diminished newspaper." Straight away, leading columnists and correspondents left for other outlets. It wasn't totally finished—it would retain a loyal core readership and survive for another decade, until Lebanon's civil war prompted its closure in 1976. But, by eliminating its founder, chief editor, and defining voice, "Nasser finished it off as a political threat."

Yet Mrowa's sons believe there was an additional, even more significant reason for Nasser to kill their father. This was what might be termed Mrowa's political activities. By the mid-1960s, Mrowa was no longer just a well-known newspaper editor but had become a person of political stature in his own right. "He was neither a parliamentarian nor a cabinet minister, but with the force of his personality, and the breadth of his contacts and influence, he was above parliament and above the cabinet," said his family's lawyer Mohsen Slim, himself a former MP.

In this capacity, Mrowa acted as something akin to a political or strategic adviser to certain regional heads of state. Not the least of these was the new Saudi king, Faysal, who broke with his predecessor Saud's occasional indulgence of Nasser when he replaced him on the throne in 1964. A photograph of Mrowa with Faysal in Jeddah in 1965, sitting side by side on identical leather armchairs, deep in conversation, gives the impression of a dialogue between equals, rather than a humble journalist before a haughty king.

Faysal would quickly establish himself as Nasser's new bête noire, taking up the mantle knocked from the hands of Iraq's Nuri al-Said in 1958. This time, the key battleground was Yemen, where Cairo and Riyadh were fighting a brutal proxy war in which Egypt's forces would become the first Arab army to use chemical weapons on the battlefield. The Yemen conflict was a costly and futile quagmire for Nasser, taking no small psychological toll on him, to the point that he described it as "my Vietnam."

In August 1965, Nasser and Faysal reached an agreement in Jeddah to bring Yemen's war to an end by the following year. Only a few months later, however, Nasser fell out with the king more violently than ever, believing he had deceived him at Jeddah in an elaborate, internationally backed conspiracy to replace him as leader of the Arab world.

The catalyst was Faysal's weeklong state visit to Tehran in December 1965, where he was warmly received by the Shah, ending a decade of frosty relations between the two largest Gulf powers. It was, in part, the Yemen war that brought them together—the Shah was also aiding the anti-Nasser forces backed by Faysal, and very much shared the Saudi king's goal of ejecting Nasser from the Arabian Peninsula. The trip ended with a joint call for a "conference" of Muslim nations in the interests of Islamic fraternity. If this sounded vague and innocuous enough on the surface, it was made clear in leaks to the press that what it really meant was a Saudi-led coalition of conservative and centrist Muslim states—Arab, North African, and Asian—against Nasserism, communism, and radicalism of all stripes.

If this were not disturbing enough by itself for Nasser, it coincided with news of a large Anglo-American arms sale to Saudi Arabia valued at several hundred million dollars, encompassing supersonic fighter planes and an advanced air defense system. Accompanying the *New York Times*'s full-page report on this was a smaller item noting that Faysal and the Shah had just signed an agreement delineating the maritime borders of their offshore oil fields.

Even an observer without Nasser's renowned paranoia might now have begun connecting dots both real and imaginary. As it happened, Nasser's mental health was already far from cloudless at this time, in the estimation of Anthony Nutting, who continued to meet him regularly. Each time he did, he found him less and less the affable, winsome young man he had known in the 1950s, and more and more an irascible, humorless figure, neurotic and ill-tempered, increasingly cut off from his closest friends and comrades. He was fast losing his common sense, even his very grip on reality:

> By the beginning of 1966 Nasser had, politically speaking, declared war on the United States and Britain, in much the same way as Anthony Eden had done against him . . . in 1956. And, as had happened with Eden, so Nasser was now to be driven inexorably towards disaster by a chain reaction of sickness and suspicion, over-reaction and misjudgement. Desperately striving to retain the initiative in the Middle East, he

committed Egypt to a series of adventures and undertakings far
beyond what her capacities could sustain; so that, instead of
moulding events to his design, he found himself reacting ever
more impetuously to the actions of others who, whether by their
own or his choosing, had become his enemies.

On February 22, 1966, Nasser broke his silence on Faysal and the
Shah, and their "Islamic Conference" proposal, in a fiery speech at
Cairo University reminiscent of the swashbuckling heyday of the
late 1950s. Assailing the Saudi king directly by name, Nasser shattered the cold peace that had prevailed between them since the previous summer, declaring in the clearest possible terms that Faysal
was now enemy number one. Saudi Arabia, he said first, had funded
the Muslim Brotherhood in Egypt, a secret armed cell of which had
been uncovered months earlier and accused of plotting terror attacks
and seeking to overthrow the regime. As for the "Islamic Pact," as
Nasser dubbed Faysal's initiative with the Shah, this was simply a
resurrection of Nuri al-Said's Baghdad Pact, this time "dressed in a
cleric's turban." Cooked up as always by the imperialists, in league
with the reactionaries, it was nothing more than the same old conspiracy to halt the march of Arab nationalism and liberation, and
subdue the Arab peoples under perpetual Western and Zionist hege-
mony. A plot "against Arabism, against Muslims, and against Palestine," it would be defeated by the Arab masses just as the Baghdad
Pact had been before it.

What did all of this have to do with Kamel Mrowa? That he was
a known associate and confidant of Faysal's would have sufficed by
itself to place him in the crosshairs. Nasser indeed referred contemp-
tuously in the same speech to the newspapers in Lebanon (without
naming names) that now supported the Islamic Pact as they had supported the Baghdad Pact in the past. Yet Mrowa's personal involvement in the story went deeper. For three years, he had been helping
behind the scenes to engineer precisely this détente between Riyadh
and Tehran, assisted in the endeavor by the influential Lebanese

Iranian cleric Musa al-Sadr. Mrowa was, in other words, a key architect of a new geopolitical alliance Nasser saw as an existential threat
to his leadership of the Arab world and railed against in public as a
conspiracy on par with the hated Baghdad Pact. Mrowa's sons are
convinced their father's assassination cannot be understood outside
this crucial context.

The timeline certainly fits with striking precision. On April 7,
1966, Nasser told the US ambassador to Cairo that his peace pact
with Faysal was "finished," and the gloves were well and truly off.
"King Faysal believed when I entered into the Jeddah agreement [of
August 1965] that it was a move from weakness, but it was not. It
was a move to avoid a clash between [Egypt] and Saudi Arabia. That
clash is now before us."

That very week, Ibrahim Qulaylat initiated contact with Adnan
Sultani to task him with assassinating Mrowa.

★

THE MURDER OF MROWA was not without precedent. The killing of Lebanese journalists was, tragically, nothing new in 1966. We
have already seen that Ghandur Karam was shot dead in 1957 by the
man who went on to lead the Nasserist "resistance" in Beirut the
following year. Slaying journalists, evidently, was a means of career
advancement in the Nasserist world. Yet an even stronger echo of
Mrowa's case was that of Fuad Haddad, a writer for the pro-Chamoun
paper Al-'Amal, who was abducted just as the Summer of Blood drew
to a close in September 1958, never to be seen again. According
to Sarraj's colleague at the Syrian Deuxième Bureau, Sami Jumaa,
Haddad's abduction was arranged by Sarraj at the personal request
of Nasser, who had taken offense at Haddad's enthusiastic mockery
of him in his column. Per Jumaa, the abductors were members of a
Nasserist militia in Beirut led by one Khalil Shihab al-Din (not to be
confused with Rasheed Shihab al-Din), who brought Haddad over
to Damascus. When Sarraj informed Nasser that Haddad was in his
possession, Nasser "ordered that he be punished as he deserved."

He was taken back to Lebanon, where Shihab al-Din killed him. A photo in Jumaa's book purports to show Sarraj introducing Shihab al-Din to a smiling Nasser, who is shaking his hand.

★

IF MROWA'S FAMILY HAD any lingering uncertainty, however slight, about Nasser's culpability for his assassination, it was laid to rest in 1974, when his widow, Salma, was given a brief audience in Cairo with Egypt's new president, Anwar Sadat. An original Free Officer, who had read out the junta's first broadcast on the morning of the 1952 coup, Sadat had known Nasser since 1938, and was his vice president at the time of his death in 1970. Receiving Salma in his office along with a delegation of *Al-Hayat* journalists, Sadat expressed remorse for Egypt's role in Mrowa's killing. Though he declined to offer details, it was nonetheless a gesture of great significance for Salma and the children.

"I think my mother's calmness after that visit seeped into us," says Karim. "That apology from Sadat was probably what ended that episode, [for us] as a family.

"But that doesn't mean that we forget."

11

A PARTING
GIFT

IN JUNE 1967, ISRAEL SIMULTANEOUSLY DEFEATED THE Egyptian, Syrian, and Jordanian armies in a blistering six-day war, seizing the Palestinian West Bank and Gaza Strip, the Syrian Golan Heights, and Egypt's Sinai Peninsula in the process. So utter and unequivocal was the humiliation that Nasser felt compelled to resign as president of Egypt. Large street demonstrations soon led him to revoke his decision, but the blow to his prestige was irreversible all the same, and his influence across the Arab world began to decline.

Lebanon was no exception. The days of Cairo handpicking Lebanon's president, dictating its foreign policy, manipulating its elections, and controlling its military intelligence were soon to be history. Before Nasser departed the scene once and for all, however, he managed to make one last major intervention in Lebanese affairs, arguably his most consequential of all, the effects of which are still felt every day in the country, more than fifty years later.

The enormity of the 1967 defeat, known euphemistically in Arabic as the *Naksa* ("setback"), shook the very foundations of Arab politics, hurling all its certainties and assumptions up in the air and triggering profound transformations. Not the least of its innumerable consequences was the rise of Palestinian militancy, which until then had been a marginal phenomenon.

From the moment of the State of Israel's establishment, and the subsequent war of 1948–49, the understanding had been that the task

of confronting Israel would fall to the regular armies of the surrounding Arab states, especially (after 1952) Nasser's Egypt. Clearly,
after June 1967, the Palestinians could no longer be expected to pin
their national hopes on the armies that had just been obliterated in
under a week, and lay still in complete ruin. Instead, the Palestinians
now resolved to take their destiny into their own hands, and the dis-
graced Arab regimes had little intention of stopping them; indeed,
they were quietly relieved to be freed of responsibility for the daunting task of liberating Jerusalem themselves.

With its large Palestinian refugee population and direct border
with Israel, Lebanon soon became a principal theater of this emerging Palestinian militancy. From the rolling green hills of its southern
border zone, extending from the foot of Mount Hermon to the Mediterranean, Palestinian guerrillas began staging small-scale strikes on
the Galilee. Meanwhile, in Beirut, radical Palestinian groups planned
and launched the dramatic campaign of international plane hijack-
ings and other attacks that would seize the world's attention into the
1970s. Israel was characteristically swift and severe in responding.
One of the more spectacular early incidents came on December 28,
1968, when sixty-six Israeli commandos—among them Israel's current prime minister, Benjamin Netanyahu—descended by helicopter on the Beirut airport and blew up over a dozen civilian aircraft
belonging to Lebanon's national carrier, Middle East Airlines. The
assault had come in response to a Palestinian attack on an Israeli El
Al Boeing 707 at the Athens airport two days previously, in which
one Israeli was killed.

Stability in Lebanon took a grave downward trajectory thereafter. Attempts by the Lebanese authorities to constrain the Palestinian militants led to armed clashes between the two. Demonstrations
in support of the Palestinians in Beirut, Sidon, and elsewhere on
April 23, 1969, turned deadly when security forces opened fire on
the crowds, killing twenty. The next day, Prime Minister Karami—
Nasser's old friend, the former leader of the insurgency against
Chamoun in north Lebanon in 1958—resigned in protest, though

he was persuaded to stay on and form a new cabinet. Subsequent months witnessed a profound deterioration on all fronts. In August, deadly clashes broke out between Lebanese security forces and Palestinian guerrillas in the Nahr al-Bared refugee camp outside Tripoli. The following month, the Lebanese army, police, and Deuxième Bureau were forcibly evicted from Palestinian refugee camps across the country. Meanwhile, Israel kept up its own attacks in parallel, launching another commando raid inside Lebanese territory that same month. October saw fierce gun battles between Lebanese and Palestinian forces all across Lebanon, from the far north to the deep south. Matters came to a bloody head when the Lebanese army encircled a Palestinian guerrilla unit near the southern border and "killed sixteen in a six-day siege."

President Helou had reached an impasse. He was powerless to restore order or bring the violence to an end. His prime minister designate, Karami, still hadn't formed his new cabinet, and now said he would not do so unless and until an agreement was negotiated with the Palestine Liberation Organization (PLO) to legitimate and regulate its armed presence and activities. In this, Karami had the firm support of Lebanon's Muslim political elites, which meant—by the quirks of Lebanon's sectarian power-sharing customs—that the (Christian) Helou could not appoint an alternative premier without sparking yet another major crisis. Paralyzed and wholly out of his depth, Helou turned in desperation to the one man who commanded sufficient authority over all concerned to bring the situation under control.

Ever since first coming to power, Nasser had towered over Palestinian politics no less than he had all other Arab affairs. Cairo had been home to most of the key Palestinian civil-society groups of the 1950s and early '60s, such as the Palestine Students Union—headed by a certain Yasser Arafat between 1952 and 1956—and the leading Palestinian workers' and women's unions. It was Nasser himself who had summoned the Arab leaders to Alexandria in September 1964 to badger them into approving the establishment of the PLO, which was at first little more than another outlet of Nasserist influence. The organization was funded, trained, and equipped by Egypt, which also hosted its radio station, Sawt Filastin ("the Voice of Palestine"). When, after 1967, the more militant Arafat moved to supplant the PLO's discredited head, Ahmad al-Shuqayri, Nasser gave the move his blessing. Arafat became his protégé just as his predecessor had been, enjoying the perks and privileges that came with the patronage of the man who was still, at the end of the day, the godfather of Arab politics. It was natural, then, that when Nasser offered to help Lebanon's beleaguered President Helou reach a modus vivendi with Arafat, Helou hastened to accept—even though it meant doing so from a position of all-too-obvious weakness.

On October 28, 1969, Helou sent a delegation led by Lebanon's army commander, Gen. Emile Bustani, to Cairo to meet with Arafat and Egyptian officials representing Nasser. It had in fact been Premier Designate Karami who was supposed to head the delegation, with Bustani merely advising him on military matters. Karami, however, failed to show up at the Beirut airport at the agreed-on time. When Bustani told Helou he would leave if Karami didn't appear, Helou replied that he had personally promised Nasser to reach a swift agreement with the Palestinians, and implored him to take the lead himself. The general reluctantly acquiesced.

In a sign of what was to come, the Lebanese were greeted at the Cairo airport by a rowdy pro-PLO demonstration staged by the Egyptian authorities, at which abuse was hurled at Lebanon's government and army. Alone but for two Lebanese diplomats and the Deuxième Bureau's leading Nasserist, Sami al-Khatib, Bustani then had to face a scrum of top Egyptian officials, including war minister Gen. Muhammad Fawzi, foreign minister Mahmud Riyadh (the notorious former ambassador to Damascus in the 1950s), Nasser's senior intelligence aide Sami Sharaf, and Nasser's personal representative Hassan Sabri al-Kholi—to say nothing of Arafat and his own six-man entourage.

The Egyptians were by no means impartial mediators standing

at equal distance from the Lebanese and Palestinians: they actively pushed Bustani and his colleagues to concede to Arafat's demands. Riyadh pressed the Lebanese to "take an active part in the resistance" against Israel. Kholi told them Syria's president had assured him that an agreement to allow the PLO freedom of action in Lebanon would resolve Beirut's problems with Damascus, which had closed its Lebanese border in protest over the bloodshed earlier in the month. Bustani was even personally received by Nasser himself on October 31 at the resplendent Qubba Palace, where the president buttered him up with friendly chatter before urging him to ensure the negotiations succeeded. The sum total of Egyptian pressure—which also included letters from Nasser to President Helou—was decisive in pushing through the final agreement.

This document, aptly named the Cairo Agreement, was signed by Bustani and Arafat on November 3, 1969, in the presence of Egypt's Fawzi and Riyadh. Subsequently approved by the Lebanese parliament, it was an accord quite unlike any other in the annals of international relations. Its terms formally awarded Palestinian militants the right to attack Israel from Lebanese territory, and to be assisted in the act by the Lebanese army, which pledged to facilitate the guerrillas' movements and military supply lines. The Palestinians were further allowed to operate from fixed military bases in south Lebanon, and to exercise autonomous rule over the refugee camps, free of any official Lebanese state presence. In exchange for these extraordinary prerogatives, they undertook to maintain discipline and avoid interfering in Lebanese internal affairs.

If there was ever a Rubicon moment for Lebanon, this was it. No other single step did more to set the country on its descent into the civil war that would erupt six years later. The attacks on Israel to which the Cairo Agreement gave official endorsement brought punishing Israeli reprisals down on Palestinians and Lebanese alike. These in turn invited yet more guerrilla operations, in a classic vicious cycle, each round of which fueled growing Lebanese discomfort with the Palestinians' armed activities.

The internal fractures that had been so imperfectly papered over after the 1958 war threatened to rupture anew. Many of the very same individuals were once again at the fore: Camille Chamoun returned from the political wilderness to join the chorus of voices denouncing the Palestinian "state-within-a-state," while against him stood Karami, Kamal Jumblatt, Saeb Salam, and Abdallah al-Yafi— erstwhile champions of Nasserism now affirming their commitment to the Palestinian "revolution."

Before long, hard-line Lebanese nationalists, most of them Christian, were building up their own militias in preparation for a showdown with the Palestinians to "liberate" what they now saw as *their* occupied homeland. On the other side, mostly-Muslim leftists and Nasserists—including Ibrahim Qulaylat—used the cover of the Cairo Agreement to arm their own paramilitaries, with which they pledged to defend their Palestinian comrades. What had begun in the late 1960s as an Israeli-Palestinian quarrel had, by the early '70s, metastasized into a three-way Israeli-Palestinian-Lebanese conflict, superimposed on top of Lebanon's preexisting internal divisions, with a religious sectarian dimension to boot. By 1975, the country was a giant Mexican standoff, with tens of thousands of heavily armed gunmen on all sides raring to go. No group was above the fray: even the tiny Armenian community, descended from refugees fleeing genocide at Turkish hands in 1915–16, acquired its own militia. The teeming tinderbox was ignited in April 1975, in an infernal blaze that would rage unextinguished until 1990.

Nasser had been dead for almost five years by the time Lebanon's war broke out, and it would obviously be unjust to attribute it all to his actions alone. Myriad other actors deserve their share of the blame for Lebanon's terrible slaughter, starting with Lebanon's own combatants and politicians, and their counterparts in neighboring Israel and Syria, and no end of other influential states across both the Middle East and the West.

Nonetheless, the case can still be made that Nasser did more than most to pave Lebanon's path to war in the years building up to it.

For a start, his central role in the 1958 conflict was, by itself, of far-reaching consequence. That violence was "a significant watershed in the political history of Lebanon . . . the first major breakdown in political order after nearly a century of relative stability," in the estimate of the prominent Lebanese sociologist Samir Khalaf. Thereafter, "Lebanon began to lose its political tranquility" as "more contentious and malevolent forms of political confrontations" were steadily normalized.

Above and beyond 1958, in creating the PLO in the particular form that it took; in backing Arafat's takeover thereof; in imposing the Cairo Accords upon the feckless President Helou, over whose rule Nasser had already cast such a heavy shadow; in having long sponsored and armed violent militants of the Qulaylat stripe since the 1950s; not to mention in precipitating and then so cataclysmically losing the Six-Day War, without which the Middle East might have taken any number of alternative historical paths—the sum total of Nasser's responsibility for Lebanon's ruin was arguably greater than that of any other single individual. Having already brought Lebanon its first civil war, his parting gift before his death was to set the country squarely on the road to its second, which was incomparably larger and more devastating, grinding on for fifteen murderous years, claiming some 150,000 lives, utterly disfiguring and transforming the country in a manner from which it has never recovered.

JORDAN

◆ 12 ◆

HIS MAJESTY'S
LOYAL OPPOSITION

T HE MORNING OF AUGUST 29, 1960, BEGAN MUCH AS
every Monday did for Jordan's forty-two-year-old prime minister, Hazzaa al-Majali. In his first-floor office in downtown Amman,
he held an open court, where anyone from senior officials to ordinary members of the public could show up for an audience with the
premier, at which he would hear their petitions and try to resolve
their problems.

Shortly before noon, he asked a young aide named Zaid al-Rifai—a
future prime minister himself in years to come—to fetch a file from
elsewhere in the building. Rifai asked if he might have a cup of coffee first. To his mild annoyance, the prime minister insisted he leave
the coffee till after he brought the file. As destiny would have it, his
demand spared the young man's life.

Moments after Rifai departed, Majali opened a drawer under his
desk, triggering a concealed explosive device that detonated, killing
him instantly. Seconds later, another bomb went off on the other side
of the room, killing all but one of those present. The lone survivor,
Abd al-Hamid al-Majali, had been standing at the moment of the
first blast by a window, through which he was thrown by the force.
By the time the second bomb blew, he was already outside the building, hurtling toward the ground below.

The twin blasts ripped out the walls of the office, caving in the
roof. It would take three hours for the prime minister's body to be
dug out of the rubble.

Yet the carnage wasn't over. On hearing the news, Jordan's twenty-four-year-old King Hussein raced to the scene, where he was prevented from approaching the building by the army's commander in chief, who insisted the risk to his security was too great. The monarch retorted that no one had the authority to stop him. As the pair were arguing, a third explosion detonated at the building's entrance, killing yet more victims. In all, eleven lives were taken by the three blasts, with eighty-five injured. Aside from the premier, the dead ranged from an undersecretary for foreign affairs to a Palestinian refugee child. The sovereign himself had very nearly been among them.

★

KING HUSSEIN BIN TALAL formally ascended to the Jordanian throne at the age of seventeen on May 2, 1953, right around the time Nasser's junta abolished the institution of monarchy in Egypt. Young though he may have been, Hussein had had a graphic early induction into the cutthroat realities of Arab politics, when his grandfather, King Abdallah I, was shot dead in the head right next to him at the entrance to Jerusalem's al-Aqsa Mosque in 1951. The gunman had also shot the fifteen-year-old Hussein himself in the chest, but the bullet bounced off a military medal his grandfather had told him to wear.

In the forty-six years for which Hussein went on to rule until his death in 1999, he would build a modern state almost from scratch; bring Jordan into the United Nations; end Britain's military presence in the country; marry four women and sire eleven children (among them Jordan's current sovereign, King Abdallah II); fend off innumerable attempted coups and assassinations; and wage bloody wars against Israelis and Palestinians alike, before patching up with both, making Jordan the second Arab state after Sadat's Egypt to sign a full peace treaty with Israel in 1994.

For much of his first two decades in power, Hussein was locked in a life-or-death duel with Nasser, in whom he had a knack for inspiring a special kind of fury. The pair began on cordial terms, and wound up reconciled again by the mid-1960s. The intervening years, however, ranked among the most tempestuous of any in the annals of Nasserism. As will be seen, it was the UAR's crusade against Amman that cost Premier Majali his life, and nearly took Hussein's own—for neither the first nor the last time.

★

ONCE AGAIN IT WAS the Baghdad Pact dispute of 1955 that formed the context of the initial encounter. With Hashemite Iraq leading the Arab contingent of the pact, it might have been expected that its Jordanian cousin and neighbor would follow suit as a matter of course. Britain, Turkey, and other pact members certainly hoped for this. Jordan was already bound to Britain through an Anglo-Jordanian Treaty signed in 1948, by virtue of which it received an annual payment of over £12 million from the Exchequer in return for granting Britain the use of two military facilities. To join the pact would amount less to a departure from Jordan's existing geopolitics than to a continuation of the status quo.

Yet Hussein was reluctant. The teenage monarch, it must be recalled, was nearly half a century younger than Iraq's sexagenarian premier Nuri al-Said, born in an altogether different era and political climate. Unlike Iraq's elder statesman, Hussein was sensitive to the charge that his army and kingdom were mere playthings in the hands of British colonialism. A proud military man himself (trained at Sandhurst), he kept a close eye and ear to the affairs of his army, and was well aware of disgruntlement in the ranks about perceived British domination and discrimination. No Jordanian officer at the time could hope for promotion to the top-brass posts, which the British reserved exclusively for themselves. Hussein shared the officers' resentment of this situation, as Britain would discover to its alarm the following year, when he unceremoniously dismissed the British commander of his army.

Indeed, as improbable as it would later seem, Hussein was in certain ways something of a Nasserist avant la lettre in early 1955. "I had for a long time been impressed by Nasser," he wrote in his 1962 memoir, *Uneasy Lies the Head*. "I felt in those early days that he was a new element in the Arab world, an element that could bring about much needed reforms. . . . I had a lot of faith in Nasser and tried to support him as much as I could."

In arriving at this position, Hussein had been encouraged by several radical young Arab nationalist officers with whom he often spent time, one of whom in particular—Maj. Ali Abu Nuwar—he appointed as his senior aide-de-camp in November 1955. These officers pressed him at every opportunity to shake off the British yoke and bring Jordan closer to Nasser's orbit. To be sure, Hussein himself had no intention of losing Britain's friendship. For one thing, he desperately needed its money. For another, he was a helpless Anglophile by both nature and nurture: a rugby-playing Old Harrovian and Sandhurst alumnus who drove an Aston Martin, acquired the stately Buckhurst Park residence near Windsor Castle, and married an Englishwoman, Antoinette Gardiner—the mother of the current King Abdallah II. Nonetheless, in 1955 he was firmly determined to "Jordanize" the armed forces, limit Britain's political sway over his government, and in every other possible sense maximize his own freedom of action and inspire the general impression of Jordanian sovereignty and independence.

He thus opted to steer a middle course with respect to the Baghdad Pact, hoping to position Jordan as the natural mediator between Egypt and Iraq. At the Cairo conference of January 1955, his delegation took a noncommittal position broadly akin to Chamoun's Lebanon and Khuri's Syria. Over the following months, Hussein paid personal visits to both Baghdad and Cairo, where Nasser awarded him the Grand Cordon of the Order of the Nile. Reconciling Nuri and Nasser was a hopeless task, however. Nuri told Hussein bluntly, "Sir, we are in the Baghdad Pact, that's that, and we are certainly not backing out of it." Nasser, of course, was equally intransigent. If Hussein failed as a peacemaker, he did at least succeed—for a time—in sparing himself the abuse dished out to Cairo's enemies over the Voice of the Arabs broadcasts.

What spoiled this calm was the stunning news in late September 1955 that Egypt had reached a landmark deal to buy arms from the Soviet bloc—the upshot of Nasser's tête-à-tête with Zhou Enlai at Bandung five months earlier. This major purchase, encompassing scores of MiG fighter planes, Ilyushin bombers, tanks, armored troop carriers, and much more, was the first of its kind in the Arab world, where such arms as existed came only from Western sources. In the charged Cold War atmosphere of the day, the news sparked intense fear and loathing in London and Washington, where it was seen as an intolerable, game-changing win for Moscow in an arena of foremost strategic importance.

By way of trying to recover the initiative, and anchor what remained of their influence before it too was swept away by the Soviet-Nasserist tide, both Britain and Turkey now renewed efforts to bring Jordan into the Baghdad Pact. In early November, Turkey's president Celâl Bayar and foreign minister Fatin Zorlu flew to Amman, where they "used every conceivable argument to convince the king and his ministers of the advantages of joining." Jordan, they said, would gain Turkey as a powerful ally and counterweight against both Israel and Syria. It would also be able to renegotiate its unpopular treaty with Britain.

The Turks were pushing an open door, for Hussein had reasons of his own for seeing the pact in a new light. Nasser's arms deal had stirred great excitement in the Arab world, not least in Jordan, and served as both an embarrassment and a challenge to all rulers who failed to secure comparable weaponry from their Western patrons. To his people—and his military officers—Hussein had now to prove that he too could deliver the goods, or else lose face to the plucky rebel in Cairo.

Pressing what he could see was his newfound advantage, Hussein told the Turks he was interested, but would require not just military but economic aid. They suggested he raise this with the British, which he promptly did, submitting a list of his needs to Britain's ambassador in Amman.

The mood in London leaned strongly in Hussein's favor. "I very much fear that if we do not get Jordan into the Baghdad Pact, she will drift out of our control," wrote an anxious foreign secretary Harold Macmillan to Prime Minister Eden, who concurred. It was decided to send in the big guns, as it were. The chief of the Imperial General Staff, Gen. Sir Gerald Templer, flew to Amman in early December with instructions to get Jordan into the pact at all costs. In his meetings with the king and senior officials, Templer offered generous quantities of arms and money, as well as an end to the Anglo-Jordanian Treaty.

Hussein was ready to accept, but, in an act of extraordinary deference to Nasser, he first sought the Egyptian president's views. "I would do nothing behind Nasser's back," he later explained. According to his account, when he informed Nasser of the terms he had negotiated, Nasser gave him his blessing, saying any gain for Jordan was a gain for the Arab world as a whole.

No sooner did this happen, however, than Cairo Radio erupted in frenzied castigation of Hussein and his conspiracy to sell out Jordan and Palestine to the imperialists. Hussein was stunned: "How could he have sent such fulsome compliments and assurances of his support and then, in a matter of hours, have tried to tear Jordan apart? I cannot recall another incident in history where a statesman has made such a *volte-face*." (In fact, Nasser had of course done much the same to Nuri al-Said, telling him in Cairo in September 1954 that he was free to join the pact if he wished, only for Voice of the Arabs to start inciting his overthrow immediately afterward.)

Charged by Cairo's propaganda, the atmosphere in Jordan rapidly soured. Four cabinet ministers resigned on December 13 while Templer was still in the country, reportedly receiving Egyptian bribes to do so. Prime Minister Said al-Mufti resigned himself later the same day, collapsing his government. Templer flew home the next morning, deeming his mission a failure.

Despite these setbacks, Hussein remained intent on joining the pact. To do so, he chose as his next prime minister none other than Hazzaa al-Majali, the man who would be bombed in his office five years later. A scion of a prominent and fiercely loyal Bedouin tribe from the town of Karak in Jordan's monarchist heartland, Majali was known to look favorably on alignment with Britain and Iraq in general, and on joining the Baghdad Pact in particular. That these were positions liable to earn him the wrath of Cairo was for him no deterrent—he was, in Hussein's words, "a man of courage, not afraid to shoulder responsibility." When Majali formed his cabinet on December 15, he did so with the express goal of bringing Jordan into the pact.

The reader may be able to guess what happened next. Violent demonstrations, organized in the main by Jordan's Baathists and communists, with Egyptian as well as Saudi Arabian encouragement, flooded Amman and every other major city in Jordan's East Bank, as well as the Palestinian West Bank (annexed by Jordan in 1950). The riots were at the time "the most serious to have taken place in Jordan's history." Consulates were attacked in Jerusalem, leaving the French and Turkish consuls wounded. As far away as Aqaba on the Red Sea at Jordan's southwestern tip, a US Point Four Program aid depot was sacked by a mob. Even the ordinarily calm Palestinian refugee camps saw disturbances, in part because a constant refrain of Egyptian propaganda was that Jordan's accession to the Baghdad Pact would spell the end of Palestine. This was "the most dangerous piece of disinformation" circulated by Jordan's detractors at the time, recalled Majali in his memoir. "Egypt and Saudi conscripted their friends, and were supported in their lies and deceit by the servants of communism, and the fiction that the Palestinian cause would be lost was on everyone's lips."

Matters grew worse still for Majali when three of his cabinet ministers were intimidated into resigning on December 19. The next day, he submitted his own resignation, after just five days in office. He claimed in his memoir that it had been within his power to crush the riots and impose the pact by force, but he had rejected this option when it was put to him, preferring to step down rather than to cause a bloodbath.

Jordan's flirtation with the Baghdad Pact had come to an end. The following month, a new government was formed under Prime Minister Samir al-Rifai, who went out of his way to stress on his first day in office that Jordan no longer sought any new alliances with anyone. Nasser had won the opening round.

★

THE LESSONS OF THE "Templer riots" were not lost on King Hussein. In the new air of calm that fell on Jordan in early 1956, he found it expedient to mend fences with Cairo, and in other ways burnish his Arab nationalist credentials to the best of his ability. In particular, he saw an opportunity to take care of an item of business that had weighed on his mind for some time.

Lt. Gen. (later Sir) John Glubb "Pasha" was a British veteran of both World Wars, based in the Middle East for over thirty years, who since 1939 had commanded Jordan's army, serving officially as an employee of the Hashemite crown. A highly capable general, he is credited with having built Jordan's army into an effective, well-trained, and disciplined fighting force. In the 1948 war in Palestine, the Jordanians under Glubb's command far outperformed their Egyptian and other Arab counterparts, successfully fending off Israeli attempts to capture the prized Old City of Jerusalem, which thus remained in Arab hands after the armistice, along with East Jerusalem and the West Bank.

In keeping with his image as a "latter-day Lawrence," Glubb's power in Jordan extended well beyond the military sphere into the political. Quite apart from his contacts in Whitehall, Glubb had spent decades building close personal relations with Jordan's leading tribes, whom he had helped rally to Abdallah I's side in the nascent kingdom's formative years. He was literally a kingmaker, having played a key role in deciding the line of succession after Abdallah's assassination in 1951. He was also the man in control of the £12 million that arrived each year from London under the terms of the Anglo-Jordanian Treaty.

While acknowledging his "personal admiration" for "all the fine work" Glubb had contributed over the years, Hussein did not conceal in his memoir that he resented the outsize influence of the Englishman over Jordanian officialdom, lamenting the way "our political leaders tended to turn to him or the British Embassy before taking the slightest decisions." Nor did it help that Egypt's propaganda had made such ecstatic hay of the fact that Jordan's army was commanded by a foreigner—an Englishman, no less—depicting the boy-king Hussein as a powerless puppet in the hands of his nefarious colonial master.

It was to answer this charge with a dramatic gesture that Hussein moved to oust Glubb in March 1956. The official pretext, per his memoir, concerned army appointments: specifically, the king's ambition to Arabize the military's upper echelons much faster than Glubb would countenance. When Hussein complained to the British about the absence of Jordanians among the army's senior posts, and urged them to expedite their promotion, the reply came that his Royal Engineers might potentially have an Arab commander by the year 1985. Needless to say, this was not the timetable the monarch had envisaged.

Hussein's deeper motive for ditching Glubb, however, was, in the words of one biographer, "his fear that if he did not place himself at the head of the nationalist movement, he would be overwhelmed by it." The king had kept up his contacts with Jordan's young Arab nationalist officers, including the aforementioned Abu Nuwar, who held a personal grudge against Glubb dating back to 1952, when the latter banished him to a diplomatic post in Paris to keep him from political intrigues at home. After Hussein brought him back to Jordan and appointed him aide-de-camp in November 1955—against Glubb's advice—Abu Nuwar was "constantly at the king's side . . . arguing for the removal of Glubb and a break with

Britain." At these gatherings with Abu Nuwar and his comrades, Hussein appears to have instinctively grasped the threat they and others like them could pose to him if he weren't careful, not least after the Baghdad Pact controversy. As many an Arab ruler was to learn the hard way in the 1950s, there was no greater danger to a regime than a disaffected officer corps.

It was, fittingly, at a meeting with just such a group of officers on the evening of February 28, 1956, that Hussein finalized his plan to remove Glubb. The venue was the house of the king's cousin and longtime friend Zaid bin Shaker. Those present included the Baathists Shaher Abu Shahut and Mahmud al-Maayta. Earlier that day, Hussein had been handed a list of officers Glubb wanted discharged from the army. Seeing the names of several friends, the king slammed the papers on his desk, refusing to sign. It was the last straw. He was ready to act.

Together with the officers at bin Shaker's home, the king hammered out the details of what they dubbed "Operation Dunlop." It was practically a full-blown palace coup: Glubb's home was to be encircled by armored cars, and his telephone lines cut. Other senior British officers were also to be kept in place, with their lines similarly severed. Trusted troops would deploy on the airport road to ensure nothing impeded Glubb's swift departure from the country. When the officers present confirmed they could execute the plan, Hussein ordered them to do so right away, with utmost secrecy.

The following morning, Hussein handed Prime Minister Rifai a handwritten order for the immediate dismissal of Glubb and other top British officers. The very next day, Glubb was gone, along with chief of staff Col. W. M. Hutton, general intelligence director Col. Sir Patrick Coghill, and, eventually, every last Briton in the army, save for a handful kept on as instructors.

In London, Glubb's dismissal met with bewildered shock and fury. Prime Minister Eden was apoplectic with rage, believing—without evidence—that the move was personally orchestrated by Nasser. This misapprehension was in fact to have serious consequences well beyond Jordan's borders, insofar as it triggered the start of Eden's obsessive vendetta against the "Hitler on the Nile" that would culminate seven months later in Britain's military invasion of Egypt in partnership with France and Israel.

Within Jordan, by contrast, Hussein's bold slap to the face of Empire proved wildly popular. For three days, his palace in Amman was swarmed with crowds of delighted well-wishers and delegations from far and wide, celebrating the monarch as never before. To underscore the army's newfound independence and Arabness, Hussein changed its official name from the British-made "Arab Legion" to the "Jordanian Arab Army." More importantly, he filled the leadership vacuum left by the departed Brits with Jordanian officers, including strident Arab nationalists. His friend Abu Nuwar was promoted straight from lieutenant colonel to major general, and made chief of staff in May. This was a decision Hussein would soon have cause to regret.

★

EMBOLDENED BY THE SUCCESS of his Glubb gamble, Hussein decided in June 1956 to roll the dice again, this time on free parliamentary elections—the first in the kingdom's history—to be held in October of that year. If he had hoped for a quiet campaign season, he was to be disappointed. No sooner had he dissolved the old parliament and announced the elections than the earthquake of Nasser's Suez Canal nationalization rocked the Arab world's tectonic plates.

Hussein quickly telegrammed his warm congratulations to Nasser, and added his voice to the loud chorus of applause for the move. The following months saw him and the country as a whole move further toward Cairo and away from Eden's Britain. At a large demonstration in August organized by the Baath, the communists, and other leftist groups, thousands of Jordanians massed in the streets carrying pictures of Nasser and proclaiming support for Egypt. A series of deadly Israeli attacks on Jordanian police stations in September and October, killing over one hundred, in response to Palestinian guerrilla raids, drove Jordanian public opinion—and with it the king—closer still to Nasser's embrace.

The net effect of these events on Jordan's electorate was as might be expected. The vote, held on October 21, brought a sizable bloc of radicals, including communists, Baathists, and Islamists, into parliament. (By way of comparison, the new parliament was both more communist and more Islamist than the Syrian parliament elected in 1954, though not quite as Baathist.) The major winners were a newly formed local group called the Patriotic Socialist Party, who took 30 percent of the total seats (twelve out of forty). The party's platform, to the extent it had one, leaned vaguely leftist and "progressive," which in the context meant primarily that it sought further Arabization of Jordanian institutions, stronger checks on the monarch's prerogatives, and alignment with the Nasser-led axis against the West, Israel, and other "reactionary" states in foreign affairs.

Having committed himself to what he later called a "period of experiment" with representative democracy, Hussein invited the Patriotic Socialists' leader, Sulayman al-Nabulsi, to form a government. Over the coming months, Prime Minister Nabulsi would stand at the epicenter of what was, at the time, the gravest turmoil in the kingdom's history.

Born in 1910 in the city of Salt, northwest of Amman, Nabulsi had been renowned for his left-wing activism ever since his undergraduate days at the American University of Beirut in the early 1930s. Upon graduating, he had briefly taught at a school in Karak, where the future prime minister Hazzaa al-Majali was among his pupils. After ruffling feathers by leading the students on a protest in the town square against British support for Zionism in Palestine, he was transferred to another school back in Salt.

By the 1940s, Nabulsi had established himself as a leading light of Jordan's loyal opposition, bouncing among government jobs, ministerial positions, and, occasionally, prison. In 1948, he was jailed for nine months for penning an article critical of that year's Anglo-Jordanian Treaty. Despite this, his energy and intelligence ensured it was never long before he was back in government again. Between 1953 and 1954, he served as Jordan's ambassador to London. On his return to Amman, he was recruited into the brand-new Patriotic Socialist Party, of which he soon became leader. For the two years between then and the party's victory in the elections, he was Jordan's most reliable rabble-rouser, marching in the streets and whipping up crowds on every occasion from the Baghdad Pact to the Suez nationalization.

For all these radical credentials, a defender as unlikely as the staunch monarchist Majali asserted that his "old friend" Nabulsi was a moderate at heart, not an extremist. He sought reform, not revolution, it has been said; a more democratic, constitutional monarchy, rather than a republic, still less a military dictatorship.

If this was the case, it was poorly reflected in the cabinet Nabulsi formed upon assuming the premiership, which was dominated by ideological firebrands. Foremost of these was Abdallah al-Rimawi, cofounder and inaugural leader of the Jordanian branch of the Baath Party, who was appointed minister of state for foreign affairs (even though the Baath had won just two of forty seats in parliament). A zealous and outspoken anti-Hashemite, Rimawi was said to make regular trips to the Syrian capital to collect cash, to the extent that it was joked that Jordan's foreign ministry was headquartered in Damascus. So devoted was he to Nasser that when the Baath later split with Cairo in the UAR years, he broke away to form his own Nasserist-Baathist splinter group in the 1960s.

Alongside Rimawi in Nabulsi's cabinet were the communist Abd al-Qadir al-Saleh as minister of agriculture, and the stalwart leftist Shafiq al-Rushaydat as justice minister. More than any others, these three militants formed the real driving force of the Nabulsi government, dragging the prime minister whether he liked it or not into ever-escalating confrontation with the palace, until it all crashed and burned in a destructive showdown in April 1957.

The king and his new cabinet did not begin on such foul terms. At first, they shared certain goals in common. The initial days were in any case dominated by the Suez War that broke out less than a week after Nabulsi took office. Hussein's instinct was to send Jordan's army to help Egypt. Ironically, it was Nabulsi, Chief of Staff Abu Nuwar, and Nasser himself who urged him against this. The war did colossal damage to Britain's name in the Arab world, and Jordan's new parliament voted unanimously two weeks after the cease-fire in November 1956 to abrogate the Anglo-Jordanian Treaty. Hussein had no objections. Britain was a spent force now anyway, and he had already laid plans to replace its patronage with that of the new top superpower: Washington.

This was the point at which his rift with Nabulsi's government began. On getting rid of Britain they were agreed. But where Hussein saw the US as Britain's natural successor, Nabulsi and his colleagues wanted fellow Arab states—Egypt and Syria above all—to fill the void in Britain's wake. Quite apart from any political reservations Hussein held about this, he had no faith these countries could make up the £12 million loss to Jordan's annual income created by the termination of the treaty. If there was one thing Jordan could not survive without, it was financial aid. For the moment, though, his preliminary contacts with Washington had not borne fruit, and so with reluctance he flew to Cairo in January 1957 to sign an agreement whereby Egypt, Syria, and Saudi Arabia pledged to collectively match the lost British payment to Jordan for ten years.

The king had by no means given up on his aim of roping Washington into an alliance, however. Around this same time, he began making forceful public criticisms of communism. His hostility to the ideology was doubtless sincere. Still, a cynic might believe these pronouncements were designed to catch the attention of the Eisenhower administration, which had that very month launched its signature doctrine offering aid to Arab states threatened by "international communism." And a cynic might well be right, for that is indeed what came to pass. When in February Hussein published an open letter to Nabulsi expounding on the mortal dangers of communism, US officials previously indifferent to the king were suddenly enthused. Secretary of State Dulles told his ambassador in Amman to convey to Hussein that "we are highly gratified at his recent public action in pointing out [the] Communist menace."

Needless to say, Nabulsi and his ministers—one a communist himself—did not share Dulles's gratification. Far from cozying up to Washington, they had spent their time in office building bridges to Moscow. Shortly before Hussein's letter, the cabinet had permitted the publication of Jordan's first legal communist newspaper, *Al-Jamahir* (The masses). The Soviet state news agency, TASS, had also been invited to open an office in Amman. This was a period, after all, when both Egypt and Syria—the two states Nabulsi's government most wished Jordan to emulate—were buying Soviet arms and signing landmark economic and other strategic agreements with Moscow. In the Cold War climate of the time, the difference between this vision for Jordan's future and the king's was not one that could be reconciled.

And so the swords were drawn. Showing he meant business, Hussein followed his letter with orders to close *Al-Jamahir* and the TASS office, to confiscate communist literature from bookshops, and to remove Soviet films from the cinemas. Later in February, Rimawi countered with a press conference denouncing the Eisenhower Doctrine and any other form of Western alliance. In March, the cabinet announced its formal recognition of Communist China, a brazen act of defiance exceeded only by its decision in early April to establish full diplomatic relations with Moscow itself.

These were high-stakes provocations. A more prudent leader than Nabulsi might have thought the point had been made, and stayed his hand for the time being. Instead, the premier—egged on by Rimawi, and apparently losing the cool head for which he was once renowned—chose to up the ante further. On April 7, the government sent Hussein a list of officials it wished to retire from office. Clearly intended as a purge of palace loyalists, it included the king's trusted director of public security, Bahjat Tabbara, whom the cabinet sought to replace with the Baathist Mahmud al-Maayta. This was a frontal assault on one of the key pillars upon which rested the king's hard power: a declaration of war in all but name. If only to buy time to ready his countermove, Hussein approved the request.

The next day witnessed what one historian has described, with scholarly understatement, as a "strange incident." From Jordan's main military base at Zarqa, twenty-five kilometers northeast of Amman, units from the First Armored Car Regiment emerged and took up positions outside the queen mother's palace and other strategic sites around the capital. The regiment's commander was none other than Capt. Nadheer Rasheed, the Nasserist who would later break Syria's Sarraj out of his Damascus jail cell in 1962.

On hearing this news, Hussein was "thunderstruck," he wrote in his memoir. "This could only mean one thing—imminent danger to Jordan, a possible attack on the Palace. Certainly it indicated that [army chief of staff] Abu Nuwar was plotting a military *coup*."

The king, it will be recalled, had been friends with Abu Nuwar since the early 1950s, and had indeed been the one who brought him home from Paris, against Glubb's counsel, then made him chief of staff once Glubb was gone. Never bashful about his Arab nationalism, since the advent of Nabulsi's government, Abu Nuwar was said to have come under the malign influence of Rimawi and other agitators. Hussein wrote that in the run-up to April 1957 he "learned that [Abu Nuwar] was making regular visits to Damascus and holding meetings with the Soviet Military Attaché there." He also happened to be a "bosom friend" of Nadheer Rasheed.

Summoning Abu Nuwar to demand an explanation for the troops outside his mother's palace, Hussein was told it was a "purely routine" exercise. He replied as calmly as he could that, routine or not, it might be best to call the exercise off. The chief of staff accepted the suggestion, and the armored vehicles were withdrawn the following day.

What was the real nature of the "exercise"? In less politically fraught circumstances, it might have been easier to accept the story of an innocent drill. But coming just one day after the ouster of

Tabbara, following weeks of confrontation between the palace and government, it is difficult not to see it as a flexing of muscles and/or a dress rehearsal for military action on the part of Rasheed, Abu Nuwar, and other Nasserist officers.

Seemingly bent on triggering a crisis, Nabulsi's government chose to escalate once again just two days later, submitting another list of loyalist officials to be dismissed. This time, the names included Bahjat Talhouni, the king's right-hand man and chief of royal court. So obviously unacceptable was this request that it could only have been made with a view to provoking what came next. Instead of accepting, Hussein sent Talhouni himself to Nabulsi to deliver the king's orders that the government resign. Sure enough—as though they were expecting it—the cabinet complied immediately without protest. Banking on their popularity in the street, and support in the army, they appear to have calculated they could prevail over the palace in an open conflict.

The next three weeks have been called "the most crucial period in the history of the Hashemite monarchy." They are also perhaps the most contested, not just politically but historically, even at the basic level of the facts of what actually happened. The central drama surrounded the events at the Zarqa military base on the evening of April 13, three days after Nabulsi's government fell.

In Hussein's telling, what occurred was nothing less than "a deeply laid, cleverly contrived plot to assassinate me, overthrow the throne and proclaim Jordan a republic." This plot's ringleader was Chief of Staff Abu Nuwar, who, the king says, had taken since Nabulsi's resignation to acting as though he were already Jordan's military dictator: chairing meetings with politicians and issuing them orders, conferring with Egyptian and Soviet officials in Damascus. The events of April 13 are described by Hussein as follows.

In the early afternoon, Abu Nuwar appeared at the royal palace and delivered an ultimatum to Talhouni, to the effect that if a government of his choosing was not formed by nine o'clock that night, the army would take matters into its own hands. In the hours that followed, numerous loyalist officers from Zarqa also showed up at the palace, warning Hussein that Nadheer Rasheed planned to move that night on the capital to seize the monarch. The good news was Rasheed's subordinates had taken a secret oath to defy his orders and stay loyal to "King and country."

Around 7 p.m., Hussein summoned Abu Nuwar to confront him with the information he had received. Before the chief of staff could reply, a phone call came in reporting chaos at Zarqa, where loyalist troops were fighting their own officers. Changing quickly into combat uniform, the king raced to the scene with Abu Nuwar and his military-veteran uncle, Sharif Nasser bin Jamil. On the roads, they encountered trucks of agitated loyalist troops, who were overjoyed to see the king and started chanting for Abu Nuwar's death. "Trembling with fright," the chief of staff begged to be let out of the car to return to Amman, a request the "disgusted" king accepted.

Once at Zarqa, Hussein restored order by the sheer force of his presence, courageously staring down machine-gun fire "so close that I not only smelt the bullets but felt their heat." Having nipped the incipient coup in the bud, he returned at midnight to the palace in Amman, where furious troops were holding Abu Nuwar captive. The king found him "in a state of complete collapse . . . crying . . . broken down . . . a pitiful sight." He chose magnanimously to spare his life, and allowed him to flee to Damascus the following day.

Perhaps unsurprisingly, this version of events has been disputed by both Abu Nuwar and Rasheed, as well as various disinterested observers and historians. Abu Nuwar claimed he was never disloyal to the king, but instead was set up by his political rivals. There had never been a coup attempt at Zarqa, only wild rumors to which the king overreacted. Rasheed too denied the existence of any kind of plot, but admitted he fled to Syria the next morning, where he met with Sarraj and was given asylum. When asked by an Al Jazeera interviewer why he fled if he had done nothing wrong, he said he did not know.

Historians themselves continue to hold contrasting interpretations of the Zarqa episode. While Avi Shlaim contends, "We may . . . confidently conclude that what took place on 13 April 1957 was not a military coup against the monarchy," Uriel Dann argues, "The evidence is convincing that Abu Nuwar did actually conspire to overthrow the monarchy . . . although he may not have intended to assassinate Hussein, and one may discount Hussein's claim that the plot was 'deeply laid' and 'cleverly contrived.' " Certainly, if it was a coup attempt, it was a remarkably incompetent one, though we have seen enough times that competence is not invariably the defining feature of such things. For whatever it may be worth, the former Syrian intelligence officer Sami Jumaa, who worked alongside Sarraj at the Deuxième Bureau at the time, wrote that Abu Nuwar told him personally when he was in Syria that he *had* been planning a coup, in collaboration with Syria's military attaché in Amman, Maj. Mustafa Ram Hamdani, but the plot was exposed to the Jordanian authorities by another Syrian official in Amman, Fuad Qodhmani.

Weighing up the competing claims, the version that comes closest to the truth may be that of Adnan Abu Odeh, a former Jordanian intelligence officer, cabinet minister, and chief of the royal court, who termed what happened a "pre-emptive coup" carried out by Hussein himself to forestall a future Free Officers' putsch that he had reason to believe was coming sooner or later. Britain's then ambassador in Amman may also have not been much wide of the mark in calling it "a confused triangular affair, a game of blind-man's-bluff with three contestants [Hussein, Nabulsi, and Abu Nuwar] bumping into each other in the dark and none knowing clearly what was happening or what he ought to do next."

Whatever exactly transpired at Zarqa, the end result was the same. Over the course of two more turbulent weeks, Hussein asserted full control over his military, shut down the political challenge from the Nabulsi-Rimawi contingent, and secured the long-term support of Washington in the process—at the price of making an enemy of Nasser.

The purge of the officer corps was a largely organic process, since most of the major figures implicated in the Zarqa events fled the country of their own accord. Beyond Rasheed and Abu Nuwar, they included the military intelligence chief, Col. Mahmud al-Musa, and Abu Nuwar's deputy, Maj. Gen. Ali al-Hiyari. Those who stayed behind were swiftly arrested. As his new chief of staff, Hussein appointed the venerable Habis al-Majali, his late grandfather's personal guard, whose loyalty was beyond question. Never again would he knowingly let the military slip into the hands of another Abu Nuwar.

The political counterattack was messier. Two days after Zarqa, a new cabinet was formed under the premiership of Dr. Hussein al-Khalidi, a former mayor of Jerusalem seen by the king as a more palatable version of Nabulsi. In a conciliatory gesture, Nabulsi himself was appointed foreign minister in the new government. Hussein's opponents, however, were in no mood for conciliation. At a large gathering in the West Bank city of Nablus one week later, hundreds of Baathists, communists, Arab nationalists, and members of Nabulsi's own Patriotic Socialists—among them twenty-three members of parliament—joined forces in a bid to bring down the Khalidi government. A statement signed by the MPs present along with some fifty other attendees contained a set of wildly unrealistic demands. These included, but were not limited to, the expulsion of the US ambassador; the federal union of Jordan with Egypt and Syria; the release of all officers arrested in connection with Zarqa; an official repudiation of the Eisenhower Doctrine; and (once again) the dismissal of the king's chief of court, Talhouni, this time with his uncle Sharif Nasser bin Jamil for good measure. As a bonus, the conference also called for nationwide strikes and protests starting April 24. The next day, Nabulsi resigned from the cabinet. The day after that, Prime Minister Khalidi tendered his own resignation.

With this, the king lost the last of his patience with the democratic "experiment" he had inaugurated with the free elections of the previous autumn. That very night, martial law was declared across Jordan. "The people of Amman came out on their balconies and leaned from upstairs windows to watch steel-helmeted troops take over the city," reported the *New York Times*. The soldiers met no resistance in the streets, which were empty but for fellow troops. The borders were sealed, and telecommunications to the outside world cut. All political parties were banned, and their assets confiscated. The coming days saw more than nine hundred arrests, according to the BBC. Nabulsi was placed under house arrest, while Rimawi managed to flee to Damascus. Trade unions were dissolved, left-wing newspapers closed, and freedoms of the press and expression sharply curtailed. "Overnight Jordan was transformed into a police state."

If in obvious ways this marked a failure of Hussein's domestic program, it was not without dividends. Watching events from Washington, President Eisenhower and Secretary Dulles were much impressed by the young king—still just twenty-one—and his forceful stand against the Red Menace. Before the month of April was out, they had approved $10 million in economic aid to Jordan, a sum followed by a further $20 million in June. At last, Hussein had secured his new superpower patron, who paid even more handsomely than Britain had. The partnership established between Jordan and the US that spring has endured ever since.

Of course, the king's troubles were far from over; in many respects, they were only beginning. On the Arab stage, the major outcome of the April crisis was the breakdown of Hussein's modus vivendi with Nasser. In a stern broadcast to the nation on the morning after the imposition of martial law, the king spoke in new tones of reproach toward Cairo, lamenting that the "brothers in Egypt" had not "cease[d] their attempts to stir up riots against Jordan and against me." He accused Egypt explicitly of links to Abu Nuwar's alleged plot to overthrow the monarchy. As the *New York Times*'s correspondent noted, "It was the first time the monarch had so openly and bitterly complained against Egypt's activities in Jordan."

For the moment, Hussein took it no further than that, and Nasser himself refrained from responding in kind. Two months later, however, Jordan expelled Egypt's military attaché in Amman, Maj. Fuad

Hilal, along with its consul general in Jerusalem, Brig. Muhammad Abd al-Aziz. Hilal was accused of tasking a Jordanian soldier with assassinating members of the royal family and government, offering him money and arms for the purpose. As for Abd al-Aziz, Hussein wrote that he was found to have organized "sabotage gangs" and smuggled weapons into Jordan from Gaza. The expulsion of the two men was followed by mutual withdrawals of ambassadors from Cairo and Amman, and the end of Egypt's (and Syria's) commitment to pay Jordan money under the agreement signed back in January.

The gloves, in other words, were fast coming off, ensuring Hussein would enjoy no respite as the storms of 1957 gave way to the momentous convulsions of 1958.

13

THE LONG ARMS
OF DAMASCUS

THE UNION OF EGYPT WITH SYRIA IN FEBRUARY 1958 perturbed King Hussein for much the same reason it did Lebanon's President Chamoun. All of a sudden, his most dangerous Arab antagonist, Nasser, was standing on his border, right on his doorstep, towering over his smaller and weaker country, shoulder to shoulder with his infamously brutal henchman, Sarraj.

Syria—or the "northern province" of the UAR, as it was now known—had already given safe haven to Jordan's "Free Officers" and other oppositionists who had fled Amman in the wake of the Zarqa saga. In the hands of Nasser and Sarraj, Hussein knew, Syria would become the inexhaustible wellspring of danger and destabilization to Jordan that it also would be to Lebanon (and Iraq). Again as in Lebanon, there was also the risk—which looked greater at the time than it does to us in retrospect—that the very entity and existence of Jordan may not long survive before being swallowed up, in part or in whole, by its aggressive neighbor.

Hussein's first instinct, therefore, was to bolster his defenses. This he did by rapidly engineering a federal union between the kindred Hashemite kingdoms of Jordan and Iraq, declared to the world as the "Hashemite Arab Federation" on February 14, 1958. It was a looser union than the UAR, with both countries largely remaining distinct sovereign entities. In theory, their armed forces, economies, and foreign policy became one and the same. Iraq's King Faysal II was the union's nominal head, while its capital would alternate every six months between Baghdad and Amman. Hussein tried his best to market the arrangement as the "true" expression of Arab unity, as opposed to Nasser's fake one, emphasizing the proud heritage of the Hashemites as historical guardians of Mecca and leaders of the Great Arab Revolt against the Ottomans. The appeal may have struck a chord in certain quarters, including among Hashemite partisans in Syria. (It's often overlooked that the pro-Hashemite People's Party won more votes than any other in Syria's elections of both 1954 and 1961.) All the same, it would be difficult to argue the federation fired the hearts of the Arab masses to the same extent that Nasser's UAR did.

Etiquette dictated that Nasser congratulate Faysal II on the new union, but it was not long at all before his feud with Hussein was resumed, this time with new intensity. Only the next month, Jordan expelled another Egyptian consul from Jerusalem, on charges of "stirring up discontent against the government." By the time summer arrived, the "cold" war between the two was on the verge of turning unmistakably hot.

In early July, Hussein received reports from US diplomats in Amman of a credible military-coup threat in Jordan, sponsored by the UAR. The plot's key figure was Lt. Col. Mahmud al-Rusan, recently returned from a posting at Jordan's embassy in Washington, where his phone had been tapped by the FBI. Fellow officers involved included his brother Muhammad al-Rusan and Col. Mahmud al-Musa. The latter had been Jordan's chief of military intelligence until fleeing after Zarqa to Damascus, where he remained, and was now said to be the link between Rusan and Sarraj, the plot's mastermind.

The basic plan was to kill Hussein in the royal palace, proclaim a republic, and—if all went well—bring Jordan into the UAR. The similarities with what did indeed transpire in Baghdad just days later may be no coincidence. Hussein charges in his memoir that the two plots were linked, and intended to be carried out simultaneously.

Rusan was swiftly arrested, along with some forty more officers of Nasserist sympathies. The immediate threat to Jordan was contained. Hussein said he then informed the Iraqis of what he had learned, but they neglected to take his warnings seriously, assuring him they were more than capable of looking after themselves. Events would very soon prove them fatally mistaken. In a striking irony, it may have been precisely the discovery of the Rusan plot that set the Iraqi Free Officers' wheels in motion on the night of July 13. A few days earlier, Hussein had requested that Iraq send military reinforcements to Jordan, which was after all its partner in the new Hashemite federation. The force chosen for the mission by the Iraqi command was the Twentieth Brigade, stationed at Jalawla by the Iranian border. It was as this brigade was en route to Jordan that the Free Officer Abd al-Salam Aref took it over and made instead for the royal palace in Baghdad.

The bloodbath in Iraq was devastating on many levels for Hussein, who had personally been very close to his cousin King Faysal II. Born in the same year, they had played together as children, attended Harrow together, and become kings on the very same day. He was "my friend and brother in all but name," wrote Hussein. That this mild-mannered, soft-spoken man of just twenty-three, who had once gifted Hussein his favorite bicycle, had been gunned down in cold blood along with the rest of his family was understandably distressing to learn.

Moreover, there were numerous Jordanians among the victims in Iraq, including the elder statesmen Ibrahim Hashem and Sulayman Tuqan, both beaten to death by the mob at the New Baghdad Hotel. They had been in Iraq in their capacities as senior officials within the Hashemite federation. Quite apart from the human tragedy involved, their killings underscored in the bloodiest possible fashion that this flagship project of Hussein's had come to a permanent end.

Or had it? The king's impetuous first reaction on July 14 was to send Jordan's army into Iraq on a quixotic mission to avenge the House of Hashem and restore its authority by force. His uncle, Sharif Nasser bin Jamil, had made it 240 kilometers inside Iraqi territory at the head of an expeditionary force before Hussein was persuaded to call him back. Had he not done so, the situation might have escalated sharply: Nasser declared two days later that he would regard any attack on republican Iraq as one on the UAR itself.

His senses recovered, Hussein's thoughts turned to shoring up his own rule at home. Martial law was declared again; the army was repurged of possible insurrectionists, and the redoubtable Habis al-Majali appointed its commander in chief. Yet the exceptional times, it was felt, called for even more exceptional measures. In Lebanon, US Marines had landed on the beaches south of Beirut on July 15, in response to President Chamoun's urgent appeal. The following day, Jordan petitioned the Western powers for a similar gesture of support. Deciding that, in the words of British prime minister Macmillan, "we would not forgive ourselves if the King were murdered tomorrow, like the Royal Family of Iraq," Britain agreed to send in two battalions of paratroopers, one artillery regiment, and six Royal Air Force Hunter fighters from its base in Cyprus. Though they did little, and left the country three months later, Hussein writes that their presence had an important psychological effect, not least on him. "The famous red berets in the streets made people realise we were not alone, that this was no time for despair."

Even so, few observers were optimistic about Jordan's prospects going forward. There was, in fact, near consensus that it was only a matter of time before its Hashemites met the same fate as their Iraqi cousins. How could they not? If a coup could happen so easily in Iraq—a far larger, stronger, and richer state than Jordan—what was to stop one happening in Amman? It was the ineluctable arc of history, against which resistance was futile. "However much one may admire the courage of this lonely young king, it is difficult to avoid the conclusion his days are numbered," said the former British diplomat Anthony Nutting, who was as sharp an observer of Arab affairs as Britain then had. The British ambassador to Amman at the time, Charles Johnston, admitted in private that "there is a school of thought in London and Washington which believes that Jordan is a dead loss and that the best thing is to . . . let Nasser have it." In the words of Hussein's nephew, Prince Talal bin Muhammad, "Our obituary was in the paper every week."

Yet Hussein clung stubbornly on, much to the irritation of Nasser, who upped his rhetorical attacks considerably in the heady wake of the Iraqi "revolution." Scarcely had the blood of the royal family members dried when Nasser declared before a crowd in Damascus on July 18 that the "banner of freedom" that now fluttered over Baghdad would soon be raised in Amman too. Four days later he went further, in an extended personal attack on Hussein, whom he compared to his assassinated grandfather Abdallah, implying none too subtly that the grandson would meet the same grisly end:

> The king of Jordan . . . has gone astray, and turned against the people and their struggle; deceived the people; and sided with imperialism, and opened his country to imperialism. . . .
>
> What is Hussein doing today, my brothers? What is he doing in his fortress in Amman? He says he is "continuing the mission"; what mission is Hussein continuing today? The mission of King Abdallah, who betrayed us in 1948. Today, Hussein—my brothers—continues the mission of his grandfather King Abdallah in 1948, who deceived us, and deceived the Arabs everywhere. . . . Hussein today continues the mission of inviting the English to occupy his country. . . .
>
> Today—my brothers—there is treason and occupation in Jordan, [but] the treason shall end, and the occupation shall end, and the people of Jordan shall be victorious.

This being the official and public stance of the UAR's president, it naturally wasn't long before Sarraj and his colleagues in the "northern province" were back to their antics.

On the morning of November 10, 1958, Hussein took off from Amman in his grandfather's old twin-engine de Havilland Dove

plane, piloting the aircraft himself. Also on board were his uncle
Sharif Nasser; his copilot Jock Dalgleish, a Royal Air Force veteran;
another British friend, Maurice Raynor, who managed the king's
cars; and two Jordanian pilots who would fly the plane home once it
arrived at its destination. The British forces that had come to Jordan
after the Baghdad coup had just departed, and, in Hussein's words,
"I felt the crisis had abated sufficiently to enable me to take a short
holiday." His plan was to spend three weeks in Lausanne with his
mother, Zein, daughter Alia, and other family members, celebrating
his twenty-third birthday at the Beau-Rivage Palace hotel overlooking Lake Geneva.

Others had different plans for the king that morning. As his plane
entered Syrian airspace and neared the outskirts of Damascus, he was
told by Syrian air traffic control that he lacked clearance to overfly,
and had to land at the Damascus airport. This was strange to hear, as
he had already been in touch with air traffic control when he crossed
the border, at which time he was given permission to proceed. He
protested that he had already received clearance and would continue
on his course toward Cyprus. When the Syrians repeated their insistence that he land at Damascus, Hussein turned the plane around
back in the direction of Amman, lowering his altitude in the hope of
avoiding radar detection.

Moments later, one of the Jordanian pilots in the back yelled that
he could see two MiG fighters overhead. As these descended toward
Hussein's plane, they "turned across our path, gained height, and
dived at us in what is known as a quarter attack." The king "tore the
old Dove round in a turn" before handing the controls to Dalgleish.
Only by taking continuous evasive action from the MiGs' repeated
dives did the Scotsman steer them back to the safety of Jordan's airspace in one piece.

As far as Hussein was concerned, this was another clear attempt
to assassinate him. "My Dove was well known and could never have
been mistaken for any other aircraft. It had the Royal Jordanian Air
Force markings and carried the royal coat of arms and the royal flag.

It had flown to Damascus several times, once with me on an official visit. . . . Only one conclusion was possible: they hoped to kill us."

Hussein never did get to Lausanne for his birthday, which he spent at home in Jordan. Nor could he long enjoy respite from the plots to knock him off his throne, which only proliferated further thereafter. In March 1959, shortly before he left on an official trip to the US, he learned from his intelligence service of a new UAR-backed coup in the works. This time, the protagonist was the army's chief of staff, Maj. Gen. Sadiq al-Sharaa, in collusion with his brother, Col. Salah al-Sharaa, a military attaché in Bonn. The plan, according to Hussein, was to seize army headquarters while he was away in the US, assassinate the army commander, and "open up with guns on the Zahran Palace, where my family was living."

As with Zarqa two years earlier, certain elements of this story have been called into question. Sharaa himself did admit to the journalist Peter Snow that he planned a coup, but claimed its target was only the army leadership, not the monarch. In any event, the brothers Sharaa were both sentenced to death, though Sadiq's sentence was commuted to life imprisonment, while Salah escaped to the UAR.

Thereafter, the attempts to kill Hussein reached a frequency and variety to rival the exploding cigars and poisoned milkshakes with which the CIA is said to have tried to eliminate Fidel Castro. "So cunning and varied and constant have been the plots against my person that sometimes I feel like the central character in a detective novel," the king wrote. There was, for instance, the time his nasal drops were found to contain an acid so powerful it peeled the metal off the fittings in one of the palace sinks. There was also the curious case of the dead cats. In the span of three days, over a dozen stray cats were found lifeless around the palace grounds. Upon investigation, one of the cooks confessed he had been recruited by Sarraj's Bureau in Damascus to poison the king's food. He had incautiously experimented on the cats to work out the required dosage.

It was in the midst of this climate, in May 1959, two months after the foiling of the Sharaa plot, that the king called on Hazzaa al-Majali—"one of Jordan's greatest patriots and one of my firmest friends"—to return for a second term as prime minister. Choosing this moment to appoint the man whose name was indelibly associated with the Baghdad Pact furor was in itself a clear statement by Hussein. The threat posed to Jordan by the UAR had never been greater, and the king needed a premier who was up to the fight. Just over one year later, that premier was blown up in the heart of the capital. Hussein called it "the worst outrage in the history of Jordan."

Before returning to the events of that day, some words should be said about the man Hazzaa al-Majali himself. As with Kamel Mrowa, we cannot understand Majali's death without first knowing something of his life. It is, in fact, an illuminating story on many levels, a microcosm of Jordan's modern history as a whole. Set alongside the biographies of Nasser and Mrowa, it underscores the striking diversity of the peoples who have come to be collectively termed "the Arabs," and how much the political differences for which these men died—or, in Nasser's case, killed—were products of the radically contrasting circumstances of their births.

★

HAZZAA BARAKAT ABD al-Qadir Saleh Muhammad Al-Majali was born on an unknown date in 1918. His father, Barakat, hailed from the small but historic town of Karak, 130 kilometers south of Amman. A site of significance since biblical times, Karak's foremost feature has long been its large stone citadel, built by the Crusaders who conquered it in the early twelfth century. This impressive structure, later used by the famous Salah al-Din (Saladin), who evicted the Crusaders in 1188, still dominates the skyline of the town today. To its east, the terrain is the rocky, gravelly moonscape of the desert that extends without interruption to the Saudi Arabian border. To the citadel's west, by contrast, one enjoys a commanding view of the dramatic swoop downward to the Dead Sea and surrounding plains more than one thousand meters below, with the peaks of the West Bank on the distant horizon.

The Majalis have been prominent in Karak for centuries, though they didn't always live there. Like many Arab tribes, they trace their earliest origins to the Arabian Peninsula; in their case, to the area of al-Hota in what is now Saudi Arabia, some 150 kilometers south of Riyadh. They belong to the broader tribal confederation known as the Banu Tamim, which makes them distant relatives of the ruling family of Qatar, the Al Thani, as well as other tribes spread across the Arabian Gulf, Iraq, Syria, and elsewhere. By the seventeenth century, they were settled in the West Bank town of Hebron. When one of their members committed a murder, however, they were banished from the area in keeping with tribal custom, and crossed the valley to settle in the nearest town on the East Bank, which happened to be Karak. This was the incident that gave them the name Majali, literally meaning "those banished for committing an offense."

Renowned for their martial prowess in battles with rival tribes, over time the Majalis established themselves as Karak's most powerful clan, and a frequent thorn in the side of their nominal Ottoman overlords. In 1910, they led a violent revolt against an effort to forcibly conscript the town's men into the Ottoman army. For eight days, Turkish troops and officials in Karak were killed or besieged inside the citadel, as their offices were sacked and their records torched. Only by sending reinforcements from Damascus were the Ottomans finally able to crush the rebellion with pitiless force.

When Ottoman rule collapsed eight years later in the course of World War I, Karak's Sheikh Rufayfan al-Majali emerged as an important ally of the emir (later king) Abdallah in establishing his new Hashemite monarchy. Majalis have played leading roles in Jordanian public life ever since. We have already encountered General (later Field Marshal) Habis al-Majali—Rufayfan's son, and Hazzaa's brother-in-law—who rose to become a storied commander in chief, celebrated as the "*beau sabreur*" of the Jordanian army. Just as Hazzaa served twice as prime minister, so did his cousin, Abd al-Salam al-Majali. One of the latter's brothers, Abd al-Hadi, became speaker of parliament, while another, Abd al-Wahhab, was an MP and cabinet minister. Three of Hazzaa's sons—Amjad, Ayman, and Hussein—have held senior military and government positions, including deputy prime minister, while Abd al-Salam's son, Samer al-Majali, is the CEO of Jordan's national airline, Royal Jordanian.

★

THE BIRTH OF BABY HAZZAA came just as the Ottomans were in the process of being driven out of Jordan in 1918. His father was away fighting in the Arab Revolt at the time, and so his mother, Amneh—a member of the Abu Wendi tribe from the Balqa region, southwest of Amman—was living with her parents in tents outside the village of Maeen when she gave birth. Once the Arab army entered Damascus in triumph in October 1918, Barakat returned to Karak and asked his wife to join him with their son, but she refused, and they divorced. The infant thus never knew or so much as laid eyes on his father. Nor would he be much closer to his mother, who soon left him to be raised by her parents when she remarried.

Unfortunate though this was for the young boy, it had certain advantages, in that his mother's father happened to be the head sheikh of his tribe. This meant Hazzaa grew up in comparative comfort, showered with gifts and treated by members of the extended clan as though he were the sheikh's own son. Still, it was hardly a life of material luxury. Theirs was a true Bedouin existence: living as nomads in tents; migrating with the seasons; raising livestock and living off its milk and meat, plus the few fruits and vegetables they managed to grow in and around Maeen. Recreation consisted of riding camels or horses, though Hazzaa recalled in his memoir that his favorite pastime was herding sheep.

At age five, Hazzaa received his first dose of education, when his grandfather brought him a cleric to teach him the Qur'an. By age ten, he had completed the holy book; memorized the seven epic poems of the classical Arabic canon; and received instruction in history, geography, and other subjects. Soon afterward, his father—who made a habit of visiting him once or twice a year—took him to live with him in Karak for the first time.

It was only here, when Hazzaa was almost an adolescent, that he first attended an actual school, where his teachers included two future prime ministers, Sulayman al-Nabulsi and Fawzi al-Mulqi. Despite this disadvantage, he quickly outpaced his peers academically, becoming the top student of the class. In consequence, he progressed to a secondary school in Salt, then the only such school in all of Jordan. Among his classmates here were the girl he later married, and another future premier, Wasfi al-Tal (who was also destined to be assassinated, in 1971).

After finishing school, he found work as a land surveyor near the northern town of Irbid, where he was briefly kidnapped by Palestinian militants. Once released, he continued surveying in and around Amman, until he resigned after a dispute with his manager.

There now began a low period for Hazzaa. He spent three months unemployed, until landing a menial job as a clerk at a court in Madaba, thirty kilometers southwest of the capital. Here, he says, his life changed completely—for the worse. He began to smoke and drink heavily. World War II broke out, bringing with it steep inflation and other economic misery. His salary could no longer sustain him. He fell into gambling, and quickly racked up hefty debts. When his boss refused to promote him, he quit his job and moved back to Karak, broke and unemployed once again, a lost young man with few apparent prospects.

He later described this time in Karak as the hardest of his life. He sank further into gambling, "night and day," frequenting the campsites of "gypsies" who invariably cleaned him out of what little he had in his pockets. His physical health declined. "My future was about to vanish altogether, until suddenly I woke up."

It was a woman who did it. Samiha al-Majali was a distant cousin of noble birth, a daughter of the Majali chieftain, the aforementioned Sheikh Rufayfan Pasha. Hazzaa had known her since their school days together in Salt, when a bond had formed between them, and they had made a mutual promise to marry one day. Hearing what had lately become of Hazzaa, however, Samiha was having second thoughts. She gave him an ultimatum: either he cleaned up his act and went to college, or she was finished with him.

This did the trick. Hazzaa persuaded his father to sell a plot of land to raise enough money to send him to study law at Damascus University (then called The Syrian University). He arrived in the Syrian capital in 1943 a new man: serious and studious, keeping away from folly and distraction. After scoring well in the first year's exams, he spent the summer break in Karak, where at last he was engaged to Samiha. "I almost flew with happiness," he wrote. "I don't think my bones have ever known that kind of ecstasy, nor has anything strengthened my confidence in myself and my future like that sublime moment."

Returning to Damascus for the new academic year of 1944–45, Hazzaa witnessed the closing act of the Second World War, including the high drama of what came to be known as the "Levant Crisis." After mass protests demanding the departure of Syria's French authorities, France responded with deadly military attacks on Damascus. These were met with British intervention to stop the French assault and, ultimately, secure Syria's independence in 1946. "When the fighting stopped, all the people came out of their homes to welcome the British forces and jeer at the withdrawing French," Hazzaa wrote. One sees here, perhaps, an early clue to the favorable light in which he later regarded British policy in the Arab world.

After another successful year of studies, he once again spent the summer in Karak, where he finally married Samiha. For their honeymoon, they toured Amman, Jerusalem, and Jaffa. The newlyweds then lived together in Damascus while Hazzaa completed his third and final academic year.

Following graduation in the summer of 1946, Hazzaa and the now-pregnant Samiha returned to Jordan. Everything was looking up at last: a degree, a wife, a child on the way, and no more war. A particular high point of the year was August 21, when he received his Jordanian law license on the same day his first son, Amjad, was born. The very next morning, he received his first case as a lawyer, representing an acquaintance at a court in Karak.

The young and ambitious Hazzaa quickly proved an effective barrister, not least in Karak, where his university education set him apart from the competition. His portrait of the legal profession in his hometown at this time makes for amusing reading. Never before had any local lawyer undertaken to actually study law in the formal sense. Most were borderline illiterate. Small wonder Hazzaa soon became the most sought-after lawyer in town, earning a handsome income.

Before long, he began taking cases elsewhere: in the towns of Maan and Tafila, and then in Amman, including at the highest court in the land, the Court of Appeals. Cutting a swath as a hotshot lawyer in the capital opened not a few doors for Hazzaa, who began rubbing shoulders with government officials and other persons of standing. By his own admission, his surname was certainly no obstacle to this rapid career advancement.

So dizzying, indeed, was his rise that in early 1947 King Abdallah asked that he work as a protocol employee at the royal palace. At first, Hazzaa was of two minds. Knowing nothing of the work, he feared he would be ill-suited to it, in contrast to his runaway success as a lawyer. His wife opposed the idea, preferring they stay in Karak "away from the spotlight." (It's sobering to reflect how prescient her instinct proved.) On the other hand, Hazzaa had begun to acquire a taste for politics in the clubs and cafés of Amman, and saw himself as a statesman in the making. The chance to work for the king was a golden ticket. At the end of the day, a royal request was not to be refused.

With a reluctant Samiha, then, he moved full-time to Amman to start his new life in the royal court. It would indeed prove the ideal launchpad for his political ambitions. Not only did he have frequent personal interactions with the king, but he met "all the politicians in Jordan." Before long, he was accompanying Abdallah on trips abroad, hobnobbing with regional leaders, and amassing an invaluable Rolodex of contacts.

First, however, came the war of 1948, in which Jordan was a frontline participant. Not being a military man himself, Hazzaa took no significant part in the combat, though he did once race to Karak with one hundred rifles to distribute to local volunteers on hearing reports the Israelis had attacked the plains by the Dead Sea beneath the town. The incursion soon ended, but a few days later Hazzaa noticed boats gathering on the other side of the Dead Sea. Fearing a second assault, he phoned Abdallah and asked if the Iraqi or Egyptian air forces might be prevailed on to strike the vessels. It perhaps says something about the overall effectiveness of the Arab war effort that when two Iraqi planes did show up, they opened fire not on the Israelis but on Hazzaa and his fellow Jordanians.

There soon came the temporary truce of June 1948, during which Hazzaa accompanied the king on an official trip to Cairo. After a day of talks between Abdallah and his Egyptian counterpart Farouk, the Jordanians were surprised to find their hosts had arranged an evening party for them at the Saffron Palace, where they were staying. Singers including the famous Umm Kulthum performed live on a stage. There was theater, music, and dance. Abdallah lasted until two-thirty in the morning before retiring to bed, but Hazzaa and the others made a full night of it. Staggering back to his room at daybreak, Hazzaa happened upon Abdallah, already awake again, performing the dawn prayer. Acting on sheer, unthinking instinct, Hazzaa rushed to join in behind him. When the rest of the Jordanians finally surfaced later that morning for breakfast, the king scolded them all for missing the prayer—except Hazzaa, whose exemplary piety he singled out for praise, and rewarded with a generous sum to spend in Cairo's shops before their departure.

After Cairo, Hazzaa again joined Abdallah on a trip to Riyadh, where they met King Abd al-Aziz (aka Ibn Saud). This was followed by a stopover in Baghdad to see the regent Abd al-Ilah. In the span of a few days, Hazzaa had shared the company of three kings and a regent—this while only thirty years old.

In late 1948, Hazzaa was appointed mayor of Amman, against the objections of then–prime minister Tawfiq Abu al-Huda, who thought him too junior in age and rank. The king overruled him, and Hazzaa's relations with Abu al-Huda would stay frosty for years to come. As mayor, Hazzaa says, he expanded Amman's roads, as well as its water network. He also kept up many of his palace duties in parallel, attending the king's gatherings every evening and accompanying him on travels both inside and outside the country.

Nor did Hazzaa's meteoric rise show any sign of flagging thereafter. In 1950, he was given his first ministerial post, in the cabinet of Premier Samir al-Rifai, who would prove his key ally against Abu al-Huda going forward. One of his fellow ministers in this government was his old teacher, the left-wing Sulayman al-Nabulsi, only recently released from nine months' imprisonment for criticizing the Anglo-Jordanian Treaty.

Rifai's cabinet endured until the assassination of Abdallah in 1951, when the premier stepped down while the crucial and sensitive question of the royal succession was resolved. A new cabinet was then formed by Abu al-Huda, from which Majali was excluded. When parliamentary elections were held weeks later, Hazzaa ran for a seat in Karak and won.

Having neither a cabinet role to keep him busy nor Abdallah's court to attend, Hazzaa returned for the time being to his legal work. Opening an office in Amman, he raked in a steady income—he says this was the first time he ever held deposits in a bank account and carried his own checkbook. The money was doubtless helpful in providing for his growing family. A second son, Ayman, had been born in 1949, followed by a daughter, Taghrid, in 1950.

It would be two years before he was back in government, this time under Prime Minister Fawzi al-Mulqi (another former teacher from his Karak school days). That cabinet fell the following year, however, to be replaced by another under Abu al-Huda.

In opposition again, it was at this time, in 1954, that Majali and a number of friends decided to form a political party, of which he became the inaugural secretary. Ironically—given its later Nasserist associations—this was none other than the Patriotic Socialist Party. He writes that its initial aims were to offer an alternative to the communists and Baathists, and to advocate for federal union with Hashemite Iraq and Syria. Clearly, the party line and ethos changed considerably once Nabulsi replaced Majali as leader.

After another round of elections in October 1954, in which Majali retained his seat, the new King Hussein invited Abu al-Huda to form another cabinet, on condition that he include several of his opponents, Majali among them. It was thus that Hazzaa came to be in government at the outset of the crunch year of 1955—the year of Nasser's emergence on the Arab stage, culminating in Majali's ill-fated first premiership.

In April of that year, Majali attended the famous Bandung Conference, where he met Nasser himself, as well as Prince (later King) Faysal of Saudi Arabia, and delegates from all over Asia and Africa. The next month, he was promoted to the significant post of interior minister in a new government led by Said al-Mufti. On a sadder note, his father passed away the same year—a deep loss for which, he says, he felt consoled by the knowledge that his father respected and admired the path his son's life had ended up taking.

It was on December 15, 1955, that Hazzaa then became prime minister himself, only to resign just five days later—as we have seen—amid riots of an unprecedented scale against his bid to bring Jordan into the Baghdad Pact.

The aftermath of that failed first premiership marked a second low in Majali's life. At first, he hardly left his house. People he had thought were friends turned their backs on him. Out of morbid curiosity, he read everything the Cairo and Damascus papers had written about him, which he described as "lies and fabrications without beginning nor end." In a mood of rare self-pity, he wondered to himself: "What crime did I commit . . . ? Was it because I strove for the good of my country? Did I truly deserve all these attacks from a people I loved with all my heart, whose demands I adopted, and whose rights I defended with all my power?"

For over two years, he drifted in the political wilderness. In 1956, he resigned from parliament, never to return. A weekly newspaper he launched in April of that year, *Sawt al-Urdun* (The voice of Jordan), lasted only a few months. It must be recalled this was the height of King Hussein's quasi-Nasserist phase, when he dismissed Britain's Glubb and moved closer to Cairo, not least after Suez. In the circumstances, it was no surprise a man of Majali's politics should have found himself out of favor.

By the same token, after Hussein's war with Nabulsi, and the Zarqa episode, and the subsequent fallout with Nasser, then the creation of the UAR, it became possible—indeed desirable—to bring Majali back in from the cold once again. It is no coincidence that Hazzaa's brother-in-law Habis al-Majali became army commander at this same time; in both cases, the king was promoting the Bedouin East Bankers who had always been the shield and backbone of the monarchy, and of whose loyalty he could be absolutely assured.

The first concrete step in Hazzaa's rehabilitation was his appointment as minister of the royal court in 1958, in another cabinet led by his old friend Samir al-Rifai. It was when Rifai stepped down as premier on May 5, 1959, that Majali took his place, reportedly with the backing of the king's influential mother, Queen Zein.

Once again, the chain of recent events preceding this moment must be recalled: the Rusan plot of July 1958, the coup in Baghdad that same month, the Syrian MiG incident of November 1958, then the Sharaa plot just two months before Majali took office. He could have been under no illusions whatever about the dangers of the times and the risks he was assuming.

It was a rocky ride from the get-go. The UAR press and radio assailed Majali from the moment news broke that he was to head the new government, alleging he would once again try to bring Jordan into the Baghdad Pact—a charge he had to explicitly deny.

By early 1960, Majali was in Nasserist eyes "an object of hate second only to Hussein himself." In March of that year, Jordan's security forces arrested two people, one a former police officer, on charges of entering the country from Syria with the intention of assassinating Majali. At a press conference in Amman, one of the men publicly asserted he had been tasked with the mission by Rimawi and Abu Nuwar—still then in Damascus, where they had fled in 1957—saying he received money, a fake passport, and a pistol for the purpose.

The foiling of a second plot against Majali's life was announced in July. Hussein recalls in his memoir that Majali was advised, in light of these discoveries, to reduce the number of visitors permitted into his office. He paid no heed.

One month later, the assassins succeeded.

★

AT PRECISELY 10:25 ON the morning of November 16, 2021, an athletic young Jordanian policeman in a light blue uniform opened the door of the brand-new olive-gray Land Rover Defender he had parked outside the entrance of my Amman hotel, and gestured for me to get in.

I had rented my own car from the airport, and was more than happy to drive myself to meet my interviewee, but he had proved conspicuously reticent about the location of his office, and insisted on arranging my transport himself. Only later did I surmise this was a security precaution.

After a drive of no more than five minutes through the residential neighborhoods of West Amman, the policeman pulled up at the side of a multistory villa. Waiting outside was a courteous gentleman in a suit jacket, who showed me indoors. He was not my interviewee. Only once the pair of us rode an elevator to an upstairs floor did I at last see the man I had flown from Beirut to meet: Gen. Hussein Hazzaa al-Majali, the sixty-one-year-old youngest son of the late prime minister Hazzaa.

Tall, with a large head and frame, Hussein is himself a prime example of the enduring prominence of Majalis in Jordanian life. A four-star general, he has held such sensitive posts as commander of the Royal Guard and head of the late King Hussein's personal security detail. When the king lay dying of cancer in Rochester's Mayo Clinic in 1998 and 1999, Majali spent more time by his side than any other person but his wife, Queen Noor. More recently, he has served as Jordan's ambassador to Bahrain, director of public security, and interior minister between the fraught years of 2013 and 2015, when the war in neighboring Syria was at its most horrific, and jihadists abruptly seized one-third of the territory of Iraq, menacing the region. When Islamic State militants infamously burned a captured Jordanian pilot to death in a metal cage in 2015, it was Majali who, as interior minister, signed the order to retaliate by executing two prominent jihadist prisoners in Jordan the next day. In person, his demeanor is affably gruff, stern yet warm, impeccably polite, but with a sense of humor the formalities could not quite stifle. Deadly serious one minute, he breaks out in a belly laugh the next. Taking me on a short drive in the Defender after our interview, he apologized for not wearing a seat belt, explaining that his security men say he'll escape faster without one if the car comes under armed attack. I asked whether I should buckle my own belt in that case. "No, no," he replied in his loud, deep voice, eyes twinkling. "We'll run together."

Over traditional Arabic coffee, we spoke for more than an hour on armchairs by the large window of his office, a modest-sized space with a contemporary feel, with artworks on the walls depicting downtown Amman and a portrait of King Hussein. On a bookshelf by his desk, I noticed Karen Armstrong's *Jerusalem*. Based on the information he provided me, plus the verdict delivered by the Jordanian court that tried those charged with killing his father at the time, and further details published in the local and international press, as well as the memoirs of various people involved, it has been possible to piece together the following about the operation that assassinated Hazzaa al-Majali.

On the night of Sunday, August 28, 1960—the last night of Majali's life—two men employed in his office entered the building and
surreptitiously planted the explosives that would detonate the following day. Their names were Shaker al-Dabbas and Kamal al-Shamut.
They had been recruited by the Deuxième Bureau in Damascus,
run by Sarraj, then interior minister of the UAR's "northern province." It is significant that Sarraj's then colleague at the Bureau, Sami
Jumaa, freely admits to this in his memoir, praising the bomber Dabbas as a "patriot," and boasting that the operation demonstrated the
"long arms" of the Bureau inside Jordan.

Having carried out their mission, Dabbas and Shamut made haste
for the Syrian border, crossing it early on the morning of the twenty-
ninth, before the bombs had detonated. Living thereafter as guests of
the UAR, the men were sheltered from arrest, prosecution, and the
death sentences handed to them in absentia by the Jordanian judiciary. It has been said they eventually relocated to Egypt.

Four months to the day after the blast, on December 29, 1960, Jordan's State Security Court delivered a guilty verdict against eleven
men charged with involvement in the crime. All were sentenced to
death: four in person, seven in absentia. Aside from Dabbas and Shamut, they included another of Sarraj's colleagues at the Bureau, Col.
Burhan Adham, previously involved in both Lebanon's 1958 Summer of Blood and Iraq's 1959 Shawwaf revolt. The court's verdict
said two of the men sentenced, Karim Shaqra and Zayn al-Din Nimr
Ubayd, were linked to Syrian-registered cars used in the operation.
Two days after the verdict came down, the four convicts held in custody were publicly hanged in the courtyard of downtown Amman's
Grand Husseini Mosque.

Among the questions I put to Hussein al-Majali was whether
it was possible to access any documents pertaining to the official
investigation into the crime, to shed light on how the authorities
came to identify these particular eleven individuals as culpable.
He replied that even he was not privy to this information. There
are, he said, two highly classified folders held by the Criminal

Information Department of Jordan's Public Security Directorate (which he headed himself between 2010 and 2013). One folder concerns the assassination of King Abdallah I; the second, that of his father.

"They're two huge files," he said. "State secrets . . . I saw the two files, but I never dared to open them."

★

IT REMAINS TO BE SAID why the UAR decided to assassinate Majali at that particular time. The broad context is, of course, the long-running feud between Cairo and Amman already explored in some detail above.

More specifically, the relevant context is the cracks that were appearing in the union between Egypt and Syria by the summer of 1960, which Amman Radio was not shy about highlighting and encouraging. It will be recalled that, in October 1959, Nasser had felt it necessary to transfer his army commander, Field Marshal Abd al-Hakim Amer, to Syria to redress the discontent that even then was an open secret. Two months later, the architects of the union themselves—Syria's Baathists—withdrew from the UAR government, emptying it of the only Syrian political force that had ever much wanted union to begin with.

As was made clear in Abu Zaabal, in Mosul, in Lebanon, and in the killings of Farajallah al-Helu and other communists in Syria, Nasser was fully prepared to shed the blood of those who threatened, or were thought to threaten, the union's prospects of survival. He was never more dangerous than when he felt his back was against the wall and his personal prestige was at stake. By June 1960, Nasser was in a foul mood indeed with King Hussein, to judge by a speech he delivered in Alexandria's Manshiya Square. Returning once again to a favorite trope, that of comparing Hussein to his grandfather Abdallah, Nasser bluntly declared that all "servants of imperialism" would be killed just as Abdallah and Nuri al-Said had been:

There remains a small group of servants of imperialism, con-
trolled by imperialism, whose fate shall be the fate of Nuri
al-Said. . . . The servants of imperialism may be able to go on
a little longer, but where is their escape from their certain fate?
The fate of Nuri al-Said, and of King Abdallah; where is the
escape from that fate? The people—my brother citizens—shall
be victorious, and shall eliminate the servants of imperialism,
just as they eliminated their grandfathers before them.

It is worth quoting some more from the speech, for it offers rich
insight into the violence of Nasser's mindset at the time, just two
months before Majali's assassination. Even by his standards, this was
fanatical language: a celebration of the murder and mutilation of
Nuri al-Said, and a broad-daylight call for the same to be inflicted
on others.

The people—brother citizens—may endure patiently for a little
while longer, and the traitors among the servants of imperialism
may feel they have won, and become powerful, but they will
find themselves suddenly in the abyss, just as Nuri al-Said did.
He was running through the streets disguised as a woman, try-
ing to flee from his certain fate. Did his disguise enable him—
brother citizens—to escape his certain fate? Destiny was waiting
for him, whether he wore men's or women's clothes, because that
destiny is the fate of traitors among the servants of imperialism.
*   The Arab nation, in order to be victorious, and to attain*
its independence, finds that its first duty is to rid itself of the
servants of imperialism. When we are rid—my brothers—of
the servants of imperialism, the path to eliminating imperial-
ism is paved before us, for imperialism can find no foothold for
itself in our countries except by depending on the traitors among
the servants of imperialism. If these traitors among the servants
of imperialism are eliminated, imperialism collapses and van-
ishes from existence. . . . The Arab people . . . have sworn

to themselves to crush the traitors and servants of imperialism
beneath their feet, and to cleanse their air and soil of every agent
of imperialism.

This, then, was the music Sarraj in Syria was hearing from the
boss back in Egypt in the run-up to Majali's killing. A fascinating further insight into Sarraj's calculus at the time is provided by
Egypt's own then chief of intelligence, Salah Nasr, in his memoir.
Candidly affirming Sarraj's responsibility for the assassination, Nasr
attributes it to the power struggle then raging behind the scenes
between Sarraj and Nasser's viceroy in Damascus, Field Marshal
Amer. The two men shared a mutual feeling that the town was only
big enough for one of them, and each did everything he could to
impress upon the boss that he alone deserved to be his right-hand
man in Syria.

The squabble reached the point that, in late August 1960, Nasser
summoned both men to his beach house in al-Maamura, Alexandria, to reach a solution face-to-face in his presence. Going into
the meeting, Nasser sided with Amer. He had tired of the endless
complaints about Sarraj's heavy hand in Syria, and agreed with his
compatriot and closest comrade that the time had come to clip the
Syrian's wings and cut him down to size.

Right as the three men were meeting, however, word reached
them of Majali's assassination. That very evening, after a break,
Nasser informed them he had decided to promote Sarraj to the head
of Syria's executive council—making him, in effect, prime minister
of Syria. In Salah Nasr's words, there is "no doubt" the decision was
a direct result of the Majali news. Soon afterward, Amer was recalled
from Damascus to spend a period back in Egypt. By killing Majali,
Sarraj had proved he was the truly indispensable man, and Nasser
paid him his due reward.

(Incidentally, this is among the clearest pieces of evidence that
Nasser not only knew all about, but fully endorsed and encouraged,
the murderous conduct of Sarraj, and was not—as is sometimes

claimed by apologists—an innocent naïf kept in the dark about the misdeeds of his underlings.)

★

THE LOSS OF MAJALI was a grievous blow to King Hussein almost equal to the murder of his cousin Faysal two years earlier. Hazzaa had been "a great personal friend of mine," he wrote in his 1962 memoir. "To think of his death even now both saddens and angers me."

Just as Hussein's first instinct in 1958 had been to send his army into Iraq to avenge the fallen Hashemites, so in the immediate aftermath of Majali's killing he again thought rashly of military adventure. Three Jordanian brigades were ordered to mobilize on the Syrian border in preparation for a march on Damascus. So serious was the king that he went as far as reaching out through secret channels to the Israelis, to seek assurance they would not exploit the operation to invade Jordan from the west. This assurance was provided. Only sustained pressure from both Britain and the US eventually persuaded the king to call the scheme off.

The counsel of restraint was soon enough vindicated. One year later came the coup in Damascus that knocked Nasser back off Jordan's border, and sent Sarraj's "long arms" to a prison cell.

14

PARTNERS IN
DEFEAT

THE COLLAPSE OF THE UAR IN SEPTEMBER 1961 HER-
alded a change for the better in relations between Cairo and
Amman, albeit not immediately. The détente was complicated by
the war that broke out in Yemen in 1962, in which the two fought
on opposing sides, though Jordan's military role in the conflict was
marginal, and came to an end two years later.

Yemen aside, the general tendency in both Egypt and Jordan after
the UAR's fall was to turn inward. Nasser embarked on a program of
domestic reforms, and Hussein did much the same. In January 1962,
he appointed the young and dynamic Wasfi al-Tal as prime minister, with a mandate to develop the economy, expand and diversify national income, root out corruption and nepotism, liberalize
politically, and improve state finances, including by cutting military expenditure. The cabinet Tal formed has been called the best
Jordan has ever had. All twelve ministers held university degrees,
three of them doctorates. Political prisoners were released (except
for communists) and restrictions on press freedom were relaxed.
The parliamentary elections held later that year were "the freest in
Jordan's history."

This liberal interlude was to be short-lived, however. Hussein
was happy to let it continue so long as neighboring Syria and Iraq
were ruled by friendly regimes (he had made his peace with Qasim
in 1960). But when both Baghdad and Damascus fell one after the
other to Baathist-Nasserist coups in the spring of 1963, the king

lost his nerve, fearing another April 1957 around the corner. This drove him back into the arms of the old-guard conservatives. Tal resigned nineteen days after the Syrian coup, to be replaced by the familiar and dependable Samir al-Rifai. In reality, there was little immediate danger to the king. The formidable-sounding three-way union among Egypt, Syria, and Iraq declared in April 1963 imploded in a matter of days, and Nasser was soon much more interested in toppling the Syrian Baathists than he was the Jordanian monarch. Indeed, as irony would have it, it was precisely their shared antipathy toward the new regime in Damascus that facilitated the historic rapprochement between Hussein and Nasser in early 1964.

The occasion was a heads-of-state summit called by Nasser in Cairo in January 1964. The official business of the summit was to discuss plans by Israel to divert the headwaters of the River Jordan from the Sea of Galilee. As always, however, Nasser was playing an inter-Arab power game at the same time. Arab politics in the mid-1960s were no longer what they had been in the simpler times of the late 1950s, when the hero of Suez had been the uncontested leader of the "revolution." The setbacks of Mosul in 1959 and, above all, the Syrian secession in 1961 had done damage to Nasser's "brand" that he could never fully undo. From Algeria in the west to Oman's Dhofar Province in the east, coursing through Beirut, Damascus, Baghdad, and the scattered Palestinian diaspora, a new self-styled radicalism, often infused with Marxism, was now on the up, threatening to leave Nasser stuck in the past, a dated and "bourgeois" relic of bygone times.

In short, Nasser needed all the friends he could get, and in this confusing environment, Hussein was starting to look suspiciously like a friend—and to act like one too. The king was naturally even more isolated than Nasser in the new militant zeitgeist, and wagered he could exploit the bad blood between Cairo and Damascus to rope Nasser into an alliance of centrists standing between the Baathists and other ultras, on the one hand, and the austere theocrats of Saudi Arabia on the other.

To this end, on January 15, 1964, while the Cairo summit was still in progress, Jordan and Egypt restored full diplomatic relations, which had been severed since 1961. Hussein agreed to all of Nasser's proposals at the summit, including the formation of a unified Arab military command under Egyptian leadership, and—most significantly for Jordan in particular—the creation of a Palestinian national entity, a precursor to the PLO, formally established later the same year. (The significance of this was that the West Bank had been officially regarded by Jordan since 1950 as its own sovereign soil, no less Jordanian than Amman and Petra. To encourage Palestinian national aspirations within the West Bank was thus to invite an inevitable clash with Jordan's own claim to the same territory, as indeed happened not long after.)

On the back of this summit, and the public friendship with Nasser it produced, Hussein enjoyed newfound domestic popularity, not least among the majority of Jordanian citizens who hailed from Palestinian roots. The hero's reception he received on returning from Cairo encouraged him to go further. In July 1964, Hussein formally recognized the Nasser-backed republican side in Yemen's war, as opposed to the royalists, leaving Saudi Arabia alone among Arab states in recognizing the latter. Perhaps more remarkably, Jordanian Free Officers, including Ali Abu Nuwar and Ali al-Hiyari, who had both fled to the UAR after the Zarqa affair in 1957, were permitted to return from exile. Salah al-Sharaa, condemned in the coup plot of March 1959, was pardoned. The Baathist Munif al-Razzaz, who would soon succeed Michel Aflaq as leader of the overall party, was freed from prison. (This last move was actually a subtle jab at Damascus, since Razzaz belonged to the faction within the Baath then at odds with the rival faction ruling Syria.)

This partnership between Amman and Cairo would endure, with only brief interruptions, for the remaining six years of Nasser's life. It was central to Hussein's decision to involve Jordan in war against Israel alongside Egypt and Syria in 1967, leading to the loss of East Jerusalem and the West Bank. It had been within Hussein's power to stay out of the war, as he had in 1956, and as another frontline state (Lebanon) did. The Israelis sent him assurances they would not attack Jordan if Jordan did not attack them. It is an arresting question to ponder: Had Hussein stayed out in 1967, would Jerusalem's Old City and the West Bank still be in Arab hands today? Would the hundreds of Israeli settlements since built on these territories, which have formed such an intractable obstacle to a final peace deal between Israelis and Palestinians, simply never have existed? It is by no means inconceivable. As it turned out, Hussein flew to Cairo on the eve of war in military uniform to meet Nasser, signed an agreement to defend Egypt should it come under attack, and handed full control of Jordan's armed forces to the astoundingly inept Egyptian high command, led by the notorious drunkard and drug addict Amer, a strong contender for the title of least competent field marshal in military history. Days later, the Old City and West Bank were lost.

Thereafter, Hussein and Nasser drew even closer. In part, this was the natural bond formed by the shared experience of war. But they were also, once again, pulling together to defend against radical maximalists on left and right, who in the crushing defeat of June 1967 heard the death knell of the existing Arab regimes, Nasser's included. Prominent among these militants were the very Palestinian groups Nasser and Hussein had both opted to empower from 1964 on, with whom they now began to collide with mounting intensity.

For Nasser, the core disagreement with the Palestinians concerned the end goal of the conflict with Israel, and the means of achieving it. While the PLO at that time sought the full restoration of every inch of historic Palestine, and the total dismantling of the Israeli state, Nasser came to endorse what is now generally referred to as the two-state solution. This consists of an agreement whereby Israel's Arab neighbors offer it full peace in exchange for the return of the territories occupied by Israel in the course of the 1967 war, leaving an Israeli state in place within the borders as they were prior to the outbreak of hostilities on June 5, 1967.

To this end, Nasser (and Hussein) accepted the UN Security Council's famous Resolution 242, passed in November 1967, which continues to form the basis of proposals for a two-state solution today. The PLO, by contrast, rejected it, as did Syria.

Undeterred, in 1970 Nasser also endorsed the so-called Rogers Plan, named after its author, US Secretary of State William Rogers, which was based on Resolution 242. This time, the PLO and other Palestinian factions came out forcefully against Nasser, denouncing him in stark terms as a coward, traitor, and imperialist agent in rowdy (and armed) street protests outside Egyptian embassies in Amman and Beirut. A furious Nasser responded by closing down the PLO's Voice of Palestine radio operating from Cairo, and ceased the funding of militants in Gaza.

Hussein's clash with the Palestinians went considerably deeper. A few weeks after the 1967 defeat, a certain guerrilla leader named Yasser Arafat slipped across the River Jordan from the West Bank to the East Bank, setting up base in the small village of al-Karameh in the agricultural plains of the Jordan Valley, four kilometers east of the river. The arrival in Jordan of Arafat and his armed *fedayeen* ("self-sacrificers") inaugurated a new phase in the conflict with Israel, transforming Jordan into the principal headquarters and staging ground for Palestinian attacks on Israeli targets.

As in south Lebanon, these attacks prompted painful Israeli reprisals on Jordanian infrastructure, both military and civilian. Before long, the entire Jordan Valley, plus nearby cities including Irbid and Salt, witnessed regular artillery battles and air strikes. But this was only half the problem for Hussein.

By early 1970, a similar dynamic to that in Lebanon had played out in Jordan. As the *fedayeen* grew in number and influence, they came to be seen as operating a parallel state-within-a-state, stoking the ire of Jordanian nationalists. Despite pledges by PLO officials to respect Jordan's sovereignty and refrain from intervening in its affairs, the ill-disciplined behavior of the guerrillas on the ground became increasingly provocative. Racing around the capital in unlicensed jeeps brandishing weapons, they ignored traffic rules and declined to stop at checkpoints. The more ideologically zealous among them, such as the Marxist-Leninist Popular Front for the Liberation of Palestine (PFLP), called openly for the toppling of the Hashemite monarchy and the conversion of Amman into an "Arab Hanoi."

Appeals from Hussein to Nasser to use his influence to curb the guerrillas' excesses met with ready cooperation on Nasser's part, but failed to translate into results. An attempt by Jordan's authorities to prohibit the carrying of arms in public places was indignantly rejected by the *fedayeen*. Loyalist army units began to seethe with rage, chomping at the bit to be let loose on the guerrillas, at whose hands they felt insulted and humiliated. They would not have to wait much longer.

June 1970 saw direct fighting break out between *fedayeen* and Jordanian troops in Zarqa. Days later, gunmen fired on Hussein himself in central Amman, killing one of his guards. Without waiting for orders, army units shelled two Palestinian refugee camps in response, sparking three days of battles with guerrillas.

Events entered a grave downward spiral thereafter. The PFLP took sixty-eight foreign civilians hostage in two Amman hotels, women and children among them, threatening to blow them all up unless the king's uncle, Sharif Nasser bin Jamil, and others were dismissed from the army. In a final act of restraint, Hussein accepted, and the hostages were released. On September 1, the king's convoy once again came under fire, triggering further clashes between the army and *fedayeen*.

As though bent on all-out war, the guerrillas chose this moment to overplay their hand spectacularly. On September 6, the PFLP hijacked three international civilian planes containing hundreds of passengers, landing two of them at an airstrip near Zarqa, to be joined by a third three days later. After removing the passengers, the militants detonated the aircraft on September 12 before the world's eyes. Three days after that, the *fedayeen* occupied the city of Irbid, declaring it "liberated" territory. The challenge to Hussein's authority could hardly get more frontal than this.

In the hours that followed, the king finalized preparations for the decisive showdown that could no longer be avoided. Already, on September 9, he had called the *grand seigneur* of Jordan's army, Field Marshal Habis al-Majali, out of retirement to reinstall him as army chief of staff. Now he dismissed his civilian cabinet, appointing a military one in its place, and declared a state of emergency.

Operations began on the morning of September 17 with tank, artillery, and mortar fire on *fedayeen* positions and Palestinian population centers across Amman, Irbid, Salt, Jerash, and Zarqa. It was an uneven fight, pitching some sixty-five thousand Jordanian troops against fifteen thousand Palestinians. Nonetheless, the army had still not fully subdued the guerrillas when, ten days later, Hussein accepted an invitation from Nasser to fly to Cairo to discuss a settlement with Arafat in person. By that point, the death toll exceeded three thousand.

The scene was understandably tense on September 26 when Hussein showed up at the Nile Hilton (now the Nile Ritz-Carlton) in combat gear and beret, a pistol strapped to his waist. Libya's Col. Muammar al-Gaddafi, who was also present, is said to have proposed shooting the king dead moments before he walked in. Despite the frosty atmosphere, Nasser succeeded the following day in brokering a cease-fire agreement, signed that evening by Hussein, Arafat, and himself.

It was to be the grand performer's final act. The very next day, after bidding his guests farewell, Nasser suffered a large heart attack, and died in his bed at home in Cairo, surrounded by his family, doctors, and friends, including the Free Officers Anwar Sadat and Husayn al-Shafii, and the writer Mohamed Hasanayn Heikal. He was fifty-two years old.

The late Malcolm Kerr wrote that the "supreme irony of Gamal 'Abd al-Nasir's career was that he died in the act of shielding his old enemy Husayn, at the expense of his old clients the Palestinians."

The second part of the sentence is less ironic than the first, for in truth the Palestinians were always a means to an end for Nasser, and he was all along more amenable to Israel's existence than is widely supposed. (One recalls his cordial meeting with Yeruham Cohen in Faluja in 1948, when he reportedly told Yitzhak Rabin that Egypt was fighting "the wrong enemy.")

Of his dramatic change in attitude toward Hussein, however, there can be no doubt. This was a man, after all, who he had previously hinted on more than one public occasion ought to be murdered and dragged through the streets. When Sarraj blew up downtown Amman in 1960, shredding Prime Minister Majali with bombs that very nearly took Hussein's life, too, Nasser rewarded him with a promotion. That he should then have gone so far out of his way to save Hussein's skin in September 1970 was a striking contrast by any standard.

There is reason to believe the change of heart was sincere, as opposed to purely cynical or tactical. If, prior to 1967, Nasser was a man drunk with hubris, seriously believing he could knock out Israel even with half his army bogged down in Yemen, the June defeat sobered his head and opened his eyes. At a summit in Rabat in 1969, he made unequivocally clear to his fellow Arab heads of state that neither he nor they were in any position to wage war on Israel in the near future. Seeing the world in this new light, he came to regard Hussein as one of the few Arab leaders capable of reading the regional situation rationally. He also felt Hussein had played the geopolitical game better than he had himself, admitting to him in July 1967 that he regretted burning his bridges so totally with the West, leaving him wholly dependent on Moscow.

This was no small confession, amounting to an indictment of much of pre-1967 Nasserism as a whole. It was not, however, the same thing as an apology, nor did it absolve the man of everything he had done. Perhaps for this reason, Hussein is said by those who knew him to have privately neither forgiven nor forgotten Nasser's shedding of his friends' blood. To Hussein al-Majali—who had spent the last seven months of the king's life by his side—I put the question of whether he had ever spoken to him about Nasser.

"He was never fond of Abdel Nasser," came the reply.

Yet Nasser, I said, changed his opinion of Hussein in his final years.

"Yes," said Majali, an amused grin breaking over his face. "But [Hussein] never changed his opinion of Abdel Nasser."

YEMEN

15

THE MOST HONORABLE BATTLE

IN THE ROCKY HEIGHTS OF THE JAGGED, CAVE-RIDDLED mountainscape of northwest Yemen sits the small village of Kitaf, around fifty-five kilometers east of the nearest city, Saada. Its few inhabitants in 1967 were tribal adherents of the heterodox Zaydi sect of Islam, living a deeply traditional existence much as their ancestors had been doing for centuries. On January 5 of that year, the villagers of Kitaf underwent an abrupt encounter with modernity in its most horrifying form, when nine Soviet-made Ilyushin-28 planes screamed overhead in three formations of three, dropping three bombs each on the village, for a total of twenty-seven.

These were no ordinary munitions. As they exploded, the bewildered villagers were plunged into clouds of peculiar, dreadful fumes and vapors, causing them to choke, vomit, and collapse on the ground. In all, between one hundred and two hundred people were killed, potentially as many as one in five inhabitants of the village, whose population numbered around one thousand. Aside from the human casualties, most of the goats, sheep, camels, and chickens in the surrounding territory were also found dead. Nearby crops and vegetation turned brown.

The massacre at Kitaf was neither the first nor the last chemical attack perpetrated by Nasser's forces in Yemen. The Egyptian army had been waging chemical warfare in the country since 1963, killing at least eight hundred people by chemical means, many of them women and children. Most of Nasser's previous chemical attacks, however, had involved the First World War–era substances mustard and phosgene. What distinguished the Kitaf strike, with its remarkably high death toll and the rapid speed with which its victims died, was the suspicion that a far more powerful and sophisticated substance—a nerve agent—may have been used. The CIA claimed to have unearthed evidence that this was the case through samples obtained from the site, though the evidence was never made public.

Nasser's forces had already earned the distinction of being the first Arab army in history to use chemical weapons on the battlefield. Egypt was, indeed, one of only two countries worldwide to have waged chemical warfare since Mussolini's invasion of Ethiopia in the 1930s (the other being Imperial Japan, which used chemicals against China in World War II). If Nasser truly did deploy a nerve agent at Kitaf, it would mark a further accolade: the first-ever wartime use of nerve agents anywhere in the world.

IN HUMANITARIAN TERMS, the war Nasser fought in Yemen between 1962 and 1967 was undoubtedly the darkest stain on his record by a considerable margin. An entirely unprovoked war of choice and aggression, which claimed an estimated twenty thousand Yemeni lives, and was later described by Nasser himself as "my Vietnam," it was the one chapter of his career no apologist, however unctuous, was able to defend in retrospect. (Even Heikal, the most servile propagandist of all, eventually conceded it had been in error, albeit only after spending years justifying it.) The war brought out the very worst in Nasser, stimulating all his most lethal instincts and sinking him to unprecedented extremes of violence. Its five long years saw him at his most unhinged, his most irrational, and most atrocious. Of the bloodbath he unleashed, it was neither Western imperialists nor Zionist usurpers who bore the brunt, but rather the blameless children, women, and men who made up the civilian population of the Arab world's most destitute country.

★

IT BEGAN, APTLY ENOUGH, with a military coup. On the night of September 26, 1962, in the Yemeni capital of Sanaa, a group of "Free Officers" led by one Col. Abdallah al-Sallal parked a tank column outside the palace of the country's theocratic ruler, the Imam Muhammad al-Badr, and opened fire. As their shells reduced the palace to rubble, fellow officers elsewhere in the city seized the radio station, telephone exchange, armory, security headquarters, and other strategic sites. Over the airwaves, they proclaimed with triumph that the "tyrant" had been killed, and a "free republic" established, promising democracy and "a socialist future." The one-thousand-year-old institution of the imamate, which had ruled parts of Yemen since the late ninth century, was no more.

For Nasser, this was the kind of welcome news that had been all too rare of late. Ever since the embarrassing collapse of the union with Syria the year before, his leadership of the Arab world had looked more tenuous than at any time since Suez. Independent Syria had escaped his orbit; Iraq was still ruled by the implacably hostile Qasim; Jordan's King Hussein was a mortal enemy. A successful Nasserist coup in the Arabian Peninsula—right on the doorstep of both Saudi Arabia and the British colonial "protectorate" of Aden—was exactly the sort of development Nasser needed to recover the initiative and prove he was still the Arabs' man of destiny.

To be sure, the Sanaa coup did not come to him as a total surprise. Yemen's Free Officers had coordinated their plans with Cairo, which had long hosted and sponsored Yemeni dissidents, not least after Nasser's public bust-up with the previous Imam, Ahmad, in 1961. Many of the key figures who founded Yemen's Free Officers movement in 1960, and went on to execute the coup two years later, such as Abd al-Latif Dayfallah and Abdallah Juzaylan, had undergone military training in Egypt, and spoke openly of emulating the Egyptian example. Sallal himself had read Nasser's *Philosophy of the Revolution* while imprisoned in the 1950s for oppositional intrigues, and left jail bent on overthrowing the imamate. Another pivotal character was Abd al-Rahman al-Baydani, the half-Egyptian, half-Yemeni brother-in-law of Anwar Sadat, who acted as a middleman between Cairo and Yemen's Free Officers, and became deputy head of Yemen's post-coup "Revolutionary Command Council," as well as deputy president of the republic and deputy prime minister. The precise details of Egypt's direct role in the coup remain a matter of debate. The likelihood, on the available evidence, is that it was roughly akin to Iraq in 1958: Nasser knew the coup was in the works, gave it his full blessing and encouragement, and made clear he would aid the officers in the event of their success. Otherwise, he left the bulk of the legwork to the Yemenis themselves, with Egyptian intelligence providing such advice and assistance as it could.

Sure enough, when the moment came, Nasser was quick to keep up his end of the deal. Three days after the coup, on September 29, Egypt's Gen. Ali Abd al-Hamid arrived in Sanaa to assess the situation. Alarmed by the fragility of the junta and nouveau régime, his first response was to ask Nasser to send a special-forces battalion to act as Sallal's personal guard, a request promptly approved. Meanwhile, Baydani traveled to Cairo to meet Nasser in person, while Sallal sent telegrams requesting Egypt's formal recognition of the "Yemen Arab Republic" (YAR), as well as military support. These too were swiftly granted. On October 6, an Egyptian steamship arrived at Yemen's Red Sea port of al-Hudaydah, carrying uniformed Egyptian troops.

At this initial stage, Nasser believed he was simply sending a token force as a symbolic gesture of "revolutionary" solidarity, to be withdrawn soon afterward once the regime had stabilized. Yemen's republicans had not yet faced meaningful military opposition; the country was not even in a state of low-level conflict, let alone civil war.

That would soon change, owing to a dramatic plot twist. Despite Sallal's claim to have killed the "tyrant" Imam on the night of the coup, the latter had in fact escaped through a rear exit shortly after the shelling of his palace began. In the days that followed, he made his way to the northern highlands—the Imams' traditional base of support—to rally loyalist tribes into armed action against the republicans and newly arrived Egyptian occupiers. In this effort, he and various relatives, including his uncle, Prince Hassan, began to receive money and light arms from both Saudi Arabia and the British in Aden.

By the second half of October, Nasser could see he was in for a bigger fight than he had bargained for. The cities of Saada and Marib, north and east of Sanaa, respectively, had fallen into royalist hands, encouraging more tribes to declare opposition to the republic. An Egyptian paratrooper base inside Saada came under siege by royalist forces, who held all the roads leading in, preventing the arrival of reinforcements. It was not until over a month later, on November 30, that the Egyptians finally succeeded in breaking the siege and relieving the paratroopers, after an intense battle requiring air strikes and heavy artillery fire, and incurring significant Egyptian casualties.

November also brought the additional bad news (from Nasser's perspective) of the confirmed survival of the Imam, who gave a defiant press conference in a tent to sixteen foreign journalists—among them the notorious double agent H. A. R. "Kim" Philby, then employed as a correspondent for *The Observer*. With "a rifle across his knees and a double bandolier of cartridges across his chest," the Imam had stern words for Egypt's forces in Yemen: "Had you come as friends we would have opened to you our homes and our hearts. But since you came as invaders we can open for you only your graves."

The situation was growing messier and more complex by the day. Nasser could, of course, have chosen this moment to bow out, citing a refusal to shed Arab blood, as he had done when he called off the deployment to Syria's Latakia the year before. But a variety of reasons kept him from doing so. By the time of the Imam's public reappearance, Nasser had not only extended formal recognition to the YAR but ratified a mutual defense pact with it, committing him to its protection. Nor was this the only sense in which his prestige had become invested in the survival of the Yemeni republic. The more the conflict was internationalized, the more it transformed in Nasser's speeches and propaganda into yet another round in the grand contest for the Arab world as a whole. The battle for Yemen, he said in a December speech, was the battle of Arabs everywhere. In Yemen, Egypt was fighting "the most honorable battle, which is the battle of Arab nationalism." It was unthinkable for Egypt to watch idly as imperialists and reactionaries defeated Yemen's "revolution," for what then would stop them trying the same in Cairo itself? "This is not the battle of Yemenis, nor the Yemeni people; it is our battle; the battle of every free people. . . . The Yemeni revolution is our revolution."

These were not statements from which one could easily climb down in a hurry. Moreover, beneath the romantic rhetoric lay hard-nosed strategic considerations. To secure the Bab al-Mandab Strait on Yemen's southwest tip would hand Egypt control of both ends of the Red Sea, rendering it master of the waters between the Mediterranean and the Indian Ocean, and allowing it (among other things) to blockade Israel's port of Eilat. The pressure Nasser could bring to bear on both Saudi Arabia and Britain (via Aden) from a firm foothold on the Arabian Peninsula would add powerful new arrows to his quiver. Above all, he desperately needed a "win" to reverse his losing streak and turn the regional momentum in his favor. Besides, how hard could it be to rout a few benighted cave-dwellers armed with muskets and daggers? Field Marshal Amer assured Nasser he could crush the Imam's tribesmen in two weeks. Sadat agreed it would be a cakewalk, remarking that Egyptian troops were so tough they could even eat snakes.

And so to war Nasser went. The man who had famously pledged that Egypt's arms would never be turned on fellow Arabs now poured his military into the very heartland of ancient Arabian civilization. In January 1963, Egypt launched a large-scale, monthslong offensive to deliver the royalists a knockout blow. Over thirty thousand Egyptian troops were brought into Yemen. The strategy was to first secure the so-called "strategic triangle" between the capital Sanaa, the Red Sea port of Hudaydah, and the city of Taiz, driving royalist forces as far north and east of this triangle as possible. At the same time, Egypt's air force—which enjoyed an absolute monopoly in the skies—would pummel the northern border zone in the hope of cutting off the royalists' supply lines from Saudi Arabia. Trapped in a pincer between the planes in the north and ground forces advancing from the south, the royalists would end up with no choice but to surrender.

At first, the plan appeared to work. The massive firepower unleashed by Egypt's aircraft and artillery succeeded in opening the road from Sanaa to Saada in the far north, and in capturing the strategic points of Marib and Harib east of the capital. Republican forces were soon in control of all Yemen's major towns and cities.

These apparently impressive gains were illusory, however. The royalists had not been defeated but had simply made a temporary withdrawal into the extensive and labyrinthine network of caves that coursed through the forbidding mountains outside the urban centers, where they were invulnerable to Egyptian air attacks. They learned quickly from their mistakes, and adapted tactics accordingly. No longer would they engage the Egyptians in large battles in open terrain. Instead, they shifted to guerrilla warfare: ambushing Egyptian convoys, sniping at soldiers from afar, mining roads, severing communication lines, and preventing deliveries of food and other essential supplies from reaching cities wherever they could.

Angered by this unexpected tenacity and ingenuity on the part of the Imam's men, Nasser upped the level of violence. Already in March 1963, Egypt's planes had bombed a hospital inside Saudi Arabia itself, in the town of Abha, more than one hundred kilometers north of the Yemeni border, killing thirty-six patients. This was followed in July with a strike on a market in Ahum, northwest Yemen, said to have claimed over one hundred civilian lives. Further air bombardments of markets were reported in November, including one in the Saudi border village of al-Khuba, which killed women, children, and men from Yemen as well as Saudi Arabia.

Arguably more chilling than even these flagrant atrocities, however, was the news in July 1963 that Egypt's air force had begun killing Yemenis with a type of weaponry never before used anywhere by any other Arab state, an infamous form of warfare immortalized in the Western imagination as the epitome of the unique horrors of World War I, a type of munition now banned by over 190 countries, and deemed a weapon of mass destruction.

★

EGYPT'S CHEMICAL WEAPONS PROGRAM came into existence no later than the early 1960s. Egyptian military officers underwent specialized chemical warfare training in Moscow at the Red Army's Academy of Chemical Defense. Scientists and engineers from West Germany were also hired by Cairo to share their world-class expertise. (It was Germans, after all, who had invented and pioneered modern chemical warfare in the 1910s, and also been the first to discover the more sophisticated—and far deadlier—nerve agents in the 1930s.)

On the back of this assistance, Egypt was able to open its first chemical weapons production facility in 1963, at Abu Zaabal, a stone's throw from the notorious prison and forced-labor complex. Given a false name and the appearance of a benign commercial enterprise—the "Abu Zaabal Company for Chemicals and Insecticides"—the facility was in fact operated by the ministry of war, and known internally as "Military Plant No. 801."

At first, production was limited to the First World War–era substances known as phosgene and "mustard." The former is a gas with an odor described as "like new-mown hay." First used by the German army at Ypres, in Belgium, in December 1915, it went on to kill more people over the course of that war than any other chemical weapon. Death by phosgene comes suddenly and unexpectedly, often hours or even days after inhalation, due to a steady build-up of yellow-colored fluid in the lungs. Soldiers often reported feeling perfectly fine one moment, only to

Gamal Abdel Nasser in his early twenties at the start of his military career, as a second lieutenant, a rank he held between 1938 and 1940. *(Bibliotheca Alexandrina)*

An Egyptian tank deploys outside the National Bank of Egypt in Cairo on July 27, 1952, four days after the Free Officers' military coup and one day after King Farouk's abdication and exile to Italy. *(Bettmann / Getty)*

The Free Officers' junta meets on July 31, 1952. Those present include Nasser (seated by the black telephone), future president Muhammad Naguib (sitting to Nasser's left), future army commander Abd al-Hakim Amer (standing between Nasser and Naguib), future president Anwar Sadat (seated fourth from left) and future prime minister Zakaria Muhieddin (seated in the foreground on the far left). *(AP/Shutterstock)*

Iraq's Prime Minister Nuri al-Said, Nasser's chief Arab adversary until his gruesome killing in 1958. "I am not a soldier in Abdel Nasser's army," he declared in 1955. "Please tell him that I will never obey his orders." *(Central Press / Hulton Archive / Getty Images)*

Nasser delivers the speech that secures his place in history, announcing the nationalization of the Suez Canal Company in Alexandria's Manshiya Square on July 26, 1956, triggering the Suez Crisis. When, three months later, Nasser survived a military invasion by Britain, France, and Israel combined, he became a hero to millions across the Arab world. *(AP/Shutterstock)*

"We are your soldiers": Iraqi troops drive an armored vehicle bearing Nasser's portrait through Baghdad during the bloody military coup of July 14, 1958. *(AP/Shutterstock)*

Syria's President Shukri al-Quwwatli votes to abolish his own office—and his country's independence—by approving union with Egypt on February 21, 1958. *(Bettmann/Getty)*

Nasser addresses a large crowd in Cairo's Gumhuriya Square upon the merger of Egypt and Syria in February 1958. *(AP/Shutterstock)*

Nasser receives his notorious Syrian security chief, Abd al-Hamid al-Sarraj, on May 13, 1962, after the latter's escape from a Damascus prison to Cairo, via Beirut. *(Bibliotheca Alexandrina)*

Farajallah al-Helu, the Lebanese communist leader tortured to death by Nasser's security forces in Damascus in June 1959. His corpse was dismembered and dissolved in an acid bath. *(Al-Helu family archive)*

Nasser receives Hafez al-Assad (center), then Syria's defense minister, in August 1969. Assad went on to rule Syria from 1970 until his death in 2000, when he was succeeded by his son Bashar. *(Bibliotheca Alexandrina)*

Lebanon's President Camille Chamoun, against whom Nasser sponsored an armed insurrection and bombing campaign in 1958. *(Philippe Buffon/Sygma via Getty Images)*

Lebanese gunmen in Beirut pose by a portrait of Nasser on June 27, 1958. The armed rebellion against President Chamoun's government received extensive support from Cairo. *(Gerard Gery/Paris Match via Getty Images)*

The Lebanese journalist Kamel Mrowa (right) with the Hollywood star Robert Mitchum (second from left) and the latter's wife, Dorothy, at Mrowa's villa in Beit Mirri, Lebanon, in September 1962. *(The Kamel Mrowa Foundation)*

Saudi Arabia's King Faysal receives Mrowa in Jeddah in 1965. At the time of his assassination in May 1966, Mrowa was assisting Faysal's efforts to lead a new regional alliance challenging Nasser's primacy in Arab affairs. *(The Kamel Mrowa Foundation)*

Lebanese Nasserist militants Adnan Sultani (right) and Ibrahim Qulaylat
(left) appear at Beirut's Higher Judicial Council on December 5, 1966,
at the opening session of their trial on charges of assassinating Kamel Mrowa.
(The Kamel Mrowa Foundation)

Nasserist gunmen
pose by a poster
of the Egyptian
icon inside Beirut's
Holiday Inn on
March 24, 1976,
after occupying the
famous hotel during
Lebanon's civil war.
*(Xavier Baron/AFP via
Getty Images)*

Jordan's Prime Minister Hazzaa al-Majali, assassinated
by a bomb under his desk in August 1960. Egypt's then
chief of intelligence, Salah Nasr, later acknowledged
that Nasser's regime stood behind the killing.
(Photo published with the permission of the Majali family)

The smoking wreckage of Prime Minister Majali's office in Amman, Jordan. In all, eleven were killed, including a child, and eighty-five wounded by the three blasts, which narrowly missed King Hussein himself. *(Central Press/ Getty Images)*

A Yemeni man displays remnants of a chemical munition fired by Nasser's air force on the village of al-Kawma in northwest Yemen in June 1963. The strike, which killed seven villagers, including a five-year-old girl, was one of scores of chemical attacks perpetrated by Egypt in Yemen between 1963 and 1967. *(© Telegraph Media Group Limited 2023)*

Victims of an Egyptian chemical attack are buried in fresh graves by the village of Kitaf, northwest Yemen, in January 1967. More than one hundred villagers were reportedly killed in the strike on January 5, which may have seen the world's first use of nerve agents in combat. *(Lancashire/AP/ Shutterstock)*

Libya's Muammar al-Gaddafi shares a laugh with Nasser, his mentor and role model, in Cairo in September 1970. The pair quickly formed a close bond after Gaddafi seized power the previous year in a military coup inspired by Nasser's own. *(Farouk Ibrahim/AP/Shutterstock)*

Nasser sits with Gaddafi (left), Jordan's King Hussein (far right), and the Palestine Liberation Organization's leader, Yasser Arafat (center), at the Nile Hilton in Cairo on September 27, 1970, one day before Nasser's fatal heart attack. *(Bettmann/Getty)*

Libyans cheer and take photos as a statue of Nasser is toppled in Benghazi on February 11, 2012, four months after Gaddafi's killing by rebels. The sculpture had been erected by Gaddafi in the 1970s as one of many public tributes to the Egyptian leader. *(Abdullah Doma/AFP via Getty Images)*

keel over coughing to death the next. When used in conjunction with chlorine on the Somme in 1916, phosgene left apocalyptic destruction in its wake, exterminating "men, horses, wildlife, insects, vegetation—virtually everything it touched." Birds and butterflies dropped dead from the skies, and trees were stripped bare of their leaves.

"Mustard," or dichlorethyl sulphide, acquired an even more fearsome reputation in the Great War. Earning its nickname from its pungent smell, it was first used in July 1917, again at Ypres, again by the Germans. Despite its late appearance in the war, it ended up accounting for 70 percent of total British chemical casualties, and more than a quarter of overall US casualties. A liquid that sprays out in a fine mist upon explosion, it seeps through clothing to wreak diabolical havoc on the body beneath. Initial symptoms may be no more than mild irritation in the eyes and throat. In the hours, days, and even weeks that follow, however, the victim undergoes a torture quite unlike any other. The eyes endure an excruciating pain, as though scratched with sand, and are often left blinded. On the skin, enormous fluid-filled blisters, several inches in width and up to a foot in length, break out all over the body, including in the most painful places imaginable: the genitals, the backs of the knees, between the thighs. If one has been unlucky enough to inhale the mustard, the coming death is slow and agonizing in the extreme, as the substance works its devastating effects inside the windpipe and lungs, swelling them up and filling them with a frothy, bloody, pus-like liquid until asphyxiation occurs.

These, then, were the first two chemicals Egypt produced at the Abu Zaabal plant starting in 1963. The phosgene and mustard were fitted into Soviet-made AOKh-25 and KHAB-200 R5 aerial bombs, respectively, ready to be dropped onto the battlefield by the Soviet-made Ilyushin-28 planes that were already part of Egypt's air force.

In time, Egypt expanded its chemical arsenal to include the nerve agents Sarin and VX. These so-called next-generation chemicals are immensely more lethal than their first-generation predecessors from World War I. First developed in the 1930s and '50s, respectively, they are colorless and odorless liquids that cause rapid death by disabling the essential functions of the nervous system. Specifically, they inhibit the action of a crucial enzyme called cholinesterase, triggering what is known as a "cholinergic crisis." The skeletal muscles begin spasming violently and uncontrollably. The stomach cramps, the pupils of the eye shrink to a pinpoint, and fluids stream from the nose and mouth. Loss of consciousness follows. If the constriction of the bronchial tubes doesn't by itself cause death from asphyxiation within minutes, the subsequent paralysis of the breathing muscles will. So deadly is Sarin that to breathe just one part of it in a million of air can be fatal. VX is three times as toxic when inhaled, and one thousand times as toxic when absorbed through the skin. The tiniest drop of VX on the skin will kill an adult male in fifteen minutes. A single liter of it is theoretically sufficient to murder one million people.

And yet, as terrifying as chemical weapons are, from the strictly military perspective they are often of dubious tactical value on the battlefield. In the open air, they disperse rapidly, making anything less than a direct hit on the enemy ineffective. Unpredictable winds can blow the chemicals away from their targets, very possibly onto nearby civilians. An especially unlucky breeze will even waft the chemicals back onto friendly forces, as was known to happen in the First World War, as well as during Iraq's war with Iran in the 1980s. Even if the weapons do successfully strike their targets, the area in question may remain contaminated with lethal chemicals for weeks afterward, making the capture of the territory prohibitively dangerous. For chemical weapons to be most effective, the enemy needs to be stationary, in a fixed position from which they cannot quickly escape, with little moving air. These conditions prevailed in World War I, when soldiers were confined to cramped trenches into which chemical clouds denser than air would sink and linger. By a similar token, in Yemen, where the royalists in their mountain caves had proved immune to conventional Egyptian air strikes, it occurred to Nasser's generals that their new chemical arsenal might offer a magic solution.

★

IN THE SUMMER OF 1963, the British *Daily Telegraph* correspondent Richard Beeston was sent by his editor from London to northern Yemen to investigate unconfirmed reports of Egyptian chemical attacks in royalist territory. At first, the very notion seemed absurd to many. No army anywhere in the world had used chemical weapons since Imperial Japan in the Second World War. "When I first heard" the rumor, recalled the *New York Times* correspondent Dana Adams Schmidt, "I did not believe it. It seemed to me quite implausible that the Egyptians would risk the obloquy which such a crime would bring upon them. In particular, I felt they would not do such a thing to fellow Arabs." Innocence of this kind did not long survive contact with Yemen's war.

From the Saudi border region of Jizan, Beeston traveled for three days by truck, by donkey, and on foot before finally arriving at the tiny hamlet of al-Kawma, a handful of stone houses huddled together at the crest of a bush-strewn mound in the high mountains, some sixteen kilometers south of Saada.

Signs of a chemical attack confronted Beeston before he had even set foot in the village, when he heard the "pitiful coughing" of its residents from over a hundred yards away. Inside al-Kawma, the evidence of mustard use was unmistakable. "The face of one woman had turned a vivid yellow and another had been blinded" after rubbing her eyes with contaminated hands, he wrote. A twelve-year-old boy, Muhammad Nasser Mansur, "had a perpetual cough and deep open wounds on his body, the size of a half-crown, from gas blisters." Of the village's one hundred inhabitants, roughly one-third had suffered the chemical's effects. Seven had been killed, Beeston was told, including a boy of thirteen and a five-year-old girl, Hadia Rashid, who "died in agony" four days after the attack.

The village chief told Beeston the bombs had produced a brown cloud with a "dirty smell. . . . Soon after, people began coughing up blood." Residents were able to show Beeston remains of the munitions responsible: a ring about the shape and size of a steering wheel, bent into an oval by the impact with the ground, bearing fifteen holes for chemical-filled canisters, some of them still attached.

Beeston's report, published on July 8, 1963, marked the first independent confirmation by an international journalist of Egypt's chemical weapons use. The attack itself was likely not the first of its kind. The sheer remoteness and inaccessibility of Yemen's northern highlands ensured that a great proportion of Egypt's atrocities went unseen by the outside world. In the same month that Beeston's report came out, a Scottish member of parliament, Lt. Col. Neil "Billy" McLean, spent weeks traveling through royalist territory, where he reported seeing evidence of chemical as well as napalm attacks in several villages other than al-Kawma. (While McLean's claims may well have been accurate, it should be noted he was not a disinterested party, but rather a paid adviser to the Imam, who lobbied Downing Street on behalf of the royalist cause.) A Dr. Bruno Beretta with the International Committee of the Red Cross (ICRC) said on July 9 that he had been receiving reports of chemical attacks for over a month.

Needless to say, these attacks, and the many more that followed them, amounted to brazen violations of Egypt's obligations under international law. In 1925, with memories of the Great War's horrors still fresh in mind, world powers gathered at a League of Nations conference on arms control in Geneva. All present were agreed that the uniquely repugnant cruelty of chemical warfare should be consigned forever to humanity's past, never to recur. The text of the resulting "Protocol for the Prohibition of the Use in War of Asphyxiating, Poisonous or Other Gases, and of Bacteriological Methods of Warfare," signed by thirty-eight nations on June 17, 1925, bound "the conscience and the practice" of its signatories to abstain evermore from using chemical weaponry, which it said had been "justly condemned by the general opinion of the civilised world."

To its credit, Egypt was among the original thirty-eight signatories to the Geneva Protocol in 1925. Three years later, it was also among the first nations to ratify it, doing so two years before the UK, and forty-seven years before the US. Evidently, the "conscience" of the post-1952 officers' republic was less troubled by such bourgeois covenants. The failure of the international community to hold Cairo to account for its repeated, systematic flouting of the protocol in the 1960s was to have grave consequences for chemical weapons proliferation—not to mention use—for many decades to come.

★

PARTLY DUE TO THE bad press generated by the strike on al-Kawma, but owing also to broader military developments, as well as US pressure exerted on Nasser in private, the Egyptians reined in the use of chemical weapons for more than three years after the summer of 1963. Some of this time coincided with a downturn in the intensity of fighting overall.

The year 1964 began with a royalist offensive that succeeded in cutting the vital road between Sanaa and Hudaydah, severing the republicans' link between the capital and the main Red Sea port. Only with difficulty were the Egyptians able to reopen the road and regain full control of their "strategic triangle." Nasser followed this up in the summer of 1964 with a determined counteroffensive in the north, aimed at striking the Imam directly in his base at al-Qarah and sealing off the Saudi border. Making full use of their unchallenged air dominance, the Egyptians and republicans managed to dislodge the Imam from his cave, forcing his relocation and capturing al-Qarah itself, while also driving large numbers of royalist fighters farther north toward the Saudi border.

It was in the immediate aftermath of this, at an Arab League summit in Alexandria in September 1964 (the same one that approved the establishment of the PLO), that Nasser approached Saudi's then-regent Faysal and proposed a cease-fire and broader resolution of Yemen's war. Having gained significant territory north and east of the strategic triangle, Nasser felt he was in a position of strength, and could secure terms favorable to himself and the YAR. The next month, he and Faysal met again in Sudan, accompanied by Yemenis representing both sides, and agreement was reached on a cease-fire effective as of November 6, 1964. This led in turn to Nasser and Faysal signing an agreement in Saudi Arabia's Jeddah in August 1965 to the effect that Egypt would withdraw its forces from Yemen by September 1966, in exchange for Saudi ceasing to arm and finance the royalists.

For a while, the cease-fire held, and Nasser even withdrew some troops. The lull in combat allowed more time for politics in Sanaa. Despised by royalists, the Sallal regime enjoyed little to no popularity or legitimacy even among republicans. A deeply repressive police state that banned political associations and executed critics, the Yemeni republic was also a vassal state undermined by its abject dependence on Egyptian support to keep it afloat. Nothing about it looked authentic: its flag, its currency, even its postage stamps were crude replicas of Egypt's own. (To this day, Yemen's flag is that of the UAR, minus the two green stars.) Nor was the widely felt insult to national pride alleviated by the ubiquitous presence of domineering Egyptian officials micromanaging all aspects of governance, not to mention enriching themselves through rampant corruption. As Nasser himself admitted to the Canadian prime minister, Egypt "[ran] the whole show."

This unhappy state of affairs led to the emergence within YAR territory of dissident republican groups opposed to Sallal and the Egyptian occupiers. Known as the Third Force, this movement included such eminent reformist figures as the future prime minister Ahmad Numan, the future president Abd al-Rahman al-Iryani, and the famous poet Muhammad al-Zubayri. At considerable personal risk, they began holding secret meetings with royalist representatives in late 1964, hoping to arrive at a formula for peace and a future state acceptable to all Yemenis. Zubayri took the further gamble of leaving Sanaa to solicit support for these efforts among the tribes of the north and northeast. The result was his assassination on April 1, 1965, almost certainly arranged by Nasser to stamp out the Third Force challenge. Numan and Iryani would later be detained in Cairo during a visit in September 1966, where they were kept under house arrest for the remainder of Egypt's occupation of Yemen.

Nasser's waning patience with Yemen's politicians was mirrored in his attitude toward the cease-fire and peace pact with Faysal. Starting in late 1965, a number of factors combined to dissuade him from delivering on his pledge to leave Yemen by the following September. For one, the royalists had violated the cease-fire several times, emerging as before from their mountain hideouts to gradually nudge the Egyptian lines back down south. The arrival of significant new deliveries of Soviet weaponry, including twenty supersonic MiG-21D jet fighters—plus Moscow's generous cancellation of $400 million of Egyptian debt—may have offered an irresistible temptation to give war another chance. The announcement by British prime minister Harold Wilson's Labour government in February 1966 that it would permanently evacuate its military base in Aden in 1968 gave Nasser a clear incentive to stick around in South Arabia until that happened, so as best to fill the impending vacuum to his advantage. And we have already seen how Nasser's ties with Faysal took a nosedive at the end of 1965, after the latter's rapprochement with the Shah of Iran, the efforts to form a Saudi-led "Islamic" alliance against Nasser, the news of the large Anglo-American arms sale to Riyadh, and the discovery of the armed Muslim Brotherhood cell in Egypt alleged by Cairo to have been funded by Saudi money.

All of this culminated in a landmark speech by Nasser in March 1966, in which he unveiled a new Yemen policy, called the "Long Breath strategy." Contrary to his pledge at Jeddah the year before, Egypt would not leave the country by September. It would not, in fact, leave Yemen until "the Yemeni revolution is able to stand on its own two feet and defend itself against the imperialist and reactionary conspiracies." Egypt would reduce its troop numbers, but this was only to trim expenses and enable it to dig in for the long haul. If Egypt's forces needed to stay twenty years in Yemen, so be it. And if anyone else dared try to intervene in Yemen, Egypt would "strike" them.

Sure enough, Nasser brought the number of troops down from their peak of seventy thousand to forty thousand, concentrating them within the strategic triangle. Somewhat paradoxically, this drawdown coincided with a marked *increase* in violence, both on the ground and in Nasser's rhetoric. The bombing of royalist territory by Egypt's air force resumed in earnest. In May, Nasser declared he would hit and even "occupy" Saudi territory itself if necessary. And, for the first time since 1963, Egypt turned once again to the use of chemical weapons, this time paying no heed to the international outcry, and perpetrating many of the most heinous atrocities of the war.

The resumption of chemical attacks began in the village of Halbal, some fifty kilometers north of Sanaa, where two Ilyushin bombers reportedly dropped fifteen chemical munitions on December 11, 1966. According to an eyewitness, 2 of the village's 150 inhabitants were killed; 3 were blinded; and 35 suffered other effects, including burns, breathing difficulties, and bleeding from the nose and mouth. The symptoms suggested the use of mustard.

This was followed on January 4, 1967, by a reported chemical strike on the village of Hadda, one day prior to the mass-casualty attack on Kitaf, previously described, in which up to 200 were killed. As noted earlier, the Kitaf strike may have been the world's first use of nerve agents in combat, though there is also reason to believe phosgene was used. Among the most significant details is the report by the Associated Press journalist David Lancashire that several victims died very soon after exposure to the chemicals. The aforementioned MP McLean asserted some were killed within just ten minutes. In the words of the late chemical weapons expert Dr. Jonathan B. Tucker, "Such a rapid onset of symptoms suggested the presence of a nerve agent, perhaps combined with other chemicals to mask its identity." Doctors in hospitals in Saudi Arabia who treated a number of Kitaf's survivors noted symptoms of "acute lung oedemata"—that is, fluid in the lungs, suggesting phosgene inhalation. Saudi officials further claimed to have found evidence of nerve-agent use, much as the CIA reportedly detected traces of nerve agents in soil samples obtained from Kitaf, though such parts of this evidence as were made public have been judged less than fully conclusive by independent specialists. Ultimately, in the words of another chemical weapons expert, Dan Kaszeta, the claims of nerve-agent use in Yemen should be taken as "possible but unproven."

Facing no consequences for its widely publicized massacre at Kitaf, Egypt continued to rain chemicals on Yemeni villages for months thereafter. The *New York Times* reported 70 killed by a strike on the village of Bani Salamah on February 9, 1967. May was an especially gruesome month, with chemical attacks reported in Bani Suraym, Bani Hushaysh, Jabal Murrah, al-Heimmah, and Sirwah—the last alone said to have killed 72 on May 28, with nerve agents once again allegedly involved. One report put the total chemical death toll for the month of May at 360.

The best-documented chemical attack of the entire war took place on the morning of May 10 in the village of Gahar, in the Wadi Hirran region northeast of Sanaa. In response to an urgent appeal by residents for medical assistance, the Red Cross dispatched a team of local and international doctors and nurses to the village, accompanied by the head of the ICRC mission in Yemen, André Rochat.

Arriving in Gahar on the night of May 15, the Red Cross heard the story of the attack firsthand from survivors and eyewitnesses. On the morning of May 10, planes had circled the village several times before dropping a total of seven or eight bombs. Residents located upwind of the bombs' impact sites were unaffected. Those downwind, by contrast, soon began to experience the telltale symptoms of mustard exposure: blinding agony in the eyes, intense chest pain accompanied by coughing and shortness of breath, and widespread swelling, especially in the face. By the time the ICRC arrived five days later, the death toll stood at 75 villagers (plus some 200 cattle, sheep, goats, donkeys, and birds). "Some of the victims were found dead in their homes," wrote Rochat, "as if they had died in their sleep."

The 75 bodies were buried in four mass graves. One of these was opened in the presence of the Red Cross team, who counted 15 corpses wrapped in shrouds. Significantly, none of the bodies displayed any "traumatic lesions," that is to say, none of the cuts or other wounds that would ordinarily accompany a violent death by conventional munitions. An on-site autopsy performed on one victim by two Red Cross doctors determined that the cause of death was "pulmonary edema"—excess fluid in the lungs—likely "caused by inhalation of toxic gas." The ICRC later sent its findings to an independent expert, Professor D. E. Lauppi, director of the Institute of Forensic Medicine at the University of Bern in Switzerland, who found their conclusion that a chemical weapon was responsible "perfectly justified," given "the total absence of traumatic lesions" and the fact there was no known "epidemical disease presenting a similar symptomatology or clinical development" to what the doctors had described. The professor added that, based on the symptoms mentioned, the chemical in question was likely to be mustard.

On June 2, 1967, the ICRC issued a public statement about the Gahar strike, which it identified as a "poison gas" attack, saying it was "extremely disturbed and concerned by these methods of warfare which are absolutely forbidden by codified international and customary law." It stopped short, however, of naming Egypt as the guilty party, instead calling on "all authorities concerned in the Yemen conflict" to refrain from using "asphyxiating gases or any other similar toxic substances"—a rather obfuscatory turn of phrase, since Egypt was the only such "authority" that possessed chemical weapons and the aircraft to deliver them. In any case, three days later, the Six-Day War broke out, changing the Middle East forever and consigning the story of chemical attacks in Yemen to the footnotes of history.

Amazingly, Egypt's chemical war in Yemen continued even after the complete and utter humiliation of the June 1967 defeat. Even as the air force back in Egypt lay in charred, smoking ruin; even as the homeland sat defenseless against an invading Israeli army that had just seized the Sinai, and now stood scarcely one hundred kilometers from Cairo itself on the banks of the Suez Canal; even as it was staggeringly obvious to all that Nasser was no longer a man in any position to export "revolution" abroad—Egyptian fighter planes were still being sent on sorties to gas civilians in Yemen. Chemical attacks were reported in the Khawlan vicinity on July 2 and 3, killing some 50 people in total. A further 30 were said to have been killed in strikes on the villages of al-Urr and al-Hamran on July 23. A large raid on the town of Hajjah on July 15, killing a reported 150, with 350 wounded, may even have been the deadliest chemical attack of the whole war.

It was not until August 1967 that the obvious futility and unsustainability of the enterprise were formally acknowledged at long last. At an Arab League summit in Khartoum, Nasser swallowed what remained of his pride and accepted an offer from King Faysal to finance Egypt's recovery from the June defeat (to the tune of £95 million per annum) and cease supporting the royalists in exchange for Egypt's full withdrawal from Yemen within three months. It was not as though Nasser had the luxury of choice. This was the best deal he was going to get; a much better deal, some might say, than he deserved. The bleak irony is that its Yemen component was essentially the same proposal first suggested by US mediators just months after Sallal's coup, in the spring of 1963. Tens of thousands of lives had been lost for nothing.

Egypt's withdrawal was completed on November 29, 1967. So unpopular had its presence become with Yemenis by then that random killings of Egyptians occurred even in the streets of republican

Sanaa. The total death toll after five years of war has been estimated at no fewer than five thousand Egyptians, and some twenty thousand Yemenis. Of the latter, at least eight hundred were killed by between forty and fifty chemical attacks, approximately two-thirds involving phosgene and one-third mustard.

Yemen's war dragged on for several months after Egypt's exit. In December 1967, a fifty-thousand-strong royalist force descended on and besieged the capital, necessitating Soviet airlifts to keep the YAR from collapse, until the royalists ran out of steam in February 1968. In the end, both Sallal and the Imam went into exile; the former in Baghdad, and the latter in Bromley, southeast London. With Sallal gone, the Third Force politicians—freed at last from their year of detention in Cairo—took office and brought about the reconciliation with royalists they had envisaged since the mid-1960s, when Nasser started jailing and assassinating them. In another irony, this republic (as Yemen officially remained) even mended fences with Saudi Arabia, now clearly established as the dominant power on the Arabian Peninsula.

On the very same day the Egyptians bade farewell at the port of Hudaydah in November 1967, the British did the same at Aden, relinquishing a once-prized outpost of empire first conquered in 1839. Britain's Aden "protectorate" was replaced by a totalitarian Soviet-backed Marxist-Leninist dictatorship called the People's Democratic Republic of Yemen. Visiting in the 1970s, the Lebanese journalist Hazem Saghieh was bemused to find that, on the one hand, his appointed Yemeni escort told him it was forbidden for Yemenis to speak to foreigners, while, on the other, when Saghieh asked for a traditional Yemeni meal in a restaurant, he was served an authentic British fish-and-chips.

The "Democratic Republic" endured until 1990, when the collapse of the Soviet Union deprived it of its patron, and it merged with the YAR to become the unified Republic of Yemen that stands today. The new state was ruled by Field Marshal Ali Abdallah Saleh, a Free Officer veteran of the 1962 coup who had already been president of the YAR since 1978, and who remained in power until his ouster in 2012, following a year of mass street demonstrations against him. On December 4, 2017, he was assassinated by militants from the same northern tribes he had warred against half a century earlier.

EGYPT II

16

ADRIFT ON
THE NILE

IN A CROWDED FIELD, THE YEMEN WAR WAS PERHAPS
the starkest of all indicators that a profound unwellness ailed
Nasser's Egypt in the 1960s. The malady, no doubt, had been present within the Free Officers' movement and regime from the start;
we have seen that no small number of Egyptians drew attention to
it early on, most memorably in March 1954. Yet it was not until the
1960s that the symptoms were aggravated to the full, and laid bare
for all to see.

Nasser's dazzling victories on the international stage in the late
1950s—Suez, the Syrian union, the Iraqi "revolution"—had made
it easy to silence skeptics at home. (Failing that, there was always
prison.) That events had rapidly gone sour in Iraq—culminating in
the Mosul bloodbath of 1959—was peripheral enough to be ignored,
or else chalked up to the eccentricities of the "madman" Qasim.

The Syrian secession from the UAR in 1961, however, was a very
different matter. Syria was no faraway country of which Egyptians
knew nothing; it had been, for more than three years, the same
country as Egypt. Syrian politicians and military men had sat in
Cairo's government offices, cafés, and country clubs, just as Egyptian officials had lived in Damascus. The collapse of the union was
a domestic affair as much as a foreign one, not least since, to Nasser's way of thinking, it raised the alarming prospect of Egypt's own
dormant opposition drawing courage from Syria's example. One
rumor held that the bar at Cairo's Gezira Club—the last bastion of

landed pashas and capitalists—raised a merry toast in tribute to the Syrian secessionists.

Embarrassed before the world by the spectacular implosion of his signature foreign policy achievement, Nasser desperately needed a new cause and battle cry to divert attention and sustain momentum. But what? He was dogged anew by the question he had tried to dodge ever since 1952, to which he may never have really known the answer himself: What did he, and his "revolution," actually stand for?

Since the mid-1950s, the answer had been "Arab nationalism," a banner to which millions across the Arab world had rallied, even if it had never fully persuaded the Egyptian public itself. September 1961 saw this wave of dreams crash ashore. In place of the grand union project that now lay in ruins, the senior theorists of Nasserism proposed doubling down on "revolution," only this time at home rather than abroad. A distinct tack inward, as well as leftward, would mark the coming phase, as the regime claimed at last to have developed its own unique school of revolutionary thought. In the sarcastic words of the public intellectual and Abu Zaabal survivor Louis Awad, the "high priests and exegetes" scratched their chins and hit upon "Arab socialism" as the new gospel and state doctrine.

An early milestone in this conversion was the speech Nasser gave in Cairo on October 16, 1961, less than three weeks after the coup in Damascus. While often described as "self-critical," on close inspection the speech is no such thing. Blame for the secession was laid squarely on Syrian "reactionaries," who had teamed up with "capitalists," "feudalists," "imperialists," and "opportunists" to strike at the "socialist revolution" set in motion by the union. If "we" were guilty of anything, it was being too gentle and accommodating with these reactionaries, who were allowed to infiltrate the National Union and corrupt it from within (as though the National Union were ever the real engine of government or policymaking).

No mea culpa was offered for the fallout with the Baath, the frictions within the officer corps, or the domineering attitude of which Syrians had long complained. The nationalization decrees of

July 1961, which had so alienated so many Syrians, were mentioned only as unequivocal examples of the union's brilliant accomplishments. Nasser didn't even pin blame on Syria's infamous intelligence chief, Sarraj, whose legendary tyranny might have served as a convenient scapegoat. No real lesson of any kind had been learned, in other words. As the Egyptian author (and socialist) Anouar Abdel-Malek put it, "At no time did President Nasser and the ruling group acknowledge the underlying cause that doomed the union in the eyes of the Syrian masses who had sought it: the dictatorial character of the government, its hatred for all democracy, its destruction of civil liberties, the dissolution of political parties, [and] the predominance of the political-military apparatus and its police forces."

The way forward now, declared Nasser in the same speech, was "socialist revolution." What this meant in practice was given solid shape six days later, when Cairo announced the arrest of forty people, including the former Wafdist secretary Fuad Sirag al-Din, and the seizure by the state of the property of 167 "reactionary capitalists" hailing from well-known families prominent since the days of the monarchy. By the following month, the latter figure had grown to 600. That many targets were members of Egypt's Jewish, Coptic Christian, Greek, and other minority communities gave the appearance of ethnic and sectarian undertones to this "liquidation of the Egyptian kulaks," as one Beirut newspaper dubbed it. The flight of these communities away from the country of their birth, already accelerated by Suez in 1956, now hastened further.

In the same month—November 1961—Nasser began discussions with a committee over the drafting of a so-called Charter of National Action, a landmark document envisaged as the definitive articulation of the program and philosophy of "Arab socialism." Six months later, on May 21, 1962, Nasser read the entirety of this twenty-two-thousand-word charter over the span of more than five hours to the members of a new body called the National Congress of Popular Forces.

Part treatise on the Nasserist version of Egyptian history, part distillation of ten years of regime propaganda, the charter was, for all its length, curiously light on concrete policy proposals. Urging a need to build further on the "glorious" decrees passed in July 1961, it stated that vast sectors of the economy, from rail transport to heavy and medium industry, mining, foreign trade and imports, banking, and insurance must all come under majority or total state ownership or control. Wherever a degree of private ownership would still be permitted, as in light industry, the state should still "maintain a role" therein.

On the political front, the discredited National Union would be revamped as the "Arab Socialist Union," to constitute the principal "authority representing the people." Half of the seats within this new union, and indeed all "political and popular organisations at all levels," would be reserved by law for "peasants and workers"—a concept borrowed, like much else in the charter, from Tito's Yugoslavia. Farmers' unions would be created, as would a "new political apparatus" within the Arab Socialist Union tasked with helping the leadership answer the needs of the masses. A passage pledging "full guarantees" for free speech and freedom of the press must have raised eyebrows among Egyptian journalists, not least those sitting in jail. On another note, it was a telling sign of the new domestic focus that only one of the charter's ten sections—the shortest—was devoted to the subject of Arab unity, while another, also brief, addressed foreign policy.

The implementation of "Arab socialism" would occupy much of the coming two years. Starting September 1962, a steady wave of new nationalizations extended to sectors as varied as shipping, cotton ginning, pharmaceuticals, trucking, river transport, glass production, farming, and book publishing. By late 1964, practically every company of significance—around eight hundred of Egypt's largest firms, representing the bulk of national output—had been taken into state hands.

What were the results? The Egyptian economy did not respond as hoped to Arab socialism. The oft-repeated goal, stated in the charter, of doubling national income in the ten years between 1960 and 1970 was not nearly attained. In its five-year plan for the years 1960–65, the regime had envisaged a growth rate of 7 percent per annum; the actual figure was less than 3 percent. Industrial output, on which Nasser had pinned especial hopes, scarcely came halfway to meeting its target over the same period. Agricultural production, which was supposed to grow at 5 percent per annum, grew in fact at 3 percent. Instead of the trade surplus of £E40 million anticipated by 1965, Egypt saw a *deficit* of £E76 million that year, bringing the total deficit for the preceding five years to over £E400 million (equivalent to $1.15 billion at the time, or nearly $11 billion today).

The failure of exports to keep pace with the imports demanded by a rapidly growing population aggravated a core problem: the acute scarcity of foreign currency. Without foreign reserves, the regime had to scale back investment in industry, which had anyway been directed disproportionately toward "expensive and relatively unproductive heavy industrial projects, especially iron and steel and such enterprises as the Nasr Motor Car works built with the help of Fiat at a cost of £30 million." Nor, without foreign currency, could state-owned factories import the essential raw materials and parts needed to operate; Nasr motors was one of many that had to either close for a period or work at reduced capacity.

By 1964, the cash crunch had led to steep inflation and unprecedented shortages of Egyptians' basic needs. Rice, meats, fats, cooking oil, sugar, soap, tea, light bulbs, and shoes all vanished at various times from the shelves, and long lines outside shops became the norm. Rationing was introduced in December 1964, when the sale of meat was banned for three days per week. That same month, Nasser tried to shrug off the crisis in a speech, claiming Egyptians were a hardy people accustomed to sacrifice. "If today we drink tea seven days a week, we'll drink it five days, until we build our country. If we used to drink coffee seven days, we'll drink it four days; if we used to eat meat four days, we'll eat it three days." Unfortunately, the problem was about to get very much worse.

Since the late 1950s, the US had sold wheat to Egypt on favorable terms—accepting payment in Egyptian currency—under the Agricultural Trade Development and Assistance Act of 1954, better known as the "Food for Peace" program. Given Egypt's foreign currency woes, the arrangement was of considerable benefit to Cairo. By 1962, Egypt was sourcing 99 percent of its wheat imports—more than half its total wheat consumption—from the US. In return for this advantageous deal, Washington hoped Nasser would extend it a minimum of political goodwill. "We didn't expect Nasser to bow, scrape, lick our boots, and say, 'Thank you, Uncle Sam,'" recalled then–Secretary of State Dean Rusk, "but we did expect him at least to moderate his virulent criticism of the United States."

Instead, Nasser did the opposite. For reasons ranging from his war in Yemen to the conflict in Congo (where he and the US backed opposing sides), Nasser's relations with Washington steadily cooled throughout the first half of the 1960s. This was especially the case after Lyndon B. Johnson took office upon his predecessor John F. Kennedy's assassination in November 1963. A growing chorus of voices in Washington asked why the US was, in effect, bankrolling its own adversary, not least at a time he was committing what one member of the Senate Foreign Relations Committee called "mass murders" in Yemen. The breach came in December 1964, when Nasser took to the podium and told the Americans to "drink from the sea"—a politer way of telling them to go to hell—and vowed to "cut off the tongue" of anyone criticizing his behavior. The following month, President Johnson suspended wheat sales to Egypt.

No longer able to import wheat in Egyptian pounds, Nasser now had to find an additional £50 million a year in already-scarce foreign currency to make up the difference. To do so, he borrowed money from Europe at extortionate rates of interest, further saddling the economy with debts it could ill afford. The Yemen war, meanwhile, was yet another bottomless pit of expenses, costing Cairo sums estimated at between $70 million and well over $100 million a year. A significant part of this bill represented payoffs to Yemeni tribes, which—like the bonuses lavished on Egyptian personnel serving in Yemen—were also paid in foreign currency.

In the face of these profound fiscal strains, Nasser enforced further austerity measures in 1965, raising taxes while slashing subsidies and imports. As we have seen, he also began looking seriously for an exit from Yemen, signing the Jeddah Agreement with King Faysal in August, and pulling some thirty thousand troops out of the country. But all was in vain. Egypt's population kept growing, its output and exports kept lagging, the cost of living kept rising, and cash kept hemorrhaging in all directions. By the end of 1966, "the national stockpile of wheat held barely enough reserves to last through January." And all this was *before* the catastrophic defeat in the Six-Day War of 1967, which cost Egypt crucial revenues from both the Suez Canal and the Sinai oil fields—two of its few remaining sources of foreign currency.

★

SO MUCH FOR ECONOMICS. In political terms, one sliver of relent provided by "Arab socialism" was the release from prison in 1964 of the leftists incarcerated since the crackdown of 1959. Their continued imprisonment had become both unnecessary—since the union with Syria was over—and an embarrassment for a regime now setting such store by its left-wing credentials. Nasser's drift ever closer toward Moscow, not least after the row with President Johnson, was another factor. The release happened in stages between March and May, coinciding with a much-hyped state visit to Cairo by Khrushchev. Out of prison, many leftists chose to make their peace with the regime, which had after all adopted much of their rhetoric and program. In 1965, Egypt's (illegal) communist party agreed to disband and join the Arab Socialist Union, though certain members objected and were jailed anew.

The case of the leftist prisoners, however, was an isolated and exceptional one; the overwhelming tendency throughout the 1960s was toward more, not less, authoritarianism. As the size of the state expanded, so did its stifling presence in citizens' lives, further shrinking what little space remained for free political or even artistic expression. A case in point was the sequestration in August 1963 of Dar al-Maaref, Egypt's largest book publisher. With newspapers and magazines already nationalized since 1960, the takeover of publishing houses left writers with no outlets free of direct state control and censorship. Much the same went for filmmakers, playwrights, and radio broadcasters. Freedom of expression, which the National Charter claimed to protect, became "a phrase without meaning," in the words of Louis Awad.

In parallel with the state's expansion was its rampant militarization, as an elite officer caste extended its influence wider and deeper than ever before. The charter itself had heaped praise on the armed forces, reminding Egyptians that it was soldiers who carried out the 1952 "revolution," and asserting that the army's role was not just to protect the nation's borders but to take an active part in the "popular struggle." In the months and years that followed, military men came to make up "the very great majority of senior diplomatic personnel; a considerable proportion of presidents, directors and members of the Boards of public corporations, etc; a very considerable number of ministers, under-secretaries of State, director-generals and directors of the various ministries; the quasi-totality of the senior personnel and administration of the security services; and a very significant proportion of the key posts in culture, the press, radio and television." The Arab Socialist Union itself was "basically run by dominant members of the officer corps, former members of the old 'Council of the Revolution' or simply functionaries in the ruling politico-military apparatus." Every prime minister of Egypt in the 1960s was of military background, while the speaker of the unelected pseudo-parliament, the National Assembly, was the Free Officer (and future president) Anwar Sadat. This aggressive elevation of a supreme military establishment, dominating officialdom at all levels, fueled popular resentment of the armed forces, whose members—especially those who served in Yemen—enjoyed all manner of salary, housing, healthcare, education, transportation, and other benefits unavailable to civilians.

It was also in the 1960s that Nasser's cult of personality, steadily built up since 1954, reached its totalitarian zenith. This was the time of blockbuster propaganda films, such as Youssef Chahine's 1963 *Al-Nasser Salah al-Din* (Saladin the victorious), a three-hour biopic on the twelfth-century Muslim conqueror who drove the Crusaders out of Jerusalem, intended all too obviously to suggest parallels with another "al-Nasser" in the modern era. Singers famed across the Arab world, from Egypt's Umm Kulthum and Abd al-Halim Hafez to Lebanon's Sabah to Syria's Farid al-Atrash were called on to perform tributes to the dear leader at the annual "Revolution Day" gala and other official events. Nasser's portrait could be seen in "every govern-ment office, store, schoolroom, and business," not to mention every newspaper. The historian Sherif Younis recalls being obliged, as an elementary school student in the 1960s, to memorize and recite songs venerating "Father Gamal," including one about the Suez Canal:

> *Gamal came along*
> *Hero of heroes*
> *Freed our country*
> *And took the Canal*
> *Long live Gamal*
> *Long live Gamal*

And another that went:

> *O Father Gamal*
> *Beloved of the [Nile] Valley*
> *You who sacrifice*
> *Your soul for my country*
> *I heard Dad*
> *Say to Mom,*
> *"It's all thanks to Father Gamal"*

The combination of deepening economic misery with an ever-more-asphyxiating political climate was perhaps the defining malaise of Egypt in the 1960s. "We have the worst of both systems," says the protagonist of Waguih Ghali's 1964 novel *Beer in the Snooker Club*. "Both the dictatorship and the starvation without any future to look forward to."

It is, indeed, in the literature of the period that one often finds the atmosphere best captured. Ghali's unsparing portrait had to be published in London; it stood zero chance of publication in Nasser's Cairo. Writers who stayed in Egypt had to tread more carefully, but this didn't always mean flinching from depicting reality. Sonallah Ibrahim published his semi-autobiographical debut novel *Tilk al-Ra'iha* (*That Smell*) two years after his release from prison with the other leftists in 1964. His protagonist, also just out of jail, finds Cairo in a bad way. The sewers are overflowing into the streets, filling the air with an intolerable stench (hence the title). Buying meat involves a two-hour wait in line. Soldiers returning from Yemen are met by the public not with a heroes' welcome but with cold indifference. On the crowded metro, everyone is always scowling, never smiling. Seeing a train driver slip a piece of opium into his mouth, our antihero envies him: he has found a way to cope.

Though the novel made no direct criticism of the regime, this was hardly the wholesome image of socialist utopia the authorities sought to promote. The book was immediately confiscated upon publication in 1966, and would not be allowed to reappear in full, unredacted form in Cairo until 1986.

Another controversial novel published in 1966 was *Tharthara Fawq al-Nil* (*Prattle on the Nile*, also translated more loosely as *Adrift on the Nile*) by Naguib Mahfouz, who later won the Nobel Prize in literature. A group of friends escape the crushing tedium of daily life by gathering each night to smoke hashish on a houseboat on the Nile. Disenchanted with everything, they seek refuge in gallows humor and cynicism. In their company, the cardinal sin is to take anything seriously. Revolution is futile; the words "Arab socialism" invite laughter; "our life" itself, declares Mustafa Rashid, "has become a tasteless joke." In perhaps the most daring passage, a stoned character imagines a conversation with the ancient Egyptian sage Ipuwer, whom he asks to recite his famous admonitions to the Pharaoh. "These are years of war and catastrophe," quotes Ipuwer. "You have wisdom, perception, and justice, but you let corruption devour the country. See how your orders are disdained; can you not order someone to tell you the truth?" One doesn't need a Nobel Prize to work out who the "Pharaoh" represents here.

It has been said that Mahfouz's novel infuriated Nasser's right-hand man, Field Marshal Amer, who may have suspected it alluded to his own notorious hashish habit. Mahfouz would later regale interviewers with tales of how Amer was about to arrest him for the book until being overruled by Nasser personally at the last moment. Another novelist, Mohamed Rabie, asserts this vignette was a fabrication circulated by officials to cast Nasser in a positive light. It might be contended the president comes off looking less than resplendent either way.

What all three of these novels put their finger on was a distinct phenomenon in the air in the mid-1960s: a widespread, grassroots disillusionment with the entire Nasserist system per se, which, after more than a decade in power, had manifestly failed to deliver the freedom and prosperity it had once appeared to promise. The "revolution" had gone rotten before it was ripe, and its leader looked less and less the man "loved by millions," as the singers had crooned in the 1950s, and more and more a garden-variety pharaoh. Since open, organized opposition was impossible, the result was a broad-based disengagement from political participation, and a withdrawal into the private sphere. As Sonallah Ibrahim wrote in his memoir, the ubiquitous "police state atmosphere" spread "apathy, negativity, and an aversion to political activity among the general populace."

The exception that proved the rule pertained to a small band of fanatics, whose faith in their own cause drew strength from the disaffection all around them. Yet another manifestation of the rot at the core of Egyptian life was the revival in 1965 of the regime's feud with the Muslim Brotherhood. That summer, security forces uncovered an armed Brotherhood cell that had quietly and systematically been preparing to assassinate Nasser and topple the regime by force.

This cell's leader was the fifty-eight-year-old Sayyid Qutb, once a secularist with literary aspirations, who held no formal religious credentials, and embraced Islamism only in the early 1950s, just in time to be swept into prison during the crackdown on the Brotherhood in 1954. A case of the convert's zeal if ever there was one, in jail Qutb developed a particularly extreme ideological doctrine, which held that Nasser, all Egyptian officials (including the religious establishment), and even most ordinary Egyptian citizens were unbelievers, heretics, apostates, and enemies of the true Islam. Nothing less than the complete destruction of the prevailing order, and its replacement by an austere Islamist theocracy, would bring harmony and justice to humankind.

During his ten years of imprisonment, Qutb's ideas found an audience among a circle of fellow inmates, as well as young Islamist activists on the outside, to whom his prison writings were secretly smuggled. After his release on health grounds in 1964, he devoted himself full-time to clandestine organizing, transforming his coterie of disciples into a deeply indoctrinated paramilitary cult. By the time of its discovery in the summer of 1965, the cell had secured arms, funds, and training, but had not yet carried out any live operations. Once exposed, its members were quickly arrested, tortured, tried, and given sentences ranging from prison to death. In a repeat of 1954, the regime also arrested thousands of other suspected Islamists more broadly across the country. "We wanted to bury the [Brotherhood], period," recalled Nasser's senior aide Sami Sharaf. "Our goal was to remove the cancer from the Egyptian body politic."

Qutb was hanged on August 29, 1966. While several of his fellow conspirators had seen their death sentences commuted, Nasser personally insisted on Qutb's execution, arguing that to cut off "the head of the snake" would deal Islamist extremism a death blow from which it would never recover. Reality, needless to say, has taken a different path. In death, the man who had known only failure when alive finally achieved the enduring celebrity he had so long craved and been denied. By paying the ultimate price for his convictions, and facing the gallows with what by all accounts was physical courage, he furnished generations of Islamists—in Egypt and well beyond—with an icon and archetype of faith-based defiance of the contemporary state system and world order. His example, as well as aspects of his doctrine itself, would go on to inspire the jihadist groups familiar to us all today, including al-Qaeda and the Islamic State.

★

A PROFOUND DISCONTENT, then, was simmering under the surface in Egypt even before the earthquake of defeat in the Six-Day War of 1967. That crushing humiliation would bring the anger out into the open at last, but only after a delay of several months, once Egyptians had had time to fully take stock of the loss and process its meaning.

In the war's immediate aftermath, Egyptians' first instinct was to cling to the comfort of the familiar. On the evening of June 9—one day after Egypt agreed to a cease-fire—Nasser gave a most extraordinary statement to the nation, broadcast on radio and television. "We cannot conceal from ourselves that we have faced a grave setback in the last few days," he said slowly, with a pained face, head drooping between his shoulders, his voice unusually frail, trailing almost to a whisper at times. Promising honesty while hiding behind the evasive "setback" euphemism, this sentence encapsulated the contradictions running through the statement as a whole. Nasser proceeded to present a grossly misleading account of the military course of events since the war had begun on June 5. He then dropped the bombshell that he had chosen to take responsibility for the "setback" by resigning from the presidency and all other official and political roles, to "return to the ranks of the masses, and carry out my duty with them like any other citizen." In accordance with the constitution, Vice President Zakaria Muhieddin would replace him as president.

No sooner had Nasser finished his words than Egyptians left their homes and flooded the streets and squares in large numbers. From Cairo and Alexandria to small towns and rural villages, impassioned crowds chanted Nasser's name and demanded he rescind his decision. The eight-kilometer stretch from central Cairo to Nasser's home in Manshiyat al-Bakri became a solid human mass, remaining in place until he announced the following day he would stay on as president after all.

What was going on? Had the crowds been genuinely spontaneous, or were they staged by the regime in an elaborate ruse? The historian Sherif Younis has written a whole book on this question, and his answer, in short, is: both.

This was, after all, the very trick the Free Officers had pulled during the great crisis of March 1954, when they pretended they were going to step aside and allow free elections, only to immediately mobilize street action to bring about the exact opposite. Just as the junta's Liberation Rally had then arranged protests chanting "Down with freedom" and "No democracy," so did its successor organization, the Arab Socialist Union (ASU), put its own formidable ground game to work on June 9 and 10, 1967. Officials from the ASU—whose head once boasted he could summon a crowd of forty thousand in Cairo in three hours—were visibly present in the midst of the demonstrations. Transportation appeared, as though by magic, to herd droves of people into the capital from other towns and villages free of charge. A number of the slogans chanted had nothing to do with the subject of Nasser's resignation, having clearly been prepared by the ASU for unrelated previous occasions (e.g., "America, gather up your money, Abdel Nasser's coming to trample you"). No Egyptian could fail to interpret the message conveyed by these and other telltale signals: the regime did not intend for Nasser to leave.

At the same time, the demonstrations cannot reasonably be ascribed to ASU orchestration alone. Plenty of Egyptians still alive today attest to taking part in them entirely of their own accord. (As have those who joined the simultaneous protests in other Arab countries.) As absurd as it seems in retrospect that a people should reject the resignation of a leader responsible for the most calamitous military defeat in their nation's modern history, the situation did not in fact look so clear-cut on June 9, 1967.

For one thing, Egyptians had still not been given anything close to the full truth of how badly the war had gone. In its first days, they were fed an outrageous stream of total lies about its progress by state media. The playwright Tawfiq al-Hakim recalled listening to the radio at the *Al-Ahram* newspaper offices on the morning of June 5, the first day, when "every fifteen minutes" brought news of dozens more Israeli planes downed by Egypt's mighty forces. By noon, the number had reached two hundred; after that, al-Hakim stopped listening, confident the war was already won. Walking from Tahrir Square to Sulayman Pasha, he saw the ASU had hung up large banners reading "To Tel Aviv!" and other slogans of triumph. He genuinely believed Egypt's army would enter the Israeli capital that night. A plethora of similar accounts from other witnesses suggests a majority of Egyptians and Arabs around the region thought much the same.

In reality, of course, it was Israel that had wiped out Egypt's air force in the opening minutes of hostilities, effectively deciding the war's outcome on the morning of its first day. Yet even in his supposedly frank heart-to-heart with the nation on June 9, Nasser did not admit to this, saying with unintentionally comic understatement that Egypt's air power had been "insufficient" to relieve its ground forces in the Sinai. Nor, indeed, did he disclose that the Sinai had been captured and occupied by Israel in its entirety, stating only that Egypt's troops had been compelled to "evacuate the first line of defence" there, before fighting fierce battles on the unspecified "second line of defence."

Worse, Nasser repeated the complete fiction (first propagated on June 6) that British and US aircraft had participated alongside Israel in the bombing of Egyptian positions, attributing the defeat to this "imperialist collusion," without which the enemy would have been "three times" weaker in the air. Egypt's forces had fought with unimpeachable skill and bravery, he said, but what could they do against a "conspiracy" as grand and "wicked" as this?

It is easy to see that, coming immediately after these remarks, Nasser's announcement of his resignation made little logical sense. If there was nothing more that could have been done against so overwhelming an array of enemies—Israel, Britain, and the US combined—and if, despite these fearsome odds, all that resulted was a partial withdrawal in the Sinai, then why the need for so drastic a step as resignation? Everything he had just said in the fifteen minutes leading up to the announcement made it seem a wholly unwarranted overreaction to a battle in which Egypt could not, in fact, have fought any more creditably, and in which it did not lose very much anyway.

Quite apart from that, who could get excited about a President Zakaria Muhieddin? It was not as though Nasser were offering Egyptians democracy, or any improvement on the status quo at all. Muhieddin, indeed, was an especially unpopular figure, associated in the public mind with the harsh austerity measures introduced while he was prime minister. There were chants against him in the streets on June 9. In any case, so long as the choice was limited to one Free Officer or another, it would always be inconceivable that the crowd would stand with anyone but Nasser. Thirteen years of relentless personality-cult promotion had made certain of that. Seeming to hint at this fact in his speech without needing to spell it out, Nasser tugged sentimentally at his audience's heartstrings, fondly reminiscing on the glories of years past before closing with the words, "My whole heart is with you, and I want your whole hearts to be with me."

Overcome with the passion of the moment, racked with profound fears and uncertainties for the future, prodded by the ASU and other regime organs, and acting in any case on incomplete information, a critical mass of Egyptians gave their leader one more chance. As Nasser would soon discover, though, this did not mean all was forgiven, or that he had carte blanche to revert to business as usual thereafter. Very much to the contrary, to the extent that Egyptians offered Nasser a mandate to stay, they did so—paradoxically—in the expectation of change. When it became apparent only months later that change was not forthcoming, it fell to a group of bold Egyptian youths to stand up and proclaim what their elders no longer had the courage to.

★

FOR A MAN WHO had just said he wanted to give up power completely, Nasser showed a remarkable readiness to take it all back again. From the moment he reversed his resignation on June 10, he proceeded as he had done after every other crisis in the past: by concentrating yet more power within his own hands. On June 19, he made himself prime minister in addition to president, as well as secretary-general of the ASU. The ethos of the coming period was summed up in two slogans that then became current, both propagated by Nasser himself.

One was that the long-awaited transition to democracy promised since the 1950s, and repeated in the 1962 charter, would have to wait once again until the "consequences of the aggression were removed," that is, until the land seized by Israel in the course of the Six-Day War was recovered. Nasser made this argument explicitly in a speech on July 23, 1967. The second slogan was that there must be "no voice louder than the sound of the battle." In other words, now was not the time for criticism. The "battle"—whatever exactly that was—took precedence over free speech and debate, indeed over "all else."

It soon transpired that a significant number of Egyptians were not prepared to play by these rules. The old arrangement by which citizens surrendered their civil and political liberties in the name of whichever grand, abstract cause the regime had last decided to champion was already under strain before June 1967. The defeat marked the ultimate confirmation of its bankruptcy. As so often in Egypt's past, it was now the youth who stepped forward and led the call for change. Specifically, it was university students—those inveterate agitators, who had sparked the great anticolonial revolt of 1919, and kept the protests going longest in the spring of 1954—who at last rediscovered their voices after fourteen years of forced silence, and reclaimed their place at the front and center of Egyptian politics.

The spark was a verdict issued by a military court trying the leaders of Egypt's air force on charges of negligence for their disastrous performance in the June 1967 war. The air force command had come to be particularly associated in the public mind with responsibility for the defeat, given the total annihilation in the war's first moments of their planes, which had been left exposed on display in the open air at their bases, sitting ducks for Israel's bombers. Nasser himself had helped encourage this perception, claiming in public that he had warned the air force commander on June 2 to expect an Israeli attack on his planes three days later. The force became the butt of routine ridicule and black humor in Egypt thereafter.

When the court's verdict came out on February 20, 1968, sentencing the air force commander and his deputy to fifteen and ten years' imprisonment, respectively, but acquitting the chief of staff and another subordinate commander, it was deemed by many Egyptians to be unduly lenient. In the industrial town of Helwan, south of Cairo, munitions-factory workers and other laborers immediately took to the streets in protest. Clashes ensued with police, causing a number of injuries.

The flames ignited in Helwan reached the gates of Cairo University four days later. A vivid firsthand account of what followed has been written by Wael Uthman, then a student at the university's engineering college, which became the epicenter of the action.

Uthman was with friends in the college courtyard on the morning of Saturday, February 24, when suddenly they heard the chants of fellow students from the law college marching past. Straightaway, he and other engineering students rushed out to join in, accompanying them to the National Assembly building five kilometers away, just south of Tahrir Square. As their peaceful procession made its way across Cairo, they were cheered by ordinary citizens—"men and women, young and old"—who waved at them and shouted in support.

Outside the Assembly, the students nominated representatives to go in and present their demands to its head, Anwar Sadat. Humoring the youngsters, whom he addressed patronizingly as "my children," the forty-nine-year-old Sadat agreed to speak with them, and pledged to "study" their demands. Matters took an ominous turn when the names of the student representatives were noted down, but Sadat gave them his word no harm would come their way.

At 3 a.m. that very night, the same student representatives were bundled into cars by intelligence agents and driven to the Citadel prison.

When word of their classmates' arrest reached the students the following morning, they erupted in fury. The hours ahead would witness the wildest scenes of domestic revolt in Nasser's Egypt since 1954.

Unlike the previous day, this time the students were met with force when they stepped outside campus onto the streets. Attempting to reach Cairo University Bridge to cross the Nile heading east, they were beaten back with police truncheons and tear gas, and could advance no farther than the end of Nahdet Misr Street, barely a few hundred meters from campus. As the volleys of tear gas intensified, they retreated back inside the engineering college.

Meanwhile, ten kilometers to the northeast, students were also pouring out of the engineering college of Ain Shams University, trying to reach the nearby Abbasiya Square. Joined by random passersby and other members of the public, they put up stiff resistance to the police's tear gas, leading security forces to eventually fire on them with live ammunition, killing three.

Back at Cairo University, the confrontation was also growing more violent. Police began firing tear gas inside the campus itself, prompting students to pick up the canisters and hurl them back whence they came. As the air grew thick with gas, some students

took refuge indoors, while others climbed up onto the college rooftops, ripped off their red clay tiles, and flung them at police in the
street below. Relief arrived in the unexpected form of teenagers
from the nearby al-Saidia secondary school, who showed up out of
nowhere and began pelting the security forces with rocks and bricks.

Around this time, Uthman and others noticed a fire truck parked
outside a side entrance to the college, one of several that had been
called in for use as water cannons against the students. They came up
with a plan. By raining rocks down on the truck and its crew, then
charging at them to force them to flee, the students succeeded in
gaining control of the truck, which they drove triumphantly into the
campus as a trophy. "We felt the thrill of victory!" recalled Uthman.

By sunset, the situation had calmed somewhat. The security
forces had pulled back to the nearby Orman Garden, and many
students had left campus. The five hundred or so who remained
decided to hold a sit-in at the engineering college until their
demands were met. Large banners were quickly improvised and
stuck on the outer walls of the college, bearing slogans "speaking
of stolen freedom, demanding the release of detainees, and attacking the dictator and his friend [Mohamed Hasanayn] Heikal," Nasser's media mouthpiece. According to Uthman, the regime ordered
public transit to avoid driving past the college, so passengers could
not read the banners. The students also printed flyers listing their
eight demands, which they distributed to members of the public in
the street.

These demands, in the order in which they appeared on the flyers,
were as follows: the immediate release of all arrested students; "freedom of opinion and the press"; a "free" National Assembly practicing "sound parliamentary life"; an end to the secret-police presence
on university campuses; the issuance and implementation of "decrees
of freedoms"; a "serious investigation" into what happened with the
workers in Helwan; "clarification of the truth regarding the case of
the air force" command; and an investigation into police attacks on
students and violation of campus sanctity.

One notices straightaway, as Uthman also observes, that the ostensible cause of the unrest—the air force trial verdict—makes up just one of the eight demands, presented second from last. All seven of the others point to far broader and deeper grievances with the repressive and antidemocratic character of the regime as a whole. These were, of course, issues long predating both the trial and the June 1967 defeat itself.

The sit-in continued for three days, sustained by food smuggled in through an adjacent zoo (until the regime closed it). On the morning of February 28, the students were invited to meet again with Sadat and other officials at the National Assembly. There they were treated to refreshments and "American cigarettes," followed by a long and condescending lecture on Egyptian history and the achievements of the Arab socialist revolution. In closing, Sadat informed them their demands were "rejected in form and substance."

To this, the students' designated spokesman responded with pluck, dismissing Sadat's oration as "empty talk" and vowing the students were committed to every word of their demands. The meeting ended with officials saying they would "discuss" the demands anew, but it was clear an impasse had been reached. The sit-in was called off, and, after ten days in detention, the students arrested on the first night were released—the only one of the eight demands the regime ever met.

On March 3, Nasser addressed the student protests in a speech, "falsifying the facts as usual," in Uthman's words. Echoing Sadat's patronizing tone, Nasser said he had followed the events closely with the concern of a "father," for "I consider every one of those children to be like my own." Portraying the regime's response on the ground as extraordinarily merciful, he claimed injuries among police were three times higher than among demonstrators. In his telling, the students were innocent victims of a misunderstanding about what happened at Helwan, on the one hand, and of exploitation by "counter-revolutionaries" on the other. Some of the slogans raised in the protests made it clear, he said, that the usual enemies of the people—feudalists, capitalists, imperialists, and reactionaries—stood behind them.

In actual fact, Uthman attests, the student movement at the time was dominated by the left, a situation that brought him no personal satisfaction, as one of the few and heavily outnumbered Muslim Brotherhood sympathizers on campus. (He laments he was almost alone among sit-in participants in observing the daily prayers at the college mosque.) In spite of this, Uthman lauds the movement of February 1968 as a rare example of honest, good-faith cooperation among Egyptians of all ideological persuasions, who set aside their differences "in the cause of freedom":

> While it distressed me that the movement's leadership was not Islamist, I feel obliged to state the 1968 movement was the only one embraced by students of all orientations. It remained clean and pure to the end. The main reason for this was it steered clear of the doctrinal differences that [later] gave rise to a violent conflict . . . which left its mark on all subsequent student movements.

Nasser's efforts to smear the protests as a conspiracy notwithstanding, the air of dissent spread outside campus walls in the weeks that followed. Leading members of the judiciary, for instance, met in March and issued a call for greater independence from the executive branch, the exclusion of judges from political organizations such as the ASU, and an end to interference by military personnel in judicial affairs. Reading the winds, Nasser switched gears, and moved to assuage the discontent. It was announced that the air force command would be retried by a different court. Nasser also appointed a new cabinet with a rare civilian majority (though he remained prime minister himself).

On March 30, Nasser then announced his version of a reform package: a "program of action" for "change." This promised a democratization of the ASU by the introduction of elections, and set out an impressive-sounding vision for Egypt's long-awaited new constitution. The latter, said Nasser, would provide "full guarantees for personal liberties," including and in addition to "freedom of thought, expression, publication, opinion, scientific research, and the press." It would also enshrine the principle of judicial immunity, create a supreme court to decide the constitutionality of laws, specify term limits for the major executive posts, and commit to "the liberation of women."

There followed another of those brief spells of comparative openness of which the regime was occasionally wont to make a display. The pages of the semi-official *Al-Ahram* newspaper, for instance, were given over to polite critiques of certain unpopular practices, such as censorship, arrests by the secret police, and restrictions on academic freedom.

As always, it was not to last. In the words of the Egyptian political scientist Ahmed Abdalla, "After a few months of liberal deeds and declarations the trend was reversed and Egyptian politics reverted to its authoritarian mould." When a second round of student protests broke out in the Nile Delta and Alexandria in November 1968, the regime's response was merciless. Twenty people were killed, including six students, as police fired live ammunition into the crowds. Hundreds were arrested, some not to be released until years later. The March 30 Program was torn to shreds, and the exciting new constitution promised by Nasser never saw the light of day.

★

THE REGIME WEATHERED THE STORM, as it always did, and hobbled forth on its increasingly aimless course. Nasser himself, on the other hand, was not much longer for the world. Afflicted with diabetes since the 1950s, his health had been in steep decline ever since, not helped in the slightest by the manic stress of the job, his lack of exercise, and the three packs of L&M cigarettes he was said to get through each day. As early as 1964, the journalist Robert Stephens thought he detected a "hint almost of physical frailty" when he met him. By the late 1960s, he was in a terrible way, with diabetic neuropathy and arteriosclerosis in his thighs causing him to drag a leg as he walked. After a physical collapse, he agreed to travel to the Soviet Union for treatment in the summer of 1968. But he suffered a heart attack the following year that put him out of action for weeks once again. By this point, "a mobile oxygen unit would follow him at a discreet distance" wherever he went. Fundamentally incapable of heeding his doctors' advice to slow down, still less of retiring altogether, he was quite literally working himself into an early grave. The final heart attack arrived on September 28, 1970, one day after he brokered the cease-fire between King Hussein and Yasser Arafat.

Yet even at his lowest and most enfeebled, in the gloomy dusk of his final year, as he lay dying and dogged by his defeats, his star eclipsed by his former Palestinian protégés, on the one hand, and his erstwhile foe King Faysal on the other, the grand old man of Arab nationalism was still to enjoy one lively final hurrah. From an unexpected direction—the desert to his west—a dashing young Nasserist firebrand suddenly stepped forth from the void, on a monomaniacal quest to follow in his hero's footsteps, raising the tantalizing possibility that the reports of Nasser's political demise may have been exaggerated after all.

LIBYA

17

SECOND TIME
AS FARCE

IN THE EARLY HOURS OF SEPTEMBER 1, 1969, IT WAS THE turn of Egypt's large, sparsely inhabited neighbor to the west, the Kingdom of Libya, to have its military coup, while the ailing monarch Idris al-Senussi was overseas. At two-thirty in the morning, a handful of junior "Free Officers" set in motion the plans they had worked on for five years.

It was not to be the smoothest coup in history. A tank driven by the man who would become Libya's defense minister for forty-one years, Abu Bakr Yunis, short-circuited and burst into flames. A convoy of jeeps led by the coup's mastermind, the wiry, young 1st Lt. Muammar al-Gaddafi, got split up at a simple fork in the road. Another officer was unable to find the radio station he was supposed to occupy in the capital city of Tripoli. Only because the resistance they encountered was so negligible did the bumbling conspirators succeed at all. In spite of themselves, they managed in under two hours to seize the key reins of power, arresting the commanders of the army and royal guard in their homes. By daybreak, Gaddafi's voice was on the airwaves, declaring the establishment of the Libyan republic, promising a glorious new era of "freedom" and "equality" devoid of all "injustice and exploitation."

Their putsch complete, the officers turned immediately to neighboring Egypt for help. That same morning, Cairo's landmark Gezira Tower received a message from the telegraph operator in Libya's Benghazi, saying an army officer had entered the building demanding to send an urgent telegram to President Nasser. Speaking in the name of "the commander of the Libyan revolution," this officer wanted Nasser to know he and his colleagues were now in full control of the country, and hoped Egypt would stand with and support them. Nasser raced to assemble a delegation of aides, including his media man Heikal, and dispatched them to Benghazi to assess the situation.

"Tell President Nasser we made this revolution for him," said Gaddafi to Heikal when they met. "Now it is for Nasser to tell us what to do."

★

IN THE FORTY-TWO YEARS he would rule Libya between his coup in 1969 and his killing at rebel hands in 2011, Muammar al-Gaddafi became a byword to many across the world for egregious despotism, garish attire, international terrorism, plane and disco bombings, the Munich Olympics massacre, and friendships with everyone from Nelson Mandela to Fidel Castro to the "Butcher of Uganda," Idi Amin. To US president Ronald Reagan, he was the "Mad Dog of the Middle East," an indelicate choice of words that underscored the infamy with which Libya's dictator was branded in the highest halls of power.

On the day of his coup, however, Gaddafi was completely unknown even to Libyans. The son of an illiterate Bedouin goat herder, he had been born in a tent in the desert south of the coastal town of Sirte, in what he said was 1941 though others have claimed was 1943. His early childhood consisted largely of helping his parents with farming and livestock duties, while acquiring a rudimentary religious education at the hands of a roaming cleric.

Not until 1954, when he was in early adolescence, did Gaddafi first attend a primary school in Sirte, sleeping in a mosque during the week and walking the thirty kilometers back to his family on weekends. Two years later, the family moved six hundred kilometers south to the remote town of Sebha, deep in the sandy wilderness of the Sahara, closer to the borders of Chad and Niger than to the Mediterranean shoreline.

It was here in Sebha, right at the time Nasser was nationalizing the Suez Canal Company and surviving the combined invasion of Britain, France, and Israel, that the teenage Gaddafi "found" the Egyptian leader as another might find Jesus, and began a lifelong worship of the anointed savior. Listening to Cairo Radio for hours on end, Gaddafi would commit Nasser's speeches to memory and perform them for friends at school. When Syria seceded from its union with Egypt in 1961, Gaddafi joined a protest in Sebha's town square, where pictures of Nasser were raised and funds collected to send him a supportive telegram. Demonstrating his budding talent for rabble-rousing, Gaddafi took the occasion to deliver a speech lambasting the Libyan monarchy's hosting of British and US military bases—a stunt that earned him local notoriety, and expulsion from Sebha's secondary school.

As the young Gaddafi exulted in the newfound gospel preached from Cairo, it was perhaps no surprise that his thoughts turned to emulating the Egyptian experience in Libya. It was also at school in Sebha that he first gathered around himself a young clique of disciples, who found his personality magnetic, with whom he held meetings in secret and waxed lyrical about revolution. After his expulsion in 1961, he made the long trek back north to the coast, this time to the town of Misrata, where he continued his missionary activities at another school. By the time he graduated, he had built a network of loyal protoconspirators extending into Tripoli itself.

Following the Nasserist playbook to the letter, Gaddafi's next step was to enroll in Benghazi's Military Academy in 1964, urging his closest comrades to do the same. Later that year, they formally established their "Free Unionist Officers" movement, holding their first meeting on a beach in Tolmetha, east of Benghazi. Already, the nucleus of the future junta was in place, with such key figures as Abd al-Salam Jalloud—Gaddafi's right-hand man for decades thereafter—on board.

The next five years were spent building up their movement's numbers and capabilities, and fleshing out the details of the master plan. D-day was initially scheduled for July 1968, but the king moved cities at the last moment, forcing the first of many postponements. Eventually, the date was fixed for September 1, 1969. In Gaddafi's telling, he spent the final hours of August 31 lying on his bed listening to Cairo Radio. When he heard the station broadcast a verse from the Qur'an—"God will not deny the faithful their reward"—he took it as a sign of divine providence. "We were assured of success," he recalled.

And so they were, though the success might have been short-lived were it not for the swift intervention of an altogether more earthly kind of power.

★

NASSER'S FIRST REACTION TO the message from Benghazi on the morning of September 1 was to wait for more information. There had been gossip in the air about a possible US-sponsored coup in Libya led by the army commander, Col. Abd al-Aziz al-Shelhi, and Nasser was wary of falling into a trap.

By the next day, however, it had become clear that this was not what had happened, and the coup was indeed carried out by earnest Nasserists. When the Libyans sent a second telegram on the morning of September 2, asking for Nasser's personal advice on handling relations with Britain, France, and the US, he decided to respond. In his reply, he suggested they contact representatives of the three states and inform them the "revolution" had solely domestic objectives and posed no threat to their interests or citizens. Nasser added they should ask the representatives for their governments' swift recognition of the new Libyan regime. Nasser was, in other words, already assisting Libya's military rulers just one day after their coup. From that moment on, for the twelve remaining months of his life, he would throw himself and all of Egypt's resources into backing Gaddafi's junta to the hilt, sparing no investment of funds, time, manpower, military assets, and personal prestige to ensure its survival.

The man appointed by Nasser as his viceroy in Libya, overseeing the day-to-day management of Egypt's support for the new regime, was Fathi al-Deeb, a North Africa specialist who had previously done extensive work in Algeria. In their telegram of September 2, the Libyans had asked Nasser to send over any person of his choosing to help them tackle the daunting challenges of the post-coup phase. Summoned to meet Nasser the next morning, Deeb was informed the president had decided he was to be that person. "Hold nothing back from them," Deeb recalled Nasser telling him. "I'm placing the reputation and future of Egypt in your hands. If you don't succeed and secure this revolution, I'll kill you with my own hands."

Deeb flew from Cairo to Benghazi that very night, accompanied by Heikal and six other Egyptians (a cryptographer, two intelligence operatives, and three men nominated by Egypt's war, interior, and media ministers, respectively). On landing in Benghazi, they were met by Maj. Adam Hawaz, the official spokesman of the Libyan "Revolutionary Command Council" (RCC), and Capt. Mustafa al-Kharrubi, an RCC member soon to be appointed head of military intelligence. From the airport, they drove to the Egyptian embassy, arriving around midnight, and immediately held a four-hour conversation with Hawaz and Kharrubi, who brought them up to speed on the latest developments and explained some of the backstory to the coup. For the first time, the Libyans divulged the name of their leader, whom they said the Egyptians could meet the following morning.

Sure enough, at 10:30 a.m. on September 4, the twenty-eight-year-old 1st Lt. Muammar al-Gaddafi strolled into the Egyptian embassy in Benghazi wearing military fatigues and carrying a rifle. Kharrubi introduced him to Deeb as the head of the RCC and "commander of the revolution." The two shook hands. Deeb congratulated Gaddafi on "the success of the revolution" and gave him a written letter from Nasser, as well as a verbal message Nasser had asked him to convey, to the effect that Egypt stood ready to place all its resources in the service of the Libyan "revolution," which was of utmost significance for the entire Arab nation.

With the pleasantries out of the way, Gaddafi told the story of the Free Unionist Officers and their coup, largely echoing what Kharrubi had said the night before, with added details. Making his Nasserist bona fides as clear as possible, Gaddafi stressed that he rejected all political parties, wished to rid Libya of Western troops, and sought the immediate union of Libya with the "United Arab Republic," as Egypt was still officially called. In what can only have been music to the Egyptians' ears, he added that Libya's vast oil wealth ought to be disbursed for the benefit of all Arabs.

The meeting lasted three hours, after which Gaddafi left to pen his reply to Nasser. Deeb took the opportunity to write his own message to the president, summarizing his first impressions. It was clear, he said, that the Libyans were extremely young and inexperienced, with no idea of what they were doing or how to run a country. The situation was far from reassuring. Gaddafi and his RCC colleagues were in urgent need of the firmest guiding hand at every step of the coming period if their regime was to last. Deeb gave his letter to Heikal, who flew back to Cairo later that day and delivered it to Nasser's secretary. Deeb himself stayed on at the embassy in Benghazi, where he would remain with only brief absences for the better part of the next two years.

Indeed, from the moment his plane touched down in Libya two days after the coup, Deeb lost no time positioning himself at the very center of events. Commanding immediate respect by virtue of having been handpicked by Nasser for his mission, Deeb was looked up to by Gaddafi and his comrades as a wise elder, an all-knowing sage of revolution, whose thoughts on any and all matters, grand and trivial, were invariably sound. Finding his advice sought on questions of every nature, Deeb was only too happy to provide it. While he took prudent pains to avoid ever giving the impression he was imposing his view on the Libyans, he found it remarkably easy to steer them at all times in directions favorable to Cairo. By the end of his first week in the country, he was already attending RCC meetings, and being kept abreast in detail of what went on in any he missed. He had also, within the first week, arranged for a Russian-Arabic translator to be sent from Cairo to enable the RCC to speak to the Soviet consul in Benghazi, and personally drafted a number of official statements issued in the RCC's name, including one addressed to the Libyan people, and another declaring Libya's recognition of Mauritania.

From that week on, until Nasser's death the following year, Egypt's involvement in Libya ballooned exponentially, extending deep into all aspects of the country's political, security, military, media, and socioeconomic affairs. Nasser's first concern was to bolster and protect the nascent regime against possible threats, both internal and external. Before Deeb had even left Cairo on the night of September 3, Nasser had tasked Egypt's war minister, Muhammad Fawzi, with moving aircraft, armored units, and mechanized infantry to the Libyan border, should the need for emergency military support arise. The following month, Nasser gifted the Libyans three naval units, free of charge, to be operated by Egyptian personnel until Libyans were trained to replace them. In December, Egypt also sent tank and special-forces brigades to Libya's urban centers, for the express purpose of helping to put down any potential countercoup attempts.

The inevitable purge of monarchy loyalists was swift in coming. Hundreds of royal family members, politicians, officials, and senior army and police officers were arrested, many then subjected to humiliating televised show trials. King Idris himself was sentenced to death in absentia. Alarmed to learn a number of top army officers were being held at a mere hotel in Benghazi, Deeb prevailed upon the RCC to move them to a secure prison outside the city.

But it went much wider and deeper than this. So green were the Libyans that the Egyptians had to walk them through such basics as the need to appoint carefully selected personal bodyguards. (Deeb advised Gaddafi to choose blood relatives, or else people with proven loyalty who had served with him previously in the military. He also

urged him to hire a full-time cook in whom he had "blind trust.")
Nasser himself fretted often over Gaddafi's well-being, imploring
him to adhere rigorously to all security measures, to look after his
health, eat regularly, and see a doctor every day. When fears were
raised over the safety of Gaddafi's air-travel arrangements, Egyptian
pilots were brought in to replace the old crew. Deeb also saw to it
that bomb-scanning equipment and detectors for listening devices
were sent from Cairo to secure the RCC's meeting locations.

Once the regime's basic, short-term security was buttressed, the
Egyptians set about building it up in their image. Among the points
Nasser personally pressed on Gaddafi was the need to create a General Intelligence apparatus on the Egyptian model. The "Colonel" (as
Gaddafi now styled himself) dutifully obliged, appointing the RCC
member Capt. Abd al-Munim al-Huni to head this new intelligence
agency, with Deeb coaching him in the role. As Deeb wrote in his
memoir, "I created an organisational structure for the [Libyan intel-
ligence] apparatus on the same bases as those upon which the Egyptian one was built in 1952." In a remark that revealed much about
the Nasserist conception of intelligence work, Deeb told Gaddafi the
apparatus would be the RCC's "eye" on the media. Soon after its
creation, thirty Libyan recruits were sent to Cairo for comprehensive
training at the hands of Egypt's General Intelligence.

Cairo was also intimately involved in the post-coup restructuring of Libya's armed forces, above and beyond the points already
mentioned. Within less than a month of the coup, the Egyptians
had studied the terms of the preexisting arms agreements reached
between Britain and Libya's ancien régime, and informed the RCC
of "the necessary amendments," in Deeb's words. Similarly, when
the Libyans entered into talks with France over what ended up being
a $300 million purchase of 110 supersonic Mirage 5 fighter jets, the
proposed terms of the deal were sent to Cairo for Nasser's review and
approval. In both cases, in other words, foreign powers that thought
they were negotiating with Libya were in fact doing so with Egypt.
There was even an Egyptian air force officer bearing a fake Libyan

passport accompanying a Libyan delegation in France to discuss the deal, much as Egyptian officers also joined an RCC member on a trip to the Soviet Union for separate arms-purchase negotiations.

On the political front, Egypt's main concern was to maintain the pro-Cairo orientation of Gaddafi and the RCC, a task that mostly amounted to pushing an open door. There were occasional challengers to be seen off, however. Two weeks after the coup, Saddam Hussein showed up out of the blue at the Benghazi airport, at the head of an unannounced and uninvited Iraqi delegation. (This sort of thing was happening a lot in Benghazi at the time: Saddam one day, Yasser Arafat the next, Algeria's Bouteflika after him, not to forget the Sudanese, always hoping for a loan the Libyans didn't want to give them.)

Saddam's all-too-apparent plan was to strong-arm the Libyans out of Nasser's orbit, and have Baathist Baghdad play the role already then being played by Cairo. To this end, he brought with him virtually an entire cabinet of Iraqis ready to get to work right away: a military officer to handle Libya's army; directors of Iraqi state radio, television, and news agencies to manage the media; the head of Iraq's national oil company; and dedicated advisers for labor, youth, and local administrative affairs. Saddam offered to send military aircraft and an armored division, to gift weapons, and to train up the Libyan army. He also distributed copies of Iraqi "revolutionary" legislation, which he proposed the Libyans apply. The pitch might have stood a higher chance of success were it not delivered in such brash, cocksure tones. When the Iraqis suggested the Libyans nationalize their oil company, the latter coolly responded that Iraq itself had not yet taken that step. Gaddafi, who already held a low opinion of Baathists, took offense at the Iraqis' arrogance, and in the end the encounter served only to push him further toward Nasser's genial embrace.

A slightly trickier problem was posed by the man the junta appointed as its first prime minister, a civilian of Palestinian origin named Mahmud al-Maghribi. Communist in sympathies, he made little effort to disguise his hostility to Nasserism, and tried to counter Egypt's influence by building up a coalition of fellow left-ists, Baathists, and Marxist Arab nationalists. Though the odds were stacked against him, he did succeed in dividing his cabinet between supporters and opponents of Cairo. This posed no existential threat from Egypt's perspective, since real power lay not in the cabinet but in the RCC, yet it was an inconvenience all the same. Deeb wrote candidly of working to "correct" the undesirable line taken by Maghribi—a bald admission of intervention in Libya's internal affairs to subvert the policies of its prime minister. As it turned out, Maghribi resigned after two months on the job, complaining the junta denied him any real authority or prerogatives.

To rectify any other "incorrect" thoughts potentially harbored by Libya's leaders, in November 1969 Deeb began a series of meetings with Gaddafi and the RCC at which he elucidated the ideological ins and outs of "Arab socialism," answering any and all questions of theory and doctrine that might occur to the young Libyans' inquisitive minds. In his telling, he dominated these hours-long symposia with Socratic virtuosity, slaying the arguments for Marxism advanced by the junta's most left-wing figure, 1st Lt. Umar al-Muhayshi, so persuasively that the latter was forced to concede total defeat.

A parallel process of indoctrination was also mounted on state media, targeting the general Libyan public, most of whom (according to Gaddafi himself) were deeply uncomfortable with the term "socialism" due to its anti-religious associations. Deeb prepared a series of explainers as to the aims and principles of the "revolution," which were broadcast on the radio and published in the press starting early October 1969. (If anyone found it unusual that an Egyptian was informing Libyans what the objectives of their own "revolution" were, Deeb does not tell us so.)

This was but one instance of Egypt's activities in the Libyan media realm, which began very early on. Accompanying Deeb on his first flight to Benghazi two days after the coup was a media specialist, Amin Basyuni (later head of Egyptian state radio), who immediately set about advising the man the RCC had placed in charge of media,

Lt. Abd al-Fattah Yunis. Within days, Egyptian-made radio material was sent over from Cairo for broadcasting on the Libyan airwaves, to diversify what had otherwise been nothing but replays of the junta's proclamations and readouts of telegrams of support. Later that month, the same was done with television programs brought out from Cairo by Deeb personally.

On the economic front, Egypt sent advisers on everything from trade to monetary policy to land reform. Never did the Libyans seem to question the wisdom of soliciting such guidance from a regime that had so woefully wrecked its own economy, any more than they queried the value of military advice from the very army that had lost the Arabs the Six-Day War.

More helpful, perhaps, were the hundreds of Egyptian doctors, nurses, engineers, and other professionals who were sent to address Libya's severe need of skilled labor. On the other hand, by Deeb's own admission, this rapid influx caused resentment among many ordinary Libyans, who complained of an "Egyptian invasion," accusing Cairo of replacing one colonial overlord with another. No decision was made in Libya, it was popularly said, without first going through "Bin Ashour Street," where the Egyptian embassy was located. Deeb himself acquired a range of unflattering nicknames, including "the High Commissioner," "the Egyptian Ghost," and "the head of the shadow government." So hostile did the atmosphere grow that there were physical assaults by locals against Egyptians in the streets, reminiscent of the last days in Yemen. All this, needless to add, Deeb blamed entirely on reactionary, imperialist, and counterrevolutionary provocateurs.

Whatever else might be said about Deeb, there could be no doubting his commitment to his job. No task was too great, nor too trifling, for this all-purpose fixer and handyman, whose patience was inexhaustible and work ethic indefatigable. On any given day, he might be found writing a speech for Major Hawaz, choosing Libya's attendees at an upcoming conference in Morocco, or booking medical appointments with Cairo's best doctors for RCC members needing healthcare. It was Deeb who arranged for an Egyptian surgeon to fly to Libya on short notice to perform an emergency removal of Gaddafi's appendix in January 1970. And it also fell to Deeb to play relationship counselor whenever the Colonel had another of his famous dustups with his colleagues, which happened with growing frequency from the spring of 1970 onward.

These legendary tantrums foreshadowed Gaddafi's transformation from the smiling, affable man Deeb had initially found "composed" into the raving, glass-eyed tyrant the world remembers today. In May 1970, RCC members confided to Deeb that the Colonel had been acting very strange of late. He had taken to swearing at them in meetings, berating and insulting them, calling them "children," saying they were useless and understood nothing. Issuing decrees without consulting them, he then blamed them when things went wrong. When his intelligence chief traveled to Cairo for medical care, Gaddafi petulantly refused to cover his bill, forcing him to borrow money from Libyan embassy employees. The Colonel was even now obliging foreign dignitaries, including a Venezuelan oil delegation invited by his government, to find and pay for their own accommodations. Another troubling new habit was his going in person with a handful of soldiers to casinos, closing them down on the spot and arresting everyone inside. When Deeb visited him at home to inquire about what was going on, Gaddafi told him he was leaving Libya to fight for the Palestinians in Jordan. It took the full extent of Deeb's Herculean powers of persuasion to effect one short-lived reconciliation after another within the crumbling junta.

Yet if there was one form of Egyptian support more important than all the foregoing combined, it was the powerful and repeated interventions undertaken by Nasser personally, both in private and—especially—in public.

We have already seen that Nasser played an active role in assisting the junta from as early as the day after the coup, when he sent advice on dealing with foreign powers. He maintained this behind-the-scenes involvement throughout the remaining year of his life, focusing on Gaddafi in particular, mentoring his young Libyan protégé in the ways of leadership and survival. At their first meeting at Nasser's Cairo home in December 1969, Nasser stressed to Gaddafi the essential importance of keeping the RCC free of all political party influence. (Three years later, Gaddafi would make party activity a crime punishable by death.) In a letter sent the following month, Nasser urged the Colonel to appoint himself prime minister as well as head of the RCC, warning that otherwise problems would spiral out of control, a lesson he said he had learned the hard way in Egypt. Nasser was, in other words, directly encouraging Gaddafi to dispense with civilian government and concentrate maximum power in his own hands. Sure enough, Gaddafi complied later that month, becoming prime minister as well as defense minister.

It was Nasser's high-profile public endorsements, however, that offered the greatest possible service to Gaddafi's image, establishing him not just as the next major act on the regional stage but as the rightful heir, in many eyes, to Nasser's own leadership of the Arab world. In December 1969, Nasser paid Libya his first state visit since the coup three months earlier. The scene recalled his triumphant arrival in Damascus after the union in 1958: jubilant crowds filling the streets and squares, screaming his name and mobbing his car, turning what should have been a short drive from the airport into an hours-long marathon.

The first order of business was an intimately personal one: Nasser attended Gaddafi's wedding ceremony, signing his own name as a witness on the marital contract. He then delivered two key speeches—one in Tripoli, the other in Benghazi—that did their utmost to legitimize the new Libyan dictator in the minds of his domestic subjects, and indeed Arabs everywhere. He thanked and praised God, he said on the podium in Tripoli, that he was standing in "the Libya of revolution, the Libya of freedom," in the presence of "the commander of your revolution," the "honourable, strong, dear, and revolutionary brother, the Brother-Colonel Muammar al-Gaddafi." Whenever he saw and listened to this Brother-Colonel, said Nasser, he felt "strength; we feel support; and we thank God we are not alone on the battlefield, but have brothers here in Libya."

In Benghazi, Nasser went further, suggesting Gaddafi had been chosen to lead Libya by the Almighty Himself:

> *What I saw when I met with your commander, the brother Muammar al-Gaddafi, makes me say to you: God has chosen for you the Arab struggler-commander who feels the feelings of this nation. God has strengthened you by choosing Muammar al-Gaddafi as your Arab leader. God has fortified you with Muammar al-Gaddafi.*

He closed with a dark warning about the unsleeping conspiracies of the imperialists, furnishing Gaddafi with the script he would use for decades thereafter, right up to the infamous speech in February 2011 in which he described his domestic opponents as "rats," "cats," and "bacteria"; accused them of seeking to bring back colonialism; and vowed to "cleanse" the country of them "inch by inch, house by house, alley by alley."

Nor was this the last of Nasser's promotion of Gaddafi in the public eye. Two months later, in February 1970, the pair rode in an open-top car through crowd-lined streets in central Cairo, after performing Friday prayers side by side at the historic al-Azhar Mosque. Four months after that, June 1970, was a particularly busy time. First, Nasser welcomed Gaddafi back to Cairo, offering him the warmest of introductions at the National Assembly before ceding the floor to the Colonel to make his own speech. Then, Nasser was back in Libya himself, joining Gaddafi and other heads of state at the ceremony marking the US Air Force's evacuation of its Wheelus base near Tripoli. Nasser's speech on this occasion was packed once again with fulsome tributes to the "hero" Gaddafi, of whom he made such remarks as:

Today, my brother Muammar al-Gaddafi said to you that free-
dom has been achieved, and he has great hopes; for an agricul-
tural revolution, and an industrial revolution, and sufficiency,
and justice, and a high standard of living for all. I was listening
to my brother Muammar al-Gaddafi saying this and I felt sure
in my innermost depths that he will achieve all these aspirations.

It was another phrase at the end of this speech, however, that would go on to form a centerpiece of Gaddafi's propaganda ever after, when Nasser closed with the words, "I feel that my brother Muammar al-Gaddafi is the custodian of Arab nationalism, and the Arab revolution, and Arab unity." In the Nasserist world, praise could come no higher than that.

Nasser would maintain this all-out backing for Gaddafi to the end, chaperoning him on the international stage until, quite liter-ally, his dying day. A well-known photo shows the two on armchairs alongside Arafat and King Hussein; it was taken at the Nile Hilton during the talks to reach a cease-fire in Jordan, one day prior to Nasser's fatal heart attack.

For his part, Gaddafi was naturally delighted to have won his idol's affections, and responded with a filial piety that lasted the rest of his own life in turn. When Britain's Royal Air Force was ejected from the RAF El Adem base near Tobruk in March 1970, the base was renamed "Gamal Abdel Nasser Airbase." The first official flag of the Libyan Arab Republic was the red, white, and black tricolor of the UAR, minus the green stars. In the years and decades to come, Gaddafi would erect lofty statues of Nasser, name streets and squares after him, and even offer Egypt $500 million to move the great man's remains to Libya for the construction of a grand "shrine for the faithful." If, when Nasser died, Gaddafi deemed himself the legit-imate inheritor of his mantle, this was an idea Nasser himself had done much to propagate. So ludicrous a figure did Gaddafi come to cut in later life that readers may struggle today to picture him as any sort of Nasser, but for years many took the notion with perfect seriousness. And it *was* a serious business. In Lebanon's civil war, the Nasserist militiamen who held almost half of Beirut at their peak— commanded by none other than Ibrahim Qulaylat—received most of their funding from Gaddafi's Libya. There can be no doubt the Colonel conceived of everything he did—from the downing of Pan Am Flight 103 over Lockerbie in 1988 to his backing of the murderers Ilich Sánchez ("Carlos the Jackal") and Sabri al-Banna ("Abu Nidal") to the slaughter of over a thousand Libyan prison inmates in a single day in 1996—as consistent with the Nasserist mission of which he was the self-appointed leader and standard-bearer. In 1981, he told an audience of students, "We, the Free Unionist Officers, are the guardians of the covenant of Gamal Abdel Nasser, the successors of Gamal Abdel Nasser, and the disciples of Gamal Abdel Nasser."

Gaddafi was, then, the head of state who most explicitly modeled himself on Nasser, building his entire image and reputation on the basis of the special relationship the pair had enjoyed. If Nasser obviously cannot be held responsible for all of Gaddafi's deeds across the forty-two years of his rule, it is equally plain that he cannot be held blameless either, given the indispensable support he provided the Libyan dictator while alive. (Nor can it be argued that Nasser was unaware of the stranger aspects of Gaddafi's character. Deeb kept him fully informed of all he saw and heard on the ground, and Nasser himself once lost his temper with him in June 1970.)

Libya is a country of immense oil reserves, a population smaller than London's, multiple UNESCO World Heritage Sites, and over 1,700 kilometers of sandy beaches. It could be, in the words of one Gaddafi biographer, "the jewel of North Africa," a thriving society combining the affluence and development of Dubai with a Mediterranean climate and a vibrant local culture. Instead, for more than half a century, it has endured an unending nightmare of tyranny and misery from which it is still yet to emerge. There is surely no more lurid example than Gaddafi of the dark side of Nasserism, and how it has all too often brought not freedom, dignity, and prosperity to the Arab peoples but the polar opposites of all three.

THE UNFINISHED
JOB

*Any revolution which fails to realise its basic objectives
inevitably lays the seeds for a subsequent uprising.*

—*Gamal Abdel Nasser*

O N FRIDAY, FEBRUARY 11, 2011, AFTER EIGHTEEN
straight days of street protests, Egypt's vice president
announced to the nation that its octogenarian ruler of thirty years,
Hosni Mubarak, had stepped down from the presidency of the republic, ceding power to the Supreme Council of the Armed Forces.

Air Chief Marshal Mubarak was as pure a product of the Nasserist
system as could be. A career air force officer, he exemplified the
caste of ambitious and avaricious military men who became Egypt's
new ruling class after the 1952 coup. In the 1960s, he led a squadron
of bombers in Yemen, before Nasser appointed him air force chief
of staff in 1969. Three years later, President Sadat promoted him to
air force commander, then vice president in 1975. When Sadat was
assassinated in 1981, Mubarak succeeded him by default. For his own
succession, Mubarak was widely believed to be grooming his son,
Gamal, named for the obvious reason.

That was not to be. As euphoric crowds filled Cairo's Tahrir
Square in jubilation on the night of Mubarak's fall, those with long
memories made the link with Nasser explicit, hailing what they
believed was the end of a dictatorship that had begun not in 1981 but
1952. With tears in his eyes, one demonstrator told a reporter how

his late father had been among the students at the Cairo University engineering college sit-in of 1968.

"His generation tell me that they were not as brave as us, but they started something and played their part," he said.

"Today, we finished the job for them."

★

EXACTLY ONE YEAR LATER to the day, on February 11, 2012, a crowd gathered in a square in downtown Benghazi, Libya. To the north, the square was bound by Gamal Abdel Nasser Street; to the south, 23 July Street, named after the date of Nasser's 1952 coup. In the center of this square was a towering stone sculpture of Nasser himself, raising a giant waving hand above his head, twice the height of the nearby palm trees, which scarcely reached to his waist.

The clue to what was about to happen next was the machine parked by Nasser's ankles: a heavy-duty, track-mounted hydraulic breaker with a pointed tip, of the sort that might be used to demolish a building.

Gaddafi had been dead for four months at this point—killed by the people he called "rats" as he himself hid in a sewer—but the physical manifestations of his regime were still everywhere in sight. The crowd had gathered that day to "remove the symbols of tyrants from the city of Benghazi," declared a middle-aged man through a megaphone, explaining that the sculpture had been erected on Gaddafi's orders in 1977. Recalling Nasser's fervent support for the Colonel, the speaker alluded specifically to the speech of June 22, 1970, in which Nasser had famously hailed his Libyan protégé as the "custodian of Arab nationalism":

> Today, we revolutionaries of 17 February [2011], and peo-
> ple of Benghazi, celebrate the removal of this false god, who
> appointed the tyrant Muammar al-Gaddafi as the custodian of
> [Arab] nationalism. Abdel Nasser destroyed Arab nationalism,

*and Muammar al-Gaddafi did the same. Both are tyrants, and
there must be no symbols of either of them.*

At that, the breaker got to work on Nasser's shins, hammering
into the stone with a loud *rat-a-tat* as people watched, recording the
scene on their camera phones. It took some time, but eventually the
sculpture keeled over, crashing into the ground with a puff of dust.
When it did, the crowd of a few hundred clapped and cheered, running and jumping on top of it with arms raised in triumph.

★

AS IT TURNED OUT, it would take more than toppling a statue, or
even a president, to banish the ghost of Nasser. The "job" had hardly
begun with Mubarak's fall, let alone finished. The democratic interlude that followed in Egypt, giving the country its first-ever freely
elected president, was not to last long. On July 3, 2013, the military brought it to an abrupt end, pouring troops and tanks into the
streets, arresting the president, and suspending the constitution. The
coup was led by the army's commander in chief, Gen. Abd al-Fattah
al-Sisi, who went on to become president himself in 2014.

A military coup in Cairo in the month of July: the parallels with
1952 were obvious, and, for his part, General Sisi was only too happy
to make use of them. The crowds that came out to cheer his coup
held up large portraits of Nasser's face next to his own. Fans hailed
Sisi as the military strongman for whom Egypt had been waiting
ever since Nasser's demise. Nasser's own son, Abd al-Hakim, got on
stage in Tahrir Square to give a speech endorsing the coup; he has
been a vocal Sisi supporter ever since. While Libyans were tearing
down Gaddafi's Nasser statues, Sisi's Egypt has erected new ones, as
in the cities of Asyut and Port Said in 2014 and 2016, respectively.

Aside from drumming up support for the coup and the idea of
military rule in general, the association with Nasser was especially
useful to Sisi in his crackdown on the Muslim Brotherhood, a group
with whom Nasser had clashed himself (even if, as we have seen, the

two were once much friendlier than either later cared to remember). The civilian president deposed by Sisi, Mohamed Morsi, came from the Brotherhood's ranks, and the group made up the lion's share of active opposition to the coup on the ground. For over a month, tens of thousands of Morsi supporters maintained a sit-in at Cairo's Rabaa al-Adawiya Square, until it was crushed in a terrible massacre on August 14, 2013, when no fewer than 817 protesters were shot dead by regime forces in the course of twelve gruesome hours. In a rerun of Nasser's campaigns in 1954 and 1965–66—but exceeding both combined in scale—Sisi proceeded to jail tens of thousands on charges of Brotherhood membership, which became a serious crime after the group was (re)banned and declared a terrorist organization in late 2013. Morsi himself was standing trial on espionage charges when he dropped dead, literally inside the court room, in 2019, having been denied vital medication for diabetes and hypertension. An estimated sixty thousand political prisoners remain behind bars in Egypt today, enduring routine torture, medical neglect, and generally appalling conditions as a matter of course. (In another macabre inheritance from the Nasser years, they are even subjected to the same "welcoming ceremony" of beatings that once greeted arrivals at Abu Zaabal.) Nor are all the political prisoners Islamists; at the time of writing, they include the British-Egyptian dual citizen Alaa Abd El Fattah, a celebrated writer and democracy activist who holds the distinction of having been jailed by every ruler of Egypt since Mubarak.

Thus was the freedom seemingly promised by Egypt's 2011 revolt cut down in a storm of bullets and pain. In retrospect, it is difficult to see how it could have ended any other way. The supremacy of the army was never in jeopardy at any moment; it controlled the streets as early as January 28, 2011, just four days into the protests, two whole weeks prior to Mubarak's departure. So long as the levers of hard power remained in the hands of the military establishment, that establishment could and would do whatever it deemed necessary to retain its primacy in political (and economic) affairs. That was the lesson of every Egyptian uprising since March 1954. It was the system as Nasser had built it.

★

THE DEMONS OF THE PAST were no more successfully exorcised elsewhere. In Libya, hopes for an orderly transition to democracy after Gaddafi were dashed by infighting between rival military factions. Before long, the country was in civil war. A key protagonist of this conflict, who at the time of writing rules vast swaths of Libya's east, including Benghazi, is the white-haired warlord and veteran army general Khalifa Haftar. A former Gaddafi loyalist who took part in the 1969 coup, Haftar now seeks to resurrect the dictatorship in his own image. Already, in those parts of Libya under his control, residents speak of a police-state atmosphere reminiscent of the Gaddafi days. Billboards of him in military uniform line the streets, to the point that locals joke the airport road is his "Instagram page." No oppositional media or political activism is tolerated. Haftar has stated that Libya is not yet ready for democracy—the same claim that Nasser made about Egypt.

In his quest to rule Libya, Haftar has enjoyed the backing of powerful friends, including Russia's Vladimir Putin, France's Emmanuel Macron, and the United Arab Emirates. Perhaps his closest ally, however, has been his fellow general Sisi in neighboring Egypt, whose ruthless seizure of power in 2013 is said to have given Haftar the inspiration to attempt something similar at home. He has, indeed, been dubbed "Libya's Sisi," and the two are on warm terms, with Sisi providing him funds, weapons, and soldiers in a manner not entirely unlike Nasser's aid to Gaddafi half a century earlier.

Another would-be dictator bidding for power today in Libya is Gaddafi's own son, Saif al-Islam, the London School of Economics–educated playboy once feted in Western capitals as the face of reform and democratization. The delusion that this friend of Tony Blair and Naomi Campbell could prove a moderating influence on his father during the 2011 uprising was dispelled when he rallied emphatically to his side, vowing in a belligerent speech on state television to "fight" the opposition "to the last man and woman and bullet."

Captured by rebels a few months later while fleeing deep in the southwestern desert, Saif al-Islam was spared the grisly treatment meted out to his father, and whisked away instead to captivity in the remote mountain town of Zintan, where, out of the public eye, he spent the next decade biding his time and patiently plotting what he intends to be his grand comeback. In November 2021, he made his first public appearance in years, sporting a bushy beard and his father's trademark brown robes in place of the clean shave and Savile Row suits of old. The occasion was his official registration as a candidate for Libya's forthcoming presidential election. (This in spite of the death sentence issued against him by a Tripoli court in 2015, not to mention an International Criminal Court arrest warrant on charges of crimes against humanity.) In his first interview with a Western journalist since his reemergence, he was utterly unrepentant about supporting his father to the end, saying subsequent events had only further proved the virtues of his forty-two-year reign. Saif al-Islam's entire sales pitch, indeed, is that the revolution was a disastrous mistake, and only a return to the past—to the glorious House of Gaddafi, Custodians of Arab Nationalism—can make Libya great again.

Meanwhile, in Yemen, the war that followed the 2012 ouster of longtime military dictator Ali Abdallah Saleh has been called a "déjà vu" of Nasser's "Vietnam" in the 1960s. Once again, the Yemeni republic is at war with the tribes of the northern mountains, now better known as "Houthis" than "royalists." Once again, foreign powers—including Sisi's Egypt—are deeply involved, each pursuing its own private agenda.

The geopolitics have changed—it is now Iran that backs the northern tribes, while their former Saudi patrons lead the "republican" fight against them, as Nasser once did. For the Yemeni protagonists themselves, the underlying dynamics remain fundamentally the same. One key difference this time is the northerners have proved far more successful than their forebears, driving deep into the old republican "strategic triangle" and seizing the capital Sanaa itself in 2014, forcing then-president Abdrabbuh Mansur Hadi into exile. In 1960s terms, it is as though the Imam's mountaineers had managed at last to overthrow Sallal and reestablish their thousand-year-old dynasty. The Houthis have not yet gone so far as to declare the imamate restored, but many Yemenis fear this is their ultimate aim. More than fifty-five years since Nasser left Yemen, the divisions he did so much to aggravate have ruptured anew with furious vengeance, claiming over three hundred thousand lives (so far) and plunging the country into what the UN has called the world's worst humanitarian crisis.

In Iraq, two decades have now passed since the overthrow of Saddam Hussein, but the shadow cast by the exceptional brutality of his long reign of terror continues to pervade all corners of life. The ethnic and sectarian antagonisms he spent over a quarter of a century stoking with genocidal ferocity between Arabs and Kurds, Sunnis and Shia, Muslims and non-Muslim minorities, formed the firewood of the horrific civil war that followed his toppling in 2003, and gave rise ultimately to the extremist Islamic State as well as the consortium of rival Islamist militias, backed by Iran, to whom the Baghdad authorities are now beholden. Twenty years on, Saddam's "republic of fear" remains alive in the minds of millions. It is telling that, when large protests against Iraq's ruling class erupted in 2019, politicians sought to scare the public off by smearing the young demonstrators as Saddam loyalists bent on resurrecting the Baath regime.

Syrians, for their part, have not even had the chance to begin grappling with the legacy of dictatorships past, for the Assad regime remains ensconced in Damascus to this day. Having inherited the torture state built on the foundations laid by Nasser and his henchman Sarraj, Bashar al-Assad has used every means at his disposal to extirpate his rebellious subjects en masse, up to and including the chemical weapons his father first acquired from Egypt. The initial success of Syria's popular uprising in toppling the regime across much of the country has now been almost entirely reversed, at a cost of well over 350,000 killed, and more than thirteen million displaced from their homes. The evidence of war crimes and crimes against humanity perpetrated by Assad's forces has been described by prosecutors as more extensive than that amassed against the Nazis at Nuremberg.

And then there is Lebanon, today a more profoundly wounded hostage than ever to the ruthless men who fought its fifteen-year civil war between 1975 and 1990. Almost all its key power brokers—including its most recent president and parliament speaker—were leading protagonists in that war, which killed an estimated 150,000 out of a total population then numbering less than three million. We have seen in these pages how Nasser bears no small responsibility for helping to set this war in motion. The large protests that swept Lebanon in 2019 were, at root, driven by the failure of its ruling class to construct a viable, functioning state atop the ruins of the old one they themselves had so recklessly destroyed.

The specifics vary, but each country has one thing in common. Seven decades since his coup, and more than half a century since his death, the Arab peoples have scarcely begun to shake off the legacy of "Father" Gamal Abdel Nasser.

ACKNOWLEDGMENTS

I T GOES WITHOUT SAYING THAT THIS BOOK COULD NOT have been written without the courage and generosity of those who agreed to be interviewed for it. It is no small thing to invite a stranger into a deeply personal and painful chapter of one's life, and I was humbled by all who gave me their time.

The first of these, chronologically speaking, were the Mrowa siblings, Malek, Karim and Lina, who extended multiple invitations to meet at their late father's extraordinary residence in Beit Mirri and offered their invaluable insights without reservation. It was over the course of several conversations with Malek in the past decade that the seed of this book was first planted, and his early encouragement was instrumental in getting the project started.

Likewise, the remarkable Selma Slim and Rasha al-Ameer took me into their own storied home in south Beirut, refusing to let me leave without a stack of volumes from the shelves of their exceptional library, including a most helpful hardback of Mohsen Slim's address to the trial of Kamel Mrowa's killers.

Nada al-Helu did much the same in Hosrayel, not just graciously taking me in off the street when I so brusquely showed up at her door unannounced, but then sending me on my way with essential and rare books on the life and death of her father, Farajallah. Nor would I have found Nada's home at all but for the charity of a passing villager—who turned out to be a nephew of Farajallah, also named Farajallah himself—who chanced to see me knocking on the wrong door and was chivalrous enough to direct me to the right one. On such felicitous happenstance do the fortunes of writers turn.

In Amman, Gen. Hussein al-Majali was munificent with his time, agreeing to meet and answer my questions before arranging, of his own accord, a visit to the home of a former prime minister of Jordan who had known both Gamal Abdel Nasser and Majali's late father, Hazzaa. My warm thanks go also to this elder statesman, whose conversation was as amusing as it was enlightening, but who, alas, spoke only on condition that his words be off the record and his name remain unmentioned.

Professors Joel Gordon and Sherif Younis gave liberally of their matchless expertise on all matters Nasser. Najem El Hachem was kind enough to share his encyclopedic knowledge of the Kamel Mrowa case. Michael Chaftari, Con Coughlin, Michael Degerald, Anthony Elghossain, Yassin al-Haj Saleh, Hassan Hassan, Rouba El Helou-Sensenig, Charles Lister, Ziad Majed, Kanan Makiya, Ayman Mhanna, Drew Mikhael, Farea al-Muslimi, Mosab Al Nomairy, Maysaa Shuja al-Din, and Michael Weiss all helpfully answered questions or in other ways enriched the book with learning and wit. I am greatly indebted to Gisèle Khoury for making one of the chapters possible.

My former colleagues at *Al-Jumhuriya* did more than they may realize to shape my thinking, not just about Nasser or Syria, but about politics as a whole, during the years we worked together, when I had the inestimable pleasure of sitting in on their wide-ranging discussions during weekly editorial meetings. Sadik Abdul Rahman, Samy Awikeh, Orwa Khalife, Nayla Mansour, Yassin Swehat and Yaaser al-Zayyat offered very helpful reading recommendations for this book in particular.

Speaking of reading, most of the books, journals, and newspaper archives that enabled my research came courtesy of the American University of Beirut, whose outstanding library never ceases to astonish in its breadth, depth, and hidden treasures. Many libraries around the world may stock Nasser's *Falsafat al-Thawra*, but only one contains the late Syrian playwright Saadallah Wannous's well-worn personal copy thereof, just as only one possesses the late Constantine Zurayk's copy of Munif al-Razzaz's *al-Tajriba al-Murra*. Special thanks must also go to Adil at Cairo's Dar al-Thaqafa al-Jadida, who went well out of his way to print a one-off copy of Ilham Sayf al-Nasr's indispensable memoir of detention in Abu Zaabal camp, which has fallen out of print since its publication in 1977.

At every step, Doug Young has been the sage counsel, firm ally, and unfailing gentleman-scholar every author would be blessed to have in an agent. Were it not for his full belief in this book from the beginning and all he has done to bring it to life, it could not have existed.

Similarly, I am more grateful than I can say to John Glusman at W. W. Norton, Ian Marshall (then) at Simon & Schuster, and all their respective colleagues for seeing merit in the idea of this book and then granting me the stupendous privilege of an offer to publish it. Helen Thomaides guided me with impeccable skill and forbearance through the many hoops and mazes of the publishing process. My copyeditor, Sarah Johnson, taught me things I had never known about the English language.

Jennifer Beeston, Kathryn Bubien, Dawn Gower, Ruth Marsh, Christiana Newton, Laura Watts, and Claire Weatherhead were all essential to the production of the book's photo insert.

The Society of Authors very kindly awarded me an Authors' Foundation grant, helping to offset some of the costs of travel, not to mention the books purchased for research.

Friends and family are the unsung heroes of every work of this kind. Fabiana and Anthony Potter made space in already-teeming suitcases to lug books from London to Lebanon at a time when COVID made flying with young children even less relaxing than usual. My parents, Barbara and John, and siblings, Emily and Josh— no strangers themselves to hauling book-filled baggage around airports—were inexhaustible wells of love and support, as ever. No man has been as fortunate in his in-laws as I have in the redoubtable

Myriam and Joe, who go far beyond the call of duty every day, sparing no effort to lighten the countless burdens imposed on my wife, Mia, by having a writer for a husband.

Mia herself may not have penned a word of this book, but it is as much a product of her own toil as mine. The task of raising a newborn son and young daughter in the collapsing state of Lebanon, amid a global pandemic, is not made easier when one parent elects to write a book at the same time. That the book is now complete owes as much to her endless talents and tenacity—as partner, reader, mother, and mentor—as anything else. If that weren't enough, she also took the photograph that appears on the book's cover, and imparted authoritative judgment on all questions of design.

As for Youmna and Paul, it is doubtless true, as the hackneyed joke goes, that without them I'd have written this book much faster, but it would also have been an immeasurably poorer work for it. Parents learn as much, if not more, from their children as the reverse. They have added to this book—and to its author—more than they can know, and, in return, it is the greatest possible joy to be able to dedicate it to them.

NOTES

PROLOGUE

1   **shot six times:** "Lebanon: Flawed Investigations of Politically-Sensitive Murders," Human Rights Watch, February 3, 2022; Marie Jo Sader, "How Lokman Slim Was Assassinated," *L'Orient Today*, February 3, 2022; Rasha Al Ameer, "The Power of My Brother Lokman's Spirit Is Stronger Than His Killers' Arms," Al Arabiya, March 25, 2021; Ahmad Mantash and Sarah El Deeb, "Prominent Lebanese Hezbollah Critic Found Killed in His Car," Associated Press, February 5, 2021; Inas Sharri, "Shaqiqat Luqman Slim la tureed tahqiqan duwaliyyan 'li-annaha ta'rif man qatalahu'" [Lokman Slim's sister does not want an international investigation "because she knows who killed him"], *Asharq Al-Awsat*, February 7, 2021, https://tinyurl.com/cch78mj5.

2   **mob gathered outside his house:** "Ba'd i'tida'at Hizb Allah . . . Luqman Slim lil-Hurra: Lan yuskitana ahad" [After Hizbullah's attacks . . . Lokman Slim to Alhurra: No one will silence us], Alhurra, December 13, 2019, https://tinyurl.com/36j9ydre.

3   **note the parallels:** In remarks to SBI (Sawt Beirut International) on February 5, 2021, available on the SBI YouTube channel: https://www.youtube.com/watch?v=-SN29-J7UGg.

4   **"He received a lot of threats":** Interview with Selma Slim and Rasha al-Ameer at the Slim family residence, al-Ghobeiry, Beirut's southern suburbs, October 5, 2021.

4   **"towering figure of American journalism":** "Wilton Wynn, Dean of Foreign Correspondents, Dies," Reuters, April 14, 2011.

6   **insulted them one too many times:** The specific trigger for the protests was the government's announcement on October 17 of a new tax to be levied on calls made through the popular WhatsApp phone application. The underlying grievances, however, included decades of misrule by a brazenly venal and violent political class content to leave citizens with daily power cuts, unclean water, dreadful roads and infrastructure, high unemployment, vast income inequality, and a chronic lack of security, marked by regular outbursts of bombings, armed clashes, and assassinations, with next to no accountability for any of the (well-known) parties responsible, among many other profound problems rooted deep in the power structures controlling everyday life.

6   **sound similar in Arabic:** *Yasqut yasqut hukm al-'askar* versus *yasqut yasqut hukm al-az'ar*, respectively.

7   **"Today, we finished the job":** Jack Shenker, "In Tahrir Square of Cairo Freedom Party Begins," *Guardian*, February 11, 2011.

7   **statue of him was torn down:** "Libya: Hadm timthal Jamal ʿAbd al-Nasir fi
Benghazi" [Libya: Gamal Abdel Nasser statue brought down in Benghazi], BBC
Arabic, February 12, 2012. A full video of the proceedings can be seen on YouTube
at https://www.youtube.com/watch?v=WBei3G8ayBk.

Introduction

9   **never a stranger to criticism:** Asher Orkaby, *Beyond the Arab Cold War: The
International History of the Yemen Civil War, 1962–68* (New York: Oxford University Press, 2017), 160; Alex von Tunzelmann, *Blood and Sand: Suez, Hungary and the
Crisis that Shook the World* (London: Simon & Schuster, 2017), 55–56; Nigel Ashton, "Hitler on the Nile? British and American Perceptions of the Nasser Regime,
1952–70," in *Scripting Middle East Leaders: The Impact of Leadership Perceptions on US
and UK Foreign Policy*, ed. Lawrence Freedman and Jeffrey H. Michaels (London:
Bloomsbury, 2013); "Egypt: The Counterpuncher," *Time*, August 27, 1956.

9   **"You meet people and discuss Nasser":** Interview with Gen. Hussein al-
Majali, Amman, November 16, 2021.

10   **comic images mocking him:** Ahmad al-Amir, "Kayfa hawwalat ʿal-komiks'
ʿAbd al-Nasir min zaʿim qawmi ila ayqunat fashal" [How "comics" turned Abdel
Nasser from a national leader into an icon of failure], Raseef22, October 14, 2019,
https://tinyurl.com/46hsdybz.

10   **"he has become a laughingstock":** Ahmed Naji, "Adab al-sukhriya min ʿAbd
al-Nasir . . . Tahaddi al-aliha al-mayyita" [The literature of Abdel Nasser mockery . . . Challenging the dead gods], Al-Modon, March 17, 2020, https://tinyurl
.com/h8rk88aj.

10   **"I do not know of a single critical biography":** Khaled Mansour, "Kayfa
nunqidh Jamal ʿAbd al-Nasir min khusoomihi wa ansarih?" [How can we rescue
Gamal Abdel Nasser from his opponents and supporters?], Daraj, October 2, 2020,
https://daraj.com/56341/.

12   **painstakingly transcribed:** The transcription process was carried out over
twelve years, between 1996 and 2008, by a team of fifteen researchers led by Nasser's daughter, Hoda Abdel Nasser. See the latter's interview with *Youm*7 published
on January 30, 2009: https://tinyurl.com/2x49w83r.

1. The Immense Secret

15   **"obstacles standing between":** Gamal Abdel Nasser, *Falsafat al-Thawra* [The
philosophy of the revolution], 10th ed. (Cairo: al-Matbaʿa al-ʿAlamiya, n.d. [first
published 1954]), 35.

15   **"How many plans":** G. Nasser, *Falsafat al-Thawra*, 35.

15   **wrongly, as it turned out:** Joel Gordon, *Nasser: Hero of the Arab Nation* (London:
Oneworld Publications, 2006), 35.

17   **brief 181-word statement:** A text of the statement can be found on the Egyptian government's State Information Service website, at https://www.sis.gov.eg/
Newvr/egyptionrevoution/januarythree.html (accessed November 10, 2021).

17   **"the creator of the modern Egyptian theatre":** Anouar Abdel-Malek, *Egypt:
Military Society; The Army Regime, the Left, and Social Change under Nasser* (New
York: Vintage Books, 1968), 204.

17 **recalled that he was pleased:** Tawfiq al-Hakim, *'Awdat al-Wa'y* [The return of consciousness], 2nd ed. (Cairo: Dar al-Shuruq, 1974), 12.

18 **"there was no one in Egypt":** al-Hakim, *'Awdat al-Wa'y*, 13.

18 **"Let us spare Farouk":** Robert Stephens, *Nasser: A Political Biography* (London: Allen Lane, 1971), 107.

19 **The family home:** It still stood in place when the author visited in 2021, renovated and converted into a public library, a quaint relic of a vanished past now squashed on all sides by dust-caked, bare concrete tenements towering over it.

19 **"a cruel blow":** Stephens, *Nasser*, 28.

19 **not without intellectual promise:** Peter Mansfield, *Nasser* (London: Methuen Educational, 1969), 19–21; Abdel-Malek, *Egypt*, 207–9.

20 **"without" . . . "having the slightest idea":** Interview with the *Sunday Times*, June 1962, a text of which can be found at http://www.nasser.org/Common/pictures01-%20sira3_en.htm and http://nasser.bibalex.org/Common/SundayTimesInterview_en.aspx?lang=en. See also Mansfield, *Nasser*, 18; and Gordon, *Nasser: Hero of the Arab Nation*, 26.

21 **boasting hundreds of thousands:** Fawaz A. Gerges, *Making the Arab World: Nasser, Qutb, and the Clash That Shaped the Middle East* (Princeton, NJ: Princeton University Press, 2018), 238; Abdel-Malek, *Egypt*, 27.

21 **"achieved nothing substantial":** Quote taken from *Sunday Times* interview of June 1962 (see above). On Young Egypt, Nasser's membership thereof, and Fathi Radwan, see Abdel-Malek, *Egypt*, 21–22, 392; Gerges, *Making the Arab World*, 61; Joel Gordon, *Nasser's Blessed Movement: Egypt's Free Officers and the July Revolution* (Cairo: The American University in Cairo Press, 2016), 18, 64, 146.

21 **A third force on the rise:** Selma Botman, "The Rise and Experience of Egyptian Communism: 1919–1952," *Studies in Comparative Communism* 18, no. 1 (Spring 1985): 49–66; Louis Awad, "Cultural and Intellectual Developments in Egypt since 1952," in *Egypt Since the Revolution*, ed. P. J. Vatikiotis (UK: Routledge, 2013), 149.

22 **"We are determined":** Jonathan Dimbleby, "On the Road to El Alamein: Winston Churchill's Desert Campaign," *Radio Times*, November 4, 2012.

23 **British tanks rolled up:** Mansfield, *Nasser*, 34.

23 **"When your letter first arrived":** Mansfield, 35.

24 **Their wedding photo:** Tahia Gamal Abdel Nasser, *Dhikrayat Ma'ahu* [Memories with him] (Cairo: Dar al-Shuruq, 2019), 10–12.

24 **Nasser's involvement with the Muslim Brotherhood:** Gordon, *Nasser's Blessed Movement*, 45; Gordon, *Nasser: Hero of the Arab Nation*, 30; Gerges, *Making the Arab World*, 72–73.

25 **Nasser was later able to deny:** See, e.g., the aforementioned interview with the *Sunday Times* in June 1962, in which he says, "I had numerous communications with the Moslem Brotherhood although I was never a member of the party."

25 **"We joined the [Brotherhood] underground":** Gerges, *Making the Arab World*, 166–68.

26 **"Our slogan shall always be":** An Arabic text of the speech is available at http://nasser.bibalex.org/TextViewer.aspx?TextID=SPCH-524-ar (accessed December 6, 2021).

26 **no enthusiasm for the fight:** Ahron Bregman, and Jihan El-Tahri, *The Fifty Years War: Israel and the Arabs* (London: Penguin, 1998), 37.

26 **"the Arabs entered Palestine":** Eugene Rogan, *The Arabs: A History*, 2nd ed. (London: Penguin, 2012), 330.

27 **not the root cause:** G. Nasser, *Falsafat al-Thawra*, 10–11, 19.

27 **"We were fighting in Palestine":** G. Nasser, 12–13.

27 **meeting with an Israeli:** G. Nasser, 14.

28 **"the wrong war":** Bregman and El-Tahri, *Fifty Years War*, 41–42; Howard

Goller, "When Towering Rivals Rabin and Nasser Met for Lunch—in Rabin's Own Words," Reuters, February 1, 2017.

29 **These were the men:** Gordon, *Nasser's Blessed Movement*, 45–47. Besides Nasser, the other seven members of the original committee were Abd al-Munim Abd al-Rauf, Abd al-Hakim Amer, Abd al-Latif al-Baghdadi, Kamal al-Din Husayn, Hasan Ibrahim, Khaled Muhieddin, and Salah Salem. In 1951, Anwar Sadat and Gamal Salem were added.

29 **they kept to vague slogans:** Sherif Younis, *Nida' al-Sha'b: Tarikh Naqdi lil-Idiyulujiya al-Nasiriya* [The call of the people: A critical history of Nasserist ideology] (Cairo: Dar al-Shuruq, 2012), 37, 42–43, 112; Gordon, *Nasser's Blessed Movement*, 49; Gerges, *Making the Arab World*, 91; *Sunday Times* interview, June 1962.

30 **a punishing assault:** Gordon, *Nasser's Blessed Movement*, 26–27; Steven A. Cook, *The Struggle for Egypt: From Nasser to Tahrir Square* (New York: Oxford University Press, 2011), 37; Claire Anderson, "The Turf Club Murders: Black Saturday for the British in Cairo, 26 January 1952" (PhD diss., University of Texas at Austin, 1996).

30 **"a vision of horror":** Abdel-Malek, *Egypt*, 37.

30 **"rioters toss[ed] cakes":** *New York Times*, January 27, 1952.

30 **running for their lives:** "Famed Hotel in Cairo Comes to Fiery End," *Washington Post*, January 26, 1952.

30 **The ugliest scene:** Anderson, "Turf Club Murders."

31 **decided on a coup:** Gordon, *Nasser's Blessed Movement*, 51–52.

32 **unsure of success:** It is said the officers thought their chances no higher than 15%; see Younis, *Nida' al-Sha'b*, 42.

2. THE TRANSITION PERIOD

33 **The fourteen-man junta:** The fourteen comprised the ten-man Free Officers' executive committee, plus Muhammad Naguib, Zakaria Muhieddin, Husayn al-Shafii, Abd al-Munim Amin, and Yusuf Siddiq, minus Abd al-Munim Abd al-Rauf, who was expelled shortly before the coup for refusing to relinquish his Muslim Brotherhood membership.

33 **"the democratic freedoms":** Abdel-Malek, *Egypt*, 12.

33 **remained the most popular party:** Even the following year, in late 1953, Nasser admitted to the French journalist Jean Lacouture that the Wafd would still win were a free and fair general election to be held. See Jean Lacouture, *Nasser* (New York: Alfred A. Knopf, 1973), 116.

33 **"a virtual 'who's who'":** Gordon, *Nasser's Blessed Movement*, 67. Unless otherwise stated, all details on the junta's early years are from Gordon's authoritative account.

34 **"grave danger":** "Egypt Bares Plot, Bans All Parties," *Washington Post*, January 16, 1953.

34 **Over two hundred arrests:** "Naguib Aide Discloses 213 Held in Egypt," *Washington Post*, January 19, 1953.

34 **"deploy thugs":** Cook, *Struggle for Egypt*, 50–51.

35 **Its purpose was to resolve:** For an excellent discussion of the junta's notion of "revolution," to which the analysis here is indebted, see Younis, *Nida' al-Sha'b*.

35 **"strike with all ferocity":** Gordon, *Nasser's Blessed Movement*, 78.

37 **"admitted any sort":** Gordon, 89.

37 **"The first objective of this revolution":** Speech by Gamal Abdel Nasser in Alexandria on November 26, 1953, an Arabic transcript of which is available at: http://nasser.bibalex.org/TextViewer.aspx?TextID=SPCH-84-ar.

39   **the depth and breadth of ill will:** Younis, *Nida' al-Sha'b*, 70.

40   **"renaissance of open political discourse":** Gordon, *Nasser's Blessed Movement*, 144.

40   **"an assault on human dignity":** Gordon, 134; Younis, *Nida' al-Sha'b*, 71.

40   **threw themselves into the movement:** Ahmed Abdalla, *The Student Movement and National Politics in Egypt, 1923–1973* (London: Al Saqi Books, 1985), 120.

41   **as many as six bombs:** "Opposition to Junta: Discord in Cairo," *Manchester Guardian*, March 21, 1954; Gordon, *Nasser's Blessed Movement*, 221; Younis, *Nida' al-Sha'b*, 73.

41   **"one of the most influential":** Nathan J. Brown, "Nasserism's Legal Legacy: Accessibility, Accountability, and Authoritarianism," in *Rethinking Nasserism: Revolution and Historical Memory in Modern Egypt*, ed. Elie Podeh and Onn Winckler (Gainesville: University Press of Florida, 2004), 135.

41   **may have lost his life:** Younis, *Nida' al-Sha'b*, 75; Gordon, *Nasser's Blessed Movement*, 135.

41   **"etched in public memory":** Gerges, *Making the Arab World*, 89.

41   **neutralize the Muslim Brotherhood:** Gordon, *Nasser's Blessed Movement*, 135.

42   **"later boasted":** Gordon, 136.

42   **The most dangerous moment:** Gordon, 128–29; Anthony Nutting, *Nasser* (London: Constable and Co., 1972), 61–63.

42   **teaching the country a lesson:** Gordon, *Nasser's Blessed Movement*, 133.

43   **British intelligence assessed:** Gordon, 138.

43   **"behind the parties and constitution":** Younis, *Nida' al-Sha'b*, 80.

44   **"the spokesman for the whole":** Abdel-Malek, *Egypt*, 95.

44   **"total contempt for the profession":** Younis, *Nida' al-Sha'b*, 83.

44   **"several times":** Nutting, *Nasser*, 68; Abdalla, *Student Movement*, 43.

45   **Nasser succeeded in extinguishing:** Gordon, *Nasser's Blessed Movement*, 140–41; Younis, *Nida' al-Sha'b*, 80–82.

45   **"From university professors to porters":** Lacouture, *Nasser*, 124.

45   **Tensions spiked sharply:** Gordon, *Nasser's Blessed Movement*, 178–79.

46   **"My blood is a sacrifice":** The full Arabic text of the speech is available at http://nasser.bibalex.org/TextViewer.aspx?TextID=SPCH-263-ar. An audio recording, in which the gunshots can clearly be heard, is available at http://nasser.bibalex.org/MediaViewer.aspx?VideoID=SPCH-AUD-23097-ar (both links accessed November 29, 2021).

46   **"confessed":** Nutting, *Nasser*, 137.

47   **"Gamal, you epitome":** Author's translation. The song title in Arabic is "Ya Gamal ya mithal al-wataniyya." For more on Umm Kulthum's "glorification" of Nasser, and her role as what he terms "an apparatus of the totalitarian Nasserist state," see Hazem Saghieh's *Al-Hawa Duna Ahlihi: Umm Kulthum Siratan wa Nassan* [Desire without its people: Umm Kulthum in life and words] (Beirut: Dar al Jadeed, 1991).

47   **"assumed the role of inquisitor":** Gordon, *Nasser's Blessed Movement*, 180.

47   **has been corroborated:** Gerges, *Making the Arab World*, 115–21; Gordon, *Nasser's Blessed Movement*, 182.

48   **"staggering blow":** Gordon, *Nasser's Blessed Movement*, 184.

48   **"in the months"** . . . **"dictatorial rule":** Gordon, 187 and 175, respectively.

48   **the number of political prisoners:** Gordon, 196. Others put the number much higher; Louis Awad, for instance, cites a figure of eighteen thousand political prisoners (Louis Awad, *Aqni'at al-Nasiriya al-Sab'a* [The seven masks of Nasserism] (Cairo: Markaz al-Mahrusa, 2014), 38.

49   **"His body is so virile":** Naoko Shimazu, "Diplomacy as Theatre: Staging the Bandung Conference of 1955," *Modern Asian Studies* 48, no. 1 (2014): 245–46. "Nehru, Nasser and Zhou Enlai easily won the popularity poll—they were the

biggest crowd-pullers and crowd-pleasers," writes Shimazu, adding that Nasser was constantly seen waving his hand and flashing his "infectious smile."

49 **fortuitous encounter:** Nutting, *Nasser*, 100–106.

49 **"Welcome, hero of Bandung":** "Triumphal Return of Col. Nasser," *Times* (London), May 2, 1955.

50 **a different man:** Gordon, *Nasser's Blessed Movement*, 189, 230.

50 **"Bandung period":** See, e.g., Abdel-Malek, *Egypt*, 116 passim.

50 **"democratic republic":** "The New Egyptian Constitution," *Middle East Journal* 10, no. 3 (1956): 300–306; Abdel-Malek, *Egypt*, 116–17.

50 **"the first of his famous":** Gordon, *Nasser's Blessed Movement*, 196.

50 **secured his place in history:** A full Arabic text of the speech is available at http://nasser.bibalex.org/TextViewer.aspx?TextID=SPCH-495-ar (accessed December 6, 2021).

52 **$30 million per annum:** For the financial year of 1955, the Suez Canal Company reported a gross profit margin of 47%, and a net profit margin of 31%, after deducting provisions for insurance, depreciation, new works, renewals, contingencies, and extraordinary reserves. The figure of $3 million cited by Nasser as Egypt's annual take represented its legal entitlement to 7% of gross profits. See "Suez Canal Company: Financial Agreement Reached with Egyptian Government," *Manchester Guardian*, June 18, 1956; and Bent Hansen, and Khairy Tourk, "The Profitability of the Suez Canal as a Private Enterprise, 1859–1956," *Journal of Economic History* 38, no. 4 (1978): 938–58.

52 **totaling $65 million:** "Accord Is Signed on Suez Payment," *New York Times*, July 14, 1958.

52 **the infamous plan was laid:** Nutting, *Nasser*, 162.

53 **The attack commenced:** Stephens, *Nasser*, 226.

53 **Nasser's worst nightmare:** Gordon, *Nasser: Hero of the Arab Nation*, 58.

53 **"contemplating":** James Barr, *Lords of the Desert: Britain's Struggle with America to Dominate the Middle East* (London: Simon & Schuster, 2018), 225.

54 **"I'm here" . . . "last drop of blood":** Arabic texts of the two speeches, delivered on November 2 and 9, are available respectively at http://nasser.bibalex.org/TextViewer.aspx?TextID=SPCH-524-ar and http://nasser.bibalex.org/TextViewer.aspx?TextID=SPCH-525-ar.

54 **"photograph was to be found":** Nutting, *Nasser*, 194.

54 **"had something of Lawrence":** Awad, *Aqni ʿat al-Nasiriya al-Sab ʿa*, 105.

55 **exodus of tens of thousands:** Gordon, *Hero of the Arab Nation*, 65; Stephens, *Nasser*, 245.

55 **The family of the famous:** See the final chapter of Edward W. Said, *Out of Place: A Memoir* (London: Granta Books, 2000), 272–95.

55 **"both invaluable economic":** Stephens, *Nasser*, 246.

55 **"Communists, progressives and leftist liberals":** Abdel-Malek, *Egypt*, 116.

55 **"enjoyed an overwhelming popularity":** Abdel-Malek, 122.

56 **not a single piece of legislation:** Irene Weipert-Fenner, *The Autocratic Parliament: Power and Legitimacy in Egypt, 1866–2011* (Syracuse, NY: Syracuse University Press, 2020), 84.

56 **"vanished in terrorism":** Abdel-Malek, *Egypt*, 129.

3. THE GRAVEYARD OF THE LIVING

57 **critics have sung his praises:** Adam Shatz, "Black, Not Noir," *London Review of Books*, March 7, 2013; Creswell, Robyn, "Sonallah Ibrahim: Egypt's Oracular Novelist," *New Yorker*, August 20, 2013.

57   **first of several brief imprisonments:** Sonallah Ibrahim, *Yawmiyyat al-Wahat* [The Oases diary] (Cairo: Dar al-Thaqafa al-Jadida, 2015), 14. Unless otherwise stated, all further biographical details are either from this source or from Sonallah Ibrahim, *Tilk al-Ra'iha wa Qisas Ukhra* [That smell and other stories] (Cairo: Dar al-Thaqafa al-Jadida, 2019).

58   **"Do you know the number":** Waguih Ghali, *Beer in the Snooker Club* (London: Serpent's Tail, 2010), 205.

58   **"Graveyard of the Living":** Arabic *Maqbarat al-Ahya'*; see Abdel-Malek, *Egypt*, 119.

58   **hauled off to detention:** Abdel-Malek, 128.

59   **"ugliest":** Fatima Khalil, "Sun' Allah Ibrahim: Ightiyal Shuhdi Attia absha' shay' fi 'ahd 'Abd al-Nasir" [Sonallah Ibrahim: The assassination of Shuhdi Attiah was the ugliest thing in the Abdel Nasser era], *Youm 7*, November 28, 2010, https://tinyurl.com/7y8t3xu5.

60   **"I can still recall":** Ibrahim, *Yawmiyyat al-Wahat*, 29.

60   **several men sat:** Ibrahim identifies these figures as including Maj. Gen. Ismail Himmat, the notorious representative of the Prisons Authority, who had overseen the briefer internment of communists in Abu Zaabal in 1954, and who was said to personally attend every reception of this kind; Saad Aql, head of the Alexandria branch of the General Investigations agency; and Aql's adjutant, al-Sayyid Fahmi, who would go on to become interior minister under President Anwar Sadat. See Ibrahim, *Yawmiyyat al-Wahat*, 29.

61   **"our national government":** Ibrahim, 27.

62   **Another inmate:** Identified only by the name "Haridi," his account is presented in Ilham Sayf al-Nasr's memoir of Abu Zaabal, *Fi Mu'taqal Abu Za'bal* [In Abu Zaabal Camp] (Cairo: Dar al-Thaqafa al-Jadida, 1977), 234–38.

62   **"took the beatings in silence":** Sayf al-Nasr, *Fi Mu'taqal Abu Za'bal*, 237.

64   **"simply left to die":** Sayf al-Nasr, 149.

64   **childhood friend of Edward Said:** Haddad's father Wadie had been the Said family's doctor in Cairo, a role Farid inherited upon Wadie's death in 1948. Said remembered him as a dedicated and benevolent physician with an "unfailingly even, kind temperament" who treated Palestinian patients free of charge, perhaps because his own father came from Jerusalem. While his communist affiliation was well known, he would demur when Said asked about it, saying, "We must have a cup of coffee together to discuss that." It's clear Haddad made a lasting impression on the younger Said, who wrote in his memoir that "Farid's life and death have been an underground motif in my life for four decades now." See Said, *Out of Place*, 121–26.

64   **"on the ground, naked":** Sayf al-Nasr, *Fi Mu'taqal Abu Za'bal*, 52.

65   **visible today with satellite imagery:** Having since filled up with water, they are now known as the "Arab al-Ulayqat Lakes." See GPS coordinates 30.28869, 31.353753.

66   **"the greatest torture":** Sayf al-Nasr, *Fi Mu'taqal Abu Za'bal*, 197.

66   **On Wednesday:** Sayf al-Nasr gives the date as February 16, which was a Tuesday. For the "Bloody Wednesday" sobriquet to make sense, the date would have to have been the seventeenth. Aside from that detail, the account presented here is his own, from Sayf al-Nasr, 108–9 and 220–28.

68   **answer questions from his hosts:** Ibrahim, *Yawmiyyat al-Wahat*, 33 and 231.

68   **"I decided to become a writer":** Ibrahim, 39.

68   **possibly at Khrushchev's insistence:** The journalist Peter Mansfield, who covered Khrushchev's visit extensively, wrote that it was "widely said that the Soviet leader had insisted on the release from prison of all Egyptian communists as a condition of his visit." See Mansfield, *Nasser*, 146.

4. THE BANNER OF FREEDOM

73   **royal palace was in flames:** The account here is based primarily on Hanna Batatu, *The Old Social Classes and the Revolutionary Movements of Iraq: A Study of Iraq's Old Landed and Commercial Classes and of its Communists, Ba'thists, and Free Officers* (Princeton, NJ: Princeton University Press, 1978), 800–803; and Justin Marozzi, *Baghdad: City of Peace, City of Blood* (London: Penguin, 2015), 326–30. The translation of the military communiqué is the author's.

73   **"hands and feet hacked off":** Marozzi, *Baghdad*, 328.

74   **"The banner of freedom":** Speech by Gamal Abdel Nasser in Damascus on July 18, 1958, a full Arabic text of which can be found at http://nasser.bibalex.org/ TextViewer.aspx?TextID=SPCH-671-ar.

74   **the intelligentsia were undecided:** Albert Hourani, *Arabic Thought in the Liberal Age: 1798–1939* (Cambridge: Cambridge University Press, 2011), 178, 330. Husayn was not alone in conceiving of Egypt as Europe. King Farouk's grandfather, the Khedive Ismail, is quoted as telling a British official in 1877 that "my country is no longer African; we now form part of Europe." See John Eliot Bowen, "The Conflict of East and West in Egypt," *Political Science Quarterly* 1, no. 2 (June 1886): 330.

74   **six-point program:** Its six points were: the elimination from Egypt of colonialism, feudalism, and monopoly; the creation of a strong Egyptian army; and the establishment in Egypt of social justice and a "sound democracy." See Awad, *Aqni'at al-Nasiriya al-Sab'a*, 49.

74   **twice offered the presidency:** Lutfi al-Sayyid was offered the presidency in 1953 and then again the following year; see Gordon, *Nasser's Blessed Movement*, 84, 186.

75   **"remarkably feeble":** Batatu, *Old Social Classes*, 679.

75   **"barefaced treason . . . or Zionism":** Patrick Seale, *The Struggle for Syria: A Study of Post-War Arab Politics, 1945–1958* (London: I.B. Tauris, 1986), 216, 223.

76   **"free to do":** Seale, *Struggle for Syria*, 207.

76   **"raise your heads":** Seale, 210.

78   **"treaty of ignominy":** Gordon, *Nasser's Blessed Movement*, 176.

78   **to whom he confessed:** Nutting, *Nasser*, 74.

79   **memorable evening of merriment:** Christopher Bromhead Birdwood, *Nuri as-Said: A Study in Arab Leadership* (London: Cassell & Company, 1959), 149.

79   **"courage, authority, and coolness":** Thomas E. Lawrence, *Seven Pillars of Wisdom: A Triumph* (London: Vintage, 2008), 558; Birdwood, *Nuri as-Said*, 59.

81   **"I am not a soldier":** Seale, *Struggle for Syria*, 217.

81   **The first secret cell:** This and all subsequent details on the Iraqi Free Officers' formation are, unless otherwise stated, from Batatu, *Old Social Classes*, 767–89.

82   **"hit [Nasser] hard":** Barr, *Lords of the Desert*, 223.

83   **"definite assurances":** Batatu, *Old Social Classes*, 795.

83   **he would supply them:** Uriel Dann, *Iraq under Qassem: A Political History, 1958– 1963* (Tel Aviv: Reuven Shiloah Research Center, Tel Aviv University, 1969), 25– 26. The source of the anecdote is Mohamed Hasanayn Heikal, Nasser's close aide and chief media mouthpiece.

84   **"Those who wish to join":** Abd al-Salam Aref, *Mudhakkirat al-Ra'is al-'Iraqi 'Abd al-Salam 'Arif* [The memoirs of the Iraqi president Abd al-Salam Aref] (Baghdad: Dar Sutur lil-Nashr wal-Tawzi', 2022), 45–46.

84   **The coup was complete:** Batatu, *Old Social Classes*, 800–803; Dann, *Iraq under Qassem*, 28–32.

84   **A scene reminiscent of Cairo's Black Saturday:** Batatu, *Old Social Classes*, 802–805; Dann, *Iraq under Qassem*, 33–34; Marozzi, *Baghdad*, 329–30; Birdwood, *Nuri as-Said*, 269. The final quote is from Rogan, *The Arabs*, 396.

5. A PROGRESSIVE PEOPLE'S REVOLUTION

86   **consigned to the dustbin:** Though it was not until the following March that Iraq officially withdrew from it.

86   **the thronging masses:** Dann, *Iraq under Qassem*, 70–71.

86   **"I felt we had known":** Aref, *Mudhakkirat*, 49–51. Subsequent quotes from Dann, *Iraq under Qassem*, 73, 80; Batatu, *Old Social Classes*, 817.

86   **following the Egyptian playbook:** Marion Farouk-Sluglett and Peter Sluglett, *Iraq since 1958: From Revolution to Dictatorship* (London: I.B. Tauris, 2001), 50, 62; Dann, *Iraq under Qassem*, 37–43, 57, 68; Batatu, *Old Social Classes*, 802.

87   **Nasser made good on his pledge:** Dann, *Iraq under Qassem*, 73–75.

87   **didn't always appear to acknowledge:** For instance, in an interview with Cairo Radio on July 24, 1958, Aref presented himself as the "leader of the command" on the day of the coup, and the foremost figure of the "revolution" in general. See Dann, 78.

88   **placed him at irreconcilable odds:** Dann, 79, 89; Farouk-Sluglett and Sluglett, *Iraq since 1958*, 59.

88   **The fall from grace:** Dann, *Iraq under Qassem*, 80–89; Farouk-Sluglett and Sluglett, *Iraq since 1958*, 59–60.

89   **The first plot was hatched:** Unless otherwise stated, all details of the plot are taken from Dann, *Iraq under Qassem*, 127–35.

91   **especially when expressed in Arabic:** Adding to the confusion is that the verbal form *ittihad*, used here to denote "federal union," is applied in the official name of the United Arab Republic (*al-Jumhuriyya al-'Arabiyya al-Muttahida*).

91   **The climate of fear:** Batatu, *Old Social Classes*, 857; Con Coughlin, *Saddam: His Rise and Fall* (New York: Harper Perennial, 2005), 20.

92   **"negative results":** Batatu, *Old Social Classes*, 829.

92   **"democratic liberties":** Dann, *Iraq under Qassem*, 157; Batatu, *Old Social Classes*, 861.

92   **"For the sake of Arab unity":** Speech by Gamal Abdel Nasser in Port Said on December 23, 1958, a full Arabic text of which can be found at http://nasser.bibalex.org/TextViewer.aspx?TextID=SPCH-695-ar.

92   **arrested by the hundreds:** Dann, *Iraq under Qassem*, 161; Batatu, *Old Social Classes*, 862.

93   **in many cases the same people:** At least six prominent officers were involved in both the Gaylani and Shawwaf plots: Rifaat al-Hajj Sirri, Tahir Yahya, Abd al-Latif al-Darraji, Nathim al-Tabaqchali, Abd al-Aziz al-Uqayli, and Abd al-Wahhab al-Shawwaf himself. See Dann, *Iraq under Qassem*, 129, 166.

93   **the key figure:** Dann, 166.

93   **"assumed the regularity":** Dann, 167, 169.

94   **"battalion of commandos":** Batatu, *Old Social Classes*, 873.

94   **a show of force:** Batatu, 879; Kanan Makiya, *Republic of Fear: The Politics of Modern Iraq* (Berkeley: University of California Press, 1998), 237.

94   **bellowed their signature rhyming chant:** Batatu, *Old Social Classes*, 880.

94   **the insurrection was underway:** Dann, *Iraq under Qassem*, 170–71.

95   **things went wrong:** Dann, 173.

95   **"completely dejected":** Dann. The wording is Dann's, paraphrasing Maj. Mahmud Aziz of the Fifth Brigade.

95   **The rebellion fizzled out:** Dann, 174.

95   **the delirium of the bloodbath:** Batatu, *Old Social Classes*, 865–89; Dann, *Iraq under Qassem*, 164–77; Farouk-Sluglett and Sluglett, *Iraq since 1958*, 66–68.

96   **regarded as a turning point:** See, e.g., Saïd K. Aburish, *Nasser: The Last Arab*, (London: Duckworth, 2004), 193.

96　**series of ill-tempered speeches:** Speeches by Gamal Abdel Nasser in Damascus on March 11, 12, and 13, 1959, full Arabic texts of which can be found at http://nasser.bibalex.org/TextViewer.aspx?TextID=SPCH-736-ar, http://nasser.bibalex.org/TextViewer.aspx?TextID=SPCH-737-ar, and http://nasser.bibalex.org/TextViewer.aspx?TextID=SPCH-738-ar, respectively.

97　**"everyone" . . . "to the floor":** Fuad al-Rikabi, *Al-Hall al-Awhad Lightiyal al-Za'im 'Abd al-Karim Qasim* [The sole solution for the assassination of the leader Abd al-Karim Qasim] (Beirut: al-Dar al-'Arabiyya lil-Mawsu'at, 2010 [first published 1963]), 24.

97　**they opened fire:** al-Rikabi, *Al-Hall al-Awhad Lightiyal al-Za'im*, 83–86.

98　**the prosecutor said:** "Iraq Ousts U.A.R. Aide," *Washington Post*, November 3, 1959; "Nasser Called 'Dog' as 57 Face Court in Kassem Plot," *Washington Post*, December 26, 1959; "Accused Iraqi Links Kassem Plot to U.A.R.," *Washington Post*, December 27, 1959; "Nasser Implicated at Kassem Plotters' Trial," *Jerusalem Post*, December 27, 1959; "Conspiracy to Kill Kassem," *Guardian*, December 27, 1959; "57 Iraqis on Trial in Kassim Attack," *New York Times*, December 27, 1959; "Cairo Tied to Iraq in Baghdad Trial," *New York Times*, December 27, 1959; "Student Bares Syrian Part in Plot on Kassem," *Jerusalem Post*, December 28, 1959; "Nasser Exposed," *Jerusalem Post*, December 28, 1959; *Al-Hayat*, December 29, 1959; *Al-Hayat*, December 31, 1959; "Mahdawi Certain Plotters Guilty," *Jerusalem Post*, January 4, 1960; "17 Sentenced to Hang for Attack on Kassem," *Washington Post*, February 26, 1960; "Iraq Court Dooms 17 in Attack on Kassim," *New York Times*, February 26, 1960; Dann, *Iraq under Qassem*, 254–59.

98　**different version of events:** al-Rikabi, *Al-Hall al-Awhad Lightiyal al-Za'im*, 42–43.

98　**In a rare interview:** Interview with Abd al-Hamid al-Sarraj by Kamal Khalaf Tawil, published in Lebanon's *As-Safir* newspaper on September 28, 2013, available at https://assafir.com/Article/322205/Archive.

99　**prior knowledge of the plot:** Dann, *Iraq under Qassem*, 255–56.

100　**Rikabi fled:** al-Rikabi, *Al-Hall al-Awhad Lightiyal al-Za'im*, 101–18.

100　**Saddam also wound his way:** Coughlin, *Saddam*, 34–39.

100　**"an undesirable person":** "Egypt Unlikely to Offer Saddam Exile Again," UPI, March 23, 1991. Batatu writes that Saddam "was released on the personal interference of President Nāṣir," in an apparent reference to the same incident (*Old Social Classes*, 1084).

101　**Just after eight o'clock:** Dann, *Iraq under Qassem*, 366.

101　**sympathetic Free Officers:** Yahya nominally joined the Baath in 1962, but was "to all intents and purposes a chance Ba'thist," writes Batatu in *Old Social Classes*, 1003. See also Batatu, 966–71; Dann, *Iraq under Qassem*, 362–65.

101　**a successful start:** Batatu, *Old Social Classes*, 975.

102　**A grim scene unfolded:** Batatu, 977–80.

102　**The final battle:** Batatu, 980–81; Dann, *Iraq under Qassem*, 367.

102　**"as only men could fight":** Batatu, *Old Social Classes*, 982.

102　**"exterminate":** Batatu.

102　**well over a thousand:** Batatu cites an unnamed "well-placed foreign diplomatic observer" as putting total deaths at 1,500, while the communists claim a figure as high as 5,000 (*Old Social Classes*, 985).

103　**Saleh Mahdi Ammash:** Batatu, 969–70. Per Rikabi, Ammash was both an informant for the hit squad at the defense ministry, keeping them abreast of Qasim's movements, and the middleman between them and the Free Officers (*Al-Hall al-Awhad Lightiyal al-Za'im*, 54, 73, 78). See also Dann, *Iraq under Qassem*, 255.

103　**again heavily Baathist:** Batatu, *Old Social Classes*, 1004–7.

103　**"found all sorts of loathsome":** Batatu, 990.

103   **hailed by Nasser:** Speech by Gamal Abdel Nasser on February 22, 1963, an Arabic text of which is available at http://nasser.bibalex.org/TextViewer .aspx?TextID=SPCH-1039-ar.

104   **thirteen trilateral meetings:** Malcolm H. Kerr, *The Arab Cold War: Gamal 'Abd al-Nasir and His Rivals, 1958–1970*, 3rd ed. (New York: Oxford University Press, 1971), 48.

104   **thirty-page agreement:** Elie Podeh, "To Unite or Not to Unite—That Is *Not* the Question: The 1963 Tripartite Unity Talks Reassessed," *Middle Eastern Studies* 39, no. 1 (January 2003): 150–185; Jay Walz, "Egypt, Syria, Iraq Sign Merger Plan," *New York Times*, April 17, 1963.

104   **"their looks of hate":** Batatu, *Old Social Classes*, 1013.

104   **"great harm":** Batatu, 990–91.

105   **incensed by the treatment:** Batatu, 1012.

105   **The inevitable rupture:** Batatu, 1022–26; Farouk-Sluglett and Sluglett, *Iraq since 1958*, 92–93.

105   **de facto province of the UAR:** Batatu, *Old Social Classes*, 1031–32.

106   **an attempt to seize power:** Interview with Aref Abd al-Razzaq by Al Jazeera's Ahmed Mansour aired in 2002, available on YouTube at https://www.youtube .com/watch?v=-uGgSfaTzCE&list=PLUxAs6a2fGkVaMcXZ198hibn4RisNIt4P &index=10 (accessed January 26, 2022).

107   **plans were set in motion:** Ibid.; Farouk-Sluglett and Sluglett, *Iraq since 1958*, 97–99.

107   **The plot began:** Interview with Aref Abd al-Razzaq by Al Jazeera's Ahmed Mansour aired in 2002, available on YouTube at https://www.youtube.com/wat ch?v=aAshBwQwOfA&list=PLUxAs6a2fGkVaMcXZ198hibn4RisNIt4P&in dex=12 (accessed January 27, 2022).

107   **had him on speed dial:** As seen by the author at Nasser's former home—now a museum—in Cairo's Manshiyat al-Bakri district, on October 13, 2021.

108   **"briefly flirted":** Batatu, *Old Social Classes*, 1074.

108   **"send us to the gallows":** Batatu, 1074.

108   **Nayef was later assassinated:** Makiya, *Republic of Fear*, 13.

108   **On the morning of July 17:** Farouk-Sluglett and Sluglett, *Iraq since 1958*, 112–13; Batatu, *Old Social Classes*, 1074–76.

109   **"Nothing will happen":** Coughlin, *Saddam*, 57.

109   **the Baath were now sole masters:** Farouk-Sluglett and Sluglett, *Iraq since 1958*, 115–17.

109   **"profound reassertion" . . . "Fulsome congratulations":** Farouk-Sluglett and Sluglett, 115–17.

110   **three successful coups d'état:** These are, respectively, the coups of July 14, 1958, February 8, 1963, and November 18, 1963; the coups attempted by Gaylani, Shawwaf, the Baath (in 1964) and Aref Abd al-Razzaq (in 1965 and again in 1966); and the October 7, 1959, attempt on Qasim's life.

110   **in at least four:** Respectively: the 1958 coup, the Gaylani and Shawwaf plots, the second Abd al-Razzaq plot, and the attempted assassination of Qasim in October 1959.

6. THE DAWN OF ARAB LIBERATION

114   **"from the doorstep":** Interview with Abd al-Hamid al-Sarraj by Kamal Khalaf Tawil conducted in 2002, published in Lebanon's *As-Safir* newspaper on September 28, 2013, available at https://assafir.com/Article/322205/Archive.

114 **"seen plenty like you before":** This and many other details here are compiled from interviews with thirty witnesses conducted in 1961–62 as part of an official Syrian investigation into Helu's killing led by Judge Maj. Ahmad Zuhayr Subhi al-Adili of the Judicial Council, as published in full in *Faraj Allah al-Hilu . . . Shaheedan: Mahadhir al-Tahqiqat* [Farajallah al-Helu . . . the martyr: The investigation documents] (Beirut: Dar al-Farabi, 2022).

116 **"three or four":** *Faraj Allah al-Hilu*, 31–32.

116 **Sarraj told an interviewer:** See aforementioned interview with Sarraj by Kamal Khalaf Tawil, *As-Safir*, September 28, 2013.

116 **Nasser maintained the lie:** Aside from the sources already cited, the account here is based on an interview by the author with Farajallah al-Helu's daughter Nada in Hosrayel, Lebanon, on August 25, 2022; Sami Jumaa's memoir, *Awraq min Daftar al-Watan: 1946–1961* [Pages from the notebook of the homeland: 1946–1961] (Damascus: Dar Tlas, 2000); Karim Mroué, *Al-Shuyu'iyyun al-Arba'a al-Kibar fi Tarikh Lubnan al-Hadith: Fu'ad al-Shimali, Faraj Allah al-Hilu, Niqula Shawi, Jurj Hawi* [The four preeminent communists in modern Lebanese history: Fuad al-Shimali, Farajallah al-Helu, Nicolas Shawi, George Hawi] (Beirut: Dar al-Saqi, 2009); Ghassan Zakaria, *Al-Sultan al-Ahmar* [The red sultan] (London: Arados Publishing, 1991); "L'Arrestation de M. Farajallah Helou," *Le Monde*, March 2, 1960; and the Alaraby TV documentary *Kuntu hunak: Ightiyal Faraj Allah al-Hilu* [I was there: The assassination of Farajallah al-Helu], available on YouTube at https://www.youtube.com/watch?v=X3onsVeTgXc (accessed February 27, 2022).

117 **happier and healthier trajectory:** Seale, *Struggle for Syria*, 132–43.

117 **"the first free elections":** Seale, 164.

118 **"constellation of parties":** Seale, 3.

119 **"Syria enjoyed what amounted":** Seale, 213.

119 **A founding father:** Sami Moubayed, *The Makers of Modern Syria: The Rise and Fall of Syrian Democracy 1918–1958* (London: I.B. Tauris, 2018), 31, 110.

120 **Khuri tendered his own resignation:** Seale, *Struggle for Syria*, 214–20.

120 **the "Nasserization" of Syrian officialdom:** Seale, 223–24, 252–54.

120 **pilot named Hafez al-Assad:** Patrick Seale, *Asad of Syria: The Struggle for the Middle East* (Berkeley: University of California Press, 1989), 50–51.

120 **"beating heart":** Zakaria, *Al-Sultan al-Ahmar*, 166.

120 **Allegations abounded:** Zakaria, 52, 166; Seale, *Struggle for Syria*, 254, 319; Hazem Saghieh, *Al-Ba'th al-Suri: Tarikh Mujaz* [The Syrian Baath: A brief history] (Beirut: Dar al-Saqi, 2012), chap. 2.

121 **it had been the officers:** Seale, *Asad of Syria*, 223.

122 **Sarraj's childhood was an unhappy one:** Zakaria, *Al-Sultan al-Ahmar*, 24–25; 142; Jumaa, *Awraq min Daftar al-Watan*, 168.

122 **a humble gendarme:** Zakaria, *Al-Sultan al-Ahmar*, 30–31, 57.

122 **Sarraj enrolled:** Zakaria, 31–32; Seale, *Asad of Syria*, 119, 245.

123 **strongest ideological currents:** Seale, *Asad of Syria*, 239–41.

123 **expunge the Syrian nationalists:** Seale, 241–43.

123 **"a year of torture":** Robyn Creswell, "The Man Who Remade Arabic Poetry," *New Yorker*, December 11, 2017.

123 **"In prison":** Quoted in the Al Jazeera documentary *Al-'Aqid al-Sarraj: Rajul al-ru'b* [Col. Sarraj: The man of terror], April 29, 2018, available at https://tinyurl.com/2ej8p3pb.

124 **Methods of torture:** Zakaria, *Al-Sultan al-Ahmar*, 33–34, 125, 247; "Torture Archipelago: Arbitrary Arrests, Torture, and Enforced Disappearances in Syria's Underground Prisons since March 2011," Human Rights Watch, July 3, 2012; "Syria: 'It Breaks the Human': Torture, Disease and Death in Syria's Prisons," Amnesty International, August 18, 2016.

124 **down a dark path:** Zakaria, *Al-Sultan al-Ahmar*, 34; Seale, *Asad of Syria*, 257.

124 **the experience was transformational:** Seale, *Asad of Syria*, 261–62; Nutting, *Nasser*, 172–73; Tunzelmann, *Blood and Sand*, 247.

125 **the real decision-makers:** Seale, *Asad of Syria*, 245–46.

125 **rising tide of communism:** Seale, 255–61.

126 **Eisenhower Doctrine was scorned:** Seale, 291.

126 **full-blown Cold War standoff:** Seale, 297–301.

126 **suddenly stepped Nasser:** Seale, 305.

126 **the time had come:** Seale, 318–19.

127 **a delegation to Cairo:** Seale, 319–20; Nutting, *Nasser*, 214–15.

127 **called it a military coup:** Seale, 319–20; Nutting, *Nasser*, 214–15.

127 **final agreement was reached:** Seale, *Asad of Syria*, 321–22.

128 **to volunteer willingly:** Saghieh, *Al-Ba'th al-Suri*, chap. 3.

128 **prepared to go along with it:** Seale, *Asad of Syria*, 322–23.

128 **"It was to be total union":** Seale, 322–23.

128 **full union between Egypt and Syria:** Seale, 323; "Egypt and Syria a 'United Republic': Nasser as First President; Single Army and Flag," *Observer*, February 1, 1958; Speech by Gamal Abdel Nasser on February 23, 1958, an Arabic transcript of which is available at http://nasser.bibalex.org/TextViewer.aspx?TextID=SPCH -580-ar.

129 **"participated in the rigging":** Bashir al-Azma, *Jeel al-Hazima: Bayn al-Wahda wal-Infisal* [The generation of the defeat: Between union and separation] (London: Riad El-Rayyes Books, 1991), 191.

129 **The official results:** "7½ Million Say 'Yes' to Nasser," *Observer*, February 22, 1958.

7. THE DAMASCENE CONVERSION

130 **swarmed by giant crowds:** Jumaa, *Awraq min Daftar al-Watan*, 294–96.

130 **"I braved the fury":** Fouad Ajami, *The Dream Palace of the Arabs: A Generation's Odyssey* (New York: Vintage, 1998), 11–12.

131 **to make up numbers:** Jumaa, *Awraq min Daftar al-Watan*, 296.

131 **clear where Nasser's priorities lay:** Kerr, *Arab Cold War*, 13; "Egyptians Head Seven of Eight 'Union' Ministries," *Jerusalem Post*, March 7, 1958.

132 **the second of four vice presidents:** Kerr, *Arab Cold War*, 11; Stephens, *Nasser*, 332–33. The other two vice presidents were the Egyptian Free Officers Abd al-Hakim Amer and Abd al-Latif al-Baghdadi.

133 **Sarraj summoned the heads:** Jumaa, *Awraq min Daftar al-Watan*, 323.

133 **the torturing to death:** Mroué, *Al-Shuyu'iyyun*, 71.

133 **the most "brutal" of all:** Interview with Riad al-Turk by Gisèle Khoury for BBC Arabic, aired April 6, 2020, available at https://www.youtube.com/ watch?v=TMdGg5JpPNQ.

133 **His name was Rafiq Ridha:** This and subsequent paragraphs from Jumaa, *Awraq min Daftar al-Watan*, 330–39.

135 **"We will be officially dissolved":** Kerr, *Arab Cold War*, 12–13.

135 **humiliations came thick and fast:** Kerr, 14–15; Nutting, *Nasser*, 250; Stephens, *Nasser*, 337.

135 **invested ever greater powers in Sarraj:** Stephens, *Nasser*, 337; Zakaria, *Al-Sultan al-Ahmar*, 201.

136 **"Minister of health":** This and subsequent paragraphs from al-Azma, *Jeel al-Hazima*, 194–219.

137 **"There is something about that club"**: Ghali, *Beer in the Snooker Club*, 126–27.

138 **turned overnight into petty tyrants**: Jumaa, *Awraq min Daftar al-Watan*, 303.

138 **was dismissed and replaced**: Jumaa, 309–10; "Bizri Replaced by His Deputy," *Jerusalem Post*, March 28, 1958.

139 **The incident was later cited**: Al Jazeera interview with Lt. Col. Abd al-Karim al-Nahlawi, aired on February 14, 2010, available on YouTube at https://www.youtube.com/watch?v=RFvJoDU-_Is&list=PLUxAs6a2fGkVB -uuRFeIJCO0z20yKStW_&index=4. Nahlawi names three of the officers imprisoned and tortured as Abd al-Razzaq al-Yahya, Samir Khatib, and Asaad Dabbur.

139 **a variety of methods were employed**: Seale, *Asad of Syria*, 59; Munif al-Razzaz, *Al-Tajriba al-Murra* [The bitter experience] (Beirut: Dar Ghandur, 1967), 87.

139 **"they spent much time lounging"**: Seale, *Asad of Syria*, 60.

139 **they comprised five key figures**: Seale, 59–64. Hanna Batatu writes that the earliest incarnation of the committee began in 1959, when it comprised Umran, Lt.-Cols. Mazyad Hunaydi and Bashir Sadeq, and Capt. Abd al-Ghani Ayyash. Only when the latter three were reassigned elsewhere in 1960 did Umran bring in Jadid, al-Mir, al-Jundi, and Assad, the five of whom then "constituted the committee's inner core or leading nucleus" (Hanna Batatu, *Syria's Peasantry, the Descendants of Its Lesser Rural Notables, and Their Politics* [Princeton, NJ: Princeton University Press, 1999], 144).

140 **"We felt the problem"**: Muhammad Umran, *Tajribati fi al-Thawra* [My experience in the revolution] (Beirut, 1970), 18.

140 **"We want freedoms"**: Speech by Gamal Abdel Nasser at the Latakia Officers' Club on February 20, 1961, a full Arabic text of which is available at http://nasser .bibalex.org/TextViewer.aspx?TextID=SPCH-962-ar.

141 **proportion of cultivated land seized**: Batatu writes (*Syria's Peasantry*, 163) that some 20% of Syria's cultivated land was affected by the 1958 law, whereas the corresponding figure for Egypt is around 10% (see, e.g., Abdel-Malek, *Egypt*, 72; Mansfield, *Nasser*, 81).

141 **"to follow the maddeningly complicated"**: Kerr, *Arab Cold War*, 24.

141 **slashing its national income**: Stephens, *Nasser*, 335.

141 **the "bombshell" announcement**: Stephens, 331, 338; Abdel-Malek, *Egypt*, 151–58.

142 **to the British diplomat**: Nutting, *Nasser*, 266.

142 **"Syrian officers felt a sense"**: Al Jazeera interview with Lt. Col. Abd al-Karim al-Nahlawi, aired in multiple episodes between February 26 and May 5, 2010, available on YouTube at https://www.youtube.com/playlist?list=PLUxAs6a2fGkVB -uuRFeIJCO0z20yKStW_.

142 **Nahlawi cited**: This and subsequent details from ibid., unless otherwise indicated.

144 **statement had harsh words**: Muhammad Saeed Ahmad Bani Ayish, *Al-Inqilabat al-'Askariyya fi Suriya min 1949–1969: Dirasa fi al-'Awamil al-Dakhiliyya wal-Iqlimiyya wal-Duwaliyya* [Military coups in Syria 1949–1969: A study of the domestic, regional, and international factors] (Irbid, Jordan: Dar al-Kitab al-Thaqafi, 2017), 211–13.

144 **"rectify the situation"**: Interview with Al Jazeera.

144 **"stabbed Arab unity"**: Speech by Gamal Abdel Nasser on September 28, 1961, an Arabic text of which is available at http://nasser.bibalex.org/TextViewer .aspx?TextID=SPCH-997-ar.

144 **Nasser did dispatch Egyptian forces**: Seale, *Asad of Syria*, 67; Stephens, *Nasser*, 340; Al Jazeera interview with Nahlawi; "Nasser Calls Off Offensive," *Guardian*, September 30, 1961.

8. N ASSERISTS AGAINST N ASSER

146 **the Nahlawi junta:** In his aforementioned interview with Al Jazeera, Nahlawi names Brig. Gen. Muwaffaq Assasa, Brig. Gen. Zuhayr Aqeel, and Nur Allah Hajj Ibrahim as the main officers (aside from himself) in charge of Syria during the period.

146 **support for the new order:** Kerr, *Arab Cold War*, 33.

147 **relatively free elections:** In his memoir, Khalid al-Azm—who received more votes than any other individual in this election—details certain restrictions imposed on candidates, including the censorship of references to the army in campaign literature. However, Azm suggests the voting itself was free and fair (as well he might). The Baath's Bitar alleged his own failure to win a seat was the result of fraud. Commenting on this, Azm contends he himself would have been unlikely to win the votes he did if the vote were rigged, given his frosty relations with the officers at that time (Khalid al-Azm, *Mudhakkirat Khalid al-'Athm* [The memoirs of Khalid al-Azm] [Beirut: al-Dar al-Muttahida lil-Nashr, 1973], 3:214–20). Hanna Batatu describes the election as "comparatively free" in his paper "Some Observations on the Social Roots of Syria's Ruling, Military Group and the Causes for Its Dominance," *Middle East Journal* 35, no. 3 (Summer, 1981): 339.

147 **The results brought a diverse spread:** Kerr, *Arab Cold War*, 34–36; al-Azm, *Mudhakkirat Khalid al-'Athm*, 220–30.

147 **fell into a major crisis:** Nahlawi interview with Al Jazeera; al-Azm, *Mudhakkirat Khalid al-'Athm*, 264–65; Kerr, *Arab Cold War*, 34–37.

147 **the almost comical experience:** al-Azm, *Mudhakkirat Khalid al-'Athm*, 266–68. The former prime ministers were Dawalibi, Kuzbari, Sabri al-Asali, Lutfi al-Haffar, and Azm himself.

148 **The new junta:** Nahlawi interview with Al Jazeera; al-Azm, *Mudhakkirat Khalid al-'Athm*, 268; "Damascus Claims Revolt Over as Leaders of Coup Flee to Geneva," *Jerusalem Post*, April 4, 1962.

148 **decided to roll the dice:** Nahlawi interview with Al Jazeera; Seale, *Asad of Syria*, 70; al-Azm, *Mudhakkirat Khalid al-'Athm*, 272; Umran, *Tajribati fi al-Thawra*, 20–21; "New Syrian Command Formed," *Jerusalem Post*, April 6, 1962.

148 **playing backgammon and chess:** al-Azm, *Mudhakkirat Khalid al-'Athm*.

148 **Azma was told:** al-Azma, *Jeel al-Hazima*, 230.

149 **ease tensions with Cairo:** al-Azma, 238; Kerr, *Arab Cold War*, 38.

149 **Cairo was not interested:** al-Azma, *Jeel al-Hazima*.

149 **"placed in one large prison":** Speech by Gamal Abdel Nasser on July 26, 1962, an Arabic text of which is available at http://nasser.bibalex.org/TextViewer.aspx?TextID=SPCH-1025-ar.

149 **"in a well-calculated needling gesture":** Kerr, *Arab Cold War*, 39; al-Azm, *Mudhakkirat Khalid al-'Athm*, 293–94.

150 **"broke down in tears":** Kerr, *Arab Cold War*, 39; al-Azm, *Mudhakkirat Khalid al-'Athm*, 293–94.

150 **The purpose of these meetings:** al-Azm, *Mudhakkirat Khalid al-'Athm*, 289–97.

150 **Azm's government was officially formed:** al-Azm, 300–302; al-Azma, *Jeel al-Hazima*, 244.

150 **marked no drastic shift:** al-Azm, *Mudhakkirat Khalid al-'Athm*, 305.

151 **"It was thought":** al-Azm, 301, 306.

151 **to their Nasserist counterparts:** Seale, *Asad of Syria*, 72–74.

152 **they seized the usual sites:** Seale, 76–77; Kerr, *Arab Cold War*, 42; al-Azm, *Mudhakkirat Khalid al-'Athm*, 438.

152 **Syria's new masters promptly set up:** Seale, *Asad of Syria*, 78–79.

153 **separated them in ideological terms:** Asked point-blank by Nasser to explain the Baath's ideological differences with him at the tripartite union talks in Cairo in April 1963, the Baath's cofounder Bitar had to admit he could think of none. See Kerr, *Arab Cold War*, 67.

153   **retained the most crucial levers:** Seale, *Asad of Syria*, 79–80.

154   **The showdown had arrived:** Seale, 82.

154   **"Nasser loyalists were purged":** Seale, 82–84.

154   **their own "National Guard" militia:** Seale, 84.

155   **"thirty percent":** Interview with Jasim Alwan in Cairo by Al Jazeera aired September 19, 2003, an Arabic transcript of which is available at https://www.aljazeera .net/programs/privatevisit/2005/1/10/%D8%AC%D8%A7%D8%B3%D9%85 -%D8%B9%D9%84%D9%88%D8%A7%D9%86-%D8%AC2.

155   **"still keen on restoring":** Ibid. For allegations of promised air and radio support, see, e.g., Al Jazeera's interview with Amin al-Hafez, aired May 21, 2001, available on YouTube at https://www.youtube.com/watch?v=3u2TxmCUWRw&list=PL UxAs6a2fGkVi9wuATt2VFXDqZa2fl8Lw&index=9.

156   **"slaughter such as Syria":** Seale, *Asad of Syria*, 83.

156   **summarily executed:** Seale, 83; Al Jazeera interviews with Jasim Alwan and Amin al-Hafez; Kerr, *Arab Cold War*, 87–88; "Mu'aridh Suri ya'ud ila Dimashq ba'da 41 'aman min al-manfa" [Syrian oppositionist returns to Damascus after 41 years in exile], Al Jazeera, April 19, 2005, available at https://tinyurl.com/yc742aat.

156   **"We have decided":** Speech by Gamal Abdel Nasser at Cairo's Gumhuriya Square on July 22, 1963, an Arabic text of which is available at http://nasser.bibalex .org/TextViewer.aspx?TextID=SPCH-1050-ar.

156   **fratricidal cannibalization:** Seale, *Asad of Syria*, 101–103.

157   **"You Baathists":** Seale, 126, 153.

157   **"undoubtedly . . . influenced by the model of Nasser":** Seale, 169.

157   **"Nasserists against Nasser":** al-Razzaz, *Al-Tajriba al-Murra*, 56, 192.

9. THE SUMMER OF BLOOD

161   **"Kamel Mrowa Assassinated":** *Al-Hayat*, May 17, 1966. An image of the paper's front page is available at kamelmrowa.com, https://www.kamelmrowa.com/copy -of-10-izdhar-alshafh-alwrqyh?lightbox=dataItem-izq1nrad. The details here of Mrowa's assassination are drawn from the official indictment issued by the Lebanese judiciary on June 23, 1966, available at https://www.kamelmrowa.com/copy -of-flstyn-walaql; a lengthy investigative report undertaken by Mrowa's son Karim in collaboration with the Lebanese journalist Najem El Hachem, published in Arabic at kamelmrowa.com; a series of interviews conducted by the author with Karim and his siblings Malek and Lina in December 2020 and January 2021, and with El Hachem in April 2022; and the address delivered by the Mrowa family's lawyer Mohsen Slim at the trial of his killers. The Sarraj quote is from an interview with Adnan Sultani by El Hachem in Beirut in 1999.

163   **as an Islamic phenomenon:** See, e.g., 11–12 in Chamoun's book *Azma fi Lubnan* [Crisis in Lebanon] (Beirut, 1977).

163   **bad blood began in 1955:** Nutting, *Nasser*, 82–87.

163   **prominent spot on Nasser's blacklist:** Nutting, 88.

164   **assistance from the CIA:** The CIA operative Wilbur Crane Eveland would later recall: "Throughout the elections I travelled regularly to the presidential palace with a briefcase of Lebanese pounds, then returned late at night to the embassy with an empty twin case I'd carried away for Harvey Armada's CIA finance-office

to replenish. Soon my gold DeSoto with its stark white top was a common sight outside the palace" (quoted in Fawwaz Traboulsi, *A History of Modern Lebanon*, 2nd ed. [London: Pluto Press, 2012], 133).

164 **"There's money for anyone":** "'Free' Election in Lebanon: But Votes at a Price," *Manchester Guardian*, June 10, 1957.

165 **security forces fired on demonstrators:** "Five Killed in Beirut Riots: Opposition rally," *Manchester Guardian*, May 30, 1957; "Six Killed in Anti-Government Riots in Beirut; Troops Called Out," *Jerusalem Post*, May 31, 1957.

165 **four bombs went off:** "U.S. and Jordan Offices Blasted in Beirut," *Jerusalem Post*, August 1, 1957.

165 **"bomb explosions and political murders":** "Violence in the Lebanon: Syrians Blamed," *Manchester Guardian*, November 7, 1957.

165 **explosion shattered the windows:** "Bomb Explosion in Beirut: British Council Hall," *Manchester Guardian*, December 20, 1957; "Three Killed in Beirut: Bomb Misses Its Target," *Manchester Guardian*, January 5, 1958.

165 **"It was natural":** Jumaa, *Awraq min Daftar al-Watan*, 258.

165 **using a donkey:** Jumaa, 259–60.

166 **Chamoun himself believed:** See, e.g., his aforementioned book *Azma fi Lubnan* [Crisis in Lebanon], in which he writes on p. 12 that, in 1958, Nasser "sought to extend his dominion over Lebanon so as to make it the third province of the United Arab Republic."

166 **"Frequent and often violent":** Kamal S. Salibi, *The Modern History of Lebanon* (Delmar, NY: Caravan Books, 1965), 201.

166 **portraits on classroom walls:** Samir Khalaf, *Civil and Uncivil Violence in Lebanon: A History of the Internationalization of Communal Conflict* (New York: Columbia University Press, 2002), 114.

166 **The Bureau began:** Jumaa, *Awraq min Daftar al-Watan*, 259–60; Nutting, *Nasser*, 232. Nutting's account is significant because he spoke in person to Sarraj, whom he said "admitted with complete candour" to the Bureau's activities (258).

167 **shot dead in southern Beirut:** The Lebanese press syndicate gives the date as November 5, 1957: http://pressorderlebanon.com/words-details.php?words=31.

167 **"in need of someone like that":** Jumaa, *Awraq min Daftar al-Watan*, 262–63.

167 **slipped quickly into rebel hands:** Khalaf, *Civil and Uncivil Violence*, 128.

167 **"on every corner":** "Chamoun May Agree to Forgo 2nd Term," *Jerusalem Post*, May 20, 1958.

168 **often in double figures:** For instance, the local English-language *Daily Star* newspaper reported more than twenty killed in Beirut and Tripoli on May 13, and ten killed in Beirut the following day.

168 **the bombings:** "Airfield Battle in Lebanon: Bombs in Beirut," *Manchester Guardian*, May 15, 1958; "Six Killed by Beirut Bomb: A Large Store Burnt Out," *Manchester Guardian*, July 8, 1958; "11 Killed by Bomb Explosion in Beirut Tram: 15 Badly Hurt; Shops Damaged," *Manchester Guardian*, May 27, 1958; "Six Killed by Bomb Meant for Premier Solh," *Jerusalem Post*, July 30, 1958.

168 **"It was incumbent on us":** Interview with Abd al-Hamid al-Sarraj by Kamal Khalaf Tawil conducted in 2002, published in Lebanon's *As-Safir* newspaper on September 28, 2013, available at https://assafir.com/Article/322205/Archive.

168 **herds of mules:** Jumaa, *Awraq min Daftar al-Watan*, 258.

168 **"four cases of bombs":** "Planes Hit Armed Donkey Caravan," *Daily Star*, May 28, 1958.

168 **"became virtually the opposition's headquarters":** Khalaf, *Civil and Uncivil Violence*, 110.

168 **"deplorably ham-handed":** Nutting, *Nasser*, 234–35.

169 **"millionaire eccentric":** "Lebanon: Bloodletting," *Time*, May 26, 1958, avail-

able at http://content.time.com/time/subscriber/article/0,33009,936911,00.html; Jumaa, *Awraq min Daftar al-Watan*, 207.

169 **the Belgian was only too happy:** Jumaa, *Awraq min Daftar al-Watan*, 266–76, 318–21; "Belgian Consul Seized with Smuggled Arms," *Daily Star*, May 13, 1958; "Belgian Consul Said 'Gun-Runner,'" *Jerusalem Post*, May 13, 1958.

169 **fell prey to scam artists:** Jumaa, *Awraq min Daftar al-Watan*, 263–65.

170 **"overt armed aggression":** Office of the Historian, U.S. Department of State, https://history.state.gov/milestones/1953-1960/eisenhower-doctrine (accessed April 11, 2022).

170 **Dulles worried privately:** Traboulsi, *History of Modern Lebanon*, 135–36.

170 **changed their calculus entirely:** Traboulsi, 137.

171 **already been floated by Nasser:** According to Nasser's senior intelligence aide, Sami Sharaf, who says he personally recorded the minutes of the conversation at Nasser's dictation (Nicolas Nassif, "Sami Sharaf yatadhakkar al-Shihabiyya" [Sami Sharaf recalls Chehabism], Part 2, *Al-Akhbar*, October 2, 2007). See also Traboulsi, *History of Modern Lebanon*, 136.

171 **insurgency was wound down:** Nutting, *Nasser*, 242.

171 **"As Chamoun goes home":** "Barricades in Beirut as Outgoing Cabinet Quits," *Jerusalem Post*, September 23, 1958.

172 **It was at this meeting:** As affirmed by Sami Sharaf; see Nassif, "Sami Sharaf yatadhakkar," Part 2.

172 **affirmed by Sarraj himself:** Aforementioned interview with Sarraj by *As-Safir*.

172 **It was Rasheed:** Interview with Nadheer Rasheed by Al Jazeera aired on September 22, 2008, available on YouTube at https://www.youtube .com/watch?v=QSzArQtMfBA; Al Jazeera documentary *Al-'Aqid al-Sarraj: Rajul al-Ru'b* [Colonel Sarraj: The man of terror], April 29, 2018, available at https://tinyurl.com/2ej8p3pb.

172 **described by Nasser's senior intelligence:** Nicolas Nassif, "Sami Sharaf yata-dhakkar al-Shihabiyya" (Sami Sharaf recalls Chehabism), Part 1, *Al-Akhbar*, October 1, 2007; Al Jazeera documentary *Al-'Aqid al-Sarraj: Rajul al-ru'b*.

173 **"political and security cover":** The quoted words are Sharaf's; see Nassif, "Sami Sharaf yatadhakkar," Part 1.

174 **on excellent terms with Cairo:** In his history of Lebanon's Deuxième Bureau, the journalist Nicolas Nassif writes that Khatib was the Bureau's "senior liaison officer with the Egyptian embassy in Beirut," with strong personal "Nasserist incli-nations" and a "special relationship with Gamal Abdel Nasser." A photo in the book shows Khatib shaking hands with Nasser at Cairo airport, both men smiling warmly. See Nicolas Nassif, *Al-Maktab al-Thani: Hakim fi al-Thill* [The Deuxième Bureau: A ruler in the shadows], 4th ed. (Beirut, 2015), 69–70; 266.

174 **interfering in everything:** Kamal Salibi, *Crossroads to Civil War: Lebanon 1958–1976* (Delmar, NY: Caravan Books, 1976), 21; Kassir, *Beirut* (Berkeley: University of California Press, 2010), 465; Traboulsi, *History of Modern Lebanon*, 140, 144.

174 **turned into Lebanese Bureau agents:** Nicolas Nassif, "Sami al-Khatib: Al-taqatu' al-mumkin bayn al-Shihabiyya wal-Nasiriyya wal-Ba'th" [Sami al-Khatib: The intersection possible between Chehabism, Nasserism, and the Baath], *Al-Akhbar*, May 27, 2019; Salibi, *Crossroads to Civil War*, 11; Traboulsi, *History of Modern Lebanon*, 140.

174 **were Nasserists:** Salibi, *Crossroads to Civil War*, 11.

174 **"maximum possible accommodation":** Salibi, 14.

174 **"summon" . . . "dictate to them his wishes":** Nassif, *Al-Maktab al-Thani*, 160.

174 **"virtually as a High Commissioner":** Salibi, *Crossroads to Civil War*, 18.

175 **Nasser pressed him in private:** Sami Sharaf says he personally delivered "more than one message" from Nasser urging Chehab to extend his term. Nasser would

even declare Chehab his preferred candidate once again in the 1970 elections. See Nassif, "Sami Sharaf yatadhakkar," Part 2.

175 **first Lebanese president to visit:** Kassir, *Beirut*, 458.

10. A MISSION VERY IMPORTANT FOR NASSERISM

176 **popped by for a shoot:** Photos of both occasions may be found at kamelmrowa .com, https://www.kamelmrowa.com/copy-of-7-mtbah-wdar-wjrydtan-jdydt (accessed January 25, 2021).

176 **recalls playing on swings:** Interview with Malek Mrowa, Kamel's son, in Mrowa Villa, Beit Mirri, December 11, 2020. Unless otherwise stated, all biographical information about Mrowa is based on this interview; a subsequent interview with Malek and his siblings Karim and Lina on December 16, 2020, also at the Mrowa Villa; another interview with Karim Mrowa by telephone on January 24, 2021; the kamelmrowa.com website; and Kamel Mrowa's memoir of the Second World War and early Cold War, *Bayrut—Birlin—Bayrut: Mushahadat Sahafi fi Uruba wa Almanya Athna' al-Harb al-'Alamiyya al-Thaniya wal-Harb al-Barida allati Talatha* [Beirut—Berlin—Beirut: A journalist's observations in Europe and Germany during the Second World War and subsequent Cold War] (London: Riad El-Rayyes Books, 1991).

180 **"painful in the extreme":** Mrowa, *Bayrut—Birlin—Bayrut*, 149.

181 **"nightmare":** Mrowa, 235.

181 **"Where were the shelters?":** Mrowa, 252.

182 **"I have come to believe":** Mrowa, 248.

182 **"I learned a lot":** Mrowa, 182.

184 **"If you wanted a piece":** Traboulsi, *History of Modern Lebanon*, 177.

184 **"had a special talent":** Kassir, *Beirut*, 466.

184 **"which he regarded":** Nutting, *Nasser*, 223–24.

184 **"It was a message":** Interview with Karim Mrowa, January 24, 2021.

185 **granted the dubious honor:** Jumaa, *Awraq min Daftar al-Watan*, 361. An arrest warrant was issued against Khatib by the Syrian judiciary in 1962, following the official investigation into Helu's killing; needless to say, he was not extradited from Cairo. (See *Faraj Allah al-Hilu . . . Shaheedan: Mahadhir al-Tahqiqat*, 188.)

185 **Qulaylat was arrested:** Nassif, *Al-Maktab al-Thani*, 69.

185 **An official party poster:** Maasri, Zeina, *Off the Wall: Political Posters of the Lebanese Civil War* (London: I.B. Tauris, 2009), 105, fig. 5.4.

185 **It was in early April:** The account here of the weeks leading up to Kamel Mrowa's assassination is based first and foremost on official Lebanese court documents, including the formal indictment against the men accused of killing him issued by the judiciary on June 23, 1966, and the final verdict delivered by Lebanon's top court, the Higher Judicial Council, on March 15, 1968, as published in full in the local press at the time. Significantly, the indictment was built around the testimony of Mrowa's killer himself, Adnan Shaker Sultani, who freely confessed to his crime and divulged a plethora of details about it, even physically reenacting much of it for the benefit of investigators. The indictment also drew on the testimony of various independent specialists, including a French military forensic expert who analyzed empty bullet casings recovered from the crime scene. This account has been further supplemented with new information uncovered by Mrowa's son Karim and the Lebanese journalist Najem El Hachem over the course of more than eighty interviews conducted in the late 1990s and early 2000s with people directly involved in or otherwise knowledgeable about the case, including the killer Sultani himself.

These findings have been compiled into a long-form investigative report available in Arabic online at kamelmrowa.com. A series of interviews conducted by this author with Karim as well as his siblings Malek and Lina, in person at the Mrowa Villa in Beit Mirri and also by telephone, in December 2020 and January 2021, and with Najem El Hachem in April 2022, shed additional light on all aspects of the Mrowa story. Last but far from least, the 160-page address delivered at the trial of Mrowa's killers by his family's lawyer, Mohsen Slim—father of Lokman Slim, the public intellectual assassinated in 2021—proved an indispensable source of further detail and clarity.

186 **"Ibrahim assured me":** "I'tirafat Sultani allati ittahama fiha Ibrahim Qulaylat bi-tahridhihi 'ala qatl al-shahid Kamil Muruwwa kama waradat fi malaff al-tahqiq" [Sultani's confessions in which he accused Ibrahim Qulaylat of inciting him to kill the martyr Kamel Mrowa, as contained in the investigation file], *Al-Hayat*, March 16, 1968.

188 **The joke that then made the rounds:** Nasser is said to have "exploded with laughter" when told this by the then-Nasserist politician Muhsin Ibrahim. See, e.g., Muhammad Hujayri, "Kamel Mrowa . . . al-istibdad wa 'al-qatl al-'adi'" [Kamel Mrowa . . . tyranny and "ordinary murder"], *Al-Modon*, May 20, 2018, https://tinyurl.com/yylqb8fz.

189 **he confessed to policemen:** Mohsen Slim, *Murafa'at al-Ustadh Muhsin Slim amam al-Majlis al-'Adli fi Qadhiyyat Ightiyal Kamil Muruwwa* [Mohsen Slim's address before the Judicial Council in the case of the assassination of Kamel Mrowa] (Beirut: Dar al-Jadeed, 1999), 55–57.

190 **a slip of the tongue:** Slim, *Murafa'at al-Ustadh Muhsin Slim*, 95.

191 *Al-Hayat* **published:** "I'tirafat Sultani."

192 **"The acquittal of Koleilat":** Airgram sent by US ambassador to Lebanon Dwight J. Porter to US Department of State, dated March 27, 1968, a copy of which the author has obtained.

194 **"He said that, at the time":** Interview with Najem El Hachem, Dbayeh, Lebanon, April 28, 2022.

194 **"He and Sarraj conducted a review":** Ibid.

194 **"had a devastating" . . . "political threat":** Correspondence with Karim Mrowa, March 8, 2023.

195 **"He was neither a parliamentarian":** Slim, *Murafa'at al-Ustadh Muhsin Slim*, 21.

195 **A photograph of Mrowa:** The photo is viewable at kamelmrowa.com: https://www.kamelmrowa.com/copy-of-10-izdhar-alshafh-alwrqyh?lightbox=dataItem-j00z81pb (accessed January 15, 2021).

195 **"my Vietnam":** Nutting, *Nasser*, 323.

196 **a Saudi-led coalition:** "King Faisal Looks to the Gulf," *Observer*, December 11, 1965; "Feisal Is Rallying Moslem Conservatives: Saudi Leader Plans Alliance to Bypass Arab League," *Washington Post*, December 15, 1965; Jesse Ferris, *Nasser's Gamble: How Intervention in Yemen Caused the Six-Day War and the Decline of Egyptian Power* (Princeton, NJ: Princeton University Press, 2013), chap. 6.

196 **it coincided with news:** "Britain Beats U.S. on $300 Million Saudi Arms Deal," *Washington Post*, December 10, 1965; "Americans Lose Competition as Indecision Is Ended," *New York Times*, December 13, 1965; "Shah and Faisal in Accord," *New York Times*, December 13, 1965.

196 **"By the beginning of 1966":** Nutting, *Nasser*, 383.

197 **Nasser broke his silence:** Speech by Gamal Abdel Nasser at Cairo University on February 22, 1966, an Arabic text of which is available at http://nasser.bibalex.org/TextViewer.aspx?TextID=SPCH-1159-ar.

198 **Nasser told the US ambassador:** Ferris, *Nasser's Gamble*, chap. 6; Laura M. James, *Nasser at War: Arab Images of the Enemy* (London: Palgrave Macmillan, 2006), 84.

198 **"ordered that he be punished":** Jumaa, *Awraq min Daftar al-Watan*, 293.

199 **Sadat expressed remorse:** Karim Mrowa clarified to the author that he heard this from his mother herself, as well as from an *Al-Hayat* journalist, Irfan Nizam al-Din, who was also present.

11. A PARTING GIFT

201 **among them Israel's current prime minister:** Anshel Pfeffer, *Bibi: The Turbulent Life and Times of Benjamin Netanyahu* (London: Hurst & Co., 2018), 79.

201 **turned deadly:** David Hirst, *Beware of Small States: Lebanon, Battleground of the Middle East* (London: Faber and Faber, 2010), 96; Traboulsi, *History of Modern Lebanon*, 154. Some accounts claim *agents provocateurs* among the demonstrators fired first on the security forces (see, e.g., Farid El Khazen, *The Breakdown of the State in Lebanon 1967–1976* [London: I.B. Tauris, 2000], 143–44).

202 **deadly clashes:** El Khazen, *Breakdown of the State*, 147.

202 **forcibly evicted:** Hirst, *Beware of Small States*, 96.

202 **another commando raid:** El Khazen, *Breakdown of the State*, 147.

202 **"killed sixteen":** Hirst, *Beware of Small States*, 97.

202 **Helou could not appoint:** El Khazen, *Breakdown of the State*, 154.

202 **Cairo had been home:** Laurie Brand, "Nasir's Egypt and the Reemergence of the Palestinian National Movement," *Journal of Palestine Studies* 17, no. 2 (Winter 1988): 29–45.

203 **outlet of Nasserist influence:** Nutting, *Nasser*, 365, 467; "Shukeiry to Use Cairo R.," *Jerusalem Post*, December 20, 1964.

203 **Nasser offered to help:** Nasser extended his offer to Helou in a letter sent on October 23, 1969; see El Khazen, *Breakdown of the State*, 159.

203 **Helou sent a delegation:** Nassif, *Al-Maktab al-Thani*, 289–90; El Khazen, *Breakdown of the State*, 155.

203 **rowdy pro–PLO demonstration:** Nassif, *Al-Maktab al-Thani*, 290; El Khazen, *Breakdown of the State*, 154.

204 **"take an active part":** Nassif, *Al-Maktab al-Thani*, 295; El Khazen, *Breakdown of the State*, 158.

204 **personally received by Nasser:** Nassif, *Al-Maktab al-Thani*, 290.

204 **decisive in pushing through:** El Khazen, *Breakdown of the State*, 159.

204 **accord quite unlike any other:** Salibi, *Crossroads to Civil War*, 42–43; Hirst, *Beware of Small States*.

205 **even the tiny Armenian community:** Kassir, *Beirut*, 508.

206 **"a significant watershed":** Khalaf, *Civil and Uncivil Violence*, 142.

12. HIS MAJESTY'S LOYAL OPPOSITION

209 **The morning of August 29:** The account here is compiled from an interview by the author with Majali's son, Gen. Hussein Hazzaa al-Majali, in Amman on November 16, 2021; further interviews with the same by BBC Arabic and Al Arabiya TV in 2015 and 2019, respectively (see https://www.youtube.com/watch?v=2UiMvp9zs20 and https://www.youtube.com/watch?v=PbAzMx5Rf0I, respectively, both accessed May 4, 2022); and newspaper reports, including "Bombs Kill Premier and 10 in Jordan," *Washington Post*, August 29, 1960;

"Hussein Charges Syrians Abetted Amman Bombing," *New York Times*, August 31, 1960; and Fathi Khattab, "Ba'da 56 'aman . . . al-Urdun yatadhakkar awwal hadith ightiyal siyasi hazz al-mamlaka" [56 years later . . . Jordan remembers the first political assassination to shake the kingdom], *Al-Ghad*, August 27, 2016, https://tinyurl.com/y22s856l.

210   **the bullet bounced off:** King Hussein bin Talal, *Uneasy Lies the Head: An Autobiography by H.M. King Hussein of Jordan* (London: Heinemann, 1962), 8; Avi Shlaim, *Lion of Jordan: The Life of King Hussein in War and Peace* (London: Penguin, 2007), 45.

212   **"I had for a long time":** Hussein, *Uneasy Lies the Head*, 86–87.

212   **Hussein had been encouraged:** Shlaim, *Lion of Jordan*, 62–63, 73, 100. Aside from Abu Nuwar, the officers included the Baathists Shaher Abu Shahut and Mahmud al-Maayta, and Nadheer Rasheed, who later helped Syria's Abd al-Hamid al-Sarraj escape Damascus's Mezze prison in 1962.

212   **Nasser awarded him:** Uriel Dann, *King Hussein and the Challenge of Arab Radicalism: Jordan, 1955–1967* (New York: Oxford University Press, 1991), 22.

212   **"Sir, we are in the Baghdad Pact":** Hussein, *Uneasy Lies the Head*, 86.

213   **the abuse dished out:** Nutting, *Nasser*, 88.

213   **This major purchase:** Nutting, 104; Stephens, *Nasser*, 161.

213   **"used every conceivable argument":** Shlaim, *Lion of Jordan*, 82.

214   **"I very much fear":** Shlaim, 82.

214   **Templer offered generous quantities:** Shlaim, 83; Dann, *King Hussein*, 27.

214   **"I would do nothing":** Hussein, *Uneasy Lies the Head*, 90.

214   **"How could he":** Hussein, 93.

214   **receiving Egyptian bribes:** Shlaim, *Lion of Jordan*, 83.

215   **known to look favorably:** Shlaim, 84.

215   **"a man of courage":** Hussein, *Uneasy Lies the Head*, 92.

215   **"the most serious":** Shlaim, *Lion of Jordan*, 85.

215   **As far away as Aqaba:** Dann, *King Hussein*, 28.

215   **"the most dangerous piece of disinformation":** Hazzaa Majali, *Mudhakkirati* [My memoirs] (1960), 171.

215   **intimidated into resigning:** Shlaim, *Lion of Jordan*, 86; Hussein, *Uneasy Lies the Head*, 92.

215   **He claimed in his memoir:** Majali, *Mudhakkirati*, 173.

216   **went out of his way:** "'No Alliances for Jordan': New Government's Policy," *Manchester Guardian*, January 9, 1956.

216   **successfully fending off:** Kamal Salibi, *The Modern History of Jordan* (London: I.B. Tauris, 1998), 158–62.

216   **"latter-day Lawrence":** Shlaim, *Lion of Jordan*, 103.

216   **Glubb had spent decades:** Salibi, *Modern History of Jordan*, 116.

217   **the man in control:** Shlaim, *Lion of Jordan*, 49–56, 80.

217   **"personal admiration" . . . "slightest decisions":** Hussein, *Uneasy Lies the Head*, 115, 125.

217   **depicting the boy-king:** Salibi, *Modern History of Jordan*, 189; Majali, *Mudhakkirati*, 184.

217   **by the year 1985:** Hussein, *Uneasy Lies the Head*, 109.

217   **"his fear that if":** Shlaim, *Lion of Jordan*, 98.

217   **kept up his contacts:** Shlaim, 62–63; Salibi, *Modern History of Jordan*, 189.

217   **"constantly at the king's side":** Shlaim, *Lion of Jordan*, 99.

218   **his plan to remove Glubb:** Shlaim, 99–100.

218   **"Operation Dunlop":** Shlaim, 100–101.

218   **immediate dismissal of Glubb:** Shlaim, 100–101; Dann, *King Hussein*, 31–34.

218   **bewildered shock and fury:** Tunzelmann, *Blood and Sand*, 20–22; Nutting, *Nasser*, 122–23, 136; Shlaim, *Lion of Jordan*, 102–104.

219 **swarmed with crowds:** Shlaim, *Lion of Jordan*, 105.

219 **Abu Nuwar was promoted:** Shlaim, 105.

219 **large demonstration in August:** Betty S. Anderson, *Nationalist Voices in Jordan: The Street and the State* (Austin: University of Texas Press, 2005), 172.

220 **closer still to Nasser's embrace:** Anderson, *Nationalist Voices in Jordan*, 107–108; Dann, *King Hussein*, 37.

220 **By way of comparison:** Jordan's communists won 3 out of 40 seats in 1956, compared to 1 out of 142 in Syria in 1954. Islamists took a total of 5 seats in Jordan (4 for the Muslim Brotherhood, 1 for Hizb ut-Tahrir), while in Syria they did not contest the election. The Baath won 2 out of 40 seats in Jordan—5% of the total— compared to 22 out of 142 in Syria, or 15% of the total. Figures taken from Shlaim, *Lion of Jordan*, 112; and Seale, *Struggle for Syria*, 180–82.

220 **Patriotic Socialist Party:** Shlaim, *Lion of Jordan*, 112. The party's name—al-Hizb al-Watani al-Ishtiraki—is often translated as the "National Socialist Party," which is problematic for obvious reasons. The author concurs with the Baathist Jamal al-Shair that "Patriotic Socialist Party" is truer to the Arabic original (see Anderson, *Nationalist Voices in Jordan*, 9).

220 **"period of experiment":** Hussein, *Uneasy Lies the Head*, 127.

220 **Nabulsi had been renowned:** Shlaim, *Lion of Jordan*, 112; Majali, *Mudhakkirati*, 18–19; Anderson, *Nationalist Voices in Jordan*, 70, 75, 138.

221 **Jordan's most reliable rabble-rouser:** Anderson, 81, 138, 162–64, 172.

221 **"old friend":** Majali, *Mudhakkirati*, 201, 208, 215.

221 **sought reform, not revolution:** Shlaim, *Lion of Jordan*, 125.

221 **dominated by ideological firebrands:** Shlaim, 113; Hussein, *Uneasy Lies the Head*, 130, 132; Anderson, *Nationalist Voices in Jordan*, 136, 159, 203.

221 **Alongside Rimawi:** Anderson, 161, 176, 181; Dann, *King Hussein*, 40–41.

222 **urged him against this:** Shlaim, *Lion of Jordan*, 117–19.

222 **he had already laid plans:** Shlaim, 121–22.

222 **his rift with Nabulsi's government:** Shlaim, 122–24.

223 **"we are highly gratified":** Shlaim, 126–27; Dann, *King Hussein*, 48.

223 **building bridges to Moscow:** Dann, *King Hussein*, 42, 49; Shlaim, *Lion of Jordan*, 126.

223 **the swords were drawn:** Dann, *King Hussein*, 49–51.

223 **chose to up the ante:** Shlaim, *Lion of Jordan*, 129–30.

224 **"strange incident":** Shlaim, 130.

224 **"thunderstruck":** Hussein, *Uneasy Lies the Head*, 135.

224 **"learned that [Abu Nuwar]":** Hussein, 130, 141; Shlaim, *Lion of Jordan*, 130.

224 **"purely routine":** Hussein, *Uneasy Lies the Head*, 135; Shlaim, *Lion of Jordan*, 130–31.

225 **bent on triggering a crisis:** Shlaim, *Lion of Jordan*, 131.

225 **"the most crucial period":** Dann, *King Hussein*, 56.

225 **"a deeply laid, cleverly contrived plot":** Hussein, *Uneasy Lies the Head*, 127.

225 **already Jordan's military dictator:** Hussein, 139.

226 **"King and country":** Hussein, 139–41.

226 **"Trembling with fright":** Hussein, 142–44.

226 **"so close that" . . . "pitiful sight":** Hussein, 127, 145–48.

226 **has been disputed:** Shlaim, *Lion of Jordan*, 133–34; interview with Nadheer Rasheed by Al Jazeera's Ahmed Mansour aired on September 8, 2008, available on YouTube at https://www.youtube.com/watch?v=32ioiS3TnEU&list=PL-8F_ zWD8Kto28r06G2RXurXP-g_1qGnD&index=2.

227 **"We may" . . . "and 'cleverly contrived' ":** Shlaim, *Lion of Jordan*, 138; Dann, *King Hussein*, 58.

227 **Abu Nuwar told him personally:** Jumaa, *Awraq min Daftar al-Watan*, 223.

227 **"pre-emptive coup"**: Interview with Adnan Abu Odeh aired in Al Jazeera's 2017 documentary, *King Hussein of Jordan*, posted February 22, 2017, available at https://www.aljazeera.com/program/al-jazeera-world/2017/2/22/king-hussein-of-jordan-survival-of-a-dynasty.

227 **"a confused triangular affair"**: Shlaim, *Lion of Jordan*, 136.

227 **purge of the officer corps**: Shlaim, 139; Dann, *King Hussein*, 59.

228 **political counterattack**: Shlaim, *Lion of Jordan*, 139–40; Dann, *King Hussein*, 57–61.

228 **"The people of Amman"**: "King Scores Cairo," *New York Times*, April 25, 1957.

229 **"Overnight Jordan was transformed"**: Shlaim, *Lion of Jordan*, 141–42, 149; Hussein, *Uneasy Lies the Head*, 151; Anderson, *Nationalist Voices in Jordan*, 185–86; "Cabinet of Elder Statesmen," *Manchester Guardian*, April 25, 1957.

229 **secured his new superpower**: Shlaim, *Lion of Jordan*, 143–44.

229 **"brothers in Egypt"**: "King Scores Cairo."

230 **"sabotage gangs"**: Hussein, *Uneasy Lies the Head*, 175; Dann, *King Hussein*, 73–75.

13. THE LONG ARMS OF DAMASCUS

231 **engineering a federal union**: Shlaim, *Lion of Jordan*, 156–57.

232 **"stirring up discontent"**: Dann, *King Hussein*, 81–82.

232 **credible military-coup threat**: Dann, 86–87; Shlaim, *Lion of Jordan*, 157–58.

232 **plan was to kill Hussein**: Dann, *King Hussein*, 87; Shlaim, *Lion of Jordan*, 157–58; Hussein, *Uneasy Lies the Head*, 160, 169.

233 **In a striking irony**: Shlaim, *Lion of Jordan*, 158–60; Dann, *King Hussein*, 87, 188; Hussein, *Uneasy Lies the Head*, 160–61.

233 **"my friend and brother"**: Hussein, *Uneasy Lies the Head*, 11, 154, 162–63.

233 **quixotic mission to avenge**: Shlaim, *Lion of Jordan*, 160–61.

234 **Nasser declared two days later**: Statement by Gamal Abdel Nasser on July 16, 1958, an Arabic text of which is available at http://nasser.bibalex.org/TextViewer.aspx?TextID=SPCH-670-ar.

234 **Britain agreed to send**: Shlaim, *Lion of Jordan*, 161–62; Hussein, *Uneasy Lies the Head*, 172.

234 **"However much one may admire"**: Dann, *King Hussein*, vii.

234 **"There is a school"** . . . **"every week"**: Shlaim, *Lion of Jordan*, 164, 169.

235 **"banner of freedom"**: Speech by Gamal Abdel Nasser in Damascus on July 18, 1958, an Arabic text of which is available at http://nasser.bibalex.org/TextViewer.aspx?TextID=SPCH-671-ar.

235 **"The king of Jordan"**: Speech by Gamal Abdel Nasser on July 22, 1958, an Arabic text of which is available at http://nasser.bibalex.org/TextViewer.aspx?TextID=SPCH-673-ar.

236 **"I felt the crisis had abated"**: Hussein, *Uneasy Lies the Head*, 179.

236 **told by Syrian air traffic**: Hussein, 180–81.

236 **"turned across"** . . . **"in a turn"**: Hussein, 181–84.

236 **"My Dove was well known"**: Hussein, 184–85.

237 **"open up with guns"**: Hussein, 196–97; Shlaim, *Lion of Jordan*, 174–75; Dann, *King Hussein*, 106.

237 **Sharaa himself did admit**: Shlaim, *Lion of Jordan*, 175; Hussein, *Uneasy Lies the Head*, 197; Dann, *King Hussein*, 106.

237 **to eliminate Fidel Castro**: Duncan Campbell, "Close but No Cigar: How America Failed to Kill Fidel Castro," *Guardian*, November 26, 2016.

237 **"So cunning and varied"**: Hussein, *Uneasy Lies the Head*, 186, 191–94.

238   **"one of Jordan's greatest"** . . . **"history of Jordan":** Hussein, 187; caption text from the photos appearing after p. 132.

238   **an unknown date:** Majali's son, Gen. Hussein al-Majali, confirmed to the author that his father's exact date of birth has never been determined, adding that, when he asked those who might have been in a position to know the month, he was told, "Thank God we knew the year!"

238   **A site of significance:** Interview by the author with Gen. Hussein al-Majali, Amman, November 16, 2021; Salibi, *Modern History of Jordan*, 22–23; "Al-Karak," *Encyclopaedia Britannica*, last updated November 30, 2016, https://www.britannica .com/place/Al-Karak; author's observations from Karak Citadel, November 16, 2021.

239   **Majalis have been prominent:** Interview with Hussein al-Majali; Salibi, *Modern History of Jordan*, 38.

239   **led a violent revolt:** Salibi, *Modern History of Jordan*, 38–40.

239   **Majalis have played:** Majali, *Mudhakkirati*, 41; Lawrence Joffe, "Habes al-Majali," *Guardian*, April 27, 2001.

240   **The birth of baby Hazzaa:** Majali, *Mudhakkirati*, 11–12. Subsequent quotes in this passage are also taken from pages 11–142 of this memoir.

246   **to form a political party:** Majali, 143; Anderson, *Nationalist Voices in Jordan*, 138.

246   **Majali among them:** Majali, *Mudhakkirati*, 148–51.

246   **he met Nasser himself:** Majali, 155–62.

246   **"lies and fabrications"** . . . **"with all my power?":** Majali, 180–81.

247   **in the political wilderness:** Majali, 182, 191.

247   **Majali took his place:** Shlaim, *Lion of Jordan*, 175; Dann, *King Hussein*, 106–7.

247   **had to explicitly deny:** "Jordan's Premier Vows Neutralism: Majali Says Commitments of Nation Will Be Limited to Arab Relations," *New York Times*, May 11, 1959.

248   **"an object of hate":** Dann, *King Hussein*, 110.

248   **arrested two people:** "Jordan Seizes Plotters," *New York Times*, March 29, 1960; "Plot to Kill Majali Uncovered in Jordan," *Daily Star*, March 30, 1960; "Al-Tahqiq yakshif kull khuyut al-mu'amara li-muhawalat ightiyal al-Majali wa Sharif Nasir" [The investigation reveals all threads of the plot to try to assassinate Majali and Sharif Nasser], *Al-Hayat*, March 30, 1960; "Jordan to Ask UAR to Extradite 'Plotters' Rimawi and Abu Nuwar," *Daily Star*, March 31, 1960; "Talab taslim al-Rimawi wa Abi Nuwar" [Handover of Rimawi and Abu Nuwar requested], *Al-Hayat*, March 31, 1960.

248   **a second plot:** Dann, *King Hussein*, 110–11; Hussein, *Uneasy Lies the Head*, 189.

249   **In person, his demeanor:** Interview by the author with Gen. Hussein al-Majali, Amman, November 16, 2021; interview with Gen. Hussein al-Majali by BBC Arabic in 2015, available on YouTube at https://www.youtube .com/watch?v=2UiMvp9zs20&t=1s (accessed May 26, 2022); Shlaim, *Lion of Jordan*, 593–94.

250   **On the night of Sunday:** Except where stated otherwise, and in addition to the aforementioned sources, these and subsequent details are from Fathi Khattab, "Ba'da 56 'aman . . . al-Urdun yatadhakkar awwal hadith ightiyal siyasi hazz al-mamlaka" [56 years later . . . Jordan remembers the first political assassination to shake the kingdom], *Al-Ghad*, August 27, 2016, https://tinyurl.com/y22s856l; "Al-Hukm bi-i'dam 11 muttahaman fi al-Urdun ba'da idanatihim bi-nasf ri'asat al-wizara" [11 found guilty of bombing prime ministry sentenced to execution in Jordan], *Al-Hayat*, December 30, 1960; and "Al-Sijn badal al-i'dam lil-Shar' wa-'Awdah ma' shanq al-Safadi wa rifaqihi al-thalatha" [Prison instead of execution for al-Sharaa and Awdah, while al-Safadi and his three comrades are hanged], *Al-Hayat*, January 1, 1961.

250 **freely admits to this:** Jumaa, *Awraq min Daftar al-Watan*, 241.

250 **All were sentenced to death:** The four men hanged were Karim Shaqra, Hisham al-Dabbas, Muhammad al-Hindawi, and Salah al-Fawrani (known as Salah al-Safadi). Beyond the aforementioned Shamut, Adham, Ubayd, and Shaker al-Dabbas, those sentenced in absentia were Bahjat Masuti (another Syrian intelligence officer), Saeed Muhammad Rasheed Barghuthi, and Zakaria "Abu al-Nasr" al-Tahir.

251 **Amman Radio was not shy:** Nutting, *Nasser*, 280–81.

252 **"There remains a small group":** Speech by Gamal Abdel Nasser in Alexandria's Manshiya Square, June 24, 1960, an Arabic text of which is available at http://nasser.bibalex.org/TextViewer.aspx?TextID=SPCH-906-ar.

252 **"The people—my brother citizens":** Ibid.

253 **"no doubt":** Salah Nasr, *Mudhakkirat Salah Nasr* [The memoirs of Salah Nasr] (Cairo: Dar al-Khayyal, 1999), 2:152.

254 **"a great personal friend":** Hussein, *Uneasy Lies the Head*, 187.

254 **Jordanian brigades were ordered:** Shlaim, *Lion of Jordan*, 176–78.

14. PARTNERS IN DEFEAT

255 **"the freest in Jordan's history":** Shlaim, *Lion of Jordan*, 184–86; Anderson, *Nationalist Voices in Jordan*, 194–96.

255 **the king lost his nerve:** Shlaim, *Lion of Jordan*, 189–90.

257 **restored full diplomatic relations:** "Egypt and Jordan Resume Diplomatic Relations," *Guardian*, January 16, 1964; Shlaim, *Lion of Jordan*, 202–5; Dann, *King Hussein*, 136–37.

257 **encouraged him to go further:** Dann, *King Hussein*, 137–38; Shlaim, *Lion of Jordan*, 202–5.

258 **The Israelis sent him assurances:** This comes on the authority of Ezer Weizman, head of Israeli army operations at the time, as quoted in Shlaim, *Lion of Jordan*, 244.

258 **Hussein flew to Cairo:** Shlaim, 237.

259 **came out forcefully against Nasser:** Shlaim, 320; Nutting, *Nasser*, 467–68; Kerr, *Arab Cold War*, 146–47; "Nasser Is a Coward, Chant Guerrillas," *Guardian*, July 28, 1970.

259 **Yasser Arafat slipped across:** Bregman and El-Tahri, *Fifty Years War*, 142–43.

259 **painful Israeli reprisals:** Shlaim, *Lion of Jordan*, 277, 303–4.

259 **state-within-a-state:** Shlaim, 312; Kerr, *Arab Cold War*, 142.

260 **began to seethe with rage:** Shlaim, *Lion of Jordan*, 313–16.

260 **June 1970 saw direct fighting:** Shlaim, 316; Bregman and El-Tahri, *Fifty Years War*, 148–49.

260 **grave downward spiral:** Shlaim, *Lion of Jordan*, 317, 322.

260 **overplay their hand spectacularly:** Shlaim, 323; "1970: Hijacked Jets Destroyed by Guerrillas," BBC.

261 **Operations began on the morning:** Shlaim, *Lion of Jordan*, 321, 324–26, 335; Kerr, *Arab Cold War*, 149–50.

261 **a cease-fire agreement:** Shlaim, *Lion of Jordan*, 335; Bregman and El-Tahri, *Fifty Years War*, 155; Nutting, *Nasser*, 472–75; "Hussein, Arafat Sign Arab Pact to End Clashes," *New York Times*, September 27, 1970.

261 **died in his bed:** T. Nasser, *Dhikrayat Ma'ahu*, 133–36.

261 **"supreme irony":** Kerr, *Arab Cold War*, 153.

262 **change of heart was sincere:** Kerr, 145–46; Nutting, *Nasser*, 454–55; Shlaim, *Lion of Jordan*, 265.

263 **"He was never fond":** Interview by the author with Gen. Hussein al-Majali, Amman, November 16, 2021.

15. THE MOST HONORABLE BATTLE

267 **an abrupt encounter with modernity:** This and the following section from Jonathan B. Tucker, *War of Nerves: Chemical Warfare from World War I to Al-Qaeda* (New York: Anchor, 2007), 192; Orkaby, *Beyond the Arab Cold War*, 138, 145; Julian Perry Robinson, "Allegations of Chemical Warfare in the Yemen, 1963–1967," in *The Problem of Chemical and Biological Warfare*, vol. 5: *The Prevention of CBW*, by Stockholm International Peace Research Institute (New York: Humanities Press, 1971), 227–28; Dana Adams Schmidt, *Yemen: The Unknown War* (London: The Bodley Head, 1968), 261; "Yemenis Say U.A.R. Killed 200 with Gas," *New York Times*, January 13, 1967.

268 **the darkest stain:** Nutting, *Nasser*, 323; Ginny Hill, *Yemen Endures: Civil War, Saudi Adventurism and the Future of Arabia* (New York: Oxford University Press, 2017), 33; Awad, *Aqni 'at al-Nasiriya al-Sab 'a*, 129.

269 **a military coup:** Orkaby, *Beyond the Arab Cold War*, 2, 6, 30–32; "Imam of Yemen Reported Slain in Coup after a Week on Throne," *New York Times*, September 27, 1962; "Imam Dies in Revolt," *Guardian*, September 27, 1962.

269 **bust-up with the previous Imam:** Ahmad had penned a poem decrying Nasser's nationalization policies as un-Islamic. In response, Nasser attacked the Imam as an avaricious reactionary stealing his people's money. See Nasser's speech of December 23, 1961, in Port Said, an Arabic text of which is available at http://nasser.bibalex.org/TextViewer.aspx?TextID=SPCH-1007-ar.

270 **Egypt's direct role in the coup:** Orkaby, *Beyond the Arab Cold War*, 9–10, 14, 19–20, 32; James, *Nasser at War*, 55–60; Ferris, *Nasser's Gamble*, chap. 1.

270 **Nasser was quick:** Orkaby, *Beyond the Arab Cold War*, 33–34.

270 **a symbolic gesture:** Orkaby, 37; Ferris, *Nasser's Gamble*, chap. 1.

270 **dramatic plot twist:** Orkaby, *Beyond the Arab Cold War*, 30–31; James, *Nasser at War*, 64–65.

271 **in for a bigger fight:** Orkaby, *Beyond the Arab Cold War*, 61–63.

271 **"rifle across his knees":** Dana Adams Schmidt, "Imam Reappears; Warns Egyptians," *New York Times*, November 10, 1962; H. A. R., Philby, "The Return of the Imam," *Jerusalem Post*, November 15, 1962.

272 **"the most honourable battle":** speech by Gamal Abdel Nasser in Port Said on December 23, 1962, an Arabic text of which is available at http://nasser.bibalex.org/TextViewer.aspx?TextID=SPCH-1035-ar; Orkaby, *Beyond the Arab Cold War*, 36.

272 **hard-nosed strategic considerations:** James, *Nasser at War*, 61, 66.

272 **now poured his military:** Orkaby, *Beyond the Arab Cold War*, 69–70; Ferris, *Nasser's Gamble*, chap. 5.

273 **the plan appeared to work:** Ferris, *Nasser's Gamble*, chap. 5.

273 **gains were illusory:** Orkaby, *Beyond the Arab Cold War*, 74–76.

273 **Nasser upped the level of violence:** Orkaby, *Beyond the Arab Cold War*, 41, 91–92, 99; "US Protests Egyptian Air Raids over Saudia," *Jerusalem Post*, March 6, 1963; Hill, *Yemen Endures*, 31.

274 **Egypt's chemical weapons program:** Tucker, *War of Nerves*, 190; Dany Shoham, "Chemical and Biological Weapons in Egypt," *Nonproliferation Review* 5, no. 3 (1998): 49.

274 **first chemical weapons production facility:** Shoham, "Chemical and Biological Weapons," 48; Tucker, *War of Nerves*, 193.

274   **"like new-mown hay"**: Tucker, *War of Nerves*, 34.

275   **"men, horses, wildlife"**: Robert Harris and Jeremy Paxman, *A Higher Form of Killing: The Secret History of Chemical and Biological Warfare* (New York: Random House Trade Paperbacks, 2002), 19–21; Dan Kaszeta, *Toxic: A History of Nerve Agents, from Nazi Germany to Putin's Russia* (London: Hurst & Co., 2020), 9.

275   **torture quite unlike any other**: Harris and Paxman, *Higher Form of Killing*, 26–33; Tucker, *War of Nerves*, 18–19.

275   **first two chemicals Egypt produced**: Shoham, "Chemical and Biological Weapons," 48.

275   **nerve agents Sarin and VX**: Tucker, *War of Nerves*, 3, 53–54, 110, 133, 158.

276   **as was known to happen**: It happened on September 25, 1915, for instance, when British forces near Belgium's Loos fired chlorine at German lines, but ended up suffering the bulk of the casualties themselves after the wind turned (Tucker, *War of Nerves*, 17). Much the same happened to Iraqi forces at al-Faw, southeast of Basra, in February 1986, who suffered the effects of mustard dropped by their own pilots (see Joost R. Hiltermann, *A Poisonous Affair: America, Iraq, and the Gassing of Halabja* (Cambridge: Cambridge University Press, 2007), 72, 166–67.

277   **"When I first heard"**: Schmidt, *Yemen*, 257.

277   **Beeston traveled for three days**: Richard Beeston, *Looking for Trouble: The Life and Times of a Foreign Correspondent* (London: Tauris Parke Paperbacks, 2006), 82–83. The book contains a photo of al-Kawma, and another of one of the spent chemical munitions used to attack it.

277   **"pitiful coughing" . . . "died in agony"**: Beeston, *Looking for Trouble*; Richard Beeston, "Nasser's Planes Use Poison Gas," *Daily Telegraph*, July 8, 1963; "Gassed Yemeni Boy, 12, Flies to London," *Daily Telegraph*, July 16, 1963; Hill, *Yemen Endures*, 29; Schmidt, *Yemen*, 257–58.

278   **"dirty smell . . . coughing up blood"**: Richard Beeston, "Nasser's Planes Use Poison Gas."

278   **not the first of its kind**: Hill, *Yemen Endures*, 30–31; Beeston, *Looking for Trouble*; Schmidt, *Yemen*, 259. Four additional villages named by McLean as having been struck with chemicals around this time were al-Ashash, al-Darb, Jaraishi, and Hassan Bini Awair.

278   **"the conscience and the practice"**: Harris and Paxman, *Higher Form of Killing*, 46–47; Tucker, *War of Nerves*, 21.

279   **Egypt was among the original**: "Protocol for the Prohibition of the Use in War of Asphyxiating, Poisonous or Other Gases, and of Bacteriological Methods of Warfare," United Nations Office for Disarmament Affairs, https://treaties.unoda .org/t/1925 (accessed June 13, 2022).

279   **US pressure exerted on Nasser**: Orkaby writes (*Beyond the Arab Cold War*, 134–35) that US ambassador to Egypt John Badeau confronted Nasser in July 1963 about his chemical attacks in Yemen, warning him they were tarnishing Egypt's image internationally. Nasser first denied using them, then obfuscated, saying he didn't know the "precise chemical content" of the munitions in question. Despite these evasions, it would seem Nasser took the ambassador's words on board, for a time.

279   **managed to dislodge the Imam**: Orkaby, *Beyond the Arab Cold War*, 77–78, 107.

280   **agreement in Saudi Arabia's Jeddah**: Orkaby, 78, 107, 110.

280   **politics in Sanaa**: Hill, *Yemen Endures*, 23, 34; Orkaby, *Beyond the Arab Cold War*, 181–82; James, *Nasser at War*, 79.

280   **dissident republican groups**: Orkaby, *Beyond the Arab Cold War*, 108–11.

281   **combined to dissuade him**: Orkaby, 111–12, 115–16; Ferris, *Nasser's Gamble*, chap. 6.

281   **"Long Breath strategy"**: Speech by Gamal Abdel Nasser on March 22,

1966, an Arabic text of which is available at http://nasser.bibalex.org/Text Viewer.aspx?TextID=SPCH-1161-ar.

282 **marked *increase* in violence:** James, *Nasser at War*, 83; Orkaby, *Beyond the Arab Cold War*, 129; speech by Gamal Abdel Nasser on May 1, 1966, an Arabic text of which is available at http://nasser.bibalex.org/TextViewer.aspx?TextID=SPCH-1163-ar.

282 **resumption of chemical attacks:** Schmidt, *Yemen*, 260; W. Andrew Terrill, "The Chemical Warfare Legacy of the Yemen War," *Comparative Strategy* 10, no. 2 (1991): 113.

282 **mass-casualty attack on Kitaf:** Tucker, *War of Nerves*, 191–92; Terrill, "Chemical Warfare Legacy"; Robinson, "Allegations of Chemical Warfare," 228–29; Orkaby, *Beyond the Arab Cold War*, 145; Schmidt, *Yemen*, 261; Kaszeta, *Toxic*, 299.

283 **Egypt continued to rain chemicals:** "Yemenis Say 70 Died in Egyptian Gas Raid," *New York Times*, February 15, 1967; Orkaby, *Beyond the Arab Cold War*, fig. 6.1; Tucker, *War of Nerves*, 191–92; Schmidt, *Yemen*, 268.

283 **The best-documented chemical attack:** Robinson, "Allegations of Chemical Warfare," 232–37; "Text of the Red Cross Report on the Use of Poison Gas in Yemen," *New York Times*, July 27, 1967; Schmidt, *Yemen*, 264.

284 **"Some of the victims":** Robinson, "Allegations of Chemical Warfare," 236.

284 **"traumatic lesions" . . . "clinical development":** Robinson, 232–37; Schmidt, *Yemen*, 267–68.

284 **"poison gas" . . . "toxic substances":** Robinson, "Allegations of Chemical Warfare," 232–37.

285 **Chemical attacks were reported:** "U.S. Is Disturbed by Yemen Report of Poison-Gas Use," *New York Times*, July 27, 1967; Robinson, "Allegations of Chemical Warfare," 234–35; Schmidt, *Yemen*, 268.

285 **accepted an offer:** Orkaby, *Beyond the Arab Cold War*, 54, 197; Nutting, *Nasser*, 434–35; Ferris, *Nasser's Gamble*, chap. 7.

286 **The total death toll:** Orkaby, *Beyond the Arab Cold War*, 138, 198; Terrill, "Chemical Warfare Legacy," 115; Robinson, "Allegations of Chemical Warfare," 236; Ferris, *Nasser's Gamble*, chaps. 5 and 7; Hill, *Yemen Endures*, 33.

286 **Yemen's war dragged on:** Orkaby, *Beyond the Arab Cold War*, 197–200; Hill, *Yemen Endures*, 35.

286 **Marxist-Leninist dictatorship:** Ferris, *Nasser's Gamble*, chap. 7; Orkaby, *Beyond the Arab Cold War*, 156; Hazem Saghieh, *Hadhihi Laysat Sira* [This is not an autobiography] (Beirut: Dar al-Saqi, 2007), 73.

287 **assassinated by militants:** "'Ali 'Abdallah Salih wal-tahaluf al-qatil" [Ali Abdallah Saleh and the deadly alliance], BBC Arabic, December 4, 2017, available at https://www.bbc.com/arabic/middleeast-42225535.

16. ADRIFT ON THE NILE

292 **raised a merry toast:** Mansfield, *Nasser*, 119.

292 **"high priests and exegetes":** Awad, *Aqni'at al-Nasiriya al-Sab'a*, 118.

292 **speech Nasser gave in Cairo:** Speech by Gamal Abdel Nasser at Cairo's Republican Palace, October 16, 1961, an Arabic text of which is available at http://nasser.bibalex.org/TextViewer.aspx?TextID=SPCH-1002-ar.

293 **"At no time did President Nasser":** Abdel-Malek, *Egypt*, 276–77.

293 **What this meant in practice:** Abdel-Malek, *Egypt*, 160; Mansfield, *Nasser*, 119–20; Stephens, *Nasser*, 346.

293 **a landmark document:** Abdel-Malek, *Egypt*, 180–86; "Nasser Presents His New Charter," *New York Times*, May 22, 1962.

294   **"glorious" . . . "maintain a role":** For a full Arabic text of the charter as read by Nasser on May 21, 1962, see http://nasser.bibalex.org/Text Viewer.aspx?TextID=SPCH-1015-ar.

294   **only one of the charter's ten:** Ibid. The titles of the ten sections were General Overview; On the Necessity of the Revolution; The Roots of the Egyptian Struggle; The Lesson of the Setback; On Sound Democracy; On the Inevitability of the Socialist Solution; Production and Society; Socialist Application and Its Problems; Arab Unity; Foreign Policy. For the influence of Titoism on the charter, see Norman Cigar, "Arab Socialism Revisited: The Yugoslav Roots of Its Ideology," *Middle Eastern Studies* 19, no. 2 (1983): 152–87.

294   **wave of new nationalizations:** Abdel-Malek, *Egypt*, 165–66; Gordon, *Nasser: Hero of the Arab Nation*, 84.

294   **Egyptian economy did not respond:** Stephens, *Nasser*, 366–70.

295   **"expensive and relatively unproductive":** Stephens, 367.

295   **"If today we drink tea":** Speech by Gamal Abdel Nasser in Port Said on December 23, 1964, an Arabic text of which is available at http://nasser.bibalex.org/ TextViewer.aspx?TextID=SPCH-1104-ar; Ferris, *Nasser's Gamble*, chaps. 5 and 7.

296   **"We didn't expect Nasser to bow":** Ferris, *Nasser's Gamble*, chap. 3; Orkaby, *Beyond the Arab Cold War*, chap. 5.

296   **"mass murders":** Orkaby, *Beyond the Arab Cold War*, 124.

296   **"drink from the sea":** Speech by Nasser in Port Said on December 23, 1964 (see above); Ferris, *Nasser's Gamble*, chap. 3.

296   **Nasser now had to find:** Stephens, *Nasser*, 370; Ferris, *Nasser's Gamble*, chaps. 3 and 5.

297   **"the national stockpile":** Ferris, *Nasser's Gamble*, chap. 7; Stephens, *Nasser*, 370–71; Avraham Sela, "'Abd al-Nasser's Regional Politics: A Reassessment," in Podeh and Winckler, *Rethinking Nasserism*, 197.

297   **sliver of relent:** Abdel-Malek, *Egypt*, 350; Ibrahim, *Yawmiyyat al-Wahat*, 189–93; Gordon, *Hero of the Arab Nation*, 90.

298   **"a phrase without meaning":** Awad, *Aqni'at al-Nasiriya al-Sab'a*, 119; Abdel-Malek, *Egypt*, 165; "Nasser Takes Over Press," *Guardian*, May 24, 1960.

298   **"the very great majority" . . . "apparatus":** Anouar Abdel-Malek, "The Crisis in Nasser's Egypt," *New Left Review* no. 45 (September/October 1967), 75–76.

298   **benefits unavailable to civilians:** Ferris, *Nasser's Gamble*, chap. 5; Gordon, *Hero of the Arab Nation*, 86.

299   **called on to perform tributes:** Joel Gordon, "The Nightingale and the Ra'is: 'Abd al-Halim Hafiz and Nasserist Longings," in Podeh and Winckler, *Rethinking Nasserism*, 310.

299   **"every government office":** Leonard Binder, "Gamal 'Abd al-Nasser: Iconology, Ideology, and Demonology," in Podeh and Winckler, 66.

299   **The historian Sherif Younis recalls:** Younis, *Nida' al-Sha'b*, 258, 264.

300   **"We have the worst of both":** Ghali, *Beer in the Snooker Club*, 203.

300   **The book was immediately confiscated:** Ibrahim, *Tilk al-Ra'iha wa Qisas Ukhra*.

300   **"our life" . . . "the truth?":** Naguib Mahfouz, *Tharthara Fawq al-Nil* [Prattle on the Nile] (Cairo: Dar al-Shuruq, 2020), 23, 107–8.

301   **Mahfouz would later regale:** Alaa Al Aswany, *The Dictatorship Syndrome* (London: Haus Publishing, 2019), 72–74; Mohamed Rabie, "Naguib Mahfouz, the Man We All Wronged," *Mada Masr*, January 7, 2017.

301   **"loved by millions":** "O Gamal, You Who Are Loved by Millions" was a hit by the popular singer Abd al-Halim Hafez.

301   **"police state atmosphere" . . . "populace":** Ibrahim, *Yawmiyyat al-Wahat*, 194.

301   **uncovered an armed Brotherhood cell:** Gerges, *Making the Arab World*, 254–56, 276; Stephens, *Nasser*, 372.

302 **the fifty-eight-year-old Sayyid Qutb:** Gerges, *Making the Arab World*, 175–86, 214–83.

302 **"We wanted to bury":** Gerges, 175–86, 214–83.

302 **"the head of the snake":** Gerges, 277–78.

303 **inspire the jihadist groups:** Gerges, 145–46, 393–94; Shiraz Maher, *Salafi-Jihadism: The History of an Idea* (London: Hurst & Co., 2016), 177–78.

303 **"We cannot conceal":** Statement by Gamal Abdel Nasser on June 9, 1967, an Arabic text of which is available at http://nasser.bibalex.org/TextViewer .aspx?TextID=SPCH-1221-ar. An almost-complete video of the address can be seen on YouTube at https://youtu.be/gIsMv5EORbo.

304 **flooded the streets:** Stephens, *Nasser*, 507; statement by Gamal Abdel Nasser on June 10, 1967, as read on his behalf by Anwar Sadat, an Arabic text of which is available at http://nasser.bibalex.org/TextViewer.aspx?TextID=SPCH-1222-ar.

304 **Younis has written a whole book:** Sherif Younis, *Al-Zahf al-Muqaddas: Muthaharat al-Tanahhi wa Tashakkul 'Ibadat Nasir* [The sacred march: The resignation demonstrations and the formation of Nasser worship] (Beirut: Dar al-Tanweer, 2012), 16.

304 **put its own formidable ground game:** Younis, *Al-Zahf al-Muqaddas*, 14.

304 **simultaneous protests in other Arab countries:** The Lebanese historian Fawwaz Traboulsi has described the "tempestuous" scenes in Beirut that day, in which he partook himself: "Beirut erupted in rage, its streets flooded with residents and others pouring in from the suburbs. Shops with signs in French or English had their glass windowfronts smashed. Motorists entering the capital or driving around in it were forced to write 'Nasser' on their windscreens in white paint, or else see their cars destroyed." See Fawwaz Traboulsi, *Surat al-Fata bil-Ahmar: Ayyam fil-Silm wal-Harb* [A portrait of the young man in red: Chronicles of peace and war] (Beirut: Riad El-Rayyes Books, 2015), 62–63.

305 **"every fifteen minutes":** al-Hakim, *'Awdat al-Wa'y*, 65–66.

306 **an especially unpopular figure:** Younis, *Al-Zahf al-Muqaddas*, 68.

306 **chants against him:** The French journalist Eric Rouleau, who was there, reported hearing the slogan "No Zakaria, no imperialism, no sterling, no dollars." Cited in Lacouture, *Nasser*, 312.

307 **made himself prime minister:** Mansfield, *Nasser*, 175.

307 **made this argument explicitly:** Speech by Gamal Abdel Nasser on July 23, 1967, an Arabic text of which is available at http://nasser.bibalex.org /TextViewer.aspx?TextID=SPCH-1223-ar.

307 **"no voice louder":** The slogan was launched in a statement by Nasser on March 30, 1968, in which he said, "There is not now—and must not be—any voice louder than the sound of the battle, and no call more sacred than its call. Any thought or calculation that does not place the battle and its needs first, before all else, does not deserve to be considered thought, and will achieve zero results. The battle takes precedence over all else. For its sake, and on the path to attaining victory therein, all else is trivial." An Arabic text of the statement is available at http://nasser.bibalex.org/TextViewer.aspx?TextID=SPCH-1234-ar.

308 **The spark was a verdict:** Abdalla, *Student Movement*, 149; Mansfield, *Nasser*, 174; speech by Gamal Abdel Nasser on July 23, 1967 (see above).

308 **took to the streets in protest:** Abdalla, *Student Movement*, 149; "Egypt's Ex-Air Chief Is Given 15-Year Term for 'Negligence,'" *New York Times*, February 20, 1968.

309 **"men and women":** Wael Uthman, *Asrar al-Haraka al-Tullabiya: Handasat al-Qahira, 1968–75* [Secrets of the student movement: Cairo Engineering: 1968–75] (Cairo, 1976), 23.

309 **"my children" . . . "study":** Uthman, *Asrar al-Haraka al-Tullabiya*, 23–24. Subsequent quotes in this passage are also taken from chapter 1 of this book.

311　**"falsifying the facts"** . . . **"counter-revolutionaries":** Uthman, 34; speech by Gamal Abdel Nasser on March 3, 1968, an Arabic text of which is available at http://nasser.bibalex.org/TextViewer.aspx?TextID=SPCH-1226-ar.

312　**"While it distressed me":** Uthman, *Asrar al-Haraka al-Tullabiya*, 31, 33, 36.

312　**dissent spread outside campus:** Abdalla, *Student Movement*, 142, 158.

312　**"program of action"** . . . **"liberation of women":** Statement to the nation by Gamal Abdel Nasser on March 30, 1968, an Arabic text of which is available at http://nasser.bibalex.org/TextViewer.aspx?TextID=SPCH-1234-ar.

313　**brief spells of comparative openness:** Abdalla, *Student Movement*, 143–45.

313　**"After a few months":** Abdalla, 145, 159–75.

313　**"hint almost of physical frailty":** Stephens, *Nasser*, 363.

314　**"a mobile oxygen unit":** Nutting, *Nasser*, 432.

314　**working himself into an early grave:** Nutting, 294, 432; Gordon, *Hero of the Arab Nation*, 117–18; Aburish, *Nasser*, 90.

17. SECOND TIME AS FARCE

317　**"freedom"** . . . **"exploitation":** Alison Pargeter, *Libya: The Rise and Fall of Qaddafi* (New Haven, CT: Yale University Press, 2012), 57–60.

317　**Gezira Tower received a message:** Fathi al-Deeb, *'Abd al-Nasir wa Thawrat Libya* [Abdel Nasser and Libya's revolution] (Cairo: Dar al-Mustaqbal al-'Arabi, 1986), 11.

318　**"Tell President Nasser"** . . . **"what to do":** Pargeter, *Libya*, 68; Dirk Vandewalle, *A History of Modern Libya* (Cambridge: Cambridge University Press, 2012), 79.

318　**born in a tent:** Pargeter, *Libya*, 61–63.

318　**in early adolescence:** Pargeter, 63–64.

319　**began a lifelong worship:** Pargeter, 49–50, 64.

319　**emulating the Egyptian experience:** Pargeter, 49–51.

319　**Following the Nasserist playbook:** Pargeter, 51.

320　**"We were assured of success":** Pargeter, 52–57; al-Deeb, *'Abd al-Nasir*, 16.

320　**Nasser's first reaction:** al-Deeb, *'Abd al-Nasir*, 11. Subsequent quotes in this passage are also taken from pages 11–165 of this book.

323　**Deeb prevailed upon the RCC:** Pargeter, *Libya*, 69, in addition to al-Deeb.

329　**mentoring his young Libyan protégé:** Pargeter, *Libya*, 72, in addition to al-Deeb.

329　**"the Libya of revolution"** . . . **"here in Libya":** Speech by Gamal Abdel Nasser in Tripoli on December 26, 1969, an Arabic text of which is available at http://nasser.bibalex.org/TextViewer.aspx?TextID=SPCH-1266-ar.

330　**"What I saw":** Speech by Gamal Abdel Nasser in Benghazi on December 29, 1969, an Arabic text of which is available at http://nasser.bibalex.org/TextViewer.aspx?TextID=SPCH-1269-ar.

330　**furnishing Gaddafi with the script:** Ibid; speech by Muammar al-Gaddafi in Tripoli on February 22, 2011, a video of which is available on YouTube at https://www.youtube.com/watch?v=RSh6QAs_my8. As well as mentioning Nasser by name, Gaddafi's speech had other Nasserist touches, such as his repetition of the phrase *al-zahf al-muqaddas* ("the sacred march"), a term used by Nasser in his book *Falsafat al-Thawra* and popularized by the Egyptian junta in the 1950s.

330　**rode in an open-top car:** "Throngs in Cairo Acclaim Nasser; Cry for Revenge," *New York Times*, February 13, 1970. Video footage of the prayers and car ride is available on YouTube at https://www.youtube.com/watch?v=Pr-AyilS3R8.

330　**the warmest of introductions:** Speech by Gamal Abdel Nasser at Cairo's National Assembly on June 11, 1970, an Arabic text of which is available at http://nasser.bibalex.org/TextViewer.aspx?TextID=SPCH-1284-ar.

331 **"Today, my brother":** Speech by Gamal Abdel Nasser in Tripoli on June 22, 1970, an Arabic text of which is available at http://nasser.bibalex.org/TextViewer .aspx?TextID=SPCH-1287-ar.

331 **"I feel that my brother":** Ibid.

331 **A well-known photo:** The image may be viewed at https://www.gettyimages .com/detail/news-photo/arab-heads-of-state-meet-at-the-nile-hilton-in-cairo-to -put-news-photo/514678234 (accessed August 2, 2022).

331 **"shrine for the faithful":** Fouad Ajami, *The Arab Predicament: Arab Political Thought and Practice since 1967*, 2nd ed. (Cambridge: Cambridge University Press, 1992), 18.

331 **with perfect seriousness:** As Ajami writes, "Many of Nasser's followers within and outside Egypt came to think of Qaddafi as the spiritual son and true heir of Nasser" (*Arab Predicament*, 143).

332 **received most of their funding:** El Khazen, *Breakdown of the State*, 303, 332.

332 **slaughter of over a thousand:** Mary Fitzgerald, "A Notorious Prison and Libya's War of Memory," *New Lines*, March 10, 2021.

332 **"We, the Free Unionist Officers":** Video footage of these remarks, indicating they were delivered at Tripoli University on January 15, 1981 (the sixty-third anniversary of Nasser's birth), is available on YouTube at https://www.youtube.com/watch?v=89y6U0gIlvM.

332 **once lost his temper:** At a heads-of-state gathering in Libya on June 21, 1970, one day after the Wheelus base evacuation ceremony, Gaddafi spoke to King Hussein in a manner Nasser deemed insulting, causing the Egyptian to bang his hand on the table and demand Gaddafi show the monarch respect (al-Deeb, *'Abd al-Nasir*, 287). Heikal, for his part, claimed to have warned Nasser that Gaddafi was a "catastrophe" after his very first meeting with him on September 4, 1969 (Kanan Makiya, *Cruelty and Silence: War, Tyranny, Uprising and the Arab World* [London: Penguin, 1993], 272).

332 **"the jewel of North Africa":** Pargeter, *Libya*, 5.

THE UNFINISHED JOB

333 **"Any revolution which fails":** Gamal Abdel Nasser, "The Egyptian Revolution," *Foreign Affairs* 33, no. 2 (January 1955): 202.

333 **Egypt's vice president announced:** The terse statement, as read on national television by Vice President Omar Suleiman, was as follows: "In the name of God, the Most Merciful and Compassionate; Dear citizens: In light of the strenuous circumstances through which the country is passing, President Muhammad Hosni Mubarak has decided to relinquish the post of president of the republic, and has tasked the Supreme Council of the Armed Forces with administering the affairs of the country. May God grant succour and success." See https://www.sis.gov.eg/Newvr/egyptionrevoution/julythree.html.

333 **Mubarak was as pure a product:** Cook, *Struggle for Egypt*, 157; Orkaby, *Beyond the Arab Cold War*, chap. 3; "Muhammad Hosni Mubarak," official website of the Egyptian presidency, https://tinyurl.com/yptbnpp5 (accessed August 8, 2022).

334 **"His generation" . . . "job for them":** Jack Shenker, "In Tahrir Square of Cairo Freedom Party Begins," *Guardian*, February 11, 2011.

335 **the sculpture keeled over:** A video of the proceedings is available on YouTube at https://www.youtube.com/watch?v=WBei3G8ayBk (accessed August 10, 2022).

See also "Libya: Hadm timthal Jamal ʿAbd al-Nasir fi Benghazi" [Libya: Gamal Abdel Nasser statue brought down in Benghazi], BBC Arabic, February 12, 2012, https://www.bbc.com/arabic/middleeast/2012/02/120212_libya_gamal_statue.

335   **troops and tanks into the streets:** "Egyptian Military Ousts Morsi, Suspends Constitution," *Washington Post*, July 3, 2013.

335   **the parallels with 1952:** Martin Chulov, "Egypt Wonders if Army Chief Is Another Nasser," *Guardian*, August 7, 2013; Sheera Frenkel, "Calls for Nasser's Son to Run for President," *Times* (London), July 5, 2013; Hassan Abbas, "Al-Sisi karikatur li-ʿAbd al-Nasir" [Sisi is a caricature of Abdel Nasser], Raseef22, October 27, 2016, https://tinyurl.com/x5jaw2ph; Muhammad Hujayri, "Tamathil Lubnan . . . Suʿood al-Nasiriyah wa ufooluha" [Lebanon's statues . . . The rise and fall of Nasserism], Al-Modon, September 10, 2017, https://tinyurl.com/2zn5wn2a.

335   **useful to Sisi in his crackdown:** "All According to Plan: The Rabʾa Massacre and Mass Killings of Protesters in Egypt," Human Rights Watch, August 12, 2014; Ruth Michaelson, "Mohamed Morsi, Ousted President of Egypt, Dies in Court," *Guardian*, June 17, 2019; Vivian Yee, "'A Slow Death': Egypt's Political Prisoners Recount Horrific Conditions," *New York Times*, August 8, 2022; Abdelrahman ElGendy, "Anatomy of an Incarceration: The Welcome Party," Mada Masr, March 28, 2021; "Alaa Abdel Fattah, Egypt's Most Famous Dissident," France 24, July 9, 2022.

336   **as early as January 28:** Ahdaf Soueif, *Cairo: Memoir of a City Transformed* (London: Bloomsbury, 2014), 157–58.

337   **A former Gaddafi loyalist:** "Khalifa Haftar: The Libyan general with Big Ambitions," BBC, April 8, 2019; Heba Saleh, "General Khalifa Haftar, Gaddafi's Old Foe, Makes a Play for Power," *Financial Times*, April 12, 2019; Patrick Wintour, "Libya: Credible Elections—or Another Failed Bid at Nation-Building?," *Guardian*, September 29, 2021; "Hifter's Rule Brings Security to Eastern Libya, at a Cost," AP, May 21, 2019. For Nasser's remarks on democracy, see, e.g., his aforecited *Foreign Affairs* essay from 1955, in which he writes of the need for Egyptians to "develop the mature political consciousness that is an indispensable preliminary for a sound democracy," adding that the political "restrictions" imposed by the junta would not be lifted until "we feel the people are no longer in danger" of being led astray by political parties (G. Nasser, "The Egyptian Revolution," 208).

337   **his fellow general Sisi:** "In lawless Libya, Egypt's Sisi becomes a star," Reuters, May 26, 2014; Khaled Mahmoud, "Sisi's Ambitions in Libya," Carnegie Endowment for International Peace, November 30, 2018.

338   **"fight" . . . "woman and bullet":** Pargeter, *Libya*, 228.

338   **his grand comeback:** "Libya Trial: Gaddafi Son Sentenced to Death over War Crimes," BBC, July 28, 2015; "Saif al-Islam Gaddafi: Son of Libya Ex-Ruler Runs for President," BBC, November 14, 2021; Robert F. Worth, "Qaddafi's Son Is Alive. And He Wants to Take Libya Back," *New York Times Magazine*, July 30, 2021.

338   **"déjà vu":** Orkaby, *Beyond the Arab Cold War*, 207–14.

338   **the underlying dynamics remain:** "The Houthi Movement from a Local Perspective: A Resurgence of Political Zaidism," Sana'a Center for Strategic Studies, November 18, 2020; Nadwa al-Dawsari, "The Houthis' Endgame in Yemen," Al Jazeera, December 21, 2017; Asher Orkaby, "The 1968 Siege of Sana: A Houthi Historical Parallel," Washington Institute for Near East Policy, November 10, 2014; "Yemen War Will Have Killed 377,000 by Year's End: UN," France 24, November 23, 2021; "Yemen: The Worst Humanitarian Crisis in the World," UN Crisis Relief.

339   **"republic of fear":** The phrase "republic of fear" was coined by the Iraqi dissident Kanan Makiya in his renowned book of the same title, first published in 1989.

339   **smearing the young demonstrators:** Sarhang Hamasaeed, "As Protests Con-

tinue in the Street, Iraq Reaches a Crossroads," United States Institute of Peace, November 8, 2019; Hassan Hassan, "How Iraq's Top ISIS Scholar Became a Target for Shiite Militias," *New Lines*, October 4, 2020.

339 **first acquired from Egypt:** Syria is said to have first acquired chemical weapons in 1972, when it purchased a $6 million arsenal from Egypt that included artillery shells and air bombs preloaded with Sarin and mustard. See Shoham, "Chemical and Biological Weapons," 49; Tucker, *War of Nerves*, 227; Kaszeta, *Toxic*, 212.

340 **well over 350,000 killed:** In September 2021, the UN declared it had confirmed the deaths of 350,209 persons, though its own High Commissioner for Human Rights, Michelle Bachelet, acknowledged this was "certainly an under-count." One leading Syrian human rights organization put the figure at over 600,000 in June 2021. See "Syria War: UN Calculates New Death Toll," BBC, September 24, 2021; "Eleven Years On, Mounting Challenges Push Many Displaced Syrians to the Brink," UN Refugee Agency, March 15, 2022.

340 **against the Nazis at Nuremberg:** "Former prosecutor: More Evidence of War Crimes against Syrian President Assad Than There Was against Nazis," CBS News, February 18, 2021.

BIBLIOGRAPHY

WORKS IN ARABIC

Aref, Abd al-Salam. *Mudhakkirat al-Ra'is al-'Iraqi 'Abd al-Salam 'Arif* [The memoirs of the Iraqi President Abd al-Salam Aref]. Baghdad: Dar Sutur lil-Nashr wal-Tawzi', 2022.

Awad, Louis. *Aqni'at al-Nasiriyya al-Sab'a* [The seven masks of Nasserism]. Cairo: Markaz al-Mahrusa, 2014 edition.

Azm, Khalid al-. *Mudhakkirat Khalid al-'Athm* [The memoirs of Khalid al-Azm]. Beirut: al-Dar al-Muttahida lil-Nashr, 1973.

Azm, Sadiq Jalal al-. *Al-Naqd al-Dhati Ba'd al-Hazima* [Self-criticism after the defeat]. 2nd ed. Beirut: Dar al-Tali'a, 1969.

Azma, Bashir al-. *Jeel al-Hazima: Bayn al-Wahda wal-Infisal* [The generation of the defeat: Between union and separation]. London: Riad El-Rayyes Books, 1991.

Bani Ayish, Muhammad Saeed Ahmad. *Al-Inqilabat al-'Askariyya fi Suriya min 1949–1969: Dirasa fi al-'Awamil al-Dakhiliyya wal-Iqlimiyya wal-Duwaliyya* [Military coups in Syria 1949–1969: A study of the domestic, regional, and international factors]. Irbid, Jordan: Dar al-Kitab al-Thaqafi, 2017.

Chamoun, Camille. *Azma fi Lubnan* [Crisis in Lebanon]. Beirut, 1977.

———. *Mudhakkirati* [My memoirs]. Beirut, 1969.

Deeb, Fathi al-. *'Abd al-Nasir wa Thawrat Libya* [Abdel Nasser and Libya's revolution]. Cairo: Dar al-Mustaqbal al-'Arabi, 1986.

Faraj Allah al-Hilu . . . Shaheedan: Mahadhir al-Tahqiqat [Farajallah al-Helu . . . the martyr: The investigation documents]. Beirut: Dar al-Farabi, 2022.

Gaddafi, Muammar al-. *Al-Kitab al-Akhdhar* [The green book]. Tripoli, Libya: al-Markaz al-'Alami li-Dirasat wa Abhath al-Kitab al-Akhdhar, 1988.

Hakim, Tawfiq al-. *'Awdat al-Wa'y* [The return of consciousness]. 2nd ed. Cairo: Dar al-Shuruq, 1974.

————. *Watha'iq fi Tariq 'Awdat al-Wa'y* [Documents on the path to the return of consciousness]. Cairo: Dar al-Shuruq, 2017.

Hilu, Yusuf Khattar al-. *Awraq min Tarikhina* [Papers from our history]. Beirut: Dar al-Farabi, 1988.

Ibrahim, Sonallah. *Tilk al-Ra'iha wa Qisas Ukhra* [That smell and other stories]. Cairo: Dar al-Thaqafa al-Jadida, 2019.

————. *Yawmiyyat al-Wahat* [The Oases diary]. Cairo: Dar al-Thaqafa al-Jadida, 2015.

Jumaa, Sami. *Awraq min Daftar al-Watan: 1946–1961* [Pages from the notebook of the homeland: 1946–1961]. Damascus: Dar Tlas, 2000.

Mahfouz, Naguib. *Tharthara Fawq al-Nil* [Prattle on the Nile]. Cairo: Dar al-Shuruq, 2020.

Majali, Hazzaa al-. *Mudhakkirati* [My memoirs]. 1960.

Mroué, Karim. *Al-Shuyu'iyyun al-Arba'a al-Kibar fi Tarikh Lubnan al-Hadith: Fu'ad al-Shimali, Faraj Allah al-Hilu, Niqula Shawi, Jurj Hawi* [The four preeminent communists in modern Lebanese history: Fuad al-Shimali, Farajallah al-Helu, Nicolas Shawi, George Hawi]. Beirut: Dar al-Saqi, 2009.

Mrowa, Kamel. *Bayrut—Birlin—Bayrut: Mushahadat Sahafi fi Uruba wa Almanya Athna' al-Harb al-'Alamiyya al-Thaniya wal-Harb al-Barida allati Talatha* [Beirut—Berlin—Beirut: A journalist's observations in Europe and Germany during the Second World War and subsequent Cold War]. London: Riad El-Rayyes Books, 1991.

Nasr, Salah. *Mudhakkirat Salah Nasr* [The memoirs of Salah Nasr]. Cairo: Dar al-Khayyal, 1999.

Nasser, Gamal Abdel. *Falsafat al-Thawra* [The philosophy of the revolution]. 10th ed. Cairo: al-Matba'a al-'Alamiya, n.d.

Nasser, Tahia Gamal Abdel. *Dhikrayat Ma'ahu* [Memories with him]. Cairo: Dar al-Shuruq, 2019.

Nassif, Nicolas. *Al-Maktab al-Thani: Hakim fi al-Thill* [The Deuxième Bureau: A ruler in the shadows]. 4th ed. Beirut, 2015.

Razzaz, Munif al-. *Al-Tajriba al-Murra* [The bitter experience]. Beirut: Dar Ghandur, 1967.

Rikabi, Fuad al-. *Al-Hall al-Awhad Lightiyal al-Za'im 'Abd al-Karim Qasim* [The sole solution for the assassination of the leader Abd al-Karim Qasim]. Beirut: al-Dar al-'Arabiyya lil-Mawsu'at, 2010. First published 1963.

Saghieh, Hazem. *Ba'th al-'Iraq: Sultat Saddam Qiyaman wa Hutaman* [The Baath of Iraq: Saddam's regime in power and in ruin]. 2nd ed. Beirut: Dar al-Saqi, 2004.

————. *Al-Ba'th al-Suri: Tarikh Mujaz* [The Syrian Baath: A brief history]. Beirut: Dar al-Saqi, 2012.

————. *Hadatha Dhata Marra fi Lubnan: Akhbar Nas wa Suhuf wa Siyasat wa Ahzab* [Once upon a time in Lebanon: Stories of people, newspapers, politics, and parties]. Beirut: Dar al Jadeed, 2022.

————. *Hadhihi Laysat Sira* [This is not an autobiography]. Beirut: Dar al-Saqi, 2007.

————. *Al-Hawa Duna Ahlihi: Umm Kulthum Siratan wa Nassan* [Desire without its people: Umm Kulthum in life and words]. Beirut: Dar al Jadeed, 1991.

————. *Al-Inhiyar al-Madid: al-Khalfiyya al-Tarikhiyya Lintifadhat al-Sharq al-Awsat al-'Arabi* [The protracted collapse: The historical background to the uprisings of the Arab Middle East]. Beirut: Dar al-Saqi, 2013.

————. *Rumantiqiyyu al-Mashriq al-'Arabi* [Romanticists of the Arab Levant]. Beirut: Riad El-Rayyes Books, 2021.

————. *Wada' al-'Urooba* [Arabism's farewell]. Beirut: Dar al-Saqi, 1999.

Sayf al-Nasr, Ilham. *Fi Mu'taqal Abu Za'bal* [In Abu Zaabal Camp]. Cairo: Dar al-Thaqafa al-Jadida, 1977.

Slim, Mohsen. *Murafa'at al-Ustadh Muhsin Slim amam al-Majlis al-'Adli fi Qadhiyyat Ightiyal Kamil Muruwwa* [Mohsen Slim's address before the Judicial Council in the case of the assassination of Kamel Mrowa]. Beirut: Dar al Jadeed, 1999.

Traboulsi, Fawwaz. *Surat al-Fata bil-Ahmar: Ayyam fil-Silm wal-Harb* [A portrait of the young man in red: Chronicles of peace and war]. Beirut: Riad El-Rayyes Books, 2015.

Umran, Muhammad. *Tajribati fi al-Thawra* [My experience in the revolution]. Beirut, 1970.

Uthman, Wael. *Asrar al-Haraka al-Tullabiya: Handasat al-Qahira, 1968–75* [Secrets of the student movement: Cairo Engineering, 1968–75]. Cairo, 1976.

Younis, Sherif. *Nida' al-Sha'b: Tarikh Naqdi lil-Idiyulujiya al-Nasiriya* [The call of the people: A critical history of Nasserist ideology]. Cairo: Dar al-Shuruq, 2012.

————. *Al-Zahf al-Muqaddas: Muthaharat al-Tanahhi wa Tashakkul 'Ibadat Nasir* [The sacred march: The resignation demonstrations and the formation of Nasser worship]. Beirut: Dar al-Tanweer, 2012.

Zakaria, Ghassan. *al-Sultan al-Ahmar* [The red sultan]. London: Arados Publishing, 1991.

WORKS IN ENGLISH

Abdalla, Ahmed. *The Student Movement and National Politics in Egypt, 1923–1973*. London: Al Saqi Books, 1985.

Abdel-Malek, Anouar. "The Crisis in Nasser's Egypt." *New Left Review*, no. 45 (September/October 1967): 67–81.

———. *Egypt: Military Society; The Army Regime, the Left, and Social Change under Nasser*. New York: Vintage, 1968.

Aburish, Saïd K. *Nasser: The Last Arab*. London: Duckworth, 2004.

Ajami, Fouad. *The Arab Predicament: Arab Political Thought and Practice since 1967*. 2nd ed. Cambridge: Cambridge University Press, 1992.

———. *The Dream Palace of the Arabs: A Generation's Odyssey*. New York: Vintage, 1998.

———. "The End of Pan-Arabism." *Foreign Affairs* 57, no. 2 (November 1978): 355–73.

———. *When Magic Failed: A Memoir of a Lebanese Childhood, Caught between East and West*. New York: Bombardier Books, 2022.

Anderson, Betty S. *Nationalist Voices in Jordan: The Street and the State*. Austin: University of Texas Press, 2005.

Anderson, Claire. "The Turf Club Murders: Black Saturday for the British in Cairo, 26 January 1952." PhD diss., University of Texas at Austin, 1996.

Ashton, Nigel. "Hitler on the Nile? British and American Perceptions of the Nasser Regime, 1952–70." In *Scripting Middle East Leaders: The Impact of Leadership Perceptions on US and UK Foreign Policy*, edited by Lawrence Freedman and Jeffrey H. Michaels. London: Bloomsbury, 2013.

Aswany, Alaa Al. *The Dictatorship Syndrome*. London: Haus Publishing, 2019.

Barr, James. *Lords of the Desert: Britain's Struggle with America to Dominate the Middle East*. London: Simon & Schuster, 2018.

Batatu, Hanna. *The Old Social Classes and the Revolutionary Movements of Iraq: A Study of Iraq's Old Landed and Commercial Classes and of its Communists, Ba'thists, and Free Officers*. Princeton, NJ: Princeton University Press, 1978.

———. "Some Observations on the Social Roots of Syria's Ruling, Military Group and the Causes for Its Dominance." *Middle East Journal* 35, no. 3 (Summer 1981): 331–44.

———. *Syria's Peasantry, the Descendants of Its Lesser Rural Notables, and Their Politics*. Princeton, NJ: Princeton University Press, 1999.

Beeston, Richard. *Looking for Trouble: The Life and Times of a Foreign Correspondent*. London: Tauris Parke Paperbacks, 2006.

Birdwood, Christopher Bromhead. *Nuri as-Said: A Study in Arab Leadership*. London: Cassell & Company, 1959.

Botman, Selma. "The Rise and Experience of Egyptian Communism: 1919–1952." *Studies in Comparative Communism* 18, no. 1 (Spring 1985): 49–66.

Bowen, John Eliot. "The Conflict of East and West in Egypt." *Political Science Quarterly* 1, no. 2 (June 1886): 295–335.

Brand, Laurie. "Nasir's Egypt and the Reemergence of the Palestinian National Movement." *Journal of Palestine Studies* 17, no. 2 (Winter 1988): 29–45.

Bregman, Ahron, and Jihan El-Tahri. *The Fifty Years War: Israel and the Arabs*. London: Penguin, 1998.

Cambanis, Thanassis. *Once upon a Revolution: An Egyptian Story*. New York: Simon & Schuster, 2015.

Cigar, Norman. "Arab Socialism Revisited: The Yugoslav Roots of Its Ideology." *Middle Eastern Studies* 19, no. 2 (1983): 152–87.

Cook, Steven A. *The Struggle for Egypt: From Nasser to Tahrir Square*. Oxford: Oxford University Press, 2011.

Coughlin, Con. *Saddam: His Rise and Fall*. New York: Harper Perennial, 2005.

Dann, Uriel. *Iraq under Qassem: A Political History, 1958–1963*. Tel Aviv: Reuven Shiloah Research Center, Tel Aviv University, 1969.

———. *King Hussein and the Challenge of Arab Radicalism: Jordan, 1955–1967*. New York: Oxford University Press, 1991.

Farouk-Sluglett, Marion, and Peter Sluglett. *Iraq since 1958: From Revolution to Dictatorship*. London: I.B. Tauris, 2001.

Ferris, Jesse. *Nasser's Gamble: How Intervention in Yemen Caused the Six-Day War and the Decline of Egyptian Power*. Princeton, NJ: Princeton University Press, 2013.

Gerges, Fawaz A. *Making the Arab World: Nasser, Qutb, and the Clash That Shaped the Middle East*. Princeton, NJ: Princeton University Press, 2018.

Ghali, Waguih. *Beer in the Snooker Club*. London: Serpent's Tail, 2010.

Gordon, Joel. *Nasser: Hero of the Arab Nation*. London: Oneworld Publications, 2006.

———. *Nasser's Blessed Movement: Egypt's Free Officers and the July Revolution*. Cairo: The American University in Cairo Press, 2016.

———. " 'With God on Our Side': Scripting Nasser's Free Officer Mutiny." In *Rebellion, Repression, Reinvention: Mutiny in Comparative Perspective*, edited by Jane Hathaway. Westport, CT: Praeger, 2001.

Hansen, Bent, and Khairy Tourk. "The Profitability of the Suez Canal as a Private Enterprise, 1859–1956." *Journal of Economic History* 38, no. 4 (1978): 938–58.

Harris, Robert, and Jeremy Paxman. *A Higher Form of Killing: The Secret History of Chemical and Biological Warfare*. New York: Random House Trade Paperbacks, 2002.

Hill, Ginny. *Yemen Endures: Civil War, Saudi Adventurism and the Future of Arabia*. New York: Oxford University Press, 2017.

Hiltermann, Joost R. *A Poisonous Affair: America, Iraq, and the Gassing of Halabja*. Cambridge: Cambridge University Press, 2007.

Hirst, David. *Beware of Small States: Lebanon, Battleground of the Middle East*. London: Faber and Faber, 2010.

Hourani, Albert. *Arabic Thought in the Liberal Age: 1798–1939*. Cambridge: Cambridge University Press, 2011.

Hussein ibn Talal, King. *Uneasy Lies the Head: An Autobiography by H.M. King Hussein of Jordan*. London: Heinemann, 1962.

James, Laura M. *Nasser at War: Arab Images of the Enemy*. London: Palgrave Macmillan, 2006.

Karam, Jeffrey G., ed. *The Middle East in 1958: Reimagining a Revolutionary Year*. London: I.B. Tauris, 2021.

Kassir, Samir. *Beirut*. Berkeley: University of California Press, 2010.

Kaszeta, Dan. *Toxic: A History of Nerve Agents, from Nazi Germany to Putin's Russia*. London: Hurst & Co., 2020.

Kerr, Malcolm H. *The Arab Cold War: Gamal 'Abd al-Nasir and His Rivals, 1958–1970*. 3rd ed. New York: Oxford University Press, 1971.

Khalaf, Samir. *Civil and Uncivil Violence in Lebanon: A History of the Internationalization of Communal Conflict*. New York: Columbia University Press, 2002.

Khazen, Farid El-. *The Breakdown of the State in Lebanon 1967–1976*. London: I.B. Tauris, 2000.

Kirkpatrick, David D. *Into the Hands of the Soldiers: Freedom and Chaos in Egypt and the Middle East*. London: Bloomsbury, 2019.

Lacouture, Jean. *Nasser*. New York: Alfred A. Knopf, 1973.

Lawrence, Thomas E. *Seven Pillars of Wisdom: A Triumph*. London: Vintage, 2008.

Maasri, Zeina. *Off the Wall: Political Posters of the Lebanese Civil War*. London: I.B. Tauris, 2009.

Maher, Shiraz. *Salafi-Jihadism: The History of an Idea*. London: Hurst & Co., 2016.

Makiya, Kanan. *Cruelty and Silence: War, Tyranny, Uprising and the Arab World*. London: Penguin, 1993.

———. *The Monument: Art and Vulgarity in Saddam Hussein's Iraq*. London: I.B. Tauris, 2004.

———. *Republic of Fear: The Politics of Modern Iraq*. Berkeley: University of California Press, 1998.

Mallakh, Ragaei El. "Economic Integration in the United Arab Republic: A Study in Resources Development." *Land Economics* 36, no. 3 (August 1960): 252–65.

Mansfield, Peter. *Nasser.* London: Methuen Educational, 1969.

Marozzi, Justin. *Baghdad: City of Peace, City of Blood.* London: Penguin, 2015.

McLean, Neil. "The War in the Yemen." *Journal of the Royal Central Asian Society* 51, no. 2 (1964): 102–11.

Moubayed, Sami. *The Makers of Modern Syria: The Rise and Fall of Syrian Democracy 1918–1958.* London: I.B. Tauris, 2018.

Musleh-Motut, Nawal. "The Development of Pan-Arab Broadcasting under Authoritarian Regimes: A Comparison of *Sawt al-Arab* ('Voice of the Arabs') and Al Jazeera News Channel." Master's thesis, Simon Fraser University, 2006.

Nagasawa, Eiji. "Communist Movements in the Era of Arab Nationalist Revolutions: The Martyrdom of an Arab Communist, Farajullah El Helou." In *Collected Essays on the Role of Marxism in the Arab World and Other Related Issues,* edited by Yoshiko Kurita. Japan, 2017.

Nasser, Gamal Abdel. "The Egyptian Revolution." *Foreign Affairs* 33, no. 2 (January 1955): 199–211.

Nutting, Anthony. *Nasser.* London: Constable and Co., 1972.

Orkaby, Asher. *Beyond the Arab Cold War: The International History of the Yemen Civil War, 1962–68.* Oxford: Oxford University Press, 2017.

Pappe, Ilan. *The Rise and Fall of a Palestinian Dynasty: The Husaynis 1700–1948.* London: Saqi Books, 2010.

Pargeter, Alison. *Libya: The Rise and Fall of Qaddafi.* New Haven, CT: Yale University Press, 2012.

Pfeffer, Anshel. *Bibi: The Turbulent Life and Times of Benjamin Netanyahu.* London: Hurst & Co., 2018.

Podeh, Elie. "To Unite or Not to Unite—That Is *Not* the Question: The 1963 Tripartite Unity Talks Reassessed." *Middle Eastern Studies* 39, no. 1 (January 2003): 150–85.

Podeh, Elie, and Onn Winckler, eds. *Rethinking Nasserism: Revolution and Historical Memory in Modern Egypt.* Gainesville: University Press of Florida, 2004.

Quillen, Chris. "The Use of Chemical Weapons by Arab States." *Middle East Journal* 71, no. 2 (Spring 2017): 193–209.

Rabah, Makram. *A Campus at War: Student Politics at the American University of Beirut 1967–1975.* Beirut: Dar Nelson, 2009.

Robinson, Julian Perry. "Allegations of Chemical Warfare in the Yemen, 1963–1967." In *The Problem of Chemical and Biological Warfare,* vol. 5: *The*

Prevention of CBW, by Stockholm International Peace Research Institute. New York: Humanities Press, 1971.

Rogan, Eugene. *The Arabs: A History*. 2nd ed. London: Penguin, 2012.

Said, Edward W. *Out of Place: A Memoir*. London: Granta Books, 2000.

Salibi, Kamal S. *Crossroads to Civil War: Lebanon 1958–1976*. Delmar, NY: Caravan Books, 1976.

———. "Lebanon under Fuad Chehab, 1958–1964." *Middle Eastern Studies* 2, no. 3: 211–26.

———. *The Modern History of Jordan*. London: I.B. Tauris, 1998.

———. *The Modern History of Lebanon*. Delmar, NY: Caravan Books, 1965.

Schmidt, Dana Adams. *Yemen: The Unknown War*. London: The Bodley Head, 1968.

Seale, Patrick. *Asad of Syria: The Struggle for the Middle East*. Berkeley: University of California Press, 1989.

———. *The Struggle for Syria: A Study of Post-War Arab Politics, 1945–1958*. London: I.B. Tauris, 1986.

Shemesh, Moshe. "The Founding of the PLO 1964." *Middle Eastern Studies* 20, no. 4 (October 1984): 105–41.

Shoham, Dany. "Chemical and Biological Weapons in Egypt." *Nonproliferation Review* 5, no. 3 (1998): 48–58.

Shimazu, Naoko. "Diplomacy as Theatre: Staging the Bandung Conference of 1955." *Modern Asian Studies* 48, no. 1 (2014): 225–52.

Shlaim, Avi. *Lion of Jordan: The Life of King Hussein in War and Peace*. London: Penguin, 2007.

Soueif, Ahdaf. *Cairo: Memoir of a City Transformed*. London: Bloomsbury, 2014.

Stephens, Robert. *Nasser: A Political Biography*. London: Allen Lane, 1971.

Terrill, W. Andrew. "The Chemical Warfare Legacy of the Yemen War." *Comparative Strategy* 10, no. 2 (1991): 109–19.

Traboulsi, Fawwaz. *A History of Modern Lebanon*. 2nd ed. London: Pluto Press, 2012.

Tucker, Jonathan B. *War of Nerves: Chemical Warfare from World War I to Al-Qaeda*. New York: Anchor, 2007.

Tunzelmann, Alex von. *Blood and Sand: Suez, Hungary and the Crisis That Shook the World*. London: Simon & Schuster, 2017.

Uwaydah, May F. "An Examination of Some Structural and Rhetorical Features in Certain Speeches of Gamal Abdel Nasser." Master's thesis, American University of Beirut, 1971.

Van Dam, Nikolaos. *The Struggle for Power in Syria: Politics and Society under Asad and the Ba'th Party*. 4th ed. London: I.B. Tauris, 2011.

Vandewalle, Dirk. *A History of Modern Libya*. Cambridge: Cambridge University Press, 2012.

———. ed. *Libya since 1969: Qadhafi's Revolution Revisited*. London: Palgrave Macmillan, 2008.

Vatikiotis, P. J., ed. *Egypt since the Revolution*. London: Routledge, 2013.

Weipert-Fenner, Irene. *The Autocratic Parliament: Power and Legitimacy in Egypt, 1866–2011*. Syracuse, NY: Syracuse University Press, 2020.

INDEX

Page numbers after 345 refer to notes.